Costume Society of America Series

AS SEEN
IN VOGUE

AS SEEN
IN VOGUE

A CENTURY OF AMERICAN FASHION
IN ADVERTISING

DANIEL DELIS HILL

TEXAS TECH UNIVERSITY PRESS

This book is typeset in Times. The paper used in this book meets the minimum
requirements of ANSI/NISO Z39.48-1992 (R1997).

Printed in the United States of America

Library of Congress Cataloguing in Publication Data

Hill, Daniel Delis.

    As seen in Vogue : a century of American fashion in advertising /
Daniel Delis Hill.

        p.   cm.

    Includes bibliographical references and index.

    ISBN 0-89672-534-0 (cloth : alk. paper)

        1. Advertising—Fashion—United States—History—20th century. 2. Fash-
ion—United States—History—20th century. 3. Costume—United States—History—
20th century. 4. Dress accessories—United States—History—20th century. 5. Vogue.
I. Title. II. Series.

    HF6161.C44H55 2004

    659.19'687'0973—dc22

                                                            2004046062

04 05 06 07 08 09 10 11 12 / 9 8 7 6 5 4 3 2 1

Texas Tech University Press
Box 41037
Lubbock, Texas 79409-1037 USA
800.832.4042
www.ttup.ttu.edu

CONTENTS

PREFACE

In the late nineteenth century, a symbiotic, tripartite relationship between clothing mass production, fashion journalism, and mass-media advertising became firmly established. Each fueled the success of the other as the three intertwined industries evolved and grew during the second industrial revolution of the 1880s and 1890s. New manufacturing technologies and distribution channels broadened the categories of apparel that could be mass produced. Timely fashion reports in the mass media spread the gospel of trends and generated a widespread awareness of style. Advertising served a triple role by inculcating consumers with a desire for fashion and modernity, by promoting product availability to audiences coast to coast, by serving as supporting style guides for what to wear and how. Fashion catalogs, for instance, were mailed to mansions in New York and San Francisco and to the most isolated prairie farmstead and the most remote cabin in the Appalachian Mountains. The wide array of fashion options produced by ready-to-wear makers season after season, coupled with the seductive images and compelling copywriting in fashion journalism and advertising, manipulated an ever-widening socioeconomic segment of consumers into aspira-

tional behavior. Increasingly, people wanted more than just basic clothing, they wanted fashion.

The significant availability and broad assortment of inexpensive ready-to-wear in the late nineteenth century are evident to anyone who flips through the mammoth "wishbooks" of the period, particularly those from Sears, Roebuck, and Company or Montgomery Ward. By the close of the nineteenth century, most every imaginable category of apparel was mass produced in affordable price ranges, and could be shipped easily and quickly to virtually every home in America. As fashion styles changed more frequently—from the biennial shows of the 1880s to the quarterly seasonal collections of the 1890s—ready-to-wear manufacturers developed ever more efficient turnaround cycles and mass produced the latest styles in short order. Editorials in mass-circulation periodicals eagerly reported on these latest styles. Retailers in turn kept the American consumer desiring the new fashion looks with illustrated catalog supplements and a barrage of magazine and newspaper advertising.

The arrangement of the categories in this study is segmented somewhat like a ready-to-wear catalog or a department store in which key fashions are on the main floor and related categories such as accessories, intimate apparel, and swimwear are in other departments. As with a catalog or store floorset, space is limited, so not every type of fashion can be featured. Some forms of clothing are too specialized for a general study, like riding habits or athletic wear. Moreover, not all categories have spanned a century. Some accessories, for example, that were once crucial to the correctly accoutered ensemble became obsolete as fashion accents: fans, parasols, and walking sticks in the 1920s, and gloves in the 1960s.

Among the themes that are explored in this study is how American fashion advertising reflected or changed society. This duality of advertising has intrigued scholars across many disciplines. On the one hand, our archives of advertising materials are documentaries of American history: what we wore and ate, how we worked and played, what kinds of houses and cars we owned, and how we viewed our social values and hierarchies. On the other hand, advertisements also show how and when marketing successfully changed consumers' behavior. For example, the massive advertising campaigns by cosmetics manufacturers within just a few years following World War I successfully overturned what previously had been a long-standing social stigma: the "painted lady" of ill repute had become the self-reliant "New Woman." Similarly, mass advertising was instrumental in launching new products or expanding style awareness for everything from new perfumes to the latest fashion trends. In 1938, *Vogue* noted:

> Drummed into all of us, young and old, is the unrelenting urge to look attractive—drummed in by that fine American invention, "fashion promotion," [which includes] blasting and gargantuan campaigns to put over ideas, our regiment of glossy fashion magazines, banners of printed words, miles of costly films, endless publicity stunts, armies of stylists, and the millions invested to induce us to wear cottons or velvets or cajole us into believing that unless we rub a specific color on our lips all chances for love will be lost.[1]

And it all worked superbly. Advertising helped the American ready-to-wear industry to become the fashion stylist for the world. Advertising also paid for the fashion writers, editors, and photographers whose work influenced and guided ready-to-wear makers, who in turn bought more advertising.

This pervasive power of advertising in American culture accounts for the selection of fashion ads as the primary sources of illustrations for this study. These vignettes of history are the true mirrors of American style across the decades. Whereas fashion journalism most often featured reports on couture, which was the domain of an elite, affluent segment of society, fashion advertising targeted a broad spectrum of the masses. Wrote fashion historian Caroline Milbank, "The aver-

age American woman found the most realistic and affordable clothes, other than those featured in the occasional 'Bargains' or 'Finds' article, in the advertisements of *Vogue* or *Bazaar*."[2] For example, few women could afford the hand-beaded gowns of Paul Poiret in 1910, but most every American woman could afford the mass-produced adaptations of Poiret hobble skirts. Nor could most American women afford the superbly cut garments from the House of Dior in the 1950s, but all American women enjoyed some form of the Dior New Look as interpreted and applied to production lines by American ready-to-wear makers.

Even beyond the influences of fashion silhouettes from innovators such as Poiret or Dior, in a great many instances, American women did not realistically want to wear most of the couture styles that featured prominently in the reports of fashion magazines. Women enjoyed looking at the high-style clothing, often with amusement, but could not imagine themselves in Mary Nowitzky's zouave trousers in 1935, or a topless swimsuit from Rudi Gernreich in 1964, or a red molded-plastic bustier from Issey Miyake in 1980. Yet these, and innumerable other high-drama costumes, have been many times the focus of fashion editorials, even to the present day.

Granted, even the most unwearable collection of Paris or Italian fashions is still, nonetheless, news. When well written, well photographed or illustrated, and well-presented in a quality format, fashion reporting will always have an audience. Few can argue that, given such high standards—and longevity—*Vogue* is the preeminent fashion publication in America.

A second point of methodology in this research is the use of advertisements from the American edition of *Vogue* as the primary source of illustrations. The foremost reason is that the periodical spans the entire twentieth century, twenty-five years longer than the British or French editions. Second, the quality of paper and printing has been exceptional from the beginning of its publication, so that reproductions of the illustrations are crisp and clear. Third, the success of the magazine has been a magnet for fashion advertisers, whose target audience is the subscription mailing list of *Vogue*. Some recent editions have approached eight hundred pages—most of which were ads.

One important distinction between this study of fashion based on *Vogue* and other similar works is that the focus here is on fashion as interpreted and worn by American women. Dior, Schiaparelli, and Saint Laurent may have been world leaders in fashion, but Macy's, Bloomingdale's, and Penney's showed in their advertising how American women adapted contemporary modes to their lifestyles. Examples of the American mass market influencing Parisian designers include the demand for shorter dress hemlines of the early 1920s, the rejection of the midi and maxi styles of the late 1960s, the resistance to the punk and Japanese Big Look of the 1980s, and the disregard of the grunge ("groonge") phenomenon of the 1990s.

In addition, the important works on fashion in *Vogue* by Jane Mulvagh (*Vogue: History of Twentieth Century Fashion),* Georgina Howell (*In Vogue: Seventy-five Years of Style),* and Linda Watson (*Vogue: Twentieth Century Fashion)* are based on British *Vogue.* Differences between the British and American editions of *Vogue* are significant. Most people might think that the British edition, and indeed, any of the other worldwide editions (Italian, Spanish, German, Australian) are simply translations of American versions. Instead, content, editorial direction, and of course advertising are unique to each edition. From a historical perspective, the trends of fashions many times were different from those in America. For example, Britain had to endure the austerity styles of the Second World War well beyond the launch of Dior's New Look in 1947. "British women had to 'make do' with their Utility

fashions," noted Jane Mulvagh. "The New Look was considered a political outrage, a calculated defiance against austerity controls."[3] But American *Vogue* raved about Dior's revolution from the start, and American ready-to-wear makers and retailers almost instantaneously presented their versions of the New Look in volumes of ads. Another example is the emergence of the mod look of the 1960s, which Americans did not accept as quickly as the British. Moreover, even with the common language of English, the fashion terminology differed in the British editions where "suspenders" meant garters, "tights" meant pantyhose, and "macs" meant trench coats.

Hence, this study provides a uniquely American perspective of fashion in the twentieth century. Not only is the evolution of fashion reviewed and illustrated, but so too are the businesses of fashion journalism, fashion advertising, and ready-to-wear manufacturing. The influence of this symbiotic tripartite has been enormous in American culture, reflecting, changing, and defining the style of each era and its generation.

"As Seen in Vogue," point-of-sale poster 1941.

1

IN THE BEGINNING

Prior to the eighteenth century, the word "magazine" meant storehouse, especially in military applications. When adapted to periodical publishing, the storehouse became the printed page with contents that often could be encyclopedic. Over the past 250 years, the subject matter of these miniature, compact storehouses reflected, influenced, and documented American society, economics, politics, science, religion, and the arts.

In colonial America, innumerable magazines were launched only to be closed after a few editions. Publishing was an extraordinarily expensive enterprise. Printing presses, spare parts, and type fonts were scarce. Paper and printer's ink were costly imported commodities that were exorbitantly taxed. With the limitations of the manufacturing processes of the time, the quality of these materials was inconsistent. Once a magazine edition was printed, distribution, even regionally, could be a nightmare, given the poor roads, limited postal routes, and interstate customs regulations.

Nevertheless, publishers with vision, editors with agendas, and writers seeking an audience persisted in their magazine ventures. Benjamin Franklin is often credited with conceiving the first magazine in the colonies, the *General Magazine and*

Figure 1-1. Nineteenth-century women's magazines provided timely glimpses of the newest styles in fashions to women of all classes across America. From *Godey's Lady's Book,* top 1849, bottom 1888.

—1—

Historical Chronicle, in 1741. In actuality, Andrew Bradford had published the first issue of his *American Magazine* a few days before Franklin's premiere edition.[1] Another notable but short-lived magazine of the period was the *Pennsylvania Magazine*, which became a persuasive voice of revolution with Tom Paine as its editor. Its final edition in 1776 contained the text of the Declaration of Independence.

By the beginning of the nineteenth century, the difficulties that plagued earlier magazine publishing were remedied by the Industrial Revolution. Affordable printing presses with machine-made parts were readily available, even to the most rural communities. Domestic manufacturing of paper and ink significantly reduced costs of those products. Railroads, canals, improved interstate roadways, and a centralized postal system made national distribution easier. An expanding frontier and increasing population created an audience of readers voraciously eager for the news of current events. As a result, new magazine titles were launched by the thousands. In one twenty-year period between 1890 and 1910, more than seven thousand magazine titles were published.[2] Even at the end of the twentieth century, despite competition from the combined mass media of television, radio, movies, and the Internet, more than forty-eight hundred American magazine titles were in print.[3]

American Women's Magazines

If asked to name an American women's magazine, most people today would cite one of the Seven Sisters: *Ladies' Home Journal, Good Housekeeping, McCall's, Woman's Day, Redbook, Family Circle, Better Homes and Gardens*. This would hardly be surprising since, by the end of the twentieth century, those seven titles reached over thirty-four million women.[4] The eldest sister, *McCall's*, began publishing in 1876, followed in 1883 by *Ladies' Home Journal* and *Good Housekeeping* in 1885. Prior to that, American women had few choices for informative, timely reading materials. Books were expensive, and newspapers were largely forbidden to women.

Some mass-circulation magazines such as *Harper's New Monthly Magazine* posed a dilemma for many patriarchal households of the mid-nineteenth century. For most Victorian men, their ladies were not supposed to be exposed to the unseemly facts of life, especially social ills, politics, business, and science. *Harper's* presented its readers with a wide variety of fiction and nonfiction subjects in all of these categories. Yet, the magazine also contained segments on family life, fashion, and other more acceptable women's topics. For instance, the August 1864 issue contained illustrations and reports on the latest fall fashions, contributions by Charles

Dickens and William Thackeray, numerous poems, and gossipy—but highly moral—letters to the editor. Dispersed amongst those features were engravings depicting nude African men and women, hospital and battle scenes from the Civil War front, and life-saving procedures for drowning victims.[5]

If a husband or father of the early or mid-Victorian era chose to deny the women of his household access to controversial magazines such as *Harper's*, then instead he might permit them to subscribe to one of the few publications specifically created for women: *Ladies' Literary Cabinet* (1819–22), *Graham's Magazine* (1826–55), *Ladies' Magazine* (1828–36), *Godey's Lady's Book* (1830–98), *Ladies' Repository* (1841–76), *Peterson's Ladies' National Magazine* (1842–98), *Frank Leslie's Ladies' Gazette* (1854–57), *Harper's Bazar*[6] (1867–present day).

These women's magazines largely followed similar formulas, with editorial content that emphasized the traditional roles of women as wives and mothers. In an 1849 issue of *Godey's*, women were advised that "every husband stands in need of encouragement, of cheerfulness, of peace in his home."[7] Advice columns and morality fiction reinforced this tenet of Victorian patriarchal society. Editions of *Godey's* also included hand-colored fashion plates, color block-printed patterns for needlework, tissue-paper inserts of interior decoration, sheet music foldouts, and floorplans for houses. (Figure 1-1.) Wrote Sara Hale, *Godey's* redoubtable editor for more than thirty years, "Our 'Book' is the mirror of woman's mind, and proud we are to show the pure and beautiful creations of her genius."[8] The appeal to women was significant, and by the 1870s, the magazine's circulation had reached 165,000.[9] So long as that genius of woman's mind did not exceed the boundaries of the nursery and kitchen, Victorian husbands and fathers were satisfied with the guidance their wives and daughters received from the pages of *Godey's* and similar women's magazines.

The first American women's magazine that focused primarily on fashion was *Harper's Bazar*. Launched in 1867, the periodical had feature departments such as "New York Fashions," "Sayings and Doings," and "Answers to Correspondents," all of which were detailed editorials on current couture styles, fabrics, and accessories. The cover layouts almost always depicted a large-format fashion plate, and the inside pages presented numerous other fashion illustrations, sometimes including men's and children's styles. (Figure 1-2.)

Although the primary focus of *Harper's Bazar* was fashion, its editorials commonly paid due attention to the roles of the Victorian wife and mother. In an 1879 article, for example, women were lectured on the dangers of neglecting housework: "In the economy of the household every disregarded

1867

1875

1884

Figure 1-2. *Harper's Bazar* was the first American women's magazine largely devoted to fashion. Launched in 1867, the periodical was originally published weekly.

duty or slighted task tells its own story in the long account, as the old geological formations have registered the rains of their period; and as every household is a fraction of the divine economy, housework in its homeliest phases is promoted from a menial, unconsidered thing to dignity and power."[10] Such seemingly gratuitous content not only enhanced the magazine's appeal to a broader audience of women, but possibly the editorials on home and hearth also assuaged a patriarch's concerns about the perceived frivolousness of a fashion magazine.

Still, fashion was the core business of *Harper's Bazar*. Women nationwide received timely reports on the newest fashion trends from the style makers in Paris, London, and New York. Women in middle America could take the highly detailed engravings to their hometown dressmakers for adaptations of Parisian couture designs from, for example, the illustrious House of Worth, couturier to the imperial French court. Descriptive text in the editorials was precise, omitting no details of the garment's silhouette, construction, fit, fabrics, and embellishments.

By the late 1860s, the publishers of *Harper's Bazar* began producing special supplements for subscribers that featured paper patterns. The fashion collections from these supplements were also reprinted in comprehensive catalogs that could be purchased by mail for ten cents. Women in small towns all across the country who could not afford or did not have access to private dressmakers now could be easily and economically dressed as fashionably as any woman in Paris or New York.

During the last quarter of the nineteenth century, numerous new women's magazines made their debut: *Delineator* (1873), *McCall's* (1876), *Ladies' World* (1880), *Ladies' Home Journal* (1883), *Good Housekeeping* (1885), and *Cosmopolitan* (1886), to name a few. Each of these periodicals regularly included feature stories on fashion. The editors of *McCall's* initially positioned their publication more in the fashion arena, with less emphasis on home-hearth-husband content through the 1890s. *Delineator* began as a promotional vehicle created by apparel pattern maker Ebeneezer Butterick to sell his paper pattern kits. Even *Ladies' Home Journal* recognized the American woman's keen interest in fashion and skewed certain key seasonal editions mostly toward modes du jour, with striking fashion plate covers. (Figure 1-3.)

1895

1896

1899

Figure 1-3. Even women's magazines such as *Ladies' Home Journal* emphasized fashion with selected seasonal editions.

Fashion Advertising

The influence of *Harper's Bazar* on the newly launched women's magazines of the late nineteenth century is significant. The early editorial model of *Harper's Bazar* featured fashion journalism, showcased ready-to-wear apparel, and encouraged fashion advertising. This tripartite model is still fundamental to fashion periodical publishing today.

By the third quarter of the nineteenth century, changes in manufacturing technologies had led to sophisticated principles of flow production—a precursor to the assembly line of the twentieth century—and of marketing distribution channels. The result was a broader array of standardized products that could be mass produced, including most every category of ready-made clothing.

Although the British had established efficient methods of manufacturing ready-to-wear clothing in the early nineteenth century, they mostly concentrated on the production of uniforms and commodity garments that did not change in style. At the other end of the spectrum were the French couture houses that created biennial fashion collections from which handmade copies were tailored for a selected clientele. With American ingenuity, U.S. manufacturers explored and developed methods of combining these two industries to mass produce ready-made fashions.

The key to success in this field of manufacturing was timing. "Modistes" (agents for the manufacturers) were sent to Paris at the beginning of each new fashion season to buy or, as many French designers complained, steal the current designs. As biennial fashion seasons became quarterly seasons, turnaround was crucial for American ready-to-wear manufacturers. To keep pace, the clothing industry constantly upgraded technologies and refined distribution channels for procuring raw materials and for shipping finished products. Receiving the new fashion designs early was essential and could give the manufacturer the edge over competitors when selling production lines to retailers or exporters. In September 1869, *Harper's Bazar* noted that as of press time for that edition, the modistes were still in Paris "in search of novelties" for the American taste. "When they return," the fashion editor wrote, "we may find further changes to record, as the original toilettes [ensembles] prepared for the Empress [Eugenie, wife of Napoleon III] to wear during her Eastern trip may affect the costumes of the winter."[11] Similarly, twenty years later, *Godey's* apologized to readers for the delay in getting the fashion plates prepared for the newest styles, explaining that the modistes had been late returning from Paris.[12]

American women responded enthusiastically to the expanding availability of ready-made clothing and, in particular, the idea of fashions for the masses. *Harper's Bazar* regularly included information and prices of ready-to-wear fashions in the same columns as reports on couture. In 1875, the fashion editor wrote that clothing stores "are providing ready-made suits at such reasonable prices and of such varied designs that something may be found to suit all tastes and purses."[13] Whereas cost estimates for couture designs in the 1870s were quoted at more than $200 per outfit, a ready-made version of a woman's three-piece wool suit was listed at $3.75.[14] Helping to fuel the interest in ready-made fashions, contributors to the fashion reports oftentimes included well-known New York retailers, including Lord and Taylor and Tiffany's.

The rapid rise and expansion of the American ready-to-wear industry in the nineteenth century was a substantial economic and social phenomenon. The notion of style and fashion increasingly appealed to a broader range of socioeconomic classes. By the early decades of the twentieth century, the abstract concept of fashion had even become a topic of scholarly research and analysis. In 1919 *American Anthropologist* published a study of fashion trends by University of California professor A. L. Kroeber.[15] The research data included the first published graphs documenting details of fashion styles that ranged from skirt lengths to décolleté necklines. Almost immediately afterward, trade publications such as *Women's Wear Daily* began including similar graphs and charts to aid ready-to-wear manufacturers and fashion retailers in projecting inventory and sales plans. In addition, the psychology of fashion became a popular academic topic. In his 1928 book, *Economics of Fashion*, Paul Nystrom devoted a lengthy chapter to this subject, covering the complexities of "human motives" and "factors that influence the character and direction of fashion movements."[16] In later years, such studies became essential to marketing strategies for apparel makers and retailers.

As the ready-to-wear industry evolved during the last quarter of the nineteenth century, a second phenomenon emerged with equal rapidity and impact on American economics, society, and fashion: advertising. Certainly the concept of sales promotion through advertising is millennia old. Rudimentary advertising techniques were familiar to shoppers in the marketplaces of neolithic communities—from barkers broadcasting product availability and quantity to visual merchandising with compelling product displays in stalls and the backs of carts. For ready-to-wear manufacturers of the nineteenth century, two key aspects of advertising developed that

dramatically accelerated consumer demand for fashion. First was the explosive growth of magazine advertising, and second was the proliferation of direct mail catalogs.

Prior to the Civil War, magazines largely disdained accepting advertising. The extent to which magazine editors might permit advertising would be an occasional page or two with a listing of books and periodicals published by their respective presses. "A publication seldom actively sought advertising," historian Frank Rowsome noted. "Publishers commonly believed that advertising was a marginal, not quite respectable business practice—a sign of commercial distress, something engaged in just as bankruptcy loomed."[17] The resistance to advertising by many magazine publishers persisted into the 1890s in some cases, despite the temptation of high gross revenues. The turning point seemed to be the Panic of 1892, which Richard Ohmann credits with inaugurating the principles of magazine publishing that are still in use today: "build a huge circulation; sell lots of advertising space at rates based on that circulation; sell the magazine at a price *below* the cost of production, and make your profits on ads."[18]

For those magazines that had accepted advertising early on, such as *Harper's Bazar*, formats for ready-to-wear ads continued in the tradition from previous decades. That is, advertising sections—usually placed in the last pages of the edition—were parceled into a mosaic of little boxes crammed tightly with as much type as would fit. (Figure 1-4.) Those apparel ads that did provide space for illustrations mostly presented product mannequins rather than images of style. The use of advertising as a branding statement of fashion or lifestyle for the apparel manufacturer would not develop as a significant competitive advantage until well into the twentieth century, led in part by beauty soap and perfume advertisers.

Certainly the cost of advertising was also an issue for ready-to-wear manufacturers. Expenses for manufacturing clothing were significantly different from those for most other industries. Procter and Gamble could manufacture Ivory Soap for many years without having to alter equipment, develop new channels of distribution to acquire raw materials, or change methods of delivery for shipping finished products. For ready-to-wear makers, however, one year's plum taffeta would be passe next season, and instead of the brass buttons that were popular six months earlier, now mother-of-pearl was the mode. Supplies of raw materials for manufacturing apparel could rarely be stocked in quantity very far in advance of production. In addition, new garment styles and fabrics might require investment in new technologies or the retooling of existing equipment to remain competitive.

A second advertising front that significantly benefited ready-to-wear makers was the direct mail catalog. Aaron

Figure 1-4. Early fashion advertising in magazines was largely confined to text wedged into a mosaic of boxes in an advertising section at the back of the publication. Detail of advertising page from *Harper's Bazar* 1878.

Montgomery Ward had started the catalog revolution in 1872 with his first slim folio of products available by mail order. Just a decade later, the Ward's catalog contained more than ten thousand items. By the end of the century, households across America could thumb through hundreds of pages of ads for ready-to-wear fashions in the annual editions of "wishbooks" produced by Ward's, Sears, Wanamaker's, and Penney's. (Figure 1-5.) Whereas in earlier decades the timeline of fashion trends in America meant a season behind Paris for New Yorkers and six to eighteen months behind for heartland cities and towns, seasonal catalog supplements kept women instantly informed of the newest trends even in the most remote communities. For a nominal shipping fee, women living in southern deltas, the Great Plains, or along the Pacific Coast could be as current in their fashion wardrobes as any of their sisters in New York.

Then Came *Vogue*

The three forces of the fashion industry in America—fashion journalism, ready-to-wear manufacturing, and fashion advertising—all were to culminate uniquely in a magazine that would epitomize women's fashion and style around the world. On December 17, 1892, the first edition of *Vogue* magazine was published.

The inception of *Vogue*, however, was less auspicious than its destiny. The founder, Arthur B. Turnure, was a Princetonian socialite who had an interest in publishing. His idea was to produce a New York social gazette. In fact, backers of Turnure's venture included members of New York's wealthiest and most influential families, including Cornelius Vanderbilt, William Jay, A. M. Dodge, and Marion Stuyvesant Fish. In addition to the notable social status of the financial backers,

Figure 1-5. Pages of ready-to-wear fashions and accessories from the Montgomery Ward catalog 1895.

Figure 1-6. *Vogue's* icon of an eighteenth-century shepherdess was created by its first art director, Harry McVickar, in 1893.

the key managers of *Vogue* were also prominent in New York society. The editor, Josephine Redding, was a socialite whose passion was animal welfare. Her most significant contribution during her eight-year tenure was to come up with the name "Vogue." The art director was Harry McVickar, a member of the same Meadowbrook hunting set as Turnure. He created the eighteenth-century-styled shepherdess with the V on her bodice that was used as a branding icon in advertising for *Vogue*. Quite possibly this trite representation was a reference to Marie Antoinette's predilection for costume parties and fancy dress balls, one of which she and her ladies had attended dressed as shepherdesses. (Figure 1-6.)

The content of *Vogue* was initially written as much for men as for women. In an 1893 *Vogue* subscription ad that ran in *Cosmopolitan*, the copy announced: "Vogue is a new weekly journal of fashion and devoted to the ceremonial side of life. It is unlike any existing periodical. Its illustrations are pictures of New York society and are strictly accurate in every detail of the prevailing mode in dress for both women and men."[19] Mostly, the contents of the first issues were as advertised. (Figure 1-7.) Topics of society and social decorum permeated most every page, including fiction and satirical cartoons. Reviews of the season's newest plays, music, art exhibits, and books reflected the upscale taste of the readers. "Society Snapshots" featured the publisher's friends and club acquaintances. Fashion articles were more in the line of wardrobe advice for social events rather than fashion journalism reporting on the latest trends from the couture houses of Paris. For example, two regular feature stories were "Of Interest to Her" and "As Seen by Him." In these columns, fashion was related to what was appropriate to wear and when. Details of garment construction, fabrics, silhouettes, and accessories were usually generalized unless relevant to the social theme.

As for advertising, securing revenue from that source of income was not a high priority for Turnure. Such mundane commercial aspects of running his little gazette were left to wage-earning employees and tradespeople. With Josephine Redding at the editor's helm, the complement of advertising and editorial was never achieved, nor actually sought. Ads for haute couture fashion houses and furriers ran adjacent to ads illustrating corsets and long johns or ads espousing cures for pimples and dyspepsia.

However, within a couple of years *Vogue* began to evolve a stronger fashion content and direction. In the tradition of *Harper's Bazar*, illustrations became more detailed, with specific descriptive text. In 1898, a *Vogue* subscription ad placed in *Life* magazine asserted: "Women who go continually into society know how to dress appropriately. They know exactly what to wear on all occasions. Such knowledge is very difficult for women who are not in society, who live away from large cities, and who do not have access to the best shops and dressmaking establishments. . . .Vogue answers questions and has the best chosen fashions with good workable descriptions."[20] Increasingly, large-format fashion plates were featured. Expanded departments, such as "Seen in the Shops," even advised of ready-made fashions and accessories, including prices. The stories for "As Seen by Him" were now often relegated to the back pages and sometimes reduced to a mere column or two instead of the full two or three pages they originally occupied.

Another change in editorial direction came in 1899 when clothing pattern maker Rosa Payne approached Josephine Redding about running a segment on garment patterns. Redding agreed, and each week *Vogue* presented one new pattern. Readers could clip the order coupon and send fifty cents to receive a pattern for garments as diverse as a Louis XV jacket,

Figure 1-7. Illustrations and topics depicted on the front covers of *Vogue* in its first full year of publication dealt more with high society than with fashions. Issues from 1893.

golf skirt, petticoat, or even children's apparel. (Figure 1-8.) Initially, Mrs. Payne hand-cut each pattern on her dining room table.[21] Soon, though, the demand for *Vogue*'s patterns grew so great that commercial services had to take over the cutting and fulfillment of orders.

The new pattern franchise was a radical departure from *Vogue*'s original editorial mission. The presumption that some of *Vogue*'s readers could not afford handmade couture fashions must have been startling to Fifth Avenue subscribers. Sensitive to this fact, the editors included a disclaimer in the opening text of each page of patterns stating, "Vogue does not publish patterns as a rule. The exception is one pattern a week."[22] The exception soon became the rule, however, despite the continual debates amongst the staff. Indeed, this dichotomy of *Vogue*, the social gazette, selling paper patterns would remain a controversy within the organization for years to come, especially during its transition into a Condé Nast publication in 1910.

Clearly, by the beginning of the twentieth century *Vogue* had become a women's fashion magazine rather than a community social gazette. Part of this repositioning strategy may have stemmed from the fact that its market had expanded far beyond New York's Fifth Avenue. The "Business Notices" index of the November 16, 1899, issue listed more than fifty U.S. cities where distributors were sent copies of the magazine.[23] By 1904, subscriptions totaled twenty-six thousand, and special editions were printed in runs of fifty thousand.[24] That same year, in an interview with *Printers' Ink,* Turnure

described *Vogue* as a "shoppers' journal" with features and advertising that were "devoted to fashion." To aid subscribers in their pursuit of the newest in fashion trends, Turnure added: "Upon sketches and suggestions from many directions, the fashion news of *Vogue* is based, and it is the quality and exclusiveness of the information underlying this news that makes *Vogue* what it is—a journal circulating among the people of taste and means who not only seek but who can appreciate the latest information about dress." He made no mention of New York society but instead noted that "the chief reason many of our readers take *Vogue* is because they live far from good dressmakers, and are thrown on their own resources."[25]

In truth, the picture was not as rosy as Turnure painted it for his interview with *Printers' Ink.* The editorial direction was still floundering, even though Josephine Redding had been let go in 1900. A year later, Turnure's sister-in-law, Marie Harrison, had been persuaded to help out as editor, but she, too, lacked the leadership to firmly establish the direction and cohesion that was needed. Harry McVickar had lost interest in the enterprise altogether and just drifted away from it. Advertising had been put in the hands of a former *Scribner*'s ad salesman, Tom McGreedy, whose priority was quantity, not quality.

Circulation numbers were actually declining, which may have accounted for Turnure's agreeing to the interview with a trade publication like *Printers' Ink.* As of March 15, 1903, a change in *Vogue*'s policy for unsold returns greatly affected nationwide distribution to newsdealers. No longer could the covers or mastheads of unsold issues be sent back to *Vogue* for credit. The intent was to increase multiple prepaid subscriptions from newsdealers. An announcement in the February 5, 1903, edition advised that "Readers of Vogue who buy papers from week to week should place a permanent order with their newsdealers to prevent disappointment and delay in being regularly shipped."[26] Such a strategy was flawed from the inception. Readers who purchased *Vogue* from newsstands most likely only occasionally wanted seasonal issues; otherwise they would already be subscribers. Dealers, faced with weekly cash losses from unsold copies, canceled or reduced standing orders immediately. After all, *Vogue* was not the only magazine with fashion news, fashion advertising, and fashion patterns.

Condé Nast

In 1905, Turnure was approached by publishing executive Condé Nast, who proposed to purchase the ailing *Vogue*. Nast was the business manager of *Collier's Weekly* and had been instrumental in introducing fresh, innovative ideas that catapulted the magazine into preeminence. Among those innovations were a complete format redesign, full-color front and back covers, and the introduction of the "special number" edition, which would be devoted to a timely topic or individual personality of the day. Nast pushed the *Collier's* editors to improve the quality of its content by featuring renowned writers such as Upton Sinclair and Booth Tarkington, and illustrators such as Frederic Remington, Charles Dana Gibson, and J. C. Leyendecker. To complement the new editorial content, Nast steered his advertising team more toward marketers of men's products at the expense of women's advertisers. The strategy worked as more and more ads poured in from manufacturers of beer, shaving products, tobacco, and automobiles.

In the midst of the lengthy negotiations for *Vogue*, Turnure died suddenly in 1906 at age forty-nine. Between considerations for Turnure's family and resolving shareholder issues, Nast continued his patient pursuit of *Vogue*.

In the meantime, Nast left his $40,000-a-year position with *Collier's* to become a vice president of the Home Pattern Company, which manufactured and distributed women's dress patterns franchised by *Ladies' Home Journal*. The significance of this new role would be twofold. First was Nast's interest in the field of fashion. He enthusiastically focused his energies on the apparel pattern business and its publications. By introducing many of the innovations he had developed for *Collier's*, Nast more than doubled advertising revenue for the company's *Quarterly Style Book* in just three years.[27] Second, his experience at the Home Pattern Company later would influence his decision to maintain and then expand *Vogue*'s

Figure 1-8. In 1899 *Vogue* created a new department offering garment patterns for sale in each edition. The editorial contrast between the elitist society stories and the proletarian pattern franchise remained a controversy within the organization for years. Shown here is the first line of patterns from 1899.

pattern enterprises. Whereas the dichotomy for Turnure's *Vogue* had been between the successful plebian pattern business versus the patrician society appeal, for Nast's *Vogue* the pattern business created a dichotomy between the high art of Fifth Avenue haute couture and the Anytown Main Street apparel trade.

Finally, in the spring of 1909, Nast closed the deal on *Vogue*. Although he had had three long years to think about the direction he wanted to take *Vogue*, changes were not immediate. Instead, for the first several months he remained virtually secluded in his office, poring over accounting ledgers and volumes of archived back issues. When at last he was ready to act, his revision plan was sweeping. In *Vogue's* fiftieth anniversary issue of 1943, the editors summed up the dramatic changes that Nast inaugurated for his magazine: "It was plump, no longer a weekly, but a semi-monthly, and its price was not ten, but fifteen cents. The most important change, however, was this: Vogue was no longer only a fashionable magazine. It was a magazine of fashion. Society belonged firmly in its pages, but clothes were the heart of the new formula."[28] Nast also brought with him many of the innovative ideas he had explored with *Collier's* and *Quarterly Style Book*. In revamping *Vogue's* editorial content, he retained many society departments such as "Seen on the Stage," "What They Read," and "Society." Fiction was eliminated entirely. News stories were usually related first to fashion, then to social events, society personalities, and travel. One totally new department about the social elite was named "Noblesse Oblige." Beneath the feature header ran an explanation of its purpose: "Under this title it is planned to publish a series of articles showing the various methods that women and men of social distinction employ in relieving the conditions under which the less fortunately placed exist."[29]

In addition, Nast enhanced the déclassé segments such as "Seen in the Shops" and "Smart Fashions for Limited Incomes" by featuring an abundance of exceptional illustrations and photography. One of the most popular additions was the "S and X" (sale and exchange) department. This was a personals and clearinghouse section for reader-to-reader notices. Categories included:

"Wearing Apparel"

> Lady desires to sell ermine muff and neckpiece costing $225; in perfect condition and of finest quality; no reasonable offer will be refused.

"Furniture"

> Wanted to sell a few charming pieces of old Southern furniture.

"Professional Services"

> Lady with rank of Princess (patent of nobility proved if desired) contemplating trip to Europe; will chaperone socially eligible ladies duly recommended.

"Miscellaneous"

> Arnold electric massage vibrator; all usual attachments; perfect condition; for circulation, complexion, rheumatism, sciatica, neuralgia, obesity, insomnia, nervous troubles, etc.; price $18.

For one dollar, anyone could publish a message of up to twenty-five words. Respondents were required to submit a stamped, unaddressed envelope in which their inquiry would be forwarded to the ad's anonymous author.[30] .

The controversy of the *Vogue* pattern department carried over from the Turnure administration to the new group of company officers and editors. Many of *Vogue's* staff felt that the paper pattern business was distasteful and lowered the image of the publication. However, Nast would not relent. He passionately defended his position to retain—and expand—this department. For him, *Vogue* appealed to women of taste, many of whom had limited incomes but still wished to be fashionably dressed. Indeed, a great many women of means and social standing who were by nature frugal also benefited from the economy and styles of *Vogue's* patterns. One of Nast's favorite stories involved an encounter with the wife of Theodore Roosevelt in which she acknowledged the importance of *Vogue's* patterns in furnishing wardrobes for herself and her children.[31]

In the course of *Vogue's* evolution, Nast took particular interest in the cover designs. He encouraged his editors and art directors to seek out the finest illustrators and photographers in the world. (Figure 1-9.) He wanted artists with a contemporary vision about fashion that matched his own. Contributors included illustrators such as Helen Dryden, Georges Lepape, Edouard Benito, and George Plank. Modern-day masters such as Giorgio de Chirico, Salvador Dali, and Pavel Tchelitchew were also commissioned to create covers for *Vogue*. From the 1920s onward the list of contributing photographers was a who's who in the field: Cecil Beaton, Horst P. Horst, George Hoyningen-Huené, Irving Penn, Clifford Coffin, and Helmut Newton.

To be assured of the finest quality printing, Nast bought a

printing company in 1921 that was located in Greenwich, Connecticut. Over the next dozen years, he expanded and modernized the facilities into one of the country's premier printers. The division became quite profitable, printing high-quality magazines such as the *New Yorker, Mademoiselle, Modern Photography,* and *Field and Stream.* Nast was so obsessed with the quality of printing that he refused to allow any color photography covers for *Vogue* until 1932, when his photoengravers demonstrated to his satisfaction that they could provide the results he demanded.

By the end of his first year as owner of *Vogue,* Nast released the good news of his success in a sales promotion piece sent to advertisers. He claimed that *Vogue* had carried over half a million lines of advertising in 1910, which topped his nearest competitor by 184,000 lines. His subscription list had doubled; newsstand sales had tripled. He concluded the promotional copy by writing: "Those who used Vogue on my first invitation eighteen months ago did so largely in my faith to 'deliver the goods.' Those who did so five months ago did so on a mixture of faith and fact. Now I ask you to come in on fact alone."[32] With such impressive results, come they did. Advertisers rushed in droves to be a part of the new *Vogue.* Prior to Nast, the regular weekly issues of the magazine contained only about three or four pages of advertising (although the special quarterly fashion issues might include up to twenty or thirty pages of ads). In 1911—the first full year after Nast converted *Vogue* from a social gazette to a fashion magazine—the key fall fashion issue in September contained 51 pages of advertising. By midcentury, the September 1, 1950, fall fashion issue featured 131 pages of advertising. In 2002, the September issue was packed with 574 pages of advertising.

It is ironic that, as with his predecessor, advertising was the one domain of his publication that Nast left to its own devices. As late as the 1930s this issue still surfaced. Editor in Chief Edna Woolman Chase commented on the subject, "We are responsible for the merchandise that we select from the shops and we are responsible for the manner in which we present it to our readers, and we are equipped to do this work editorially, but we are not equipped in this capacity in the Advertising Department."[33] The result was yet another one of those peculiar dichotomies of *Vogue.* Amongst editions with glamorous stories on fine dining, social decorum, and elegant lifestyles were full-page ads for Campbell's soups, Kotex feminine hygiene products, Listerine mouthwash, Zip hair removal cream, Fleischmann's Yeast laxative, and Lysol douche, to name a few.

More important was the dual personality of *Vogue*'s fashion image decade after decade. On the one hand were the reports of current fashion trends supported with high-fashion art and photography. On the other hand were the hundreds of ads annually from ready-to-wear makers and retailers—sometimes complementing and sometimes conflicting with *Vogue*'s editorials. The former represented the dreams and aspirations of American women; the latter depicted the reality of what they bought and wore. The phrase "as seen in Vogue" provided both advertisers and consumers with a halo effect by association with America's preeminent fashion publication. Advertisers enjoyed an implied endorsement, and consumers felt confident that their fashion choices were timely and correct.

Conclusion

The successful symbiotic relationship between ready-to-wear manufacturing, fashion journalism, and advertising, as we know it today, has its roots in the second industrial revolution that swept America following the Civil War. Primary contributors to the development of this tripartite business model were *Harper's Bazar* in the nineteenth century and *Vogue* in the twentieth.

Harper's Bazar had broken new ground in three key areas of periodical publishing when it was launched in 1867. First, its editorial content focused principally on fashion rather than the usual home and hearth topics of women's magazines. Second, from the start, its editors encouraged journalistic contributions from American ready-to-wear makers instead of concentrating solely on modistes' reports from Paris. Third, it accepted advertising at a time when publishers disdained the practice, thus helping sustain the embryonic advertising industry.

When *Vogue* began publishing in 1892, the list of women's magazines in print was extensive. Among the well-entrenched titles that specialized in fashion besides *Harper's Bazar* were *McCall's* and *Delineator.* Most other women's magazines also included regular and extensive articles on fashion trends, particularly *Ladies' Home Journal* and *Good Housekeeping.* In addition to fashion journalism, women received timely news of trends from mass marketers such as Sears and Montgomery Ward, whose annual wishbooks and frequent seasonal supplements carried the fashion message to the remotest corners of America.

With such fierce competition in the fashion market, *Vogue* concentrated on its debut as a social gazette, limiting its reports on fashion to the interests of high society. As its distribution expanded nationally, though, it began to focus more on fashion beyond that of the elite. By the turn of the century, *Vogue* regularly reported on ready-to-wear and even began to include a paper pattern service for home sewing. When Condé

Nast acquired the magazine in 1909, he transformed its look and editorial content into a fashion magazine that transcended the style gulf between Paris couture and American Main Street ready-to-wear. Across the decades of the twentieth century, *Vogue* set high standards for fashion journalism that appealed to a broad audience. Its editorials not only provided notoriety and branding for French haute couture but also spotlighted American ready-to-wear makers. As a business success, *Vogue* delivered the fashion messages of advertisers directly to their target market and collected substantial fees from satisfied marketers.

By the time *Vogue* celebrated a century of fashion and style in America in 1992, it was widely regarded as the preeminent fashion authority by journalists, clothing makers, advertisers, and most especially, its readers—a status it holds still in the new millennium. Whenever a poster, mailer, or newspaper ad proclaimed "as seen in Vogue," the featured fashion or accessory received instant credibility—and sales.

A.

B.

C.

Figure 1-9. Condé Nast took a keen interest in the cover designs for *Vogue*. He encouraged his editors and art directors to seek out the world's best illustrators and, after 1932, photographers to create visions of fashion.

(Issue date and cover illustrator):
A. March 15, 1912; George Plank
B. June 1, 1913; Helen Dryden
C. April 15, 1914; E. M. A. Steinmetz

D.

E.

F.

G.

(Issue date and cover illustrator):
D. July 1, 1914; Helen Dryden
E. July 1, 1915; Helen Dryden
F. June 1, 1915; Helen Dryden
G. April 15, 1915; George Plank

H.

I.

(Issue date and cover illustrator):
H. March 1, 1915; Helen Dryden
I. April 15, 1916; George Plank
J. April 1, 1916; Helen Dryden

J.

K.

L.

M.

(Issue date and cover illustrator):
K. June 1, 1917; Helen Dryden
L. April 1, 1917; Helen Dryden
M. October 1, 1917; Helen Dryden

OPPOSITE PAGE
(Issue date and cover illustrator):
N. March 15, 1918; Helen Dryden
O. June 15, 1918; Alice de Warenne Little
P. May 1, 1918; Porter Woodruff
Q. July 1, 1918; Helen Dryden
R. March 15, 1919; Helen Dryden

S. March 1, 1919; George Plank
T. July 1, 1919; Helen Dryden
U. October 15, 1919; George Plank
V. April 1, 1920; George Plank
W. February 15, 1920; Helen Dryden
X. December 15, 1920; Helen Dryden
Y. January 1, 1920; Georges LePape

N.

O.

P.

Q.

R.

S.

T.

U.

V.

W.

X.

Y.

2

VICTORIA THROUGH WORLD WAR I

On January 22, 1901, Queen Victoria died. The monarch for whom an era was named had reigned sixty-four years. The social influence of her personal demeanor and conduct crossed generations and all classes worldwide. The political and economic influence of her imperial dominion was global; the sun truly never set on the British Empire of the nineteenth century. Through that network of colonialism streamed the modes of social thought and behavior that would become characterized as Victorianism. Immigrants by the millions brought it with them to America. The socially elite of the United States looked to the titled aristocracy of England for social guidance, despite their steadfast assertions of republican nationalism when in their peer cliques.

By the dawn of the twentieth century, science, medicine, engineering, technology, and the arts all had made tremendous leaps in progress. The telephone and electric light bulb were decades old by then. The first American automobiles had been built in 1893, and barely ten years later man successfully flew in an aeroplane. Skyscrapers had changed the skylines of cities, and massive bridges spanned the widest rivers. Cubist and Fauve painters gave the world new visual experiences. Louis Pasteur had revealed the realm of microbes. Charles Darwin's *On the Origin of Species* had shaken religious dogma to its foundations. Havelock Ellis and Sigmund Freud had published studies avowing that sexuality was a fundamental characteristic of all normal women.

Yet, society as a whole responded slowly to these momentous changes. From the perspective of the masses, these advances were remote, with little impact on their daily lives. In 1925, historian Mark Sullivan compared his modern America with that at the turn of the century:

> In 1900, "short-haired woman" was a phrase of jibing; women doctors were looked on partly with ridicule, partly with suspicion. Of prohibition and votes for women, the most conspicuous function was to provide material for newspaper jokes. . . . The hairpin, as well as the bicycle, the horseshoe, and the buggy were the bases of established and . . . permanent businesses. Ox-teams could still be seen on country roads; horse-drawn streetcars in the cities. Horses or mules for trucks were practically universal; livery stables were everywhere.[1]

Indeed, in 1900 few American homes had electricity or indoor bathrooms. Automobiles were toys for the wealthy, and telephones were conveniences for prosperous urban businesses.

Figure 2-1. Corsets of the nineteenth century were designed to constrict a woman's abdomen into a tiny, cinched waist to achieve the desired hourglass silhouette. Ads 1894.

Doctors and modern medicine were only to be called upon in dire emergencies. Freud and Ellis were unknown outside of professional circles. Darwin was universally suppressed. Women in the workplace were acceptable only in the case of justifiable financial needs. Women in higher education were rare. Women in competitive sports were mostly confined to girls' school events that were usually closed to the public. Gender role socialization taught little girls to prepare to be wives and mothers, and boys to be familial patriarchs. Victorianism continued to thrive in the fabric of American daily life well into the first decades of the twentieth century.

Although historians can point to a number of socioeconomic changes, including some of those mentioned above, that created the first fissures in the solidity of Victorianism, two uniquely modern industries were at the forefront of the assault: advertising and fashion. As a unified force, the influence of these two marketing juggernauts was pervasive and percolated rapidly through all strata of American society. "When advertising and sales promotion ride in the tide of fashion," wrote economist Paul Nystrom, "they undoubtedly supplement each other very effectively."[2]

As was discussed in the preceding chapter, the groundwork for what would become a symbiotic relationship of fashion and advertising was laid in the second industrial revolution of the nineteenth century. With improved manufacturing technologies, new ideas of flow production, and more efficient distribution channels, the fashion industry began to evolve from the limited market scope of handcrafted couture to mass production of ready-to-wear styles. Unlike with standardized products such as soap or toothpaste, fashion created new product models each season. The challenge then was to expand a consumer market not only to sustain mass production, but also to generate a high turnover of product lines. To achieve this, ready-to-wear manufacturers increasingly turned to advertising to get their ephemeral messages before a mass audience of consumers. Across the decades of the twentieth century, the coalition of fashion and advertising sometimes altered, sometimes simply reflected, the landscape of American society.

The Interlude that Was Edwardianism, 1900–1908

The heir to Queen Victoria was Edward VII. His consort, Queen Alexandra, was a tall, slender beauty who would be the last royal to showcase fashion until Princess Diana in the 1980s. Although Alexandra patriotically patronized British fashion houses, the prevailing trends she wore still originated in Paris.

The first and most dramatic change in fashions at the turn of the twentieth century was the introduction of an entirely new silhouette created by a redesigned corset. For decades prior to

that, corsets had been laced up tightly to produce an hourglass figure with a constricted, tiny waist. (Figure 2-1.) All manner of health risks were endured to achieve this fashionable look. A doctor writing in 1870 complained, "Why is it, by what strange freak of fashion and blindness to artistic rules, women of the present day think that a deformed and ill-proportioned waist is a requisite of beauty, we do not know."[3] In response to the health issue, French designer Mme. Gaches-Sarraute introduced a completely reengineered corset in 1900. The new design was structured to relieve pressures exerted on a woman's diaphragm and internal organs by the prevalent styles of the day. Instead of having a curved, concave front, the new corset had a straight-line busk that began lower on the chest and extended more deeply over the hips. The resulting S-line thrust the bust forward into a pouter pigeon profile and forced the hips back into an exaggerated kangaroo stance. Unfortunately, the "health corset" did not achieve its intent. Pain and

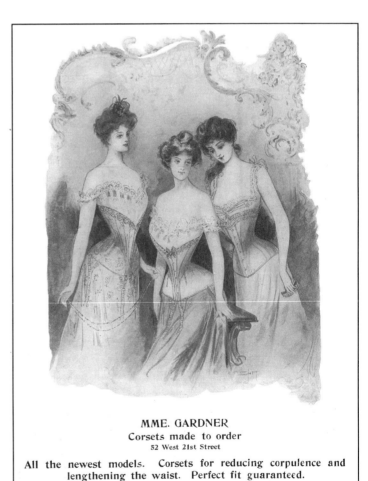

MME. GARDNER
Corsets made to order
52 West 21st Street
All the newest models. Corsets for reducing corpulence and lengthening the waist. Perfect fit guaranteed.

Figure 2-2. The S-bend corset was originally introduced to relieve the unhealthy constraints of earlier styles. Instead, it forced the hips back and the bust forward into an exaggerated kangaroo stance. Ad 1900.

Fall Opening

Mme. E. Morrison
Importer of
ROBES AND MILLINERY

The illustrations here shown represent some of our importations this season.

We shall be pleased to have you inspect the others.

7 West 32nd Street, New York
Near Fifth Avenue

Figure 2-3. Modes of the Edwardian period largely continued in the styles of the 1896–98 seasons. For example, the bishop's sleeve and the bell-shaped skirt remained popular for more than a decade. Changes in Edwardian fashions were subtly governed by fabrics, ornamentation, and accessories. Ad 1901.

innovative fashion styles. In fact, Edwardian fashion designs continued to be modeled on many of the stylistic changes that had occurred in the 1896–98 seasons. For example, the huge leg-of-mutton sleeves that had been popular in the early 1890s were at first moderated in size and then inverted into the bishop's sleeve with the fullness at the wrist rather than at the shoulder. The bishop's sleeve continued to be popular for years afterward. Similarly, the gored, bell-shaped skirt with a close fit over the hips also remained constant from the 1890s till around 1910, especially in ready-to-wear. (Figure 2-3.) Instead of innovative designs, the three changing modes that governed fashion styles of the Edwardian period were fabrics, ornamentation, and accessories.

During the closing dozen or so years of the nineteenth century, Parisian couturiers designed fashions in the style tapissier. That is, the favored fabrics used in fashions paralleled those used for interior upholstery and draperies: stiff satins, taffetas, plushes, jacquards, toiles, and tapestries. The Edwardian lady, however, preferred to adorn herself with deli-

KEISER HAND-DRAWN COLLARS, CUFFS AND STOCKS
COLLARS, 50¢
STOCKS, 75¢ AND UPWARDS

Guaranteed
Handwork

EVERY PIECE BEARS ABOVE LABEL

Figure 2-4. The exuberance of ornamentation, rich fabrics, and an abundance of accessories hallmarked the fashion trends of the Edwardian upper classes. Ad 1903.

discomfort from the stress on the spine, lower back, and hip and shoulder joints were common. Nevertheless, the radical proportions of the S-bend created a dynamic new look that swept the world of fashion. (Figure 2-2 and color plate 1.)

Almost immediately, corset makers saturated magazines and direct mail catalogs with depictions of their versions of the S-bend look in fashion. Illustrators had to rethink the new representation of the female fashion silhouette. Across the board, from the simplicity of the shirtwaist to the opulence of evening gowns, the S-bend was uniformly applied despite its seemingly impossible and unnatural configuration. Simply put, "the fashionable Edwardian lady did not want to follow nature," noted historian Elizabeth Ewing.[4]

Ironically, though, the S-bend silhouette did not inspire

cate silks, soft faille, crepe de chine, froths of chiffon, laces, and airy netting.

Exuberant ornamentation was another distinguishing feature of Edwardian fashion. (Figure 2-4.) In a 1902 report from Paris, *Vogue* noted: "Everything is still trimmed with silk cords and tassels, or bobbing pompoms strung on long fringes. Sleeves are slashed and laced with these, falling four or five inches from the forearms. Cloaks especially are smartly fastened with these passementerie trimmings which bob and dangle with fascinating coquetry."[5] Another report from Paris a few months later emphasized still more variations of ornamentation. "Egypt, Japan, China, Persia, the peasants of Europe, the redskins of America are all consulted, metaphorically speaking, for ideas in the arrangement of borders, designs and harmonious colorings."[6] All these decorative excesses provided subtleties of change without the drama of innovation.

Finally, the greatest fashion extravagance was manifested in the Edwardian lady's choice of accessories. (See chapter 8.) The Paris correspondents for *Vogue* during this time frequently devoted extensive editorial space to detailed descriptions of accessories that they had glimpsed at social events such as the 1903 Grand Steeplechase at Auteuil. Gainsborough hats, lace scarves, pompadour hair bows, pearl-encrusted belts, and art nouveau hair combs were described in exacting detail and duly credited to the wearer, especially if titled.[7]

Such lavish excesses as ornamented lace teagowns and art

Figure 2-5. American department and specialty stores advertised tailor-made replications of Parisian originals. Fullaytar and Keen ad 1902, Oatman ad 1903.

"ISN'T HEAVEN IN THERE?"
"YES, BUT THIS IS THE LADIES' ENTRANCE."

Yet for all it seems that she
Girlish ways would banish,
Knickerbockered to the knee
In a manner mannish—
Give me Her! I little care
So we go out "biking;"
What she chooses she may wear,
It quite suits my liking!

Felix Carmen.

THE SPINNING WHEEL.
(NEW AND OLD.)

Fickle custom! Nothing stays!
There is no controlling
Fate or Fortune in these days,
Now the wheel is rolling.
Here's Priscilla in a gown
Nothing less than shocking—
Short?—It hardly reaches down
To Priscilla's stocking!

Years ago when at the wheel
Sat Priscilla spinning,
Exercising toe and heel,
And the homespun winning—
That was different from this
Spinning home, and saying:
"Miles are good for any miss"—
With the proverb playing.

Figure 2-6. In the 1890s, women by the thousands joined in the bicycling craze. Ready-to-wear and corset manufacturers introduced radically new styles designed specifically for this New Woman. Cartoons from *Life* 1896.

nouveau hair combs were for the exclusive enjoyment of the upper classes. Ready-to-wear manufacturers could not replicate the many details of tucks, pleats, insets, appliques, hand embroidery, and border treatments that distinguished these garments. American department stores and specialty shops that advertised variations of these costumes usually had the staff and facilities for tailoring custom-fit replications of Paris or London originals. (Figure 2-5.)

The S-bend silhouette of the Edwardian period represents the last time in fashion history that the mature, full-figured woman was the ideal. The emphasis on ample breasts and rounded hips configured by the S-bend corset was a direct descendant of nineteenth-century modes created by Parisian couturiers such as Charles Worth and Jacques Doucet. Even as the S-bend silhouette took hold and became the first sweeping trend of the twentieth century, on the horizon was a new ideal in feminine beauty and fashion from America that would eclipse that of the European aristocracy. Wrote Elizabeth Ewing of the Edwardian lady, "she was blissfully unaware . . . that hers was a sunset song, and that, even in her own time, she was becoming an anachronism."[8]

The Gibson Girl and American Fashions

In 1848, a group of women met for a conference in Seneca Falls, New York. Among the issues that attendees considered was dress reform. Although some nineteenth-century women abandoned their corsets and a few even donned a style of Turkish pantaloons called bloomers, these feminists were considered fringe extremists and were unable to generate much interest in their crusade. Still, the issue of dress reform remained a cause for progressive women's organizations.

Around 1890 two unrelated phenomena originated in America almost simultaneously that would influence dress reform more than all the combined efforts of feminists during the preceding forty years. One was the development of the safety bicycle, and the other was the publication of drawings depicting the New Woman as envisioned by illustrator Charles Dana Gibson.

Although versions of the bicycle had been around for decades, only in the 1890s did the introduction of the safety bicycle generate mass appeal and, consequently, mass production. Unlike the earlier "boneshaker" models, the new safety bicycle featured inflatable rubber tires, a chain drive, and a padded seat. Advertising from bicycle manufacturers extensively targeted women by promoting the benefits of recreation and health. Women responded enthusiastically to the bicycling craze.

For proper breathing during bicycle excursions, many

women abandoned their corsets for the first time. For those who were reluctant to go that far, corset manufacturers provided alternative designs that were shortened to the waist and constructed with a less-constricting fit. In addition, skirt hemlines rose as much as three inches to create the "rainy daisy" styles, so named because the hems could be kept dry on rainy days. By the middle of the 1890s, some daring women even rode their bicycles in divided skirts or breeches called knickerbockers. (Figure 2-6.)

Another indirect but significant influence on American women's fashions was the image of the Gibson Girl. Charles Dana Gibson was a prolific illustrator for advertising and mass-circulation magazines such as *Life*, *Harper's Weekly*, and *Ladies' Home Journal*. In 1890 he introduced his first pen-and-ink drawings of the New Woman. She was taller than most women depicted in illustrations of the era, many times shown at about the same height as her male companions. Her facial features were solidly articulated: heavy-lidded eyes, sometimes with a defiant glint, arched eyebrows, full lips, and a strong jawline. Her hair was most always piled atop her head in twists, rolls, and chignons, usually casual in look but sometimes formal when appropriate. She played golf, hunted, canoed, bicycled, and rode horseback—often hatless and jacketless in only a shirtwaist. She also dined with titled aristocrats and wore sumptuously accoutered evening gowns. (Figure 2-7.) Art historian Susan Meyer described how the Gibson Girl was perceived in her time: "She was the flowering of the pioneer spirit that had accomplished the security and freedom

Figure 2-7. The Gibson Girl epitomized the ideal beauty of American women from the 1890s through the early 1910s. Illustrations by Charles Dana Gibson from *Ladies' Home Journal* 1902.

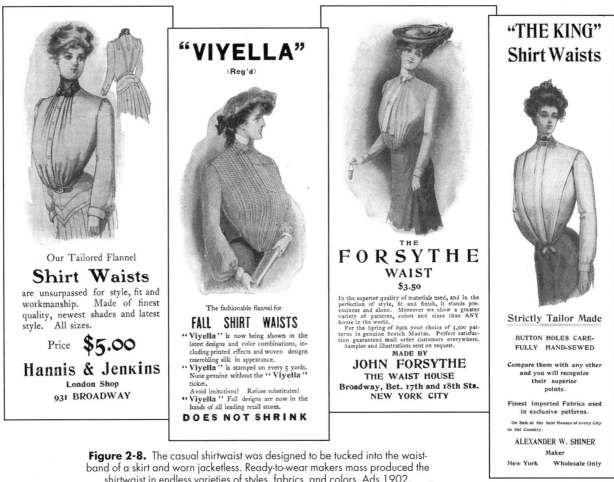

Figure 2-8. The casual shirtwaist was designed to be tucked into the waist-band of a skirt and worn jacketless. Ready-to-wear makers mass produced the shirtwaist in endless varieties of styles, fabrics, and colors. Ads 1902.

making her arrival possible. She set a style in looks and dress but—even more significant—she brought about a change in social attitudes. . . . The Gibson Girl established a new set of feminine values: by emphasizing self-reliance and gallantry as charming and legitimate feminine characteristics."[9] For an entire generation of American women, the Gibson Girl was a role model and an icon of aspiration.

As noted above, two key elements of change in fashion— the Gibson Girl's shirtwaist and the rainy daisy skirt—were to carry into the Edwardian years with two very different results. The former would continue to grow in popularity and actually extend to the present day in thousands of variations on the theme, and the latter would dramatically influence couture fashions in the 1908–10 seasons.

The shirtwaist was an informal, simple style originally based on menswear shirts. Basically, it was a blouse tucked into the waistband of a skirt that could be worn jacketless. The concept of the waist and skirt duo was the birth of the "sepa-rates" category of ready-to-wear manufacturing—garments that could be bought as an ensemble or separately. Unlike the

complicated, lavishly embellished designs of Edwardian cou-ture, the shirtwaist blouse could be mass produced in an end-less assortment of fabrics, colors, and styles. (Figure 2-8.) The newest looks in the shirtwaist were frequently reported in *Vogue,* including feature articles on elaborate collars, cuffs, and bodice treatments that elevated the utilitarian garment to the status of haute mode. Several versions of the shirtwaist were even offered by *Vogue*'s pattern department.[10]

As with the shirtwaist, the new, plainer styles of skirts had popular appeal and were easily mass produced. They were comfortable, easy to launder and iron, and inexpensive, even when tailor-made. The shorter varieties of the rainy daisy skirt, sometimes called the golf skirt or walking skirt, were cut simply and made without embellishments that could get caught in the mechanisms of a bicycle or in the branches of shrubs along hiking trails. Even so, the shorter skirts were not worn strictly for physically exerting activities. In large cities, as the work force of women began to grow, the shorter skirts were increasingly popular for street wear since they were eas-ier to maneuver on mass-transit vehicles and office building

Binner
Corſetiere

Is

Cultivating Figures

with Her

Famous Corsets

The New Beautiful FALL
MODELS, ORIGINATED
and PATENTED by Mme.
Binner, will show the Features
confined exclusively to the
FAMOUS BINNER
CORSETS

───────────

Custom made under Mme. Binner's personal supervision at

**18 East 45th St.,
New York**

(Booklet Free On Request.)

(Patented)

Figure 2-9. In 1908 Parisian couturier Paul Poiret introduced the directoire style, which draped fluidly over the body. The fuller bustline and rounder hips of the S-bend silhouette were replaced with an emphasis on a narrow, girlish figure. Ad 1909.

elevators, not to mention on densely crowded sidewalks.

Vogue noted in its Paris report of 1907 that "Americans have been responsible for the innovation of several fashions among the Parisiennes," of which first on the list was "the shorter skirt."[11] The impact of that influence would be especially significant in how the shorter hemline would be integrated into the radical new looks from the couturiers the following year.

Hemlines and Hobble Skirts

In the Paris collections of 1908–09, designers presented a sweeping transformation of fashion, led principally by couturier Paul Poiret. Almost in an instant the S-bend silhouette and the frilly excesses of Edwardian designs were superseded by dramatically new looks. Three key changes formed the basis of the new fashion drama.

First, the contrived S-bend corset was discarded in favor of a version that more naturally comported with the body. Corsets became longer, extending below the hips and even to

midthigh. (Figure 2-9.) Women could stand upright again, and the constricted waist was eased. The result was a slim, youthful look. The curvaceous ideal of the full-figured, mature woman now passed into fashion history forever.

Second, the baroque opulence of shape and decoration of the Edwardian styles was supplanted by simpler, more vertical lines. Revivals of the columnar, high-waisted silhouettes of the directoire era (c. 1795–99) were especially suited to the new narrow contours. Instead of pouter pigeon chests and robust hips, the contours of the body were more revealed by dresses that fluidly draped across the figure. Hemlines also began to rise above the vamp of the shoes. By the end of 1908, the first glimpses of this radical style change amongst the American elite were observed by *Vogue* as "ultra fashionable," with gowns that were "skimpy" and "fitted like a glove."[12] Shortened hemlines, "scarcely to the ankles," were likewise worthy of note, as *Vogue* reported from the Twenty-Fifth Annual Horse Show in Madison Square Gardens in 1909.[13]

Third, the layers of frilly petticoats were eliminated as a requisite for the narrower silhouette. In place of multiple petticoats, a simple chemise-style slip provided opacity beneath fine silk skirts while allowing the fabric to drape unimpeded in soft, vertical lines.

Another significant contribution from Poiret was his inventive and influential use of vivid color. He was one of the first designers to have his showroom models discard the traditional black or white stockings and wear hose of scintillating hues that flashed bright accents of color from beneath shortened hemlines. Among Poiret's inspirations for the use of color were the avant-garde circles of the visual and performing arts in Paris at the time. An exhibition of paintings in 1905 by les Fauves—translated as "the beasts"—presented the world of modern art with the bright colors and abstract images of Matisse, Vlaminck, and Derain. During the Russo-Japanese War of 1904–05, Paris bookshops, stationers, home and garden retailers, and textile shops abounded with products and wares decorated with Japanese or Russian motifs. In 1909–10, Sergei Diaghilev presented performances of *Cléopatre* and *Schéhérazade* by the Ballets Russes, which showcased exotic sets and costume designs by Léon Bakst. Around the same time, decorative patterns and design elements taken from the artwork of the Viennese Sezessionists, such as Gustav Klimt, were widely popular in the design of French fashion accessories, jewelry, and interiors. From these and similar sources, Poiret received energy and inspiration for the colorations of his trend-setting fashions. Purples and oranges, jewel-tone greens and reds, and shimmering golds and silvers were rampant in his favorite textiles. Vividly hued embroidery, beading, and trimming hallmarked his creations.

Fashion editors, though, did not quite know what to make

of the new couture styles from Paris. In October 1909, *Vogue* declared that the couturiers were "becoming more individual" by introducing "new customs and new ideas more in touch with modern needs, views and demands." Furthermore, "no one will be able to criticize upon the ground . . . that such and such a gown is not in the highest fashion as there will be a dozen leading models where once there were but two or three to choose from." [14]

Meanwhile, Main Street U.S.A. embraced many of the bold changes from Paris while retaining some elements of Edwardian style. (Figure 2-10.) *Ladies' Home Journal* reported in September 1910 how American style had adapted the innovations from Paris: "Never has there been so much simplicity in so many types of clothes. . . . It is nothing but short skirts, short jackets, little round bodices, small, narrow shoulders, short sleeves, and the slim, graceful silhouette." [15] Contrary to Parisian fashion trends, though, was the American resistance to the use of color. In the same edition of the *Journal,* Lou Eleanor Colby wrote that readers should use "Dame Nature" as a guide to color choices in fashion. "We shall find that the softer grayish colors or the rich, dark tones should form the main portion of our [ensembles], and that the

V 9. See description opposite.

V 11. See description opposite.

Figure 2-10. Although the slender, more youthful silhouette and shorter hemlines were adopted by American ready-to-wear manufacturers and retailers, Edwardian styling and embellishments remained popular into the 1910s. Franklin Simon ad 1909, Stern Brothers ad 1910.

stronger notes of vivid, pure color should be small."[16] The accompanying color plates in that issue, as well as those in American fashion catalogs of the period, confirmed that women were not ready for the startling use of color and textile prints that the sophisticated Europeans were relishing.

Ironically, during this time when American women were only occasionally accepting the fashion direction from Paris, the U.S. fashion industry failed to capitalize on the open opportunity. Even when magazine editors and journalists urged apparel and textile manufacturers to take leadership action, few mobilized. *Ladies' Home Journal*, especially, led the crusade for American fashion preeminence. In the 1909 "Autumn Fashion Number," Anna Westermann posed the editorial question, "Can America originate its own fashions?" She answered that regardless of how innovative and artistic French designs might seem, "they are not for us." Furthermore, she roundly criticized American clothing makers, retailers, and consumers for lazily acquiescing to the fashion dictates of Paris. "So positive has become both the need and desire in the evolution of an American style of dress," she insisted, "that we shall not only be co-equal with Paris, but perhaps excel it in cleverness and originality."[17] The following year, the *Journal*'s publisher, Edward Bok, went one step further when he offered to buy and publish fashion designs by Americans. "Are the only clever women in the world in Paris?" goaded Bok. "That is what we are told apropos of our American fashions—that the American woman cannot trim a hat in a new way—create a new frock—design a new shirtwaist—tie a jabot in a new way."[18] Unfortunately, though, this flurry of nationalistic campaigning failed to stimulate a creative force that would catapult America ahead of Paris in the arena of fashion design. By the beginning of World War I, such efforts had largely faded. Economist Paul Nystrom lamented a decade later, "Thus, at the very time when it might have attained its greatest importance, due to the isolation of France from the rest of the world by war, the movement itself had been deemed hopeless by American producers and distributors."[19] It would take another generation and another world war before American designers were again challenged to be free of Paris.

Surprisingly, though, the one trend that American women did accept almost immediately was Paul Poiret's hobble skirt. Although introduced in 1908 for a selected clientele, the slim, tubular shape of Poiret's narrow skirts became a key feature of most 1909–10 Paris collections. The contours of the hobble skirt were tapered from the hips to the ankles in such an extreme line—some with barely more than a twelve-inch opening at the hem—that women had to walk in short, mincing steps, or as some cartoonists captured, even hop to descend stairs or curbs. (Figure 2-11.) Stepping over streetside

Figure 2-11. The narrow, constraining hobble skirt was grist for the cartoonist's pen of 1909.

puddles or climbing into a carriage often required a woman to suffer the embarrassment of pulling up her skirt almost to the knees to keep from falling.

One reason for the instant success of the hobble skirt in America was mass production and mass marketing. Variations of the simple, narrow skirt were easily mass produced by American ready-to-wear makers. Subdued colorations and textile patterns were tailored to the taste of American women. Fashion retailers and catalogers eagerly bought up the production runs of the manufacturers and quickly began to promote the new look in their advertising. (Figure 2-12.) Versions of the slim, narrow skirt would remain popular until the beginning of World War I, especially varieties with kick pleats and side or back slits that eased the difficulty of mobility while maintaining the youthful, trim silhouette. (Color plate 2.)

World War I

In June 1914, Archduke Ferdinand, heir to the Austro-Hungarian Empire, was assassinated in Sarajevo by a Serbian nationalist. When the outraged Vienna government moved against the tiny Balkan country, czarist Russia promised

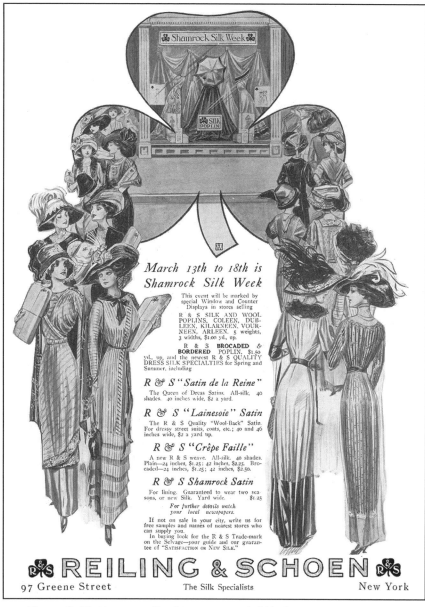

Figure 2-12. Variations of Paul Poiret's narrow hobble skirt were easily mass produced by American ready-to-wear manufacturers. Versions remained popular until the start of World War I. Reiling and Schoen ad 1911, Bergdorf and Goodman ad 1912.

support to its Slav neighbor. Germany's Kaiser Wilhelm then entered the conflict on the side of Austria-Hungary and quickly struck against its archenemy France by invading through unsuspecting Belgium. With her shores now jeopard-ized by Germany, Britain allied with France and Russia, and World War I erupted.

The United States remained neutral for the time being. Meanwhile, the war was actually an economic boon for Americans. Immigration virtually ceased, so an important source of cheap labor dried up. Manufacturers had to pay ever-higher wages as the demand for export goods rapidly increased. Unskilled workers left their positions as servants and laborers to join factory assembly lines. An enormous pop-ulation of African Americans from the South migrated north into the vacuum of the labor shortage.

In Paris, the fashion industry was impacted immediately. Some couturiers, such as Paul Poiret, Edward Molyneux, and Jacques Worth, left their salons to join the military. Others converted their businesses into factories for the war. In Sep-tember 1914, *Vogue*'s correspondent from Paris wrote, "When the [couturier] was not away on affairs of war, his assistants were; his designers were enlisting; little sewing girls were with the Red Cross or he had set them to work in his ateliers making bandages; his [sales staff] were with their families, helping in the preparations for war; approached on business, they could only weep."[20] Shortages of fabrics and related materials for apparel became more severe as European factories were destroyed and imports declined. Everyone suffered from restrictions on travel and shipping.

Condé Nast and his new editor in chief of *Vogue*, Edna Woolman Chase, were panic stricken at the thought of no more Parisian fashions for the duration. To be assured that fashion news, editorials, and advertising continued to fill the pages of *Vogue*, Chase hit on an idea to feature American designers. Topmost in New York at that time was Henri Bendel. She approached the designer with a plan for a war benefit to showcase American fashions. When Bendel agreed, other design shops jumped on the bandwagon. Chase also enlisted the support of women from New York's most socially prominent families—Vanderbilt, Whitney, Astor, Belmont—who deigned to socialize with dressmakers and other fashion tradesmen for this charity event. The three-day Fashion Fete was held in November 1914 and was a huge success. Thousands of dollars were raised for the Committee of Mercy, which would provide relief to women and children left destitute by the war in Europe. Emily Post wrote for *Vogue* about the "fashionables" who were in attendance, noting that "each woman in the audience delightedly applauded her own dressmaker, heart and hand, and each had a rather protective feeling toward the Estelle, or Mary, or Rose, who wore the dresses of the establishment she patronized most, and Rose, Mary, and Estelle as they saw the faces of the women before whom they were accustomed to exhibit gowns, smiled a delighted recognition."[21] Also, the Fashion Fete provided *Vogue* with enough material to fill fifteen pages in the December 1, 1914, edition, and another twelve ensembles were featured in the December 15 issue. (Figure 2-13.)

Notable in the photographs and drawings of the designs from the Fashion Fete was a dramatically new silhouette. Despite the difficulties created by the war, Parisian couturiers continued to design new collections and export models when possible. In response to the zeitgeist of war, several new developments in couture styles occurred rapidly. Changes in style now reflected women's everyday needs rather than the glamour or mystique of fashion. Clothes that provided comfort and freedom of movement were necessary for a great number of women who had to undertake all sorts of activities for the war effort, from volunteer work with emergency agencies to full-time employment filling vacancies for men away in the military. Narrow skirts and fitted bodices disappeared almost

Figure 2-13. At the beginning of World War I, *Vogue* sponsored a fashion fete to spotlight American designers. Proceeds from the three-day event in November 1914 went to a war charity. Shown here are two of the dozens of designs donated by American designers and featured in *Vogue*: left, fur trimmed velvet afternoon dress by Henri Bendel; right, fur trimmed coat by Thurn.

immediately. Hemlines continued to rise and would be about eight to ten inches from the floor by war's end. Skirts became fuller, almost voluminous initially, despite fabric shortages, although materials were of poorer quality. Jackets and coats were as shapeless and simple as menswear of the time. Military motifs such as wide, loose belts, epaulets, capelets, metallic buttons, and big patch pockets were liberally incorporated into the new styles. Beading, fringe, embroidery, and other such opulent embellishments were minimized. Colors were muted. "Striking costumes do not meet with favor in Paris at present," *Vogue* reaffirmed in 1915.[22] With the world at war, conspicuous consumption and self-indulgent behavior were viewed as unpatriotic. "Social affairs in Paris are at a standstill," wrote a *Vogue* correspondent in June 1915. "Occasionally one finds a handful of people gathered together over a cup of tea, but instead of the usual merry tea-table gossip nothing is heard but

Figure 2-14. Within the first few months of the start of World War I, fashion styles changed dramatically to reflect the zeitgeist of war. Fuller skirts, shorter hemlines, and baggy menswear jackets afforded comfort and ease of movement. Epaulets, patch pockets, capelets, and other military embellishments replaced lace, beading, and embroidery. Textile patterns and colors were more subdued. Ads 1915.

businesslike plans for Red Cross work, and stories of the war." [23] In neutral America of 1915, too, social events not linked to war benefits became much subdued.

American ready-to-wear makers did not suffer the same shortages and hardships as did the fashion leaders in Paris. Textile mills in the South and New England ran at full production throughout the war years. The economic boom in the U.S. created a leap in mass consumption. In addition, as the editors of *Vogue* happily discovered, there was no interruption in the news of fashion direction from Paris after all. By the start of 1915, American fashion advertising and retail catalogs reflected how quickly U.S. ready-to-wear makers had responded to the stylistic changes introduced by the French just a few months earlier. (Figure 2-14.)

By 1917, America could no longer enjoy the luxury of neutrality in the global conflict. The sinking of the *Lusitania* by a German U-boat had killed 128 Americans, the destruction of unarmed U.S. merchant ships by German submarines accelerated, and Allied propaganda against "Hunnish" barbarism in Belgium and France abounded in American media. A reluctant President Woodrow Wilson convinced Congress to declare war in April.

During the war years of 1917–18, fashion styles continued an evolution toward economy. As U.S. textile mills converted to wartime production and fabric exports to France virtually ceased, Paris designers shortened hemlines and narrowed skirts. The looser fit and other design features of menswear and military uniforms continued to influence the plainer look of most women's apparel. Germany had been a major source of dyes, so dark colors and simpler textile patterns prevailed. (Figure 2-15.) "Long, slim, dark and very clever are these new frocks;" observed *Vogue* in the fall of 1918, "with true wisdom, they take the line and let the trimming go."[24] Dresses with sleeves shortened above the elbow became more acceptable in warm weather daytime. Eveningwear collections offered fewer models, and those were almost severe in simplicity compared to the sumptuousness of prewar tastes.

American ready-to-wear manufacturers and retailers carefully balanced their advertising messages with reinforcements of restraint and conservation while at the same time promoting consumption of each season's newest fashions. "Betty

Figure 2-15. By the fourth year of World War I, severe limitations in fabric imports led French designers to narrow skirts and shorten hemlines even more. Loose-fitting jackets, somber colors, and other influences of menswear styling remained prevalent in women's apparel. Ad 1918.

Figure 2-16. As large numbers of women entered the work force during World War I, job-safety issues forced changes in social conventions that were to profoundly affect fashion. Women cut their hair and wore trousers into the workplace. Although sports pants for women, such as riding habits, were statements of fashion, work pants were not. Nevertheless, the parallel paths of the two styles paved the way for greater acceptance of women wearing trousers. Ads 1918–19.

Wales knows that wartime dresses should conform to the rules of fabric conservation, and should be practical, durable and economically priced," declared the body copy in a 1918 ad for the dressmaker.[25] Typical headlines of ads from that year included:

"Appropriate attire for war-time social activities"
"The most beautiful, durable, economical war-time fabric"
"Authorized new fashions planned to meet war-time expenditures"
"War conservation frocks"[26]

One other significant change in the wardrobe of American women that occurred during the 1910s was a broad, general adaptation of trousers. In the early part of the decade, women's trousers were limited to designs for elite or esoteric cliques, such as knickerbockers for bicyclists, jodhpurs for riding clubs, and Poiret's jupe-culottes for socialites in the vanguard of fashion. Women rarely wore these trouser styles beyond the activity or environment for which they were designed. However, necessity changed this social protocol during the war years. Women by the millions entered the work force as huge numbers of men left for war. Long skirts—and

long hair—proved dangerous for certain jobs, the remedy for which was to shed both. Suddenly, women were seen in all sorts of public places wearing pants, and not just on the job. Obviously, these women had to make their way to and from places of employment. They had to take care of domestic errands on the way home from work and were commonly seen in banks, post offices, and stores still dressed in their pants.

Although work pants for women were not regarded as fashion, ready-to-wear makers included the emotional appeal of style in their advertising. For example, the copy in a 1918 Finck and Company ad emphasized that the company produced pants for women that were "necessary because women workers must adopt an efficient work-garment to produce effective results. Modest because they are made along lines that are essentially feminine, having been designed by women who know how to put style even into a work-garment. . . . Safe because there are no loose ends or cumbersome skirts to become danger-points."[27] Despite the claim of style in the copy, though, the photo of the woman in baggy overalls was still far from the fashion presentation of the figures in the Bonwit Teller "equestrienne" ad of the same year. (Figure 2-

16.) Work pants were not regarded as fashion, unlike trouser styles such as those for riding habits or cocktail pyjama suits. In addition, apparel makers and retailers advertised women's work pants in mass publications whose readership was largely from the middle and working classes, while ads for equestrian breeches were featured in fashion and society magazines.

Nevertheless, the advent of trousers as a mainstream garment for women was a significant change in American social conventions. In the postwar years, women continued to adopt forms of trousers for daywear, such as beach pyjamas, and for specialized attire, such as menswear-styled swimsuits and boudoir pajamas—all of which paved the path in the 1920s for an even-wider acceptance of women's trousers as a fashion style.

Conclusion

As the twentieth century dawned, a new era in fashion and consumerism emerged in America, fueled by ever-faster cycles of fashion change combined with mass production and mass marketing. The introduction of the S-bend corset in 1900 coincided with the start of the Edwardian era. During this period both fashion and society were transformed from an easy, Victorian provincialism to the frenetic, technology-driven modernism of a new century. The S-bend silhouette was fresh and exciting, and provided a clear delineation in style from that of the late nineteenth century. Most importantly, it was a fashion trend in which virtually all classes of women could participate fully. Ready-to-wear manufacturers mass produced the newly engineered corsets and the Edwardian fashions that went with them, making the styles broadly affordable. Marketers made the fashions readily available on a national scale by mass distribution through retail chains and direct mail catalogs. Advertising widely publicized the new looks, educating the masses and creating aspirational wants.

As the Edwardian period ended, pivotal new modes from Paris swept away the S-bend styles. Skirts became narrow, columnar, and youthful. The simple designs were easy for ready-to-wear makers to produce, and advances in distribution methods and the growing reach of advertising fed a burgeoning consumerism.

When World War I erupted, the priorities and mores of most women changed almost overnight. Fashion makers and marketers were quick to respond by producing clothing that women needed—comfortable, durable, and functional styles for their wartime activities. Advertisers tailored their fashion messages to the times with patriotic themes and advice on conservation and shortages. As women went to work in factories and services to fill the labor shortage, they required clothing that was practical and safe around machinery and equipment. Apparel manufacturers quickly produced new forms of functional work trousers for women. Advertisers helped dispel the social stigma of women wearing trousers by asserting the modernity and femininity of the styles. And American society was reluctantly thrust down the uncertain road of progress once again.

When the war ended, fashion makers, marketers, and advertisers were poised to serve the pent-up demand for the new, the modern, and the innovative. Consumerism was about to soar to unprecedented heights in the coming decade.

3

HIGHS OF THE TWENTIES AND
LOWS OF THE THIRTIES

Following the Armistice in November 1918, and victory celebrations in the spring of 1919, Americans looked for a return to normalcy in the new decade ahead. But the Great War had changed everything in such a short time: social mores and attitudes, politics, regional economies, medical science, and technologies. On the threshold of the 1920s, the doughboy came home to a postwar economic depression, a nationwide Prohibition, the hysteria of the Red Scare, and most notable, a new American woman. The mothers, sisters, wives, and sweethearts who had been left at home to tend the hearth fires instead had been transformed. A nation in crisis had called upon them to work in offices, operate heavy equipment in factories, learn industrial skills, and organize and supervise other workers. They had earned a paycheck, and with it, economic independence. They had discovered a purpose and a new self-esteem not tied to the kitchen and nursery.

In the 1920s, American women continued to achieve even-greater independence and self-reliance. Many chose to continue working, even as government agencies urged them to relinquish jobs to returning soldiers. Manufacturers and retailers developed installment credit plans, which allowed women to purchase their own cars, giving them unprecedented freedom of mobility. The Nineteenth Amendment was passed in 1920, granting women the right to vote. Margaret Sanger and Marie Stopes introduced methods of birth control to the masses, freeing women from unwanted child-rearing responsibilities. Enrollments at universities soared as women sought advanced education. Women athletes set records, won championships, and broke stereotypes. The modern woman of the 1920s smoked cigarettes in public. She experimented with her sexuality. Feminine beauty was redefined: instead of the demure, alabaster lady of Edwardian times, the New Woman now bobbed her hair and wore lipstick, cheek rouge, and mascara.

Modern mass media and mass production helped change the American cultural landscape at a dizzying pace during the 1920s. Mass production made radios affordable to large segments of consumers. The immediacy of radio broadcasting instantly brought into homes coast-to-coast news of current events, innovative sounds of Jazz Age music, and new methods of advertising. Movies educated and influenced women in the ways of a rapidly moving, contemporary society. Improvements in printing technologies made possible an avalanche of color magazines, catalogs, and all manner of advertising print materials for every American home. Increased production of electric irons, washing machines, refrigerators, toasters, and a host of similar products improved the quality of life for a growing middle class. Telephones for home use became a common necessity. The cost of a new automobile dropped to less than four hundred dollars, creating an explosion in travel and vacation-related businesses. "The inhabitants of our country are stimulated to new wants in all directions," President Calvin Coolidge remarked in a 1926 speech.[1]

Fashion before the Roar

During the months following the end of the war, the United States briefly suffered an economic downturn. War industries had to shut down or convert back to the production of consumer goods. As a result, raw materials for manufacturing had to be rechanneled or warehoused. Exports were still limited due to bankrupted European economies. Unemployment rose and wage levels dropped.

Soon, though, consumer spending began to fuel a recovery. Soldiers returning from military duty were eager to doff uniforms for civvies. The sacrifices and privations endured by the home-front populace were relieved by an indulgence of consumption. Americans began restocking, repairing, or replacing the old with everything new: new cars, new home improvements, new appliances, new personal care products, and new fashions.

In Paris, the new in fashion meant new names at the forefront of design. Although the stars of a decade earlier—Poiret, Worth, Pacquin, Doucet—resumed designing after the war, they ceased to be the leaders of innovation. Poiret, for example, picked up where he had left off in 1914 by ornamenting

Figure 3-1. By the start of the 1920s, a confusing myriad of fashion styles were advertised by ready-to-wear makers and retailers. Ads showed that skirt silhouettes could be either full or narrow. Revivals included the directoire waistline, the pannier, and the crinoline. The one common stylistic element was the short hemline. Ads 1920.

women with sumptuous fabrics and decorative embellishments. His failure to understand that women now wanted comfort and ease in their fashions, not artifice, eventually led to his bankruptcy and the permanent closing of his shops before the end of the decade.

The rising stars of Parisian fashion in 1920 were enthusiastic proponents of comfort chic: Jean Patou, Madeleine Vionnet, Edward Molyneux, and Gabrielle "Coco" Chanel. The common denominator amongst the leaders of French fashion in the 1920s was simplicity. Patou took his influence from elements of art deco design, incorporating that purity of line into garments that epitomized modern sportswear. Vionnet's approach to simplicity was to cut fabric on the bias for a flowing fluidity of garments reminiscent of those in a neoclassical frieze. Chanel, though, best understood the modern woman's desire for comfort and style. She created sports suits, dresses, and pullovers of jersey knits, which had primarily been used for swimwear and underwear before that time. When she became mistress to the Duke of Westminster, she introduced the combination cardigan jacket and softly pleated skirt made of English tweed. Her clothes were so comfortable because she tried them out herself rather than merely sketching concepts on paper. "Delightfully wearable clothes are always to be found in the collection of Chanel," rhapsodized *Vogue* in 1921.[2] Chanel's influential personal style included an abundance of oversized costume jewelry, print scarves, and men's cardigans, jackets, and belts.

The problem for consumers was that, except for short skirts and the beginning of the lowered waistline, fashion designs were all over the chart. (Figure 3-1.) Although *Vogue*'s Paris reporter questioned in 1920 "whether or not the mode of full skirts is accepted as a whole," skirt silhouettes were widely advertised as both full and narrow.[3] Equally baffling for the editors of *Vogue* in 1920 was the myriad of "clever ideas, old and new," including revivalisms and theatrical costume influences.[4] The return of the Ballets Russes and a magnificent production of *Aida* that season in Paris inspired fashions decorated with elements taken from Egyptian, Persian, Turkish, and Chinese motifs. Historical influences included "bodices quaintly second empire and silhouettes of 1885," with attempts to reintroduce hooped skirts and even the bustle.[5] Also revived were the directoire waistline and panniers.

Eveningwear designs, especially, exhibited the more extreme versions of the historical costumes and revivalisms. Many evening gown styles of 1920 seemed to be throw-backs to the tapered hobble skirts of a decade earlier, only with much-longer trains or trailing swathes of material draped from the shoulders, waist, or hips. (Figure 3-2.) "Some of the houses show gowns with immense trains, such as we have not

seen in many seasons," noted a *Vogue* Paris report.[6] However, Vionnet's simplistic Grecian-styled gowns were as readily worn to society events as were the crinolined and ornamented dresses by Worth or Doucet. "Greater variety, indeed, appears in these evening costumes" observed *Vogue*, "than in any other phase of the mode and in none of its phases is the mode unanimous in favor of any given period."[7] Therein lay the dilemma for ready-to-wear makers and advertisers who needed clear direction of fashion styles.

Consequently, few of the exaggerated revivalisms and theatrical influences translated into a broad appeal with American women. Variations of the pannier and other hip treatments were popular for a couple of years, as was the continued preference for the peplum in assorted cuts and lengths. Ready-to-wear makers and retailers discovered, almost belatedly, that what American women wanted most were short skirts, whatever the style.

Battle of the Hemline

Ironically, one of the most notable marketing failures of Paris couturiers was the hemline of the early 1920s. By the fall of 1921, designers such as Lanvin, Molyneux, Chanel, and Lelong dramatically dropped the hemlines on dresses. In its report on the Paris collections of that season, *Vogue* declared that "modes at the openings show the influence of many periods and countries and disagree as to silhouette, but agree as to . . . longer skirts."[8] For the winter of 1921–22, the fashion editors predicted that "the tendency is more marked towards the ankle-length skirt."[9] *Vogue*'s patterns, too, illustrated the longer hemline throughout 1922, 1923, and into the beginning of 1924. "What smart New York women consider chic," avowed *Vogue* in July 1923, were skirts that "reach to just above the ankle."[10] Even a year later, *Vogue*'s reference to the short skirt still meant a length to only just above the ankles, as depicted by the editorial illustrations.

American ready-to-wear manufacturers, always eager to follow the dictates of Paris, produced lines of dresses, coats, and skirts with the longer length well into 1924. Textile manufacturers were ecstatic. Retailers bought what the makers produced, which they promptly displayed in their windows and featured in ads. (Figure 3-3.) American women, though, rejected the longer skirt, year after year. As stores became backlogged with alterations orders for shortening hemlines, they demanded that apparel makers produce styles with shorter skirts.[11]

By the end of 1924, French couturiers finally began to respond to the marketplace with much shortened hemlines. Autumn collections that year exhibited skirts even shorter than those of just six months earlier, and within a year hemlines were to the knees. (Figure 3-4.)

Panoply
A new creation
by
The Shelton Looms

THE distinctive texture of this new fabric makes it especially desirable for the most charming of costumes.

Panoply—beautiful in its sheen of silky meshes—a fabric as magnificent as velvet, as clinging as satin—unrivalled for wraps, evening gowns and smart costumes for the country club and beach.

Pan Ondulay, also a new creation, is similar to Panoply in texture. Instead of a smooth surface, however, it boasts a fascinating undulating weave.

Mandarin, a third member of this unusual fabric family has all the beauty of Panoply and in addition a gold and silver design threading its way over the surface.

You will find these beautiful fabrics fashioned into the smartest garments —or by the yard at the better stores.

SIDNEY BLUMENTHAL & CO. Inc.
"Fabrics of Distinction"
395 FOURTH AVENUE   NEW YORK

Evening Wrap of Panoply Made by H. SAMUELS & SON NEW YORK

Figure 3-2. Eveningwear styles of 1920 were as varied and confusing as daywear. Couturiers attempted to reintroduce crinoline hoops of the Second Empire, bustles of the 1880s, and immense trains of the Edwardian years. At the same time, some designers took inspiration from the theater and incorporated Egyptian, Persian, Turkish, and Chinese motifs and styles into their collections. Ads 1920.

Two other fashion developments of the 1920s that were embraced by American women included the dropped waistline and a wide assortment of hip treatments. Both design elements would remain popular throughout the entire decade.

The waistline of couture designs actually had begun a move downward as early as 1919. Within the year, American ready-to-wear makers had adopted the new look as one of the many styles then in production. In the 1920 ad for Rosemary Dressmakers shown in figure 3-1, the longer bodice is already in evidence, with some models showing a blouson of fabric slightly above the hips. Within the next two years the line would

Figure 3-3. One of the most notable failures of the French couturiers was the reintroduction of ankle-length hemlines in the collections of 1921, 1922, 1923, and even into early 1924. Although ready-to-wear makers and retailers followed the dictates of Paris, American women rejected the look and flooded the alterations departments with orders for shorter hemlines. Bonwit Teller ad 1923, Blackshire ad 1924.

continue downward until it was universally applied across the center of the hips. The resulting look, which fashion editors called the "straight silhouette," emphasized a youthful, willowy slenderness. *Vogue* complained that only "a figure five feet six inches in height, weighing one hundred and twenty pounds might get away with this fashion, provided . . . that a plumb-line dropped from her seventh vertebra to her heels did not vary anywhere from the absolute perpendicular."[12] By 1924, fashion editors were already describing the straight silhouette as "boyish" in appearance.[13]

The short dress, the dropped waistline, and the boxy, boyish silhouette would unite into a style that, combined with bobbed hair, skin-tone hosiery, and liberally applied makeup, would come to epitomize the look for women of the Roaring

Twenties. (Figure 3-5.) This was the "flapper uniform," as Bruce Bliven called it in a 1925 article for the *New Republic*. But the look was not exclusive to the boyish nineteen-year-old "Flapper Jane." Instead, Bliven maintained: "These things and none other are being worn by all of Jane's sisters and her cousins and her aunts. They are being worn by ladies who are three times Jane's age, and look ten years older; by those twice her age who look a hundred years older."[14] The reason for such a broad appeal of the flapper look was simple enough to understand. It was fresh, comfortable, and most importantly, it was youthful. The term "flapper" has been credited to a number of origins. One was the wildly flapping motion of a woman's arms as she danced the Charleston. Another was the nickname for young women who brazenly rode the flapper bracket of a motorbike. Yet another even preceded the First World War and was derived from a German word for a young woman of loose morals.[15] Whatever the source of the word, the meaning was universally understood. The flapper style—both in look and demeanor—reflected the exuberant, fast pace of modern America, with its mass production, mass marketing, and mass consumption.

Seventh Avenue

American fashion on a mass scale came into its own during the 1920s. But the evolution had been slow and painful. During the nineteenth century, ready-to-wear manufacturers frequently opened and closed shops with uninhibited rapidity. Often they had just enough capital for a single season's production line. Start-up expenses were controlled by setting up operations in low-rent facilities and by employing low-wage workers, especially vulnerable immigrant women who were highly skilled at sewing and other garment-related work.

As the nineteenth century concluded, labor reform movements led to increased unionization and, for those members of unions, somewhat improved conditions. However, the labor forces of most garment factories remained nonunion well into the twentieth century, so the plight of their workers remained abysmal. Writing for *Popular Science* in 1913, Malcolm Keir detailed many of the egregious conditions under which employees worked in those early years. In many companies, for example, a female factory worker was not permitted to stop work even to "attend to her natural bodily needs." Breaks from repetitive motion routines were infrequent, and long hours of standing during sixty-hour work weeks were common. The piecework systems that were prevalent in factories, Keir noted, caused all manner of health problems for workers, ranging from "nervous tension and strain" to "functional abnormalities" such as anemia and "chronic inflammatory disease in the pelvis."[16]

Safety issues, too, were a significant concern of factory workers and labor reformers. Besides the dangers from machinery and tools, fire was a particular terror, most especially for urban workers who labored in multistoried buildings constructed before fire codes. The nation was horrified in 1911 by the news of one such fire in New York at the Triangle Shirtwaist Company in which 146 girls died when they were trapped by blocked doors or fell from upper stories trying to escape.

In 1900, the International Ladies' Garment Workers Union was founded to challenge these labor practices in the ready-to-wear industry. Despite their aggressive efforts, though, sweatshop working conditions persisted until the midteens, when legislation and a labor shortage forced factory owners to make concessions.

Figure 3-4. Responding almost belatedly to demands from women and retailers, couturiers began shortening skirts in 1924. By the following year, hemlines had risen to the knees. Ads 1925.

Figure 3-5. Representations of the flapper with her short skirts, bobbed hair, and makeup were favorites of satirists and social cartoonists.
Illustrations by:
A. Ann Fish 1921
B. Harley Stivers 1926
C. John Held, Jr. 1926

One result of the American fashion industry's attempt to get organized and clean up its image was the founding of "Fashion Avenue" in New York. At the close of the First World War in 1918, a group of investors and about fifty ready-to-wear manufacturers joined forces to build a fireproof complex of showrooms and workshops on the west side of Seventh Avenue. At the time construction got underway, the United States had more than 7,600 clothing manufacturers, employing 165,000 workers and producing more than $1.2 billion in goods.[17] In 1921, buildings 498 and 500 Seventh Avenue opened to full occupancy. Within the next three years buildings 512, 530, and 550 were finished and leased to ready-to-wear manufacturers who moved their businesses from the slums of East Broadway, Prince Street, and lower Madison Avenue. Some apparel makers even relocated their entire operations from as far away as Brooklyn. However, tenancy was strictly regulated by the venture capital group. Occupants were limited to certain price ranges and categories of apparel they could produce. The idea was to create a convenient one-stop buying source for out-of-town merchants. Almost immediately manufacturers began advertising their new address. (Figure 3-6.) Today, buying staffs for retail operations from coast to coast refer to Seventh Avenue simply as the "market." Trade publications such as *Women's Wear Daily* use the abbreviation

Figure 3-6. The first buildings of what would become the New York ready-to-wear market opened at 498 and 500 Seventh Avenue in 1921. Tenants immediately began advertising their new address. Ads 1922–23.

"SA" in headlines and text as an all-encompassing handle for what would quickly become America's "Garment Center Capital." [18]

Seen in the Shops

For many ready-to-wear makers, success came in the 1890s with the enduring popularity of the shirtwaist and skirt ensemble. The two garments could be cut from simple patterns, were easy to mass produce, and required minimal stylistic changes season after season. As sewing machine technologies improved, fancy applications and embroideries could replicate elaborate hand needlework at a fraction of the cost. Celluloid simulations of expensive tortoiseshell or mother-of-pearl buttons were plentiful and cheap. A larger

segment of the American population could now enjoy a sense of style and fashion rather than merely satisfying the needs of warmth and modesty with basic clothing.

Mass production of ready-to-wear was further bolstered by the mass distribution to consumers by catalogers and apparel retailers. In turn, clothing shops and department stores utilized mass marketing to sustain high-volume turnover of inventory. In 1904, one entire issue of *Printers' Ink* was devoted to the highly sophisticated principles of marketing and merchandising employed by retailers. Even at this early date seasonal and sale pricing plans and shoppers' incentive programs such as trading stamps were firmly established. Direct mail programs effectively segmented customers by their purchasing habits. Newspaper advertising schedules conditioned customers to shop certain days of the week for

Figure 3-7. Sports apparel manufacturers revived bicycling costume styles from a generation earlier, including the split skirt and knickerbockers. Jersey Silk Mills ad 1922, Golflex ad 1923.

specific categories of merchandise: Mondays, women's ready-to-wear; Tuesdays, household furnishings; Wednesdays, dry goods and piece goods; Thursdays, general merchandise; Fridays, men's goods. One store in Philadelphia even put a representative of its target customer—the married woman—at the helm of its advertising department and its $100,000 budget.[19] A decade later, department stores began employing the "secret shopper" to go out into the streets, restaurants, and other shops to see what average women were buying and wearing.[20]

As a result of these refined marketing strategies, department stores and apparel retailers began to follow the lead of the catalogers and included a stronger presence of ready-made clothing in their inventories. Fashion advertising in mass-circulation women's magazines persuaded consumers that ready-made clothing was just as stylish as any made-to-order copies of Paris originals, and much more affordable. Increasingly, fashion editors included reports on ready-to-wear styles and availability. For instance, one of the standard departments of *Vogue* from its very beginning in the 1890s had been "Seen in the Shops," which provided information on the most current trends of ready-made apparel and accessories. By the 1910s, the magazine had begun publishing retail prices with the illustrations of garments, and even offered a mail-order shopping service at no charge to women who did not have access to the featured fashions. *Vogue* regularly began to acknowledge the quality of American ready-to-wear clothing with editorial endorsements. Suggested the editors in 1920: "Fastidious though she may be, the woman who dresses smartly does not hesitate at all to purchase ready-made blouses, one of the things that have been brought to a very high degree of excellence."[21]

Women's Sports and Sports Clothes

In addition to the high quality of ready-made blouses and skirts, the production of sports apparel became a specialty of American ready-to-wear manufacturers. This should not be confused with "sportswear" as applied generically today, which encompasses a broad mix of garments including separates (matching skirts, pants, and tops), casual jackets and blazers, and knitwear. Sports apparel, on the other hand, refers to clothing that is appropriate for athletic activities. During the 1920s women's sports became one of the most notable forces in America's social evolution, and ready-to-wear makers responded with an endless variety of specialized clothing for that burgeoning market.

The youth-oriented zeitgeist of the decade brought with it radical changes that permeated virtually every aspect of American society. These experiences were not just the domain of the socially savvy, but were adopted by most every Main

Street nationwide. The mass media of magazines, newspapers, radio, and movies presented to national audiences the rapid pace of change week after week: the newest looks in makeup, hairstyles, and fashions; the latest models of cars, radios, and home appliances; the fast sounds of jazz and contemporary slang.

Yet, these were but the surface embellishments of the era. The core fundamentals of American society were being swept up in a bewildering vortex of change unlike anything experienced since the Civil War. From the full-color pages of magazines and the silver screens of movie houses, Americans were introduced to new ideas of social order, religion, politics, science, and economics. Women especially were besieged with new challenges and opportunities. Wrote one editor for *Physical Culture* at the time:

> Life has become a swift business. The auto, the films, the stupendous modern output of books and magazines and papers, the radio—each had popped in upon the American home and helped create an ever-widening horizon. Where Grandmother could slowly steer each girl along the path of propriety, today a girl has so many ideas and emotions and reactions flung in front of her that by sixteen she knows many things Grandmother was still wondering at sixty.[22]

Even Grandmother, though, could not remain impervious to the shifting sands of change in the Delirious Decade.

One particular challenge that great numbers of women enthusiastically took up in the 1920s was athletics. Barely a generation earlier, women's intramural sports were usually played in closed gymnasiums with spectators restricted primarily to their own sex. For girls and young women to run or leap about in sports competitions wearing loose middy blouses and knee-high bloomers in front of men was unseemly. The very concept of athletic competition for women was regarded by most with suspicion and doubt.

Indeed, only a few sports for women were narrowly acceptable in the nineteenth century. Competitive golfing, bowling, and lawn tennis were tolerable, but just barely. When Pierre de Coubertin revived the Olympics in 1896, he called the athletes of the world to Athens, but invited no women to compete. Eight years later, for the St. Louis Olympics of 1904, the U.S. Amateur Athletic Union (AAU) reluctantly allowed women to participate in one event: archery. But when the Stockholm committee agreed to permit women's swimming in the 1912 games, the AAU blocked American women from competing by refusing official sponsorship of national championships.[23]

World War I helped change these constraints, however, and women broke through the barriers of competitive sports just as they had those of employment, politics, education, and society. In a rapid succession of well-publicized sports events, women proved their athletic skills and competitive spirit. In the Olympic aquatic competitions of 1920, American women won all but one of the events. Two years later the National Amateur and Athletic Federation was founded to assure that standards and regulations were applied to both boys and girls in competition. Throughout the decade women set new records in sports: Gertrude Ederle swam the English Channel, beating all previous times by two hours; Glenna Collett became the first woman to break eighty for eighteen holes of golf; Hazel Wrightman won four U.S. national championships in tennis; and Floretta McCrutcheon defeated bowling champion Jimmy Smith.

The successes of women athletes and the publicizing of their achievements contributed to the era's sense of youthful vitality. Women wanted to look young, act young, and dress young. To this end, more and more women joined golf and tennis clubs or attended swimming and exercise sessions at their local YWCA. This quest for youthful vitality also meant dressing the part of the active woman. For ready-to-wear makers, the call to action was clearly heard, and they responded with comfortable, easy-care sports clothing that looked as good at a backyard barbecue as on the tennis court or driving range. Wrote one fashion editor, "It has been said, with more or less truth, that the ultramodern woman wears only two types of clothes in summer: sports things all day and dance frocks all night."[24]

Besides the traditional sports clothing ensembles of skirts, pullovers, blouses, and cardigans, ready-to-wear makers rediscovered variations of bicycling costumes from a generation earlier. The split skirt was a welcome solution to flying hemlines on the tennis court, and in 1921, *Vogue* reported that the knicker suit had "invaded the golf links."[25] (Figure 3-7.)

Of significant credit to American sports clothing designers and manufacturers, the flow of fashion influence was in reverse to its usual path in the 1920s. For instance, cotton ready-to-wear exports grew from a market value of $242,000 in 1919 to $14 million in 1928.[26] As a result of this phenomenal success, Paris began to cast an eye toward America for inspiration. *Vogue* observed in 1922 that "a few years ago the sports costume was ignored by the French couturier; now it appears in the collection of almost every house."[27] Kilts and pleated skirts abounded in the 1924 collections. Lelong introduced his version of the split skirt, called culottes, that year. Patou, Molyneux, Chanel, and most all the other big names in fashion offered variations of American sports clothing. "Never have the couturiers paid so much attention to sports clothes," commented a *Vogue* Paris reporter, "a striking sign of the times, for, nowadays, even those who only stand and watch wish to be dressed more or less like actual players."[28]

Expo '25 and Art Deco

Fashions of the second half of the 1920s can be summed up in one garment: the short, straight, drop-waist chemise. The most popular fabrics for the style were soft, flowing silks or the newly developed synthetics, particularly rayon. The straightline silhouette and the fluid fabrics complemented the desired figure of the era, which fashion historian Jane Mulvagh described as "the physique of a young boy, straight, hipless, bustless, waistless." [29] For women who were full figured, elasticized bands were used to flatten breasts and narrow hips to better approximate a boyish figure. The total look of short skirts and sensuous fabrics provided young women with a shock value especially aimed at the older generations.

Other shock values of women's modern dress included Chanel's mounds of costume jewelry, which either were viewed as flashy or cheap. Short hair, accentuated by the introduction of the cloche in the late 1910s, refuted the Victorian notion that a woman's hair is her glory. Additionally, young women further shocked the older generations by discarding their corsets, girdles, and brassieres. All in all, as Bruce Bliven observed in 1925, Flapper Jane "isn't wearing much." He noted that her clothes "were estimated the other day by some statistician to weigh two pounds. Probably a libel; I doubt they come within half a pound of such bulk. . . . If you'd like to know exactly, it is: one dress, one step-in [one-piece underwear], two stockings, two shoes." [30] Certainly Bliven's satirical look at women's fashions of the 1920s is an oversimplification, but not by much. This basic costume of flaming youth would remain constant from 1925 through 1929. The most notable variations of the look occurred in color, texture, and textile patterns. Across these years all three of these elements were influenced by what we call today the art deco movement.

In the simplest terms, the masculine, geometric shapes and purity of line of art deco embodied the Machine Age. Like all pervasive art movements, the style was one of total design. An art deco office building, just as with a baroque church or a neoclassical villa, was a total visual experience of the elements that defined that style. From the architecture to the interior fixtures to the decorative furnishings, the design was comprehensive.

However, the origins of art deco as a definable style actually preceded the 1920s by decades and stemmed from a number of schools of design and art movements. During the late 1890s, the Viennese Sezessionists, led by Gustav Klimt, began to distill the organic undulations of art nouveau into the simplified, geometric patterns that would come to characterize art deco. At the same time in Scotland, the Mackintosh school similarly stripped art nouveau of its gratuitous ornamentation and emphasized simplistic linearity. By the first decade of the twentieth century, Le Corbusier and Walter Gropius of the German Bauhaus expanded upon this purity of line for everything from architecture to teapots. Cubism, Fauvism, and Futurism redefined imagery and color in painting and sculpture. The costumes and set decorations of the Ballets Russes inspired bold applications of vivid color and ethnic decorative motifs. The discovery of Tutankhamen's tomb in 1922 launched a mania for Egyptian, Turkish, and other exotic styles of ornamentation. All of these influences, inspirations, and insights culminated in the famous 1925 Exposition Internationales des Arts et Décoratifs et Industriels Modernes hosted by Paris.

Although the 1925 Paris Expo was an international event, conspicuously absent from the exhibition were American designers and artisans. The U.S. had declined participation, according to art historian Alastair Duncan, because "Secretary of Commerce, Herbert Hoover, felt that it could not meet the Modernist requirements laid out in the Exposition's charter." [31] The art deco movement in America, better known as moderne, was more prevalent in the 1930s. Those early masterpieces of American moderne architecture and interior decoration, New York's Chrysler Building, Empire State Building, and Radio City Music Hall, were all completed between 1930 and 1932. Some might argue that in America the style actually endured through the 1950s, given the look of automobiles, architecture, and furniture of that time.

Nevertheless, contemporaries of the Paris Expo recognized the significance of this visual phenomenon. Paul Nystrom acknowledged in 1928 that the Paris Expo had an "enormous" influence "not only in the field of pure art, but also in the field of production and style goods." [32] Since the term "art deco" was not coined until the 1960s, [33] designers, journalists, and scholars of the 1920s used the generic term "modernistic." Nystrom concluded that "The modernistic art movement seems destined to have a very important influence over much of what goes into use and consumption all over the world, and the prestige of Paris has been heightened very greatly by the fact that the first general exhibition of works of art of this genre was held in Paris." [34] Editorials in fashion and style periodicals used comparable language. For example, the bold art deco patterns of textiles and paper goods illustrated in 1926 *Vogue* articles are generically described as "modern designs" or having "modernistic influence." [35] Today, when we thumb through design books and issues of home and fashion magazines of the late 1920s and 1930s, we clearly see the profound impact of the art deco movement in all arenas of design—from the fine arts of architecture, painting, and sculpture to mass-consumption products like food packaging, kitchen appliances, and automobiles.

In America, the two industries that were immediately

Figure 3-8. Following the 1925 Paris Expo, American marketers quickly adapted art deco design formats and motifs to give their ads and products a sense of modernity. Even the most mundane items could be elevated to works of art. Ads 1925–29.

influenced by the Paris Expo were advertising and fashion. Advertisers discovered that even the most mundane, utilitarian objects could be glorified with a halo of modernity when enthroned on an art deco stage. (Figure 3-8.) Likewise, American fashion immediately imported this energetic high style from Paris. By the autumn of 1925, the influences of art deco in American ready-to-wear were already noticeable. Emphasis on straightline forms of garment construction such as crystal pleats, triangular gores, diagonal yokes, handkerchief hemlines, and squared necklines reinforced the geometric look of art deco. Textile patterns reinterpreted traditional depictions of flora and fauna into hard-edged, stylized representations. Graphical diamonds, chevrons, and other rectilinear shapes were used as all-over designs or accent trimmings. (Figure 3-9.) American variations of art deco even incorporated the geometric flat patterns and primary colors of native Indian

decorative motifs. (Color plates 4 and 5.) The style also quickly came to dominate virtually every category of fashion accessories, particularly jewelry, compacts, handbags, hats, and print scarves. (See chapter 8.)

As the decade came to a close, a startling new look in fashion was introduced by Paris. In the September 1929 issue of *Vogue*, readers were advised:

> We are on the brink of a new mode—really new, not merely one composed of variations of the clothes we have been wearing. . . .When the waistline is high, other lines will be altered proportionately. If skirts are longer, waist-lines will move, too. Neck-lines that are softer are merely parts of a greater femininity throughout the costume. . . . And each of these points has a definite relation to the fabric, the color, the texture, the feeling—and even the wearer—of a costume.[36]

By the end of the year, the new look was already evident in

ℐTS CARESSING WARMTH
ITS FLATTERING GRACE
assure unending satisfaction

AMONG the exotic negligées of the new mode none are more popular than luxurious coats with silken pajamas. A coat of Waterside completed with trousers of the most modern of prints to match its facings, makes the smartest of lounging costumes.

FOR the smart combination of coat and dress Waterside offers beautiful sombre shades with the lustrous richness of pile and texture to give the smart lines you require.

WITH its wide range of colors to clothe every mood, Waterside answers every negligée problem. For the comfortable dressing gown with its simple lines and sheer trimmings no fabric combines beauty and practicability in so delightful a way.

THE shimmering colors that beguile you into a care-free mood, the luxurious texture that lures you to relax—they are so necessary for your lounging robes!

You'll find exquisite boudoir shades in Waterside Corduroy—suggesting deliciously feminine touches of ostrich or satin or lace! And there are Waterside's more brilliant colors for the new exotic pajama negligée!

Supple, rich, softly draping—Waterside has a charming manner all its own of clinging gently to graceful curves, of tactfully masking sharp angles. Its lus-trous pile with soft shadows melting into its velvety texture is irresistibly flattering! Waterside Corduroy is so luxurious, so colorful and so moderate in price that women are using it both indoors and out. And they are as practical as they are smart, those frocks for street or sport, for Waterside wears wonderfully, tubbing or cleaning like new.

You will find Waterside Corduroy in all the better department stores—the same delightful Waterside great couturiers have used—the same luxurious corduroy that leading negligée designers choose for their smartest models. Howlett & Hockmeyer Co., Fifth Avenue at 26th Street, New York.

UUATERSIDE CORDUROY

1925

A GOLFLEX COAT
for Every Winter Hour

A color symphony — the rich silver-flecked worsted with its facings of silver grey squirrel! Elegant enough to wear with party frocks; but of a sturdy integrity of material and making—a gracious simplicity of design—that recommend it for daily service! Insist on the Golflex label!

Wilkin & Adler, Inc. 500 Seventh Avenue, N. Y. C.

For sale only at Department and Specialty Stores

1925

"ONE HUNDRED YEARS OF BUILDING FOR TOMORROW"..1826-1926

The cape-coat for sports or travel, sketched left, is of imported plaid in black and white with kit fox collar $195.

The sports costume, center, has imported tweed coat frock of silk in pattern to match and collar of Mongolian chipmunk $295.

The riding habit, right, is correct in cut, tailored of brown wormebo, fastidiously finished at every point $69.50.

A SPORTS SHOP
for Sports Lovers and Onlookers

The smart golf outfit—the comfortable frock for tennis—the correct riding habit; these for active sports women. And for those who enjoy their sports from the sidelines: frocks, suits and wraps in the colors and fabrics approved by fashion. This is the two-fold story of the new Sports Shop opened on the Third Floor.

Lord & Taylor
FIFTH AVENUE · NEW YORK

Our personal shopping bureau is prepared to fill mail and telephone orders promptly and carefully

1926

The *Smartest Silk Frocks*
Under Summer Skies
are Made in Paris

Handmade and handdrawn in decorative lines, squares, circles, in all the new Parisian summer shades. Only Paris could make them so exquisitely—and only Stewart & Co. present them so inexpensively.

Geraldine—at the left, wears a one-piece frock. The lines of the handdrawn work give her a bewitchingly slender appearance. Only 33.00

Marie—with the parasol, affects polka dots applied with handdrawn work on her two-piece frock. Pleats, of course, like every smart Parisienne. Only 38.00

And the Countess—seated. Her two-piece frock features handdrawn and crocheted squares in self color. The pockets and cuffs are squared. Only 48.00

PARIS **Stewart & Co.** NEW YORK
Correct Apparel for Women & Misses
Fifth Avenue At 37th Street

1926

Figure 3-9. The modernity of the art deco movement translated easily and effectively into fashion designs, accessories, and textile patterns. During the second half of the 1920s, hard-edged pleats, yokes, and other rectilinear garment constructions were complemented by geometric prints, textures, and contrasting colors.

Mrs. Franklin INC.

*Introduces a new evening coat of quilted green velvet,
trimmed with blonde fox .... Original hand-knitted
frocks for sports and informal daytime wear in specially
dyed colorings .... Wraps .... Hats .... Accessories.
The New York Shop is at 16 East 53rd Street.*

All genuine Franklin hand knitted [logo] sweater suits bear this label.

NEW YORK · PHILADELPHIA · PALM BEACH · BAR HARBOR

1927

Mangone Models
for Resort Wear
now being displayed by
over two hundred stores in the
United States and Canada

FOR INFORMATION WRITE MANGONE, NEW YORK, N. Y

1927

BERGDORF
GOODMAN
616 FIFTH AVENUE
NEW YORK

*A new hand-loomed sport coat of white
wool with green and yellow flowered
border. As shown by Bergdorf-Goodman.*

1927

"A Garment is no finer than its Fabric"

The Satin Ensemble

as preferred by the well dressed woman achieves its
loveliest expression in Haas Brothers'

Moleskin Superior

The satin crepe famous for its brilliant lustre, suppleness of
texture and the crystal clearness of its colors

Produced by

These fabrics by the yard
at retail silk departments—
also in made-up garments

Haas Brothers
FABRICS CORPORATION

Fifth Avenue
New York

928

BONWIT
TELLER
FIFTH AVENUE AT 38TH STREET

SPORTS CLOTHES
WORN WITH APPRECIATION
BY WOMEN NOTED FOR THEIR
SMARTNESS

SPORTS ATTIRE FOR WOMEN AND MISSES ... Fourth Floor

1928

The
MODE REVEE

COAT FASHIONS
THAT HOLD A
HIGH DEGREE
ON THE CAMPUS
AND WITH
TRAVELWISE
WOMEN

FABRICS
BY FODIER
AND OTHER
MASTER
WEAVERS ..

NOW OBTAINABLE AT YOUR FAVORITE SHOP

L.J.RUBIN & CO.
1412 BROADWAY, NEW YORK

1928

Mildred Louise Bedell presents these

Early Spring Frocks of Soft Crepes ... $25

The advanced and authoritative style conceptions of the new season's silhouette, depicting the discriminate and fascinating fashion versions in Flat Crepes...at the specialized Bedell price of $25

The chosen colors are Patou Blue, Chanel Red, Imperial Jade, Carnelian, Cliquot Beige and Black

Featured at all Bedell Fashion Shops in the ronupt cities from Coast to Coast

Boston	Cleveland		Newark	Providence
Bridgeport	Detroit		Oakland, Cal.	Rochester
Brooklyn	Los Angeles		Philadelphia	St. Louis
Buffalo	Milwaukee		Pittsburg	Syracuse
Chicago	New York		Portland, Ore.	Worcester

BEDELL

Figure 3-10. By the end of 1929, ready-to-wear makers already advertised the totally new look in fashions. Almost overnight, the boyish silhouette of the flapper had given way to a return of the waistline, feminine curves, and much longer skirts. Ad 1929.

the ads from American ready-to-wear makers and retailers. (Figure 3-10.) Initially advocates of the short skirt railed against the threat of long hemlines from Paris. Novelist Fannie Hurst led a campaign to resist the new look. She insisted that "we are going right back to where we started from—and yet we laugh at the 'quaint' fashions of the 1890's!"[37] But this was not like the hemline battles of 1921. The departure of fashion styles in 1929 from those of the preceding four years not only signaled the conclusion of an era, it coincided with an economic calamity on a global scale. Inevitably, all women were swept along on the tide, surrendering in the end to the new look.

Hard Times and Soft Curves

In October 1929, the U.S. stock market crashed. Few people actually understood what that meant at the time. Most average Americans were not attuned to the complexities of national or world economics. All they knew was that as a result, U.S. banks and businesses failed; mortgages were foreclosed, displacing many thousands of families; unemployment rose to over eight million; breadlines formed throughout the country; and labor riots left hundreds dead or wounded from the violence. The United States—and the world—plunged into an economic depression that would last almost ten years.

The fashion industries of both America and Paris were especially hard hit. On Seventh Avenue, numerous ready-to-wear businesses went under between 1929 and 1933. Many of those that managed to survive operated on the slimmest of margins by mass producing low-end apparel mostly for the budget and discount retailers. In Paris, Poiret went bankrupt and closed his salons. Prominent houses such as Doucet and Doeuillet were forced to merge to reduce costs. Chanel cut the prices of her clothes by half. Designers who had premiered up to five hundred models in each collection instead presented as few as a hundred. American retailers tightened the budgets of their buying staffs. Ready-to-wear and made-to-order makers bought only one or two models from each season's collection. French dress imports had peaked at more than $80 million in 1926, but by 1935 they had dropped by 70 percent.[38]

Women's magazines, including upscale fashion publications, frequently featured tips for economizing on clothing. In May 1930, *Vogue* advised:

> It has suddenly become chic to be poor. . . . Nobody bothers any more to camouflage poverty. Quite the contrary . . . going to cheap shops is a fetish. Snooping at Woolworth's is the latest indoor sport. The fashionable woman's jewels may come from Cartier's, but her gown is quite likely to be a gem from nowhere. She may eat her squab off Crown Derby, but her cocktail glasses will quite probably be from a "Five and Ten."[39]

Such commentary may seem to have trivialized the scope of the trauma that the nation was experiencing, but in the spring of 1930, few could have predicted that the Great Depression would extend from months into years. In fact, *Vogue* soon expanded its editorial campaigns of thrift advice. New departments such as "Tips on the Shop Market" by "Shop-Hound" were introduced, in which readers were informed of affordable ready-to-wear labels and trends, cost-effective home decorative fixtures and accessories, and even the availability of discount merchandise by store name. Other 1930 articles that related to frugal shopping were headlined:

"Chic at a Price"
"Practicality by Day for Limited Incomes"
"Unlimited Smartness at a Limited Cost"
"Accessories of Small Expense and Great Chic"
"Wise Economy of Clothes for the Country"[40]

The Depression brought a sobriety to fashion. Short skirts,

1930

Figure 3-11. The look that was to prevail in American fashions throughout the 1930s was a soft, curvaceous silhouette with a natural waistline and new emphasis on the bust and hips. Unconstructed neckline treatments such as cowls and shawl collars coupled with soft fabrics like rayon and knits reinforced this new look of femininity.

1931

1933

rich fabrics, and vivid colors were almost instantly démodé. "The red-hot baby had gone out of style," wrote historian Frederick Allen in 1931.[41] In her place emerged a more mature ideal of feminine beauty. With the return of the natural waistline, most often belted, a new emphasis was placed on the curves of the hips and bustline. Yet, it was not the voluptuousness of the Edwardian belle. Instead, an almost severe silhouette prevailed during the early thirties. The favored look became a tall, somewhat emaciated figure. Fashion illustrators elongated the human form into an exaggerated El Grecoesque interpretation. The reality, though, as demonstrated by movie star Thelma Todd in the 1931 Jeunesse ad, was a soft, curvaceous slenderness. (Figure 3-11 and color plate 8.) Garment construction became softer as well. Rounded collars and scoop necks, along with unconstructed neckline treatments such as cowls, oversized fur collars, and softly draped bowfronts, reinforced the new femininity.

Legs virtually disappeared beneath the longer, slimmer

1932

1938

skirts. Early in 1930, *Vogue* advised readers of hemline lengths in precise measurements: "Skirts for an average figure stop sixteen inches from the ground for sports. For general wear, they are from thirteen to fifteen inches from the ground—fifteen for tweeds, thirteen for silks."[42] For women who wore high heels, that general guide placed hemlines just a few inches above the ankles. On the other hand, the long, narrow cut of skirts, when combined with soft fabrics such as knits and synthetic silks, created a new feminine sensuality. Hips and thighs were visibly contoured when a woman moved or stood outdoors in a breeze.

Intimate apparel underwent redesigning and reengineering to minimize bulk but still accentuate a woman's curves. The corset evolved into the lightweight girdle made of new elasticized fabrics. Camisole-style brassieres were reduced in design—and name—to the halter bra types with alphabet cup sizes that are still the standard model today. Formfitting panty briefs replaced baggy step-ins and bloomer underpants.

Another technological change in garment construction that occurred in the 1930s was an improved design of the zipper. (Figure 3-12.) Although versions of mechanical hook-and-eye fasteners were invented in the 1890s, they were neither reliable nor well accepted. In 1913, a version with interlocking metal teeth affixed to fabric was introduced. However, it, too, often broke easily and rusted shut. During the 1920s, an executive at the rubber manufacturer B. F. Goodrich added an improved form of the device to galoshes and gave it the onomatopoetic name by which it is known today. By the 1930s, reengineered versions of the zipper were stronger and more rust-resistant. Couturiers, tailors, and ready-to-wear manufacturers increasingly replaced cumbersome snaps or hook-and-

Figure 3-12. Early versions of the zipper invented in the 1890s replicated hook-and-eye fasteners. In 1913 a "slide fastener" with metal teeth affixed to fabric was introduced. B. F. Goodrich attached the device to galoshes and gave it the onomatopoetic name by which it is called today. By the 1930s, improved designs reduced problems with breakage and rusting. Increasingly, couturiers and ready-to-wear makers began to utilize the zipper in fashion designs.

1935

Figure 3-13. The backless evening gown became especially popular in the early years of the 1930s. Versions of the style would be a perennial favorite of designers throughout the twentieth century. Franklin Simon ad 1931, Lord and Taylor ad 1933.

eye closures with the zipper. Side-zip dresses were immensely popular since they eliminated the need for assistance or con-tortionist reaching to close bodices from the back. Men's trousers, especially, benefited from the addition of a reliable zipper to fly fronts, replacing the gaping button closure forms. Couturiers such as Charles James and Schiaparelli even began using zippers as intriguing design elements.

For eveningwear, one of the newest looks of the early 1930s was the backless gown. (Figure 3-13.) As if the vast expanse of bare flesh would not attract enough attention, designers embellished the back openings with all manner of fussy detailing, including cascading ruffles, garlands of silk flowers, wings of accordion pleats, and oversized bows. Two double spreads of backless gowns that were illustrated in the October 1933 *Vogue* featured "one of the most dramatic backs in Paris" from Jean Patou—a plunging halter design that lay bare the entire back, shoulders, and arms.[43]

Couturiers addressed such décolleté challenges by con-structing internal bras into their dresses. By the 1930s, ready-to-wear makers and made-to-order retailers could enjoy an equal advantage to this customization by the couturiers. The engineering of intimate apparel styles had evolved to such a specialized degree that lightweight, strapless bras with front underwire supports were mass produced to suit most every décolleté design.

A New Deal, New Times, and New Looks

In 1932, Americans went to the polls and voted out the Republican president, Herbert Hoover, and with him the Republican congressional majority. Into the vacuum were swept Franklin Delano Roosevelt and a Democratic Congress. In the first hundred days of the new administration, an

Figure 3-14. Franklin Roosevelt's New Deal recovery plans inspired hope in the depression-weary nation. Fashion designers began to reintroduce some fun and frivolity into clothing. Special emphasis on the shoulderline ranged from the exaggerated pagoda shoulders to the more popular padded and puffed silhouettes. Ads 1936.

unprecedented avalanche of legislation was quickly passed to set in motion the three R's—relief, recovery, and reform. New Deal legislation included unemployment insurance, minimum wage regulations, and child labor laws. Banks were reopened under the new Federal Deposit Insurance Corporation. Alphabet agencies such as the CCC (Civilian Conservation Corps), CWA (Civil Works Administration), PWA (Public Works Administration), and WPA (Works Progress Administration) put millions of the unemployed back to work.

Condé Nast and his circle of associates most likely did not vote for Roosevelt. Still, his magazines began to reflect the initial optimism that Roosevelt's New Deal inspired in the nation during those darkest days of the Depression. Three months before the election, *Vogue* had run an editorial on the "Follies of 1932." The point of the article was that the time had finally come when women should stop being "dazzled by the price tags." The consumer of the early 1930s had become so used to bargain shopping that she lost sight of the difference between value and cheap, asserted the editor. Women shoppers of the time, though, were understandably sensitive to costs, given the three years of severe economic conditions they had endured. In *Vogue*'s view, this made consumers particularly vulnerable to "alluring advertisements" inviting them "to come in and see . . . what little bargains could be had." The poor workmanship and low-quality materials of bargain clothing inevitably led to disappointment, continued *Vogue*, or even pain, given the shoddy construction of a three-dollar pair of shoes. Moreover, it was no bargain if the garment required additional expenses for alteration, or worse, barely lasted the season intact. The lessons that were learned may have been costly to consumers during those early years of the Depression, but "women have emerged wiser," concluded *Vogue*. "They have learned that the bottom does not have to mean the ditch—and that you can not go on wearing very cheap dresses, and very cheap hats, and very cheap shoes and stockings without beginning to look just a little cheap yourself."[44] After all, happy days were here again, so women should be encouraged to look at quality and branded labels once again rather than solely at price tags.

As the New Deal began to generate a slow but perceptible recovery in 1933, *Vogue*'s editors pronounced that "human patience can stand just so much frugality and no more."[45] In response to the renewed optimism, fashion began to show some stylistic opulence. A boldness of color and prints returned. (Color plate 9.) Fun, and frivolity was expressed especially with accessories. "Silly hats—they are the fashion," declared *Vogue* that spring.[46] In a tribute to the end of Prohibition, one chapeau sported a band made of the metal caps from champagne bottles. Meanwhile, to the theatrical extreme, Schiaparelli took influence from the Surreal-

ists and created hats shaped like inverted shoes, gloves with gold fingernails attached, padlock-shaped handbags, and transparent collar necklaces bespeckled with realistic-looking plastic insects.

By the mid-1930s, the frivolity of fashion was especially expressed by exaggerated shoulder and sleeve dimensions that had not been seen since the early 1890s. (Figure 3-14.) "Here is the new silhouette," observed *Vogue* of the fall collections in 1932, "broad of shoulder, deep of armhole, with a slim shaft below."[47] The following year, that special interest grew into the pagoda shoulders from Schiaparelli, which swooped down from the neckline and then rose to sharp pinnacles at the shoulder seam. Other versions of shoulder treatments included fluted or corrugated sleeves that dropped from extended shoulderlines, and flaring tabs or double revers that rose up over the shoulders, broadening the silhouette. Although these exaggerated proportions of shoulder interest were short lived, puffed sleeves and padded shoulders would remain popular into the early forties.

West Coast Influences

Fashion historian Jane Mulvagh noted that prior to the late 1920s, to comment on an outfit with "Whew! Pretty Hollywood" was an insult.[48] When Cecil B. DeMille ordered fashions from Paris for Gloria Swanson, he specifically requested theatrical exaggeration, not current couture styles. However, all that began to change, partially at the insistence of the stars themselves. At first Hollywood imported the French couturiers to work on film projects at the studios. Chanel, Molyneux, Lanvin, and Schiaparelli all made the trek westward. When Chanel visited in 1929, she created elegant, sophisticated wardrobes for movies that ended up being shelved because of the abrupt drop in hemlines the following season. In addition, movie directors and executives discovered that many couturiers' designs may have looked stunning in person but seemed flat and unmemorable on film.

The solution was for studios to seek out indigenous talent to head up house wardrobe departments. The most famous of these designers were (Gilbert) Adrian, Edith Head, and Howard Greer. Their challenges were vastly different from those of Parisian fashion designers. Hollywood costumers, wrote Margit Mayer, "were not couturiers in the European sense; rather, they were art directors of femininity."[49] They knew the importance of image and how to create illusion to achieve it. To optically lengthen Norma Shearer's short legs, MGM's Adrian raised the waistlines of her dresses. To disguise Barbara Stanwyck's long waist and low behind, Paramount's Edith Head constructed a belt that was wider in the front and fitted to be worn higher on the waist. Just as

Figure 3-15. Period costume designs from historical-themed movies influenced many mainstream fashion styles of the 1930s. Designers reintroduced new adaptations of the bustle, cinched waistline, and high collars, to name a few. Coca-Cola ad 1934, Velveteen ad 1936.

important to movie producers as the look of fashions on film was to avoid a repeat of the expensive Chanel disaster of 1929. Consequently, studio designers not only had to fuse style and glamour with the star's personality, they also had to make contemporary clothes that would not look outdated during the film's expected run—perhaps two years.

Studio wardrobe designers also had to be adept at period costuming. Although historical accuracy was not always a governing factor, the styling of the costumes had to be convincing. For hit movies, the influence of the costumes on mainstream fashion styles was sometimes significant. (Figure 3-15.) For instance, in designing costumes for *Gone with the Wind* in 1939, Walter Plunkett submitted antebellum material samples from the 1850s and 1860s to a northern textile mill for replication. As part of the agreement with the manufacturer, licensed *Gone with the Wind* cotton fabrics were widely distributed.[50] In addition, designs of prom dresses of the fol-

lowing spring were replete with wide crinoline skirts. Similarly, a number of other historical-themed movies of the 1930s directly influenced American fashions. *The Merry Widow* inspired versions of the bustle in 1934. In that same year Mae West starred in *Belle of the Nineties* and revived an interest in the cinched hourglass waist. Capes and high collars reappeared after the release of *Mary of Scotland* in 1936. Indeed, throughout the decades since the 1930s the impact of period movie costuming has been felt repeatedly in the American fashion arena.

In addition to inspiring revivals of historical costumes, the studio designers also influenced contemporary American fashions with stylistic interpretations that appealed to a broad spectrum of women. Joan Crawford's tailored suits with padded shoulders were a staple model for ready-to-wear makers throughout the late 1930s and into the 1940s. The tapered trousers worn by Katharine Hepburn and Marlene Dietrich

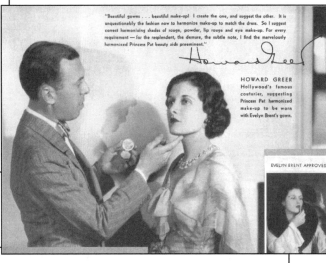

were widely copied. Versions of Adrian's white satin gown, made for Jean Harlow in *Dinner at Eight,* were seen at many social events of 1933. Some studio head designers such as Academy Award–winning Edith Head, Adrian, and Howard Greer even attained celebrity status and were as eagerly courted by advertisers as the stars they dressed. (Figure 3-16.)

One other West Coast influence that began to make its presence known in American fashion was the California style. Whereas New York clothiers largely conveyed an urban look in their collections, California makers emphasized sportswear. Names still familiar to us today, such as Cole, Koret, White Stag, and dozens of others, began to promote their California origins in logos, on garment labels, and especially in advertising. (Figure 3-17.) At their peak in the 1960s, more than six hundred garment manufacturers on the West Coast produced about $200 million dollars in apparel—almost one-third of the total ready-to-wear business in the United States at the time.[51]

Although there were a significant number of dress, suit, and coat makers on the West Coast, the specialties of the larger firms were centered on sportswear, notably swimwear, slacks, and shorts. (See chapter 7 for swimwear.) Fashion styles of slacks and shorts for most American women, though, were not broadly accepted initially, even in California. The styles of pants introduced for women by the Paris couturiers in the 1920s, particularly Chanel and Patou, were innovations of their resort wear collections. These casual types of trousers were worn by sophisticated socialites who gathered in St. Tropez, Monte Carlo, and Palm Beach to escape winter. Only gradually did the styles of menswear trousers, sailor's gobs, shorts, and pyjamas begin to appeal to American women, and then primarily through sports clothing such as golf and tennis apparel. By the mid-1930s, though, slacks and shorts had

Figure 3-16. Hollywood costume designers began to influence American fashion design and style in the 1930s. Some costumers achieved celebrity status and were eagerly courted by advertisers. Details of ads featuring Adrian 1931, Howard Greer 1931, and Edith Head 1938.

1936

1937

1937

Figure 3-17. California apparel makers promoted their West Coast origins in their logos, garment labels, and especially advertising.

become fairly common in the wardrobes of most women. Ready-to-wear makers routinely included models in their spring lines. (Figure 3-18.) However, the debate continued about when and where women could or should not wear pants. In 1936, *Vogue* offered specific advice:

> In Florida and California they play golf in tailored slacks like a man's flannel trousers. But conservative Easterners say they don't like them on Long Island courses. Slacks for fishing? Yes, everywhere—from deep-sea fishing off Montauk to marlin fishing at Bimini. Slacks for boating? Decidedly yes, whether you're handling your own sail or cruising on a Diesel-engine yacht. Slacks for gardening and country loafing? By all means. And now, rumours drift about that America may take up the fashion of Continental women at Cannes—that of wearing slacks at night to dance in casinos or yacht-clubs.[52]

By the close of the decade, though, *Vogue* acknowledged that pants were "an accepted part of nearly every wardrobe today." Most especially, the editor noted, "in California [they] go in for them wholeheartedly."[53]

American Designers

As mentioned previously, in the years immediately following the Wall Street crash in October 1929, imports of French couture designs dropped by as much as 70 percent. Huge tariffs on foreign-made clothing were imposed, retail buyers' budgets were severely cut, and consumers themselves adopted a commiserative frugality. Moreover, fashions of the post-chemise days required much more careful, time-consuming fitting, so made-to-order tailors and retailers had greater difficulty selling French couture styles.

As a result of these developments, the American fashion industry began to embrace and encourage native designers. In 1932, Lord and Taylor vice president Dorothy Shaver began to feature the names of American designers in the store's advertising. The promotional campaign also included display windows on Fifth Avenue and special shops set up inside the store devoted to each designer's collection. Following Shaver's lead, more and more fashion editorials and advertising included the names of American designers. (Figure 3-19.) Not since the editorial campaigns of Edward Bok and his supporters in the years preceding World War I were American fashion designers featured in the press and promoted by advertisers to this extent.

The year after Lord and Taylor's American designer ad campaign, *Vogue* examined the status of American fashion in a special issue. The editors insisted that despite a renewed sense of nationalism, and "the faint 'hissing' noises . . . when the word 'import' is mentioned, . . . politics had best be left out of art—and we consider clothes a Fine Art." Furthermore, asserted *Vogue*:

Unquestionably, if you want to see the largest number of good clothes in any season, you must turn to Paris. If you want to see the birth of radical changes that affect the mode of an entire year or decade, you must turn to Paris. . . . Let us admit that Paris sets the mode, and that the majority of American designers interpret it. They are nonetheless creative for taking an established trend as the basis of their work. . . . But, largely, it is the American designer's job to look over the shoulder of Paris, to come home and write his or her own versions of the mode, as has been established there.[54]

To some degree, this attitude is understandable, given that American designers who established shops operated their businesses quite differently from the French couturiers. Whereas the fashions of Paris houses were exclusive to the designer, most New York shops were likely to offer for sale as many French models as they did styles by the house designer.

1934

Figure 3-18. When introduced to American women in the 1920s, fashion styles of pants and shorts were initially acceptable only as sports clothing for tennis courts or the beach. By the mid-1930s, though, both styles were more common in women's everyday wardrobes.

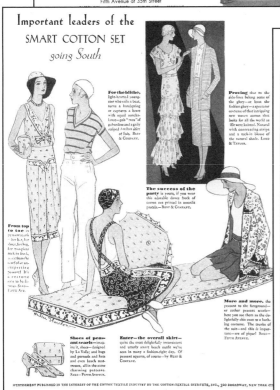

1930

1931

1939

Figure 3-19. Beginning in the 1930s, some American department stores began to credit their house fashion designers by name in advertising. Ads 1938.

For instance, imports from Schiaparelli, Vionnet, Patou, Molyneux, and Chanel were as available in the salons of Henri Bendel, Frances Clyne, and Sally Milgrim as were their own labels. This tradition would continue in America for another three decades before native designers began to adopt an exclusive brand marketing strategy for their stores.

Even when *Vogue* issued the first of its Americana editions in 1938, American designers still were viewed primarily as stylists of French modes. Only Hattie Carnegie and Henri Bendel were showcased with a full page each. Most of the fashion editorial space went to the department stores, which featured their private labels, house designers, and better ready-to-wear brands. In answering the question of why American women were the best dressed in the world, *Vogue* credited the nation's vast ready-to-wear industry, rather than the creative forces of U.S. designers: "Though half the country doesn't know it, most of the ready-made dresses bought in the shops of Fifth Avenue or Main Street come from the West Side of New York City—from that small area colloquially known as 'Seventh Avenue,' or the 'wholesale market.' Here, in chromium-plated, white-carpeted, thirty-story skyscrapers (rabbit-warren, sweat-shops have almost disappeared), more than 5,000 wholesalers make most of the nation's clothes."[55] The adaptive and versatile nature of fashion design in America, coupled with the increasingly sophisticated mass production and mass marketing of Seventh Avenue, accounted for the growing success of the U.S. ready-to-wear industry in the 1930s, despite the economic conditions.

The constellation of American fashions was not without its stars, however. (Figure 3-20.) Prominent names included Jessie Franklin Turner, Elizabeth Hawes, Muriel King, Hattie Carnegie, Peggy Hoyt, Frances Clyne, Mrs. Franklin, Sally Milgrim, Jay-Thorpe, Claire McCardell, and Henri Bendel. Of these designers, *Vogue* noted that "many of these people have sponsored new fashion ideas practically simultaneously with Paris, the result of something in the air, perhaps intangible or actual." Nevertheless, *Vogue*'s editors had a vested interest in the international politics of fashion and did not wish to offend the highly temperamental couturiers of Paris. Thus, acquiesced the editors, "We refuse to enter into any international controversies, however, as to who did what first."[56] Still, the recognition from the world's premier fashion magazine was significant to American designers.

Among those Americans featured by *Vogue* was Hattie Carnegie. Austrian by birth, she came to America with her family in 1889 and received her training in the ready-to-wear industry of New York. She opened her own shop in 1909 specializing in millinery, but within a few years began importing Parisian couture to include with her own fashion collections. By the 1930s, her clients included Joan Crawford and Con-

Cheerio!

BY

HATTIE CARNEGIE

INCORPORATED

42-46 East 49th Street · New York

Palm Beach, Fla. · Boca Raton, Fla. · Paris

1931

By **SALLY MILGRIM**

Essentially smart and eminently useful...a town costume in black that can well be the very backbone of your wardrobe. Soft little caracul jacket, with nonsensical ruffle to match and meet the frock's high fur cuff. Cloth dress tailored with Milgrim finesse. And silver buttons that look like heirlooms.

MADE-TO-ORDER · now from $85
READY-TO-WEAR · now from $55

MILGRIM

6 West 57th Street, New York

Cleveland   Detroit   Miami Beach

1932

Peggy Hoyt INC.
16 East 55th St · New York
New York's Leading Dressmakers

Peggy Hoyt, Inc. has at all times maintained a standard of excellence that remains unquestioned. The superior chic and beauty of the dresses and hats is conceded by all smart women.

There is no substitute for Quality.

1932

MRS. FRANKLIN has designed the perfect first dress for Autumn . . . of hand-knitted bark-brown and nubby, white wool . . . with a hint of orange in its depths. The green of the belt is complemented by the bright green beret. Here is a classic, in a season when correct clothes are not merely smart but essential. Its price is equally modern.

Mrs. **Franklin** *inc.*

TOWN AND COUNTRY CLOTHES

NEW YORK, 56 EAST 53RD ST.
PHILA., 260 S. 17TH ST. · JENKINTOWN, PA. · HAVERFORD, PA.
BAR HARBOR · YORK HARBOR · WATCH HILL · PALM BEACH

1932

Frances Clyne

ANNOUNCES

THE OPENING OF
HER NEW ESTABLISHMENT

where she now presents her collections with all the *éclat* of the Continental designers—Gowns, Hats and Wraps created by Frances Clyne in her own workrooms. Also imported models.

FRANCES CLYNE

6 East 56th Street
NEW YORK

1933

Gowns designed and made to order by
Jessie Franklin Turner
25 East 67
New York

1933

JAY·THORPE
57TH STREET WEST, NEW YORK

APRIL AFTER THIRTY-FIVE . .

Jay-Thorpe have developed a type of fashion for women who conquer years with poise and graciousness. This corded-sheer black dress, accented with sheerest white organdie, is typical of the ageless chic in our Matron's collection for April-into-Summer, 65.00. Sizes to 44.

MATRON'S COLLECTION . . SECOND FLOOR

1933

AS DESIGNED BY

Henri Bendel, Inc.
Ten West fifty-Seventh Street

THE PRINTED EVENING GOWN

Black background with scattering of daisies in moderne red and white. The soft neckline and graceful appliquéd hem are both smart and youthful.

The Spring Collection of
Exclusive Bendel Offerings
in all departments is now being shown

1934

Figure 3-20. Advertising in magazines helped market the names of American designers as fashion brands.

stance Bennett. *Vogue* assessed her as a designer who "does sophisticated clothes in a superlative way."[57]

Sally Milgrim was a designer for both the couture and the ready-to-wear markets. She created inaugural-ball gowns for First Ladies Florence Harding, Grace Coolidge, and Eleanor Roosevelt. Under the label name of Salymil, she distributed a line of fashions to retailers all across the country. *Vogue* described her "fresh young clothes" as "complicated and unusual, and more often than not, very jeune fille."[58]

Peggy Hoyt arrived in New York from Michigan with her widowed mother just before World War I. Apprenticed to a milliner as a teenager, she scraped together three hundred dollars and opened her own shop on Fifth Avenue. Within a few years, she, too, began to import French originals to show with her own fashions. In 1924 she introduced a line of fragrances named for various flowers that became quite successful. *Vogue* declared that she "expresses fashion in a completely feminine way, with an attention to detail that is remarkable in this, the machine age."[59] Such attention to detail was made possible by dozens of employees who hand stitched the embroidery and beadwork that hallmarked her designs.

Mrs. Franklin was personally interviewed by *Vogue* for its 1933 report. The editors concluded that they were unsure how to list her, "for she is unique."[60] Her specialty was knit fashions. Although she imported some Paris designs from the lesser-known houses, she much preferred to explore the use of new knit fabrications with her own designs. "Heavy, soft, tweedy-looking fabrics, cut like ordinary yards are actually made by loving hands…on actual needles," explained *Vogue*.

Frances Clyne had just opened her new Fifty-sixth Street salon in 1933, which *Vogue* described as "very swish with leopard satin and shining mirror panels." Clyne's "distinguished gowns and her unusual authoritative country things" were featured along with the latest styles from Lanvin, Schiaparelli, Chanel, and Molyneux.[61] Her clients included Ethel Barrymore and Broadway star Katharine Cornell.

Jessie Franklin Turner had begun her career as one of the many anonymous department store designers in the 1920s. Her "precious imagination," commented *Vogue*, produced some of the most enchanting tea gowns of the era.[62] She designed many of her own fabrics and combined them in visually intriguing ways with other fabrics imported from around the world. Unlike most of her contemporaries, Turner's shop was exclusive to her designs. In fact, when she visited her country house in France, she avoided the Paris salons to keep from being influenced by their current trends.

Jay-Thorpe was already well established when he opened his department store-sized salon on West Fifty-seventh Street in 1920. In addition to an extensive millinery and negligee collection, his shop even included a beauty salon. His sense of design was more avant-garde than that of his fellow American designers. When he began to import French couture, he favored Mirande, Augustabernard, and Premet. Like other large fashion establishments, Jay-Thorpe also employed house designers, such as the "diminutive Miss Montague," whose creations, according to *Vogue*, especially suited "knowing ones both in society and the theatre."[63]

For decades, Henri Bendel had been the preeminent fashion designer in America. As World War I began in 1914, *Vogue* had approached him first to participate in its Fashion Fete benefit, knowing that the rest of the American designers would follow his lead. Besides his couture work, he also wrote numerous magazine articles on fashion trends. His imports of French designs included styles by Yvonne Carette and Lucille Paray, along with representations from Schiaparelli, Chanel, and Molyneux. In 1931, he expanded his business to include a department of ready-to-wear.

A number of other American designers were also making names for themselves in the 1930s. Elizabeth Hawes made headlines in the fashion press when she took her collection to Paris for a Fourth of July showing in 1932. She wanted to prove that non-Parisian designers could create exceptional fashions, but later complained to reporters that she was not well received. Muriel King understood "how to take one good costume and turn it into six by clever capes and scarfs and such," mused *Vogue*.[64] Mary Lewis was the exponent of "typically American clothes" such as the "shirtmaker frock."[65] Jo Copeland started out as a fashion illustrator but then began to sell her designs to ready-to-wear maker Patullo. Philip Mangone was a seventh-generation tailor whose ready-to-wear label, Mangone Models, was sold in more than two hundred stores.

The majority of American fashion designers—sometimes disparagingly referred to as "stylists" by the more supercilious couturiers—worked anonymously for ready-to-wear manufacturers and made-to-order salons of department stores. The branded labels that went into the completed garments were those of the retailer or wholesaler. Observed *Vogue* in 1938: "customarily the dress you buy carries the name of the store in which it is sold, rather than the label of the [designer] who made it. All in all, there's very little glory in the work—terrific gamble, stiff competition, and money only if you never grow stale."[66] A few years earlier, in its 1933 report on American fashion design, *Vogue* acknowledged a few of these designers who worked outside of the fashion spotlight. Among those featured were Mr. Newman at Bergdorf Goodman, Miss Martha at Bonwit Teller, and Mrs. Gimble at Saks Fifth Avenue. Even with this notoriety and the advertising efforts of the salons and department stores, this was not the coming of age of American

Figure 3-21. New silhouettes of 1939 included fuller and much shorter skirts. Oversized shoulder treatments remained popular. The exaggerated, cinched waistline that had been so prevalent in Paris collections that year failed to ignite interest as the war progressed. Ads 1939.

fashion, regardless of the innovation and creativity of the designers. The allegiance and reliance upon the French couture industry by fashion journalists, ready-to-wear makers, and retailers remained constant well into the 1960s.

Celebration and Tumult in 1939

In 1939, two major U.S. expositions opened on opposite coasts: the New York World's Fair and the San Francisco Golden Gate Expo. The fact that America hosted these international events simultaneously was regarded by *Vogue* as a reflection of the nation's "exuberant extravagance." Whereas the Golden Gate Expo represented "a passion for our past," the New York Fair provided "a drawing of the future." [67] Exhibition pavilions gleamed with glass towers, steel turrets, and aluminum bricks and were accented with moderne murals and sculptures. The futures of aviation, transportation, electricity, communications, and entertainment were forecasted in daz-

zling scale models and life-sized exhibits. One glimpse of America's future was presented in a multimedia diorama representing a 1960s "city of tomorrow" with its talking robot and rocket airport.

For a futuristic perspective of fashion, *Vogue* contracted nine industrial designers to each create a costume for the year 2000. The men chosen for this assignment were noted for designs of locomotives, aluminum appliances, or plastic furniture. Now, they explored the challenge of new silhouettes for apparel and the potential applications of modern materials to clothing such as Plexiglas, cellophane, Lucite, and glass filaments. Viewed today from the perspective of the twenty-first century, the outfits were pure theater, irrespective of the designers' intended principles of form and function. Indeed, elements of their creations would be quite familiar to us today from science fiction movies of the 1950s and 1960s, or even from the costumes of rock music performers like Madonna and Cher.

Silk for beauty—

An evening gown of gold silk taffeta and gold silk lace with its pattern outlined in metal thread.

Silk for beauty—beauty that not only is satisfying to the eye but beauty that has for its foundation a heritage of satisfying service. When you buy a dress that looks like silk and feels like silk at a price for which you have a right to expect silk do not take for granted that it is silk but ask to have "Silk" written on your sales check. There are added values in a good silk dress—inherent qualities of strength and elasticity which mean longer wear and greater clothes satisfaction.

INTERNATIONAL SILK GUILD · 250 FIFTH AVENUE · NEW YORK

Figure 3-22. As World War II began, eveningwear reflected a marked interest in fanciful escapism with revivals of Renaissance and rococo finery. Ads 1939.

HOYNINGEN-HUENE

Balenciaga evokes an era of minuets and marble stairs in this sumptuous gown of palest *café au lait* faille, pointed up by black velvet bows and basque. From our Made-to-order Salon.

ON THE PLAZA · NEW YORK
BERGDORF GOODMAN
5TH AVENUE AT 58TH STREET

In 1939 Americans looked to the future with such effervescent optimism largely because the economy had substantially improved and the Great Depression was perceived to be at an end. Unemployment numbers had dropped by more than four million from their peak in 1932 and would continue a rapid decline to less than 4 percent the following year. In addition, neutrality acts passed by Congress, combined with the high-profile influence of isolationist groups, gave Americans a sense of security in a turbulent world already at war.

Fueling the U.S. economic growth were the insatiable appetites of the war machines of Nazi Germany, Fascist Italy, and imperial Japan. Millions of tons of raw materials and manufactured goods were imported by each to sustain their expansionist agendas. Millions more were shipped to adjacent countries that were mobilizing for defense. Between 1936 and 1938 Germany had marched its army into the demilitarized Rhineland and annexed German-speaking Sudetenland and

Austria. Italy had invaded Ethiopia with tanks and aerial bombardments in an attempt at colonization. Japan had occupied China in a quest for natural resources.

These events were but a prelude to the global tumult of 1939. On September 1, Germany invaded Poland. Honoring their alliance agreements with Warsaw, Britain and France declared war on Germany. The conflagration of World War II had begun.

Thus, it was not without great irony that the Lagoon of Nations at the New York Fair was fringed with weeping willow trees. Germany had declined to participate in the fair. Italy used its pavilion as a propaganda display with the motto "Obey, Believe, Fight" chiseled on the facade.

Despite the beginning of war in the fall of 1939, the Paris openings were well attended. *Vogue* reported that the great majority of skirts were full and short. (Figure 3-21 and color plate 10.) Even so, "individual proportions should be studied," suggested the editors, "every woman taking a good look at her legs before she decides where her skirts should end."[68] Variations of the skirt also included revivals of the pre–First World War hobble skirt and versions of the hoop skirt just ahead of the release of *Gone with the Wind*. The most notable change of the fashion silhouette, though, was the tiny, cinched waistline that most all of the couturiers emphasized in their collections. *Vogue* even ran a double-page spread about the new corsets that would allow women to "build" the "ring-size waist" for Molyneux's suits, or the "caved-in waist" for Schiaparelli's jackets, or the "moulded torso" for Chanel's gowns.[69] However, the war needs of the time sent fashions in another direction entirely so that the corseted waists were quickly forgotten—at least for the time being.

In eveningwear, French designers looked back to period costumes from the sixteenth and eighteenth centuries. (Figure 3-22.) *Vogue* called these fanciful creations "escapism." "Retrospective eyes were turned backwards toward paintings, toward the Arabian nights, toward the past for these imaginative clothes—possibly because those eyes dared not look forward."[70]

Truly, this latter sentiment was sincere. As France braced for a German invasion in the autumn of 1939, *Vogue* reminded readers of the conditions that had so adversely affected the fashion industry during the four long years of World War I. Labor shortages, the lack of materials, and the challenges to the creative spirit were duly noted. By October, Lelong, Barbas, and Creed had already left their Paris salons for military duty. Molyneux had just shipped his last clothes to America before converting operations to the production of uniforms. "Just how long Paris will go on designing clothes, one can only hazard a guess," lamented the editors.[71]

Conclusion

Following the First World War, fashion styles began to turn on ever more rapid cycles of change. Advances in technology during the Machine Age made possible a faster response for ready-to-wear makers. Mass marketing became even more immediate with the advent of commercial radio in the early 1920s. Not only were the newest trends in fashion sent to market sooner, but advertising got the message out faster to a broader demographic of American consumers.

Following World War I, Paris designers were initially unsure how to design for the modern, postwar woman. Molyneux, Patou, and Chanel led the way in the early twenties with the comfortable fit and fresh look of the dropped-waist chemise. After adjusting to market demands for shorter hemlines, by middecade fashion makers succeeded with the boxy, straightline silhouette of dresses belted at the hips and cropped to the knees—the quintessential style of the flapper era.

With the opening of the 1930s, the Great Depression spread globally, and the silhouette of women's fashions was transformed. Emphasis on feminine curves returned. The waistline was shifted back to its natural position, though not cinched, and a new focus was placed on the hips and bust. Hemlines dropped nearly to the ankles, but the legs remained defined by the slim skirts and soft, fluid fabrics. Throughout the 1930s, the quest for comfort and ease in dressing introduced adaptations of sports apparel into everyday wardrobes, including shorts, culottes, and slacks. As the Depression eased, designers expressed a renewed optimism with fun and frivolity in fashion. Exaggerated details such as puffed sleeves and wide shoulders redefined silhouettes, and fanciful revivalisms were favorites for eveningwear.

This was also a period of importance for the emergence of the American designer. Retailers and ready-to-wear manufacturers began to promote the names and labels of homegrown fashion makers. In addition, the influence of movie fashions and historical costumes established Hollywood designers like Adrian and Edith Head as famous brands. The star of American fashion design had at last begun to rise, if not to challenge Paris, then at least, and significantly, to shine with a home-court advantage for the American woman.

4

WORLD WAR II THROUGH THE FASHION-CONSCIOUS FIFTIES

In the weeks preceding the German occupation of Paris in June 1940, a group of couturiers moved their operations to Biarritz on the Bay of Biscay in southwestern France. Schiaparelli, Patou, Lanvin, Lelong, Balenciaga, Molyneux, Pombo, Piguet, and Heim all endured severe hardships to transport equipment, materials, and staff across roads clogged with military transports and refugees. Their common purpose was to sustain the survival of the French couture industry by shipping new collections to its only remaining customer, the United States. All hopes were abruptly dashed, though, when France capitulated and exports were immediately frozen.

Just before the borders were closed, Elsa Schiaparelli escaped into Spain and on to America as the goodwill ambassador for the Chambre Syndicale de la Couture. As her close friend Lucien Lelong departed for the front, he urged her, "Please go for all of us. Try to do all that you can so that our name is not forgotten. . . . You must represent us over there. Assure everybody that our work will start at the first opportunity."[1] Upon her arrival in New York, a journalist asked her about the bird brooch she wore. She declared that it was the "symbol of France"—the phoenix.

Writing for *Vogue* in September 1940, Schiaparelli recounted the difficulties that she and her fellow couturiers had been dealing with since war had been declared. Leather and metals for shoes, accessories, and trimmings all were taken for the military. Wool was needed for uniforms and blankets, and silk for parachutes. Even color options became limited as the use of certain dyes became proscribed. Labor shortages were felt immediately as men were called up for military duty. "Not a tailor was left, not one," bemoaned Schiaparelli.[2] Then, too, there were the distress and anxiety of war news and the uncertainties of wartime that were felt by everyone.

More important, Schiaparelli emphasized, was that the "tricks of our own invention" had risen to the challenge. When buttons became unavailable, she had set chains through buttonholes and attached fasteners originally made for dog leashes. She explored creative uses of material substitutions for wool and silk such as fabric blends, nonessential synthetics, and cotton. Even when materials were available, government restrictions on the amount of fabric that could be used in any respective garment narrowed the range of design possibilities.

The Last Paris Collections

In the winter of 1939–40, World War II in Europe was largely fought by air and at sea. Poland was subdued by Germany, and Finland surrendered to Russia. Germany's aggression against its western neighbors did not commence until April, when Norway and Denmark were invaded, followed in May by Luxembourg, the Netherlands, Belgium, and France. During the winter lull, sometimes referred to by historians as the "phony war,"[3] French couture prepared for the openings of the spring collections.

"Paris presents: narrower and narrower silhouettes," declared a *Vogue* headline in March 1940.[4] The "pencil slim" suits and "needle-thin" dresses that were so prevalent in the showings were the result of strict fabric rationing. Hemlines remained short, and padded shoulders were ubiquitous. (Figure 4-1.) Military motifs were conspicuously absent from any apparel category. By a stretch, the exception might be the occasional textile pattern, such as Balenciaga's cannon-print peplum dress. In fact, print fabrics were widely used by most all of the couturiers to appeal specifically to American buyers. "Prints were prominent at the collections," reported *Vogue*, "beautifully detailed prints that the French couture does so well, that American women love so well to wear."[5]

However, eveningwear designs presented a host of full skirts and swathes of drapery at hiplines, in bustles, and for oversized bows. Rayon and synthetic blends such as acetate and Celanese replaced silk and pure wool in tulles, chiffons, crepes, and jerseys.

Figure 4-1. The Paris shows of early 1940 reflected the wartime restrictions on fabric use. Narrow suits and dresses with short skirts and padded shoulders were represented in most every couturier's collection. Even though no restrictions were in place in the United States at the time, American ready-to-wear makers and retailers adopted the dictates of Paris. Ads 1940–41.

Straight—

Cool

Slim—

Lord & Taylor

Brown—

Advance summer guise of a great fall fashion – slim-skirted dresses. In brown rayon bengaline, cool as ice coffee. With puff crown felt hats in café au lait. Original collection by the Misses' Dress Salon, Third Floor, 39.95. Hats, 18.50. Lord & Taylor, Fifth Avenue, New York

Glenurquhart Plaid from the Looms of Strook

It's our pet Glenurquhart plaid turned out in an ensemble that for crisp tailoring challenges all comers. Note the feminine curves of the jacket—the new waistline buttoning. The flared skirt has inverted pleats both before and aft—the casual coat is broad-shouldered and also boasts an inverted back pleat. In a soft, luxurious fabric—loomed by Strook. Suit, $49.95 . . . Topcoat, $49.95.

Peck & Peck

NEW YORK • BOSTON • CHICAGO • CLEVELAND • DETROIT • MINNEAPOLIS
HARTFORD • PHILADELPHIA • ST. LOUIS • PALM BEACH • MIAMI BEACH

Bonwit Teller

Anthony Blotta

From an Academy of Fine Art's training in Rome, to one of America's most modern designers. Here is the success story of a sculptor, which Anthony Blotta still remains . . his media now the shears instead of the chisel, fabric instead of clay. Here is the kind of gallant costume which is his special flair. This season's most important fashion . . the cape . . done, with the dashing air of a highwayman, in ginger-colored wool. Over a two-piece dress of gray plaid Linton tweed, with big stag-at-eve buttons. Misses' sizes, 215.00

DRESS SALON—SIXTH FLOOR

FIFTH AVENUE • NEW YORK

SPRING FASHION COMMUNIQUÉ: For Madame, the versatile dress with young bolero jacket and alluring skirt drama of pleats . . TOUJOURS—a sheer crepe classic by DUPLAN—woven for lasting loveliness of TUBIZE Abrazed Acetate Rayon Yarn. Seen at B. ALTMAN & CO., New York; L. BAMBERGER & CO., Newark; T. A. CHAPMAN CO., Milwaukee; MARSHALL FIELD & COMPANY, Chicago; FILENE'S, Boston, HALLE BROS., Cleveland; J. L. HUDSON CO., Detroit; KAUFMANN'S, Pittsburgh; LIVINGSTON BROS., San Francisco; J. W. ROBINSON CO., Los Angeles; WOODWARD & LOTHROP, Washington, D. C.   *Reg. Trademark

*toujours** . . . *fabric distinctively DUPLAN*

Despite the wartime conditions, the spring showing was one of the most successful in almost a decade. *Vogue* hastened to acknowledge the adversities under which the couturiers and their production teams had worked on the collections. "To have made them at all is heroic," the editors marveled. "To have made them so beautiful is an epic victory."[6]

Unfazed by travel dangers, American retailers and ready-to-wear makers made significant purchases from the Paris openings. Despite submarine warfare throughout the Atlantic, boatloads of shipping crates arrived safely in New York in time for spring production lines. Thinking themselves secure behind the imposing Maginot Line of forts along the German border, neither the couturiers nor their American buyers suspected that the 1940 spring opening would be the last major French showing for the next four years. Many retail buyers and private clients "were sorry later that they had not bought more generously," Schiaparelli was to write from the U.S. that autumn.[7]

For the First Time on Their Own

Even before Paris was occupied, speculation was rampant in the U.S. as to what might happen to American fashion without direction from the French couturiers. Although twenty years had passed since the founding of "Seventh Avenue" as the fashion center of America, native designers were still viewed mostly as stylists of Parisian designs rather than fashion innovators. This attitude had moderated somewhat during the 1930s, when retailers and fashion publication editors featured the work and names of American designers in formats comparable to those usually reserved for French haute couture. Still, industry leaders had their doubts.

When the French borders closed in June 1940, the issue was moot. Many Parisian couturiers continued to produce limited collections for French and German buyers, but very little information about the designs reached America. Condé Nast wired Michel de Brunhoff, his editor in chief of French *Vogue,* that he approved in advance of any operational decisions he made on behalf of Nast Publications.[8] When the Germans insisted that de Brunhoff prove there were no Jewish attachments to the publication by providing biographies of all staff and outside resources, he instead shut down operations and fled to America. French *Vogue* did not resume publication until 1945.

In the fall of 1940, *Vogue*'s editors noted that "the fashion spot-light turns on New York, and our title changes from 'Paris Openings' to 'American Openings.'"[9] Page after page of headlines in the September fashion issue emphasized the words "America" and "American." A feature article on "who's who in American design" cast the mold for future reports on current

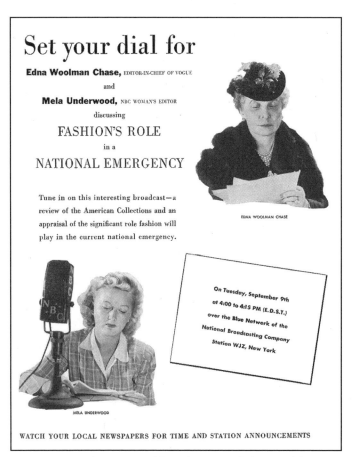

Figure 4-2. *Vogue* publicized American fashions and the names of native designers to a broader consumer market with segments on radio broadcasts. Ad 1941.

trend makers. Even mainstream, mass-circulation publications recognized the significance of the change of venue for the multimillion-dollar American fashion industry. For example, *Ladies' Home Journal* proclaimed: "America claims its own! This year, as never before, all eyes turn to New York for fashion guidance. We of the *Journal* cover the collections as we would in Paris—with eagerness, and a sense of news emerging!"[10] Similarly, *Life* featured ten American designers with brief biographies, photo portraits, and accompanying fashion shots of their recent creations. Wrote the editors: "The U.S. fashion world is becoming very proud of U.S. clothes designers. As long as Paris ruled in the realm of style, Americans were apologetic about their designers. But when Paris fell Americans began to appraise and appreciate their own."[11] In addition, fashion editors such as Lois Long of the *New Yorker* and Virginia Pope of the *New York Times* redoubled their efforts to champion American designers, both in the couture and the ready-to-wear arenas. Eleanor Lambert, one of the first fashion publicists for American designers, spread the news about native fashions by sending press releases and photographs to newspapers around the country. By the 1940s her semiannual press weeks in New York were eagerly anticipated. Going one step further than the printed fashion report, *Vogue's* editor in chief, Edna Woolman Chase, even began taking the news of American fashions to the masses with segments on the radio. (Figure 4-2.)

Unlike with Parisian haute couture, in America the lines between a couture designer, a made-to-order designer, and a ready-to-wear designer were blurred by advertising and fashion editorials. For most American women, the only difference was in production quantity. The couturier may sell only one, or at best just a few copies, of each model; the made-to-order designer may make dozens of copies; and the ready-to-wear designer may produce thousands of copies. To most consumers, advertisers, and journalists the argument was a distinction without a difference. Fashion was fashion, and a designer was a designer.

The war allowed these versatile and talented designers to enjoy the limelight without having to compete with the French on French terms. In fact, in 1943, *Life* reported on the "first sizeable collection of French creations to reach the U.S. since the occupation of Paris." The new fashions were from the wardrobe of a visiting French aviator's wife. The editors observed that "in normal times the arrival of a new collection of French clothes in New York would greatly stir the trade and press." These clothes, however, were viewed as merely "vulgar exaggerations of famous silhouettes" that "created barely a ripple" against the showings of the American fall collections.[12]

Many of the best-known names in American fashion of the early 1940s had already gained prominence during the preceding decade. Hattie Carnegie, Henri Bendel, Sally Milgrim, Philip Mangone, Adrian, and Muriel King were just a few of the established designers who continued to lead the American fashion industry. Some new names that achieved prominence during the late 1930s and especially in the 1940s were Germaine Monteil, Nettie Rosenstein, Sydney Wragge, Norman Norell, Adele Simpson, Clare Potter, Lilli Ann, and Claire McCardell. (Figure 4-3.)

The name Germaine Monteil is best known today as a line of cosmetics and skin-care treatments. During the late 1930s, Monteil had begun to experiment with fragrances and skin preparations as a sideline to her fashion business. By the end of the 1940s, her cosmetic division had achieved such success and demanded so much of her attention that she eventually abandoned fashion designing. Despite her French name, her clothing styles of the early 1940s appealed to a broad American market, especially her use of prints. Her dresses featured slender silhouettes with flared skirts that were pleated or circular-cut. Monteil's classic styling and use of easy-care fabrics, such as rayon, were ideally suited to the wartime needs of American women.

Nettie Rosenstein is credited by many fashion historians as having "invented the little black dress."[13] Because her versions were made in daytime lengths of black crepe and other supple fabrics, they served effectively for day-into-evening functions. Rosenstein worked by draping her designs directly on live fit models. This allowed her to best use the tricks of the trade to create illusions of femininity for women who did not possess the ideal figure. Her print fabrics were often complemented by her accessory designs that included matching gloves, handbags, and costume jewelry.

The name B. H. Wragge was the ready-to-wear label of designer Sydney Wragge. His collections were centered on the concept of separates—garments designed as units of an ensemble that could be purchased separately. Retailers' ads that featured B. H. Wragge fashions often depicted several photos to emphasize the interchangeable wardrobe options and to encourage multiple purchases. Each season, Wragge devised a theme for his collection, such as the South Wind group shown in Figure 4-3. Textile patterns and colors would be coordinated around these themes. Price points for his clothing were moderate for the 1940s, mostly in the five-dollar to twenty-five dollar range, so consumers could afford to buy several pieces from each group.

Norman Norell began his fashion career as a costume designer for Astoria Studios in the 1920s. During the 1930s he worked for a wholesale dress company and then joined the salon of Hattie Carnegie, who taught him to curb his penchant for Hollywood theatricality. In 1941, he partnered with the ready-to-wear manufacturer Traina to form the Traina-Norell label. Although his eveningwear often revealed his early training in Hollywood, he actually became more noted for his simpler designs, especially suit blouses and shirtwaist dresses. His favorite textile prints were basic checks, stripes, and polka dots.

Adele Simpson emerged from the anonymity of designing for wholesalers in the 1930s to own her own company in the 1940s. Her fitted suits, cut with narrow waists and flared skirts, were feminine and flattering to the proportions of the American woman. She was one of the first designers to treat cotton seriously as a fashion fabric, including its use in eveningwear. In later years she created wardrobes for First Ladies Mamie Eisenhower and Rosalyn Carter.

Clare Potter enjoyed the distinction of being America's most prolific casualwear designer of the 1940s. She lived on a farm in rural Rockland County, New York, where she raised Dalmatians and gardened. Her fashions reflected the ease and casualness of her personal lifestyle. *Life* reported that Potter's collections "have an informal, comfortable look, plus an elegance achieved by combining odd and delicate pastel colors."[14]

Lilli Ann established her ready-to-wear business in San Francisco in 1942. Despite her West Coast location, her exquisitely detailed coat and suit designs were versatile and sophisticated. Many of her suit styles were elegant enough to wear to the theater or cocktail parties. Lilli Ann ads of the period reflected this elegance through the dramatic fashion images created by the great Hollywood photographer George Hurrell. Writing in her book *Ready-Made Miracle*, former *Vogue* editor Jessica Daves noted that in 1967, Lilli Ann was the largest American manufacturer of coats and suits in the price bracket of $69.50 to $250.[15]

Claire McCardell made her name in sportswear. She deliberately omitted design pretensions such as shoulder pads, restrictive foundations, and superfluous decorative treatments. Her silhouettes were simple, inventive, and multifunctional. In 1942 she designed an inexpensive "popover" dress made of quilted denim that sold in the tens of thousands for $6.96.

Numerous other designers achieved renown and success during the 1940s. Howard Greer was another former movie costume designer who, like Adrian and Norman Norell, abandoned Hollywood for New York. He specialized in expensive ready-to-wear evening gowns that were priced in the $200 to $650 range. Coty Award–winner Pauline Trigére had been trained in Paris as a couturier but chose to work in American ready-to-wear during the 1930s. After establishing her own

Figure 4-3. Following the German occupation of Paris in June 1940, French fashions ceased to be available to the U.S. market. American designers were, as *Vogue* noted, "for the first time on their own." Without the inspiration—and competition—from Paris, new American talent emerged into the limelight.
Ads these two pages 1940–44.

business in 1942, she soon gained recognition for her scarf-tied suits and superbly cut wool dresses. Her high-styled suits were worn by Patricia Neal in *Breakfast at Tiffany's*.

The most notable new name on the American fashion front of the 1940s was Mainbocher. Born Main Rousseau Bocher in Chicago in 1891, he came to fashion design in a roundabout way. In his early years he worked as an illustrator in Munich, Paris, and New York. When America entered World War I, he volunteered as an ambulance driver and was sent to France. After the war he stayed on in Paris as a fashion illustrator for *Harper's Bazar*. In 1922 he became the fashion editor for French *Vogue*, where he remained at the helm for seven years. In 1929 he decided to try his hand at fashion

Nettie Rosenstein

B.H. Wragge

matched wardrobe in South Wind colours

Bonwit Teller

Bonwit Teller

Traina-Norell

The House of Traina-Norell comes on the season like an electrical storm. Its designer, young Mr. Norell, creates a collection so alive that everyone's talking. Photographed his Salome, a silk jersey in molten beige, purple, baroque pink, 135.00. Headdress, 25.00.

An Adele Simpson original

New suit silhouette in an Adele Simpson original in pure wool. Fuchsia, beige, bride blue, black, with braid buttons. Suit under seventy dollars. Blouse separate. At Saks Fifth Avenue and other leading stores.

Bonwit Teller

Clare Potter

button-up dresses 25.00

It's an amazing talent that can design a classic dress and still have it tell the name of its creator as clearly as a signed portrait. Clare Potter has done two classics as American as an army's buttons... of one of her pet fabrics, a chalky rayon she calls "Ranna." Casual, easy lines, good shoulders. Rose-red, white, blue, daisy-yellow. 12 to 20, 25.00.

BONWIT TELLER · TOWN & COUNTRY DRESSES, FIFTH FLOOR · FIFTH AVENUE, NEW YORK · WHITE PLAINS · MIAMI BEAI

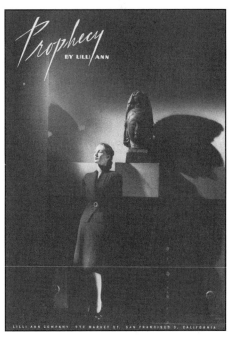

Prophecy
BY LILLI ANN

LILLI ANN COMPANY · 973 MARKET ST. SAN FRANCISCO 3, CALIFORNIA

designing and set up his own Paris salon in Avenue George V. He bought a sewing mannequin, pins, and yards of muslin and taught himself the fundamentals of draping. At this time he also contracted his name into Mainbocher.

His first collection in the fall of 1930 was not a commercial success. However, his efforts were favorably reported by his former colleagues in the fashion press, lending a cachet to his salon that usually took years to achieve. As a result, his openings soon were crowded to overflowing. He even

required attendees to guarantee the purchase of one dress at minimum to gain admittance in an attempt to prevent copyists from stealing his ideas. From sales of 16 million francs in 1930, his business leaped to 100 million francs in 1939.[16]

Mainbocher's dress designs were simple. He followed Vionnet's tradition of cutting fabric on the bias for easy, fluid draping that flattered the slender, feminine figure. His reductionist evening gowns were afforded variety and imagination with the addition of his little "tie-ons" such as swags, aprons, and full overskirts. His great love was the luxury of fabric, which he imported from all over the world.

This luxury of fabric and simplicity of design greatly appealed to Wallis Simpson. When she consented to marry the Duke of Windsor in 1936, she commissioned Mainbocher to design her wedding gown and trousseau. The pale blue wedding dress had a floor-length skirt with rows of tiny self-buttons at the waist and wrists, and a jacket that was not meant to be removed. Both Mainbocher and the Duchess benefited immensely from their collaborative relationship. He received world fame, and she was catapulted into the role of a supreme arbiter of fashion taste.

When Paris fell to the Germans in the summer of 1940, Mainbocher closed his maison de couture and returned to the United States. He set up a new salon in New York and resumed his couture business. Unlike most of his American contemporaries, he remained strictly a couturier and never mass produced or mass marketed his label. Despite his continued financial success, Mainbocher was viewed less and less as a leader in American fashion. His classic and simple styling seemed repetitive and uninspired to many of those in the fashion press. Yet, when he closed his business in 1971, his profits were greater than they had ever been.

The War Years, 1942–1945

Although American isolationist organizations had been successful in their lobbying efforts during the early years of the war in Europe, everything changed in a moment on December 7, 1941, when Japan attacked Pearl Harbor. Four days later, Germany and Italy declared war on the United States, and suddenly America was thrust into World War II.

Since the clouds of conflict had first appeared on the European horizon in 1938, the Roosevelt administration had been cautiously preparing for the inevitability of war. Diplomatic lines of communication hummed with negotiations, government agencies outlined contingency plans, and the military stepped up recruitment efforts and combat training. In a bolder move, the president persuaded Congress to pass the Lend-Lease Act of 1940, which was devised as a way to send arms, equipment, and supplies to a nearly bankrupt Britain without generating additional foreign debt on either side. This sweeping legislation put American manufacturing plants into full production—a circumstance that made U.S. mobilization much easier in the transitional months following Pearl Harbor.

In the early months of the war, American mass media alerted the populace about the lifestyle changes that they were about to confront. Not only were the civilian wartime condi-

tions from the First World War still in living memory, but for two years Americans had witnessed the challenges experienced by the besieged British via news reports, photo journalism, movies, and radio broadcasts.

When it came to fashion, *Vogue* acknowledged in February 1942 that American women would "clothe themselves in sackcloth" if that were needed to help win the war. Rather than go to that extreme, though, the editors instead advised readers: "The makers of fashion—of shoes and hats, gloves and bags, of dresses and coats and suits—all these makers are operating with full Government approval. Whatever is on sale in a shop is there to be bought, with the Government's full permission. Refusal to buy only helps to dislocate the public economy."[17] Still, *Vogue* warned, changes other than just fashion styles were imminent. First of the losses were rubber and silk. Although the significance of rubber in the fashion industry was primarily its use in the making of foundation garments, *Vogue* suggested that manufacturers knew how to make corsets before elasticized fabrics were invented, and they could do so again, if needed. Besides, there were "large stocks of foundation garments to carry us through a long season of adjustment." Silk was thought to be in plentiful supply—perhaps two or three years' worth before its loss would be noticed, and then rayon or cotton would suffice as a substitute. Wool already had been rationed for a while, so consumers were prepared for "adulterations" such as wool blends and synthetics. The wide range of rayon yarns was expected to be reduced to a few variations that could be produced in greater quantity. Too, color dyes were projected to be limited in variety, although *Vogue* hastened to point out that "you never bought those hundreds of mutations anyway." Finally, copper, brass, tin, and other metals needed by the government would disappear from costume jewelry, buttons, buckles, and trimmings. But accessory designers became quite creative with "hundreds of other unsuspected materials . . . where whimsy has always been of more importance than raw materials."[18]

Indeed, these predictions turned out to be fairly accurate. An enormous array of raw materials and manufactured goods were immediately rationed for war needs. For the American fashion industry, the challenge was as cheerfully accepted by designers and ready-to-wear manufacturers as it had been in France and England. Under its L-85 regulation, the U.S. War Production Board (WPB) set strict guidelines for the kinds and quantities of materials that could be used in almost every category of apparel and accessories. Exceptions included religious vestments, wedding gowns, maternity clothing, childrenswear, and burial shrouds. One of the primary purposes of the regulation was to standardize apparel silhouettes to

conserve materials and to prevent retooling or adjusting of production equipment that might require new machinery and additional labor. As material shortages occurred, the WPB revised its regulations, to which designers and ready-to-wear manufacturers complied without complaint.

For women's clothing, the L-85 regulations restricted skirts to seventy-two inches at the hem. Although this still afforded fullness, the circle skirt and the dirndl skirt disappeared from design collections. The hemline return of skirts could not exceed two inches. The length of suit jackets was limited to twenty-five inches, which hit just at the hips of average women, and the circumference of pant legs was restricted to nineteen inches. For blouses and coats, design features such as double yokes, back pleats, wide cuffs, hoods, scarves, and sashes were prohibited.

American designers had already previewed what these austerity measures would mean in fashion styles two years earlier with the last collections from France. In addition, the British had also established similar regulations for their

Figure 4-4. Unlike their counterparts in Paris and London, American fashion designers incorporated silhouettes, trimmings, and details from military uniforms into their collections.

Figure 4-5. Even before America entered the war, conservation measures were encouraged by government agencies.
As foreign imports of heating fuels diminished, fashion designers
and ready-to-wear makers produced versatile and comfortable
sweater sets. Tish-U-Knit ad 1940, Caerlee ad 1941.

wartime needs and produced clothing silhouettes that forecast
those of America in 1943.

The noticeable difference between the fashions of 1940,
shown in Figure 4-1, and the styles of 1942 and 1943 was the
predicted reduction of silhouette. "New collections narrow the
line, widen the use," read a headline in the September 1943
issue of *Vogue*.[19] (Color plate 12.) Certainly the intention was
far more than merely providing a fresh look or versatile
styles. In fact, a *Vogue* editor reminded readers:

> No law compels us to wear clothes as narrow as these. L-
> 85 allows much more generous measurements. Of our
> own free will, we're wearing them. Voluntarily, a group
> of American designers have pledged themselves to use
> less fabric than L-85 allows—in order to save every
> yard. . . . The British, who have felt the pinch of fabric
> shortages longer than we, practically live in slim coat-
> dresses. They call them austerity fashions, but if this is
> austerity, let's have more of it.[20]

American designers were so successful in creatively adapt-
ing the restrictions on fabric use that more than fifteen million
yards of material were saved for the war efforts.[21]

Unlike with the fashion houses of Paris and London,
American designers unhesitatingly took inspiration from the
styles of military uniforms. Many collections of late 1942 into
early 1944 included silhouettes, trimmings, and other details
taken directly from the uniforms of the WAVES, WACS,
SPARS, and other similar women's military and war service
organizations. (Figure 4-4.)

Even before America entered the war, conservation was
the guideline for daily life. From as early as 1938, imports of
coal, oil, and gas began to diminish as foreign producers were
invaded and ocean trade routes were disrupted. In answer to
the lowered thermostats and shortages of home heating fuels,
American designers and ready-to-wear makers expanded the
varieties and price point ranges of sweater styles. The layered
twin set—a pullover and matching cardigan—became especially popular. (Figure 4-5.) Not only did the garments help
ward off the chill of colder seasons, but they also afforded
women wardrobe options for numerous looks. The cardigan
and pullover could be worn together as a set or separately
over a blouse with pants or a skirt, creating a different look
each time. Mainbocher even created a collection of handmade
sweater sets that were ornamented with beading and costume
jewels for eveningwear.

As during the First World War, vast numbers of women
entered the workforce to ease the labor shortage. They cut
their hair and stepped into trousers to work in factories, operate machinery, and manage service tasks more safely. By the
1940s, though, women's trousers were tailored to the feminine form with a more flattering fit than the utilitarian styles

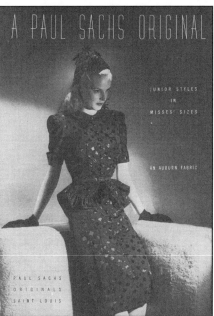

Figure 4-6. Following the end of World War II, American designers celebrated the lifting of restrictions on fabric use with modes that featured capacious sleeves, fuller skirts, and exaggerated peplums. Ads 1945.

of the 1910s. The convenience, comfort, and variety of slacks increasingly appealed to a broader spectrum of women, and the look became widely acceptable for day and evening wear. (Color plate 13.)

In August 1944, Paris was liberated by the Allies. In *Vogue*'s "first report from the French couture since 1940," the editors noted that "the clothes made during the German occupation were intended by the various dressmakers to be deliberately fancy and exaggerated in order to taunt the Germans." Upon seeing the Parisian fashions, one German commander declared, "If they wear such gay monstrosities in defeat, what can they possibly think up for their victory?"[22] Because sav-

Stern's newest print... Paris-
inspired... scoop-necklined,
wisp-waisted, soft-shouldered,
swirl-skirted... dramatic silhouette in a dramatic season! Fluid
black rayon crepe splashed with
white, 10 to 16, 35.00. Third Floor

Stern's

1947

I live

in California

WHERE THE FIRST COOL DAYS
OF FALL FIND ME IN ONE OF GENE SHELLY'S
MASTERFULLY DESIGNED, DISCREETLY
UNDERSTATED GABARDINE SUITS, WHICH
I FIND AT ONLY ONE PLACE IN LOS ANGELES,
MAY CO. OF COURSE. 175.00

MAY CO. LOS ANGELES

1948

Capri Original

MONTALDO'S
Denver · Colorado Springs · Bartlesville, Okla. · Columbus, Ohio · St. Louis
Richmond, Va. · Charlotte, Winston-Salem and Greensboro, N. C.

Bird-Speakman Inc.
Wilmington, Del.

Deep's
East Orange, N.J.

1948

Figure 4-7. The 1947 debut collection from Christian Dior inspired a pivotal change in women's fashions. This New Look provided women with fashion drama, exaggerated femininity, and the luxury of volumes of material. A cinched waist, rounded hips, and long hemlines were key to the silhouette. The New Look was accented by an abundance of accessories, including hats, gloves, masses of costume jewelry, fur pieces, handbags, and even parasols.

ing fabrics and labor only aided the Germans, Paris designers reputedly created models that intentionally used materials extravagantly. Enormous capes, full peplums, overskirts, hip swags, shirred bodices, and balloon sleeves all contributed to the frivolity.

Almost immediately, though, the French couturiers shifted their stylistic directions to those of the narrowed, austere designs of the American and British modes. Since the war was still far from over and the French were back in the field with the Allies, fabric rationing now benefited the home cause. The Chambre Syndicale de la Couture set up conservation restrictions similar to those of America's L-85 and Britain's Utility regulations. As materials became scarcer, French inventiveness led to wool blends made of rabbit hair and velvet woven from wood-pulp yarns.

After the War, a New Look

Victory in Europe was achieved in May 1945 with the surrender of Germany at Rheims, followed by victory over Japan in August 1945. Gradually, rationing was phased out as war production converted back to consumer use. By the autumn of that year, American fashions celebrated the increased availability of fabric. (Figure 4-6.) Huge sleeves and oversized peplums were especially prevalent in the collections of most all American designers. Particularly notable, though, was the reintroduction of the cinched waist that had briefly appeared in Paris in 1939. Wrote *Vogue* of the new silhouettes: "Waists are as small as inner or outer lacing can make them. They look as small as panniers, peplums, hip padding or leg 'o mutton or puffed sleeves can make them seem. The illusion that a figure is as small as its smallest visible point prevails."[23]

Ironically, Paris couture had not yet recovered sufficiently to take the forefront of international fashion design once again. *Vogue* reported that "there is little in Paris to inspire creative effort; no exciting fabrics, no brilliant accessories, no enthusiasm from the workers in the ateliers, no smart restaurants or parties to whet an appetite for elegance, few smart women to put fashions over . . . and a crushing luxury tax to kill buying enthusiasm."[24] Still, one hint of things to come was noted from the 1945 fall collection of Balenciaga. He had dropped hemlines as low as fifteen inches from the floor. This longer dress length and the reappearance of the cinched waistline, coupled with the pent-up desire of women around the world for luxury and femininity in fashion, culminated in the sweeping New Look of the 1947 debut collection of newcomer Christian Dior.

Prior to establishing his own salon, Dior had studied political science at college, served in the military, run an art gallery, and worked as an illustrator. In the late 1930s he joined the house of Lelong as a designer, where he met textile magnate Marcel Boussac. So impressed was Boussac with Dior's talent and driving ambition that he offered to back the designer's launch of his own label. With his very first collection in 1947, Dior soared straight to the pinnacle of French fashion design. Paris couture once again took center stage in the world of fashion.

Dior's New Look was one of those pivotal events in fashion that dramatically altered the course of style. After nine years of masculine, narrow L-85 and Utility clothing, women were suddenly provided an indulgence in all things that were most feminine and forbidden. "I designed clothes for flower-like women," Dior avowed, "with rounded shoulders, full, feminine busts, and hand-span waists above enormous, spreading skirts."[25] Hemlines were dropped to twelve inches from the floor, even lower than Balenciaga had attempted the previous year. The tiny waist was applied to virtually every mode, reversing the long-standing fashion freedom initiated by Poiret and expanded upon by Chanel two decades earlier. Contorting corsets were in favor again, especially the

Figure 4-8. The Infanta silhouette was named for the seventeenth-century portraits of the Spanish princess painted by Diego Velazquez. The style featured a tight bodice or jacket with a wide, full skirt. Adele Simpson ad 1948, Jack Herzog ad 1947.

Sportleigh

THOROUGHBRED GREATCOAT

Born to travel roll-front coat in
kitten-soft pure wool Harrod-tweed.
Tanbark or fieldstone gray. Misses' sizes
8 to 18, junior sizes 7 to 15.
At one leading store in your city.
America's greatest coat value — $40

TAILORED AT SPORTLEIGH HALL · HARRODSBURG, KENTUCKY

Adrian's new shoulder movement on a striking herringbone tweed greatcoat...over a
miniature-check worsted suit ... from an exclusive collection, in Philadelphia at **NAN DUSKIN**

Figure 4-9. Greatcoats of the late 1940s were designed in
the triangle silhouette to allow sufficient room to cover the
accentuated busts and hips and the full, long skirts of the New
Look suits and dresses. Nan Duskin ad 1947,
Sportleigh ad 1948.

guepiére that cinched the waist, emphasized the bust, and rounded the hips. (See chapter 7.) Dior took advantage of the increasing availability of luxurious fabrics at the time when many women still contended with ersatz wartime materials. His fashions featured full drapery, gathers, pleats, gores, flounces, and oversized bows. The pleated skirt from his Bar suit required twenty yards of material. To complete the appeal to women's fantasies, Dior's salon models were abundantly accessorized for each outfit they demonstrated.

Opening day of Dior's spring collection was so successful that his staff remained on duty until the early morning hours to complete the flood of orders. Major American department and specialty stores took upward of forty toiles each, ensuring that the New Look would be seen everywhere in the United States by Easter. The Duchess of Windsor and Eva Peron were among Dior's first famous customers.

Few British women got to enjoy Dior's New Look as soon as the French and Americans had. The war-torn nation remained under strict rationing and conservation regulations well into the early 1950s as it rebuilt cities and the infrastructure devastated by Nazi bombs. Even though the Labour Party had insisted that the Guild of Creative Designers make every effort to keep the Utility suit and short skirts popular, there were exceptions. By the fall of 1947, even the queen's couturiers, Molyneux and Hartnell, had created variations of the New Look for the women of the royal family, most especially vivacious Princess Margaret.

In America, some groups of women resisted the long skirts, a reaction reminiscent of 1921 and 1929, when hemlines abruptly dropped. In some instances stores that advertised Dior's New Look were picketed by women carrying placards proclaiming:

> Mr. Dior,
> We abhor
> Dresses
> To the floor.

Nonetheless, the New Look rapidly swept America. *Vogue* noted that "people are talking about . . . the New Look, and with pontification."[26] The square-shoulder jackets and dresses and the short skirts that hung in every woman's wardrobe closet suddenly looked demodé. Most wartime styles did not have enough fabric or hemline returns to even attempt makeovers into the New Look. U.S. ready-to-wear makers and designers quickly adapted the mode for three camps of American women: those who continued to like the slim, tailored silhouette; those who preferred a casual sportswear look; and those who embraced the curvaceous femininity of Dior's models. (Figure 4-7 and color plate 15.) In all three cases, the tiny waist, longer hemline, and complete coverage of accessories governed the total look. "Every woman's a woman again," declared *Vogue* about the New Look.[27] American milliners, jewelers, corset makers, and accessory manufacturers were ecstatic about the increased demand for their goods. (Color plate 16.)

One of the key variations of the New Look that became especially popular in America was the Infanta silhouette. Named for the Velazquez portraits of the seventeenth-century Spanish princess, the styles featured tight, almost tubular bodices joined to wide, very full skirts. (Figure 4-8.) *Vogue* called this look the "flatterer of the season" because it could "flow over—gloss over—larger than ideal hips" and, as a result, could make "almost any waistline seem small by comparison."[28]

The one category of clothing that evaded the influence of the cinched, curvaceous New Look was that of coats and jackets, particularly the greatcoat. (Figure 4-9.) The triangle coat silhouette, according to *Vogue*, was designed to be "ample enough to flow over accented hips and full skirts."[29] In one respect, though, these oversized coats complemented the New Look in that they were an indulgence of rich fabrics, fur trims, capelets, big pockets, and turned-back cuffs—most all of which had been denied to women during the privations of wartime.

Segue to the Fashion-Conscious Fifties

When feminists criticized Dior's New Look as negating much of what women had achieved for themselves across two World Wars, the designer responded demurely, "I brought back the neglected art of pleasing."[30] Indeed, this simple statement would define not only Dior's fashions in 1947, but it would become the perspective of most women for the next fifteen years.

During the Second World War, American women had experienced social and economic changes unparalleled in American history. Whereas their mothers and grandmothers had endured World War I for only eighteen months, the women of the 1940s had faced a national crisis that lasted almost four years. In response to the needs of their country, women in huge numbers had joined the labor force in munitions plants, airplane factories, mass-transit systems, government agencies, military offices, and all manner of service-sector businesses. They had compromised, conserved, rationed, and, at times, managed to do without even fundamental necessities throughout the whole ordeal. They had also witnessed unprecedented horrors on a global scale: wholesale slaughter of humanity, the destruction of entire cities all across Europe and Asia, the displacement of entire populations, the Holocaust, the atomic bomb.

When at last the war was won, all Americans longed for a return to normalcy, to perhaps rekindle the optimism they had enjoyed with the predictions and promises of the 1939 World's Fair. Yet, uncertainties did not evaporate when the surrender pacts were signed in 1945. Franklin Delano Roosevelt, who for twelve years had guided them all through the Great Depression and a World War, died suddenly, leaving an unknown entity, Harry Truman, at the nation's helm. A postwar economic downturn, fueled by rampant inflation, hit every American household. Labor unrest boiled over into violence. Decisions on racial issues from all three branches of government affected laws in the South and social order in the North. The cold war created a new evil bogeyman lurking just behind an iron curtain. China fell to the Communists. The Soviet Union exploded the atomic bomb. "Perhaps out of fear that there were so few roots in modern America and things were changing so fast, people found solace in doing what they were supposed to do, whether as 'gray-flannel organization men' climbing the corporate ladder together or as 'organization women' holding down the home front and providing a bedrock of security in a world of competition and chaos," concluded William Chafe in his book *The Paradox of Change: American Women in the Twentieth Century.*[31]

Amidst this global chaos of the late 1940s, a renewed debate on "woman's place" emerged. Mass media besieged women with messages that urged and manipulated them into regressive conventions and conformity. Advertising represented women as the new social order required them to be: devoted wives, homemakers, and mothers. To help women achieve and successfully maintain these goals, the beauty and fashion industries poured billions of dollars into new product development and marketing. Businesses reinstated policies against hiring married women, especially those of childbearing years.[32] Higher education was but an interlude before marriage for many women. As one college president noted in 1952, curriculums of the time were revised to "educate women as women," offering courses in applied and decorative arts, textiles, ceramics, clothing design, child psychology, nursery care, marriage, and family life.[33] The new medium of television provided sanitized programming that reinforced traditional ideals of white, middle-class women to millions of households.

On the fashion front, *Vogue,* too, joined in the regressive social campaign to redefine the modern American woman in patriarchal terms. Articles highlighting women's domesticity became more frequent. In comparing the issues of 1940 with those of 1950, twice as many articles on homemaking targeted the postwar woman. Although not abandoning features on elegant flatware and fine china, gourmet multicourse menus, or sophisticated interior decoration, which had been standard copy in 1940, the editorial content of 1950 also included articles such as:

"The Three 'I's' of Parenthood"
"A Child's Reputation"
"The Fine Art of Being a Stepmother"
"Wonderful 'Average' Woman"[34]

Even the fashion cover for December that year yielded to a close-up photo of a mother cuddling a chubby, happy baby—a sentimental image that resembled those more commonly used on the covers of *Ladies' Home Journal* and *McCall's* at the time.

A few years later *Vogue* wrote about the "different kind of woman" in postwar America. The "statistical" differences reflected a swing back to the traditional, almost stereotypical Victorian woman. She was 11 percent more likely to be married and 77 percent more likely to have three or more children than at the start of the war. In 1954, only three in ten women had jobs, 6 percent less than the female work force peak of 1945. As for being "different individually," *Vogue* suggested to readers that "no woman wants to be wholly different—a certain basic loyalty to our personalities is the wonder, and delight, of psychoanalysts; but in all of us there's a constant urge toward the ideal."[35]

That ideal—a "feminine mystique"—was the subject of much pioneer research and analysis by Betty Friedan, who published her findings in 1963. Basically, Friedan maintained that most American women of the 1950s strove for a common ideal. "Their only dream," Friedan wrote, "was to be perfect wives and mothers; their highest ambition to have five children and a beautiful house; their only fight to get and keep their husbands."[36]

Part of that "urge toward the ideal" that *Vogue* had articulated in 1954 included achieving the new definition of female beauty. The one woman of the era who best exemplified this beauty perfection was Audrey Hepburn. That year Cecil Beaton wrote in *Vogue*: "Nobody ever looked like her before World War II; it is doubtful that anybody ever did. . . . Yet we recognize the rightness of this appearance in relation to our historical needs. And the proof is that thousands of imitations have appeared. The woods are full of emaciated young ladies with rat-nibbled hair and moon-pale faces." The one difference between Audrey Hepburn and most of her beauty peers was sex appeal. Her beauty seemed ethereal and precluded any hint of the earthy, sensual attributes that might be attached to Marilyn Monroe, Grace Kelly, or Elizabeth Taylor. In fact, Beaton's lengthy tribute to Hepburn used phrases such as "natural grace," "innate elegance," "rare phenomenon," and "incandescent glow," but never once described her as sexy.

Nevertheless, Beaton concluded, Audrey Hepburn was the "public embodiment of our new feminine ideal."[37]

By no means did this model of beauty perfection mean women were expected to be put on a pedestal and worshiped from afar like their Victorian predecessors. Indeed, *Vogue's* editors had been quick to emphasize the sex appeal of the New Look fashions. For example, in their trend report for spring 1948, the cover headline read: "New fashions chosen with a man in mind." Foremost on the list of criteria for women to consider in choosing fashions for sex appeal was that "men really like some indication of the female figure beneath the clothes." In 1948 that female figure ideally possessed "the rounded bosom, indented waist, and rounded hips" of the ultrafeminine New Look. In addition, the editors insisted, high heels were a must. "The curving instep, the pointed toe, above all, the vault of a slender heel: these, men notice and remember."[38]

By the end of the 1950s, ready-to-wear designer Anne Fogarty summed up the typical view of the American woman in her book *Wife Dressing*. Despite the old adage that women dressed for women (and men dressed for women), Fogarty insisted that, when selecting what to wear, a woman should always think of herself first as a wife—either as her goal or as her vocation. To achieve success in either case, she must place complete femininity at the top of her list of priorities, especially "the selection of clothes as an adornment, not as a mere covering." This notion extended even to the point of wearing a girdle under everything, including casual apparel worn for cooking and cleaning. "The kitchen is your natural setting as a woman," Fogarty advised, "and you should look beautiful, not bedraggled, in it."[39]

The Second Half of the Century Begins

Despite the uncertainties and fears of the postwar years, the American people emerged into the 1950s with a collective feeling of optimism and world preeminence. Americans elected the avuncular Dwight Eisenhower as their president in 1952 and again in 1956. Production and consumption of new goods and services during the decade surpassed that of any era in U.S. history. The population soared with the baby boom, and continued to climb until the early sixties. Jonas Salk found a vaccine against polio. *Brown v. Board of Education at Topeka* set in motion the dismantling of segregation laws and policies. The U.S. flag got two more stars when Alaska and Hawaii became states.

World crises were either brief or too remote to impact most Americans. The Korean War was touted as a "police action" in conjunction with the United Nations and lacked the cachet of a national emergency. McCarthyism whipped up

Figure 4-10. The "most important single day fashion" of 1950, according to *Vogue*, was the sheath. Featured in the Dior Vertical Line collection that year, the sheath would remain popular through the entire decade and inspire later variations that included the chemise revival, the trapeze, and the sack dress.

mass hysteria with its highly publicized witch hunts, but was soon dispelled when people of reason prevailed. The USSR successfully launched its Sputnik satellite, and the United States answered with its first satellite a few months later. Distant rumblings in Suez, Hungary, and the assorted colonies of European powers were largely out of sight and out of mind to most Americans. A burgeoning middle class was too self-absorbed and complacent in its world of prosperity and respectable conformity to be troubled by such remote storms. Economist John Kenneth Galbraith wrote of the period:

> These are the days in which even the mildly critical individual is likely to seem like a lion in contrast with the general mood . . . when men of all social disciplines and all political faiths seek the comfortable and the accepted; when the man of controversy is looked upon as a disturbing influence; when originality is taken as a mask of instability; and when, in modification of the scriptural parable, the bland lead the bland.[40]

Americans had endured a tumultuous world of back-to-back crises in the 1940s and now, in the fifties, were content with the calm and predictability of the bland.

With the dawning of the new decade, and a revitalized economy, the American fashion industry jumped at every hint of a style change coming from Paris. To compete in the ready-to-wear market, manufacturers and retailers had to react quickly to fashion barometers. Turnover of inventory was crucial, so consumer demand was kept sharp by rapid American production and instantaneous advertising.

In the 1950s, fashion drama from Paris occurred with just about every collection. For the major houses that usually meant two primary season collections and two midseason collections, each featuring hundreds of models. Unlike in earlier years when French couture was primarily a business tailored to an exclusive, trend-setting clientele, Paris designers of the 1950s instead looked to commercial buyers as their key target market, especially American ready-to-wear manufacturers, made-to-order retailers, and department stores. In the U.S. some Paris modes were copied exactly, including construction, fabrics, and trimmings, and were sold with labels confirming "from an original by" Dior, Fath, Balmain, or whomever. For important silhouettes that were too costly or complicated to mass produce, French models were modified to suit the needs of the ready-to-wear manufacturing processes.

Before the openings of the first French collections of

Figure 4-11. Two of the favored jacket silhouettes for the new sheath and suits of 1950 included the cropped bolero and the longline tunic. Ads 1950.

1950, the January issue of *Vogue* predicted what the "body line" was to be for midcentury fashions: "an unexaggerated bosom, a concave middle, a close hipline, a seemingly long leg." If the reader was not born with this figure, the editors advised, she could achieve it in one of three ways. First was a regimen of dieting (a ten-day diet plan booklet was available for ten cents), exercise, and a "new attitude of posture." Second was figure control with the newly styled corsets and bras. Third was "the cut of the new fashions themselves, with bulk placed one way or another, above the waist, attenuating the line below."[41]

Certainly Parisian designers did not wait for indicators from fashion magazines of what American women expected or desired in clothing. The conceits of style were confidently charted by the couturiers. Sometimes, their ideas failed to connect with consumers, such as the hemlines of the early 1920s. Other times, their visions swept away prevailing modes with their newness, such as Poiret's hobble skirt and Dior's New Look. Because Dior's innovation was so prolific, he set the frenetic pace that most fashion designers would follow for the next thirty years. Following Dior's debut in 1947, designers no longer could coast along for several seasons, simply modifying styles from earlier collections, as many previously had done. Now, each collection had to offer something fresh season after season. Exceptions were rare, and then only for couturiers such as Mainbocher or Chanel, who had ceased to be innovators by this time.

The first new look of the fifties was Dior's Vertical Line. Unlike the narrow, boxy silhouette of the L-85 styles from World War II, the Dior Vertical Line collection maintained the emphasis on femininity that the designer had initiated with his fitted and shaped New Look. In addition to narrowed lines, the style featured horseshoe collars, draped aprons, cutaway box jackets, and crystal-pleated skirts. Of all the new silhouettes in the collection, asserted *Vogue*, the "most important single day fashion [was] the straightline sheath."[42] (Figure 4-10.) The contouring dress style was flattering to slim, curvaceous figures, whether corseted or natural. Ready-to-wear makers liked the timeless simplicity of the style because it was so easy to manufacture and could be renewed each season with different color palettes or fabrications. In addition, the sheath afforded women innumerable looks with the change of accessories such as scarves and belts or the addition of jackets, aprons, or overskirts. American women agreed with Dior and *Vogue* and bought tens of thousands of sheaths throughout the 1950s.

Among the favored jackets of 1950 for suits and jacket-dresses and as an accessory for the sheath were the bolero and tunic styles. (Figure 4-11.) Versions included the box jacket silhouette as well as cutaway and buttonless models. The popularity of these two jacket styles would continue well into the midsixties.

In the 1950 fall collection from Dior, the Oblique Line was presented to rave reviews. Many of these styles were reappearances from earlier collections but with greater emphasis on the asymmetrical elements. Diagonal tucks swirled around bodices and skirts. Jackets, coats, and dresses fastened or wrapped to one side. Oversized Oblique Line collars slanted outward into exaggerated points. American ready-to-wear makers could not match the complicated cuts and superlative construction of Dior's Oblique Line collection. Instead, the designers for American manufacturers modified simpler versions with asymmetrical motifs to simulate the Dior look. (Figure 4-12.)

By 1950, American designers once again had been relegated to second-place status by following innovations from Paris. Fashion editors, enraptured with Paris style, diminished

Figure 4-12. Dior's collection for the fall of 1950 was called the Oblique Line. American ready-to-wear makers instantly produced variations of asymmetrical necklines, bodices, peplums, and skirts to create the Dior look without having to exactly replicate the complicated cuts of the originals. Ads 1950.

does mobile* clothes for summer living

Cool traveler, carefree stay-at-home . . .
B. H. Wragge's no-sleeved sheath of fine pure
linen underscored in silk-honan. Twilight
pink, summer sky, ocean floor, deep . . .
Sizes 10 to 16. $45.00. THE TRIBOUT SHOP.

John Wanamaker
PHILADELPHIA

In pure worsted Juilliard Planeteon.
Sizes 10 to 20. About $85.
Prices slightly higher west of the Rockies.
At one leading store in your city.
The House of Swansdown, Inc.,
500 Seventh Avenue, New York 18, N. Y.

Swansdown.

Figure 4-13. Dior's Oval collection of 1951 featured a softer, more rounded silhouette. As part of this smooth, ovoid look, elements of traditional Chinese garments, particularly the stand-up mandarin collar, were adapted to a wide assortment of garments.
Ads 1951.

their focus on U.S. designers. The American fashions featured in *Vogue*'s Americana issue for that year were, ironically, photographed in Paris. In fact, the accompanying editorial emphasized that "American clothes" meant "American in character—and some of them have been made by the great [French] couture houses." Dior, Fath, and Molyneux were represented as designers of American clothing. "Some of the French designers came, looked, and returned to us beautiful, free translations of our clothes ideas," explained *Vogue*.[43] There was no mention of a single American designer in the editorial. Similarly, subsequent Americana editions only generalized about new styles as they were interpreted for the U.S. market. When American fashions were featured in the articles and photographs, the styles were more likely to be credited to department stores that carried the collection or to the ready-to-wear makers that manufactured the line, rather than to the designer by name.

Nevertheless, some American designers continued to maintain a high profile, especially through advertising. As with today's market, many women of the fifties liked the look or fit of styles by their favorite designer and shopped specifically for that label. In addition, the American Fashion Critics Awards gave native designers recognition for excellence. Established in 1943, the awards were familiarly known as the Cotys, named for the event's sponsor. By 1950, award winners had included Adrian, Norman Norell, Claire McCardell, Pauline Trigére, Hattie Carnegie, Clare Potter, Nettie Rosenstein, and Adele Simpson.

Of the new names that emerged in American fashion of the 1950s, some were veteran designers and others were foreign imports. Adolfo Sardiña was born in Cuba and apprenticed in Paris. In 1954 he opened a millinery shop in New York, and he won a special Coty the following year. Geoffrey Beene left his medical studies in 1927 to learn fashion design in Paris and at the Traphagen School of Fashion in New York. By the 1950s his name was featured in the ads of ready-to-wear makers such as Hamay and Teal Traina. Oleg Cassini closed his couture house in Rome at the height of the Fascist regime in 1936 and moved to New York. He worked for various ready-to-wear makers before going to Hollywood as one of Edith Head's assistants. In 1950 Cassini returned to New York and started his own ready-to-wear firm. Bill Blass had begun designing for ready-to-wear makers in the 1930s. When he joined the Anna Miller Company in the 1950s, Blass began to receive recognition for his glamorous, Hollywood-inspired designs. Anne Fogarty began her career as a designer of junior fashions for teenagers. She then joined the Margot Company and designed dresses for which she won a Coty Award in 1951. James Galanos was a California designer who began to receive recognition for his fabric virtuosity only when he began showing in New York. He won both a Coty and a Neiman Marcus Award in 1954. The Scaasi label was derived from Arnold Isaacs, who reversed his first name as his logo. Apprenticed to the House of Paquin in Paris, Isaacs came to New York in 1951 to work with Charles James for two years before setting out on his own.

These are but a few of the notable leaders of American fashion during the 1950s. The contributions of these and the many dozens of other outstanding American designers often went unrecognized or were minimized by the fashion press due to the obsession with Paris. The wide range of apparel needs of consumers was another reason American designers of the time often appeared to be in a supporting role on the fashion stage. Caroline Milbank noted that "because there were so many different types of American women and so many requirements across the country for different types of clothes, most American designers offered multiple silhouettes at any given time."[44] Consequently, the impact of a single, innovative theme, such as those created by Dior, was missing from most of the collections produced by American designers.

Fifties Themes and Variations

In 1951, Dior and Balenciaga offered collections that were uncharacteristically similar in line. The Spanish couturier had never liked the artifice of Dior's designs, preferring instead to accentuate the natural contours and movement of the female figure. Jane Mulvagh wrote of Balenciaga's craftsmanship, "While other designers used geometry for sensationalism, defying rather than enhancing the body, Balenciaga applied radical shapes to flattering ends, for his clothes echoed movements and gestures, never determined them."[45] Whether subconsciously influenced by Balenciaga or not, for the first time

Dior completely abandoned the padded hips, bustline, and shoulders of his previous collections for a softer, rounded look. It was the Oval Line theme. Garments fit snugly at waistlines, curving out over the hips in a tight contour or in a gathered fullness of skirt. Shoulders were made narrow with raglan sleeves, small collars, or collarless cuts. The Chinese motifs from the Oval Line collection, most particularly the mandarin collar and the edge-to-edge version of the box jacket, were adapted to a host of garment styles by American ready-to-wear makers. (Figure 4-13.) The coolie hat complemented the Chinese look, even when decorated with a baroque excess of bows, ribbons, and other ornamentation.

Balenciaga continued to dominate the fashion headlines over Dior into 1952, when he featured styles with a dropped waistline called the middy. This startling new look set fashion journalists' tongues—and pens—to speculating on where the waistline might be heading across the board. Many people feared that the middy was a forecast of a revival of the universal look from the 1920s. The *New Yorker* even weighed in on the middy controversy with its perspective:

> Vogue presents this ugly revival boldly and mentions a fellow named Balenciaga as being back of it. . . . It was one thing for us to cope with baggy, malformed women when Scott Fitzgerald was around, cheering us on . . . but nowadays, when males are pushed pretty hard anyway, and with Scott dead, it is too much to ask us to accept girls whose pelvis appears to start just below the chin and who look as though they had been hacked out of an old elm stump.[46]

However, dress styles of 1952 with the middy waistline bore little resemblance to the ubiquitous dropped-waist chemise of twenty-five years earlier. The main difference between the two styles, *Vogue* pointed out, was that with the modern-day middy "the waist is marked, above a defined hipline."[47] In fact, the middy silhouette snugly contoured the natural curves of the waist and sometimes was even accented by a cinchbelt. (Figure 4-14 and color plate 18.) Other examples of the silhouette included middy-length tops and suit jackets that were cropped at the hips and tightly tapered at the waist.

Dior's collections for 1952 were a continuation of his natural, contouring designs, only this year he moved even more into a subdued mood with soft fabrics and pastel colors. His Sinuous Line collection featured some of the simplest silhouettes of his career. Soft dressing hallmarked the group, especially unconstructed cardigan jackets and crepe pleated skirts.

However, by 1953 Dior brought back the kind of complicated, precision construction that had made him famous. Silhouettes from his Tulip Line collection were molded to the body from just under the bustline to the hem. Shoulder and neckline interest prevailed, with padding, puffed sleeves,

GO..........to Cartagena for a sunset sip in **DAVID CRYSTAL'S** dress, pleated, below
the belt, for a peplum effect. Black-etched stripes
of grey, red, royal or brown on
Roberson's white silk shantung, sizes 8 to 16, 49.95.

eight styles shown on these pages are available at all eight stores.

Carson Pirie Scott&Co
CHICAGO

Lanz

*Subtly shaped in a
daisy strewn print, imported
Lanz Continental cotton.
Sky blue, pink or black 7-15 $25
All Bonwit Teller stores
L. S. Ayres . . . Neiman-Marcus
OR WRITE TO LANZ, 6900 WILSHIRE BLVD.,
LOS ANGELES 48, CALIF.
OR 1357 BROADWAY, N. Y.*

Figure 4-14. Balenciaga introduced the middy look in his
1951–52 collections. The waistline was dropped to the hips, sparking
much debate about a revival of the 1920s style. Instead, Balenciaga's
versions included an emphasis on the defined waistline, sometimes
accentuated with a belt. Carson Pirie Scott ad 1953,
Lanz ad 1955.

and off-the-shoulder treatments. These feminine, curvilinear
details gave dresses and jackets a unique, top-heavy look.
Even so, American ready-to-wear designers created adaptations
that captured the flavor of Dior's Tulip Line without the
costly couture construction.

At the same time that Balenciaga and Dior were blazing
new trails with their midcentury collections, a new group of
designers from Italy entered the international arena with their
first collaborative showing in 1951. Couturier Giovannia Battista
Giorgini had visited the better-known salons in Florence,
Rome, and Milan to persuade designers to stop copying the
French and to create their own unique styles. Fourteen
designers then joined Giorgini at his villa in Florence to present
their collections to an international audience. Most
notable among those collections were the stunning architectural
ball gowns by twenty-two-year-old Roberto Capucci.
Within a couple of years, *Vogue* covered the Italian openings
with as much interest as it did the French showings. In 1953,
Vogue's editors remarked that "the couture in Rome and Florence
and Milan has been a volcano in constant eruption of
ideas, some wonderful, some not, all of them executed with
the inventiveness and superb working materials—fabric,
leather, straw—that are as indigenous to Italy as olives."[48]
Americans responded to the Italians as selectively as had
Vogue's editors. Italian leather goods, especially shoes and
handbags, had always been recognized for their quality and
design. Italian fashions, however, more often than not had a
less-broad appeal to American women than those from Paris.

Between the spring of 1954 and autumn of 1955, Dior
dominated French couture with his alphabet collections. In
rapid succession he presented the H Line, A Line, and Y
Line. (Figure 4-15.)

The H Line of 1954 with its exaggerated body contortions
generated considerable negative publicity. The design shifted
the bosom up and incorporated the hipline of the middy as
the crossbar of the H. Dior's intention had been to create the
illusion of a longer, leaner look. The controversy primarily
centered on the treatment of the bust. The constricting
bodices pushed up the breasts, sometimes resembling the sixteenth-century
Tudor-style costumes of Anne Boleyn. (Color
plate 17.) For American ready-to-wear designers, the H Line

The H Line, 1954

The H Line, 1954

The Y Line (inverted), 1955

The Y Line, 1955

The A Line, 1956

Figure 4-15. Between 1954 and 1955, Dior introduced his alphabet lines: the H Line, the A Line, and the Y Line. The H Line was characterized by the controversial Tudor bodice and dropped waistline of the middy. The triangular A Line of 1955 was a huge success and has remained a constant silhouette of fashion ever since. The Y Line did not translate as easily into American ready-to-wear versions. Basically it was a slender body with a top-heavy Y look. Some versions were inverted, with a slender top leading to a Y bottom profile.

Figure 4-16. Despite a love of French haute couture, the majority of mainstream American women opted for comfortable, casual adaptations of the Paris modes. The shirtdress, for example, reflected the femininity of the fitted bodice, cinched waist, and full skirts of Dior's New Look, and yet still afforded the wearer a sense of casual comfort. Mission Valley ad 1955, Chemstrand Nylon ad 1954.

did not have a noticeable impact since the Tudor bodice required such precise construction and fit that it could not be mass produced. The middy waistline at the hips, though, continued to provide manufacturers with the opportunity to produce affordable versions of the Dior look. Similarly, American-made overblouses, tunics, and sweaters cropped at the hipline captured the feel Dior had intended with his H Line without having to impose a constriction of the bustline. "A wonderful, long slenderness... to mold the torso and fit snugly around the hips," stated the copy in a 1954 ad for a Dior-label sweater licensed by Lyle and Scott.[49]

Dior had much greater success with his A Line collection of 1955. The silhouette was revolutionary. It marked a radical departure from the cinched waists and full, bell-shaped skirts that he had continued from the New Look eight years earlier. Dresses, jackets, and coats were narrow at the shoulders and flared into a triangle at the hem. The negligible waistline of the A Line look set the stage for the reintroduction of the loose-fitting chemise, which in turn led to the sack dress in 1957. For American women, the A Line silhouette fulfilled two desires—it provided an exciting new fashion profile and freedom from binding, cinched waist corsets, bodices, and belts. To this day, the A Line is as popular as when introduced.

The Y Line created for the autumn 1955 collections was basically a top-heavy Y treatment at the neckline or shoulders, leading to a slender body. Wide collar revers and similar neckline or shoulder details achieved the silhouette. Some styles featured an inverted Y profile with slender tops and slit skirts. The look did not translate well into a wide range of ready-to-wear versions.

At the same time Dior was presenting his alphabet collections, his antithesis, Coco Chanel, opened a salon in Paris after a ten-year absence. Following the liberation of Paris in 1944, Chanel had closed her couture house and moved to Switzerland. Rumors were that she had collaborated with the occupying Germans and feared reprisals from French patriots. At age seventy-one, Chanel supposedly returned to fashion design because she was incensed at the continued popularity of Dior's New Look. She was once observed loudly condemning women on the street for being fools who let "queens" dress them to look like transvestites.[50] Unlike with Dior and those couturiers in his camp, Chanel's style had always been to put the woman first and the clothes second. Her contention was that a wasp waist was a pretentious exaggeration even on a wasp. After the showing of Chanel's first collection in 1954, *Vogue* reminded readers of why she had been so successful in the 1920s and 1930s: "Her clothes always had that supple, unpinched, flexible look and, more important, feel."[51] Immediately Chanel reintroduced the masterfully tailored suits for which she had become famous. The perception amongst fashion journalists, though, was that Chanel had merely repeated old lines from the thirties rather than translating them into contemporary versions. Given that the fashion industry and its mass-marketing initiatives had conditioned women to expect rapid innovation and change of styles, this timelessness of Chanel's designs kept her in the shadow of Dior.

American women adored the innovative creations from the House of Dior. Yet, as consumers, they were not purists in wearing the French modes exactly as designed, for two reasons. First, the massive ready-to-wear industry could not match Dior's superlative garment construction, such as the H Line bodice or the exaggerated collars of the Oblique Line. Second, in spite of the prevalence of corsets, the legacy of American fashion since the 1890s had been one of casual comfort, even in many categories of formalwear. For example, the restricted bodices, cinched waists, and full skirts of Dior's New Look translated easily into the shirtdress, which had been a constant in American women's wardrobes since the Gibson Girl wore it. Also, American women of the 1950s increasingly donned versions of sports clothing for city wear. Instead of tailored menswear styles of trousers, the casual looks of capri pants, clam diggers, knit stirrups, or culottes were acceptable for errands downtown or at the nearby shopping center. (Figure 4-16.) At the 1958 Brussels World's Fair, *Vogue*'s team of editors even selected many of these styles (including jeans!) for the American fashion exhibit in the U.S. Pavilion. Nevertheless, most Parisian silhouettes and key design features were eagerly appropriated and successfully adapted to American versions.

In 1957 Christian Dior celebrated the tenth anniversary of his salon with a collection called the Libre—Free Line. He had arrived at the exact opposite of his New Look, with its padded, structured, ultrafeminine styles. Now, Dior presented designs such as the vareuse, a simple tunic smock traditionally worn by Breton fishermen. Although he preferred to show his versions belted, American ready-to-wear adaptations of the smock top were worn loose. (Figure 4-17.) For those who wondered how a baggy, masculine garment could become so popular with American women, the answer was threefold. It was new; it hid a lot of physical anomalies, especially those of larger-sized women; and, according to *Vogue*, the smock top gave "the woman inside a look of delightful, wonderfully appealing fragility."[52]

The following autumn, Dior continued to emphasize freedom in fashions with a reinterpretation of the loose-fitting, unwaisted chemise. (Figure 4-18.) Accessories were more important than ever, providing innumerable looks with the addition of a scarf, belt, or garlands of costume necklaces.

I. Magnin & Co. likes the young chic of the tunic dress by Traina-Norell, exclusive with I. Magnin

SAN FRANCISCO • OAKLAND • PALO ALTO • SACRAMENTO • FRESNO • LOS ANGELES • BEVERLY HILLS • PASADENA • SANTA BARBARA • LA JOLLA • SANTA ANA • SEATTLE

Figure 4-17. The collections from Dior's final year were exactly opposite of where he had begun ten years earlier. In place of the padded, ultrastructured clothes of the New Look, the 1957 styles were loose and easy fitting such as the vareuse (fisherman's smock top). Ad 1958.

Figure 4-18. Continuing his emphasis on freedom in fashions, Dior reinterpreted the chemise in the fall of 1957. The simple garment with its unstructured waistline was an immediate hit in America. Ready-to-wear makers could easily mass produce innumerable variations ranging from daytime sack dresses to adaptations for eveningwear. Ads 1958.

The simplicity and softness of the style even inspired milliners and shoe manufacturers to soften their creations at the time.

The end of Dior's extraordinary leadership of style came in October 1957, when the master couturier died suddenly of a heart attack. Not only had his vision and talent restored French couture to its preeminence, but he had also built a $20 million fashion empire. (Figure 4-19.) Dior's original three-room salon had grown tenfold into a complex, vastly successful business, including licensing agreements with makers of perfume, hosiery, scarves, costume jewelry, gloves, furs, and lingerie.

At the corporate offices of 30 Avenue Montaigne, the immediate question was who, if anyone, could step into the role of head designer. For three years, Dior had been cultivating the talents of a young man from Algeria, Yves Mathieu Saint Laurent. Although it was widely known that Dior was homosexual, his relationship with his twenty-one-year-old protege was paternal. Remarkably, Dior had even planned to

introduce Saint Laurent to the press as a co-designer that following spring. Since Saint Laurent had collaborated so closely with Dior, management took a chance and made him successor to the salon's founder.

In the spring of 1958, Saint Laurent launched his first solo collection, the Trapeze Line. Following the path begun by Dior with the A Line, Saint Laurent's trapeze designs continued the loose-fitting and waistless silhouette, this time, though, with hemlines that peaked at the knee. The collection was a resounding success. The following June, *Vogue* predicted: "This year's swing-over to shape couldn't be timelier. Among the trapeze endowments, reckon this: a good sound circulatory system—air is part of the shape, and the coolness. And reckon, also, on the trapeze being the shortest dress you own."[53] American ready-to-wear makers went into full production of trapeze cut garments. (Figure 4-20.)

Unfortunately for Saint Laurent, soon after he assumed Dior's chair he was conscripted into the French military service—a mandatory duty at the time. The board of directors at

Figure 4-19. When Dior died suddenly of a heart attack in 1957, he left behind a ten-year legacy of fashion innovation and leadership that would never again be equaled. Above, Dior fashion show featured in a Cadillac ad 1956; right, Marshall Field's ad 1957.

Dior immediately imported Marc Bohan from the London branch to take over the design reins. Saint Laurent then had a nervous breakdown after only two months in the military and was discharged. Dior's management could not have foreseen this turn of events and had already made Bohan permanent head designer. There was no position left for Saint Laurent. After a bitter lawsuit, Saint Laurent agreed to a settlement with Dior's board and opened his own salon in 1962.

However, the spotlight on Paris had dimmed considerably after Dior's death and would seldom be as brilliant again. From the late 1950s forward, fashion became increasingly international, with designers from New York, London, Milan, and Paris all fully sharing the stage.

Conclusion

With the German occupation of France during World War II, American fashion designers were freed from the laconic comfort and convenience of the style dictates of Paris. Among

AVISCO

FASHION-SHAPED FOR FALL, the new trapeze by Nelly Don. Starts out now in the fabric that knows no season ... a happy blend of Avisco rayon and cotton called Tamale by Fabrex, woven of Bucaron+ yarn. Demurely collared, buttoned down the front, and bred to be a stand-out success in your wardrobe. Fall shades of ... Pueblo Red, Indigo Blue, Yucatan Purple. Sizes 5 to 18 under $20. ... STERN BROS., New York City; ... JELLEFF's, Washington, D C ... DAYTON's, Minneapolis; ... FROST'S, San Antonio; ... BURGER-PHILLIPS, Birmingham. AMERICAN VISCOSE CORPORATION, 350 Fifth Avenue, New York 1, N. Y.

Figure 4-20. The loose-fitting, waistless styles of Dior's final collection in 1957 were a striking contrast to the cinched, fitted fashions of his New Look a decade earlier. U.S. ready-to-wear makers easily and quickly produced adaptations of Dior's chemises and Saint Laurent's trapeze dresses for the American market. Ad 1958.

those designers who gained prominence during this period were veterans such as Adrian, Henri Bendel, and Hattie Carnegie, and newcomers like Norman Norell, Adele Simpson, and Clare Potter. In response to the austerity restrictions on most materials of the fashion industry during the war years, designers created narrow and trim looks with hemlines at the knees. Fashion journalists and advertisers showed their support of the American designers with publicity about their work—and their names—that showcased their talents and bolstered their credibility.

Despite this era of achievement and notoriety, American fashion design was eclipsed once again by Paris after the war. In 1947 Christian Dior presented a collection of ultrafeminine designs that collectively were dubbed the New Look by the fashion press. After almost a decade of wearing simplistic, functional clothing, women were offered glamour and luxury with Dior's fashions. The silhouette featured a cinched waist, fitted bodice, rounded hips, and yards of fabric in long, sweeping skirts. An almost Edwardian excess of head-to-toe accessories was revived, including even parasols. Throughout the ten years Dior dominated the fashion stage, he created innovative collections that subtly evolved from the previous styles into a fresh look.

In America, most of Dior's ideas were adaptable to ready-to-wear versions or interpretations, from the earliest innovations of the New Look to the later looser chemises and A Line styles. Fashion advertisers readily promoted the mass-produced versions with photographs and artwork that projected the essence of Paris to a mass market. Retailers stocked the styles with all the accessories, and American women eagerly bought. Even at the dawn of the 1960s, when something revolutionary was afoot in London and the Dior mantel had passed to the young genius, Yves Saint Laurent, American women continued their adoration of the New Look and its variants.

YOUTHQUAKE IN THE SIXTIES AND SCHIZOPHRENIA IN THE SEVENTIES

As the 1950s closed, the first of the baby boom generation became teenagers. By the end of the succeeding decade, almost one-third of the American population would be under the voting age. The very notion of a teenager as a significant, independent segmentation of society is uniquely American in origin. In the Old World order, teenagers—or youths, as they were collectively called—hardly differed from any of the pre-pubescent categories of childhood. This was not the case in America, due largely to consumer marketing. (Figure 5-1.) Movies such as *Rebel without a Cause* (1955) depicted the vast purchasing power of suburban, white, middle-class teenagers of the 1950s: radios and hi-fi's for their rock and roll music; jeans, circle skirts, and saddle oxfords that differentiated their wardrobes; soft drinks and fast food at neighborhood soda shops and drive-in theaters. In urban areas teenagers became more individual in their personal style, exploring avenues quite new and apart from their conventional counterparts in suburbia. City teens were more receptive to cultural and social influences from a diversity of economic classes, ethnic communities, and the street scenes of Britain and Italy.

One of the first splashes of America's youth tidal wave occurred with the presidential election of 1960. The oldest man ever elected to the presidency, Dwight Eisenhower, was replaced by the youngest man ever elected to that office, John F. Kennedy. At his side as First Lady was the beautiful, poised, and cultured Jacqueline Bouvier Kennedy, whose personal style and sense of fashion would be scrutinized the world over. The couple epitomized the promise and optimism of youth. Their domain was a romantic "Camelot," so named because JFK used to play a record of that musical for his children. Their vitality, casual manner, and good looks enthralled

Figure 5-1. American teenagers of the 1950s became a significant consumer group that was aggressively targeted by marketers. Ads 1952–55.

Non-stop fashions by Toni Hunt to take you beautifully across the seasons.... In silken-touch prints of 59% rayon/41% cotton. Left, bow-bright charmer in beige and blue, sizes 12-20, 14½-24½; center, pocket-perfect shirtwaist in plum and caramel, sizes 10-18, 7-15; right, casually clever daytimer in teal and periwinkle, sizes 10-18, 12½-20½...*under $10*

THAT WONDERFUL
TONI
HUNT®
LOOK

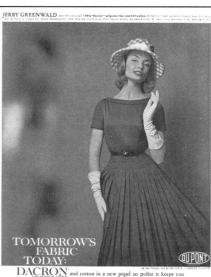

TOMORROW'S
FABRIC
TODAY:
DACRON
POLYESTER FIBER

and cotton in a new piqué so polite it keeps you unfussed, unmussed the livelong day. Pleats behave immaculately. Neatness lasts and lasts! And ironing's so rare, you're free of care. Isn't it just like "Dacron" to bring you tomorrow's piqué—today!

GO GLENHAVEN

TEAL TRAINA

Himelhoch's

Figure 5-2. American fashion styles of the early 1960s continued many of the silhouettes that had originated from Dior's New Look more than a dozen years earlier. The chief difference was the knee-length hemline, which itself had been introduced by Paris in 1957. The shirt-dress, middy line, Chanel suit, and sheath were simultaneously part of most women's wardrobes. Ads 1960.

the nation. From their national forum in the White House, the young First Family set a high-profile tenor for America's changing society.

Yet the dawning of a new decade did not mean that Kennedy got a fresh start. He had inherited much unfinished business from the Eisenhower administration, both domestic and international. The cold war grew even more intense as America and the Soviet Union faced off over Cuba, bringing the world to the brink of nuclear war. The Berlin Wall was built. Red China threatened Southeast Asia, to which Kennedy fatefully committed an increased presence of American "military advisers" in tiny Vietnam. At home, the snail's pace of desegregation in the South led to massive protests and marches by African Americans. Violence erupted. To enforce a federal court order to integrate the University of Mississippi, Kennedy sent in federal marshals to escort its first black student to classes. The Twenty-third Amendment was passed outlawing poll taxes.

Cultural changes of the early sixties began to reinforce the growing predominance of a youth-oriented society. The Beatles' first record hit American charts in 1962 and launched a six-year British invasion of pop music. But these early years of an evolving pop culture were still enveloped in innocence. Whereas Elvis's erotic gyrations had shattered mores of the 1950s, the Beatles only wanted to hold your hand. Even after the birth control pill was introduced in 1960, American youth still continued to observe the conventional rituals of dating as reflected in movies and TV programming of the time. The "youthquake," as *Vogue* editor Diana Vreeland called the cultural upheaval of the midsixties, exhibited only mild rumblings in the early years of the decade.

The Beige Years

Reading the feature headlines of *Vogue* from the first three years of the sixties, one might imagine that changes in fashion were as dramatic and rapid as when Dior reigned supreme. "New" and "change" were the operative words in fashion editorials. On the front cover of the January 1960 edition, for example, a column of boldface banners proclaimed: "New Ideas," "New Ways," "New Beginnings," "New Series," "New Visions," "New Year," "New Decade." In actuality, though, nothing could be further from reality. In a call directly out of Dior's 1947 playbook, *Vogue* reported that "a little waist is a lot of charm" and the "fit of the new fitted clothes" was the "female-feminine" look of "gently curved proportions."[1] This was hardly new at all—nor were the styles the editors had selected to illustrate "news in the shape," many of which were still in women's wardrobes from several seasons back. Sleeve interest was the key change. However, unlike the theatrical

pagoda shoulderlines, batwings, and balloon sleeves of the 1930s, the sleeve drama of the early sixties was the three-quarter cut. Indeed, as if a portent of what American fashion would be like for the first years of the 1960s, *Vogue* featured a six-page report on the importance of the color beige.

How did this status quo take effect so completely, considering how avidly American women had pursued the drama of fashion change through most of the 1950s? One answer lay in the continued popularity of such a vast variety of styles. (Figure 5-2.) Fashion ads in the January 1960 issue of *Vogue* depicted predictable shirtdresses, peplum suits, Chanel jackets, sportswear separates, chemises, crinoline skirts, narrow skirts, and dirndl skirts. As long as women bought such a wide assortment of styles, ready-to-wear makers and retailers continued to market them all. Newness, as *Vogue* would repeatedly emphasize, mostly came with palette changes and the introduction of fresh textile prints or fabric textures.

Another contributing factor to the conservative trend in American fashions of the early 1960s was the lack of style leadership. The most innovative creations from American designers were to come in the mid to late years of the decade. Meanwhile, the great names in American fashion tended to produce versions of styles that had already become mainstream. Mainbocher was still occasionally featured in *Vogue*, but his designs had ceased to be innovative twenty years earlier. Claire McCardell, Pauline Trigére, Adolfo, Oscar de la Renta, Galanos, Norman Norell, and Adele Simpson were all top names in American fashion of the early 1960s, but each of them largely focused on traditional silhouettes with simplicity of line and detail.

Fashion had also been impervious to the influences of Hollywood. Even with fashion-plate movies like *Gigi, Breakfast at Tiffany's, Funny Face,* and *My Fair Lady,* Hollywood was not viewed as the beacon of fashion trends it had been in the 1930s. Neither did television provide much fashion-forward insight, especially given the innocuous programming that filled the networks' schedules. If anything, both movies and television programming perpetuated the beigeness of American fashions of the late 1950s and early 1960s.

The one icon of fashion taste and style of the time was Jackie Kennedy. However, the First Lady's personal look was elegant when official but not trend setting, and quite mainstream casual for leisure hours. In 1961, *Vogue* featured sketches of her inaugural gown and three evening gowns by Oleg Cassini. "Evident in each choice is her first clothes-requirement: strong simplicity," wrote the editor.[2] Later that summer, when Jackie Kennedy toured Europe, *Vogue* reproduced photographs of a dozen of her outfits, ranging from a riding habit with boots to a brocade dinner suit. The accom-

Figure 5-3. Oleg Cassini became the exclusive designer for First Lady Jackie Kennedy. In this role he changed his fashion style from the decorative femininity that characterized his previous collections to one of simplicity and comfort. Ad 1961.

panying editorial noted that "the clothes were so unobtrusive that the wearer was far more significant than what was worn. And while the applause sounds lovely, we're fully aware that the look being applauded isn't essentially new."[3]

Ironically, Oleg Cassini actually changed his fashion perspective when he became the costumer to the First Lady. (Figure 5-3.) Previously, his ready-to-wear collections had been noted for their decorative femininity. When he was invited to submit sketches from his 1961 collection to the First Lady, Cassini instead specially designed a group of simplified dresses that he thought would particularly suit her. Along with his portfolio of sketches and fabric samples he also submitted an ultimatum. He would completely furnish her wardrobe with exclusive designs, provided she wore only his clothes. She agreed, and he immediately set to work, creating her white satin rosette evening gown for the inaugural ball, and her mink pillbox hat and muff worn with a Cassini wool coat to the swearing-in ceremony. Having Jackie Kennedy as a client catapulted Cassini to the forefront of American fashion design. Although the clothing he designed for the First Lady was exclusive, his ready-to-wear collections became a high-demand commodity. He later expanded into sportswear, swimwear, accessories, and menswear. By the late 1960s, he disbanded his ready-to-wear lines and concentrated on the highly profitable licensing arrangements.

Even though American fashions of the early 1960s were mostly repetitive and unmemorable, the international fashion industry continued to produce glamorous and exciting collections each season. In the major fashion centers of Europe, new names emerged that would be at the forefront of the decade's fashion innovations. Styles reflective of the escalating youth movement were already selling in the shops and on the streets of London and Paris in 1960.

London especially seized the leadership of the fashion world, with Mary Quant en point. Although Quant is often credited with inventing the miniskirt, she denied the assertion, noting that she merely popularized a style that was on the streets at the time. Quant later recalled: "We were at the beginning of a tremendous revolution in fashion. It was not happening because of us. It was simply that, as things turned out, we were part of it. . . . All a designer can do is to anticipate a need before people realize that they are bored with what they have already got."[4] In 1955 Quant had opened a boutique called Bazaar in Chelsea's King's Road. There she originally sold ready-to-wear clothing from assorted manufacturers, but soon began making her own fashions for the shop when she could not find the young styles she and her clients really wanted. Initially she modified Butterick patterns to suit her design ideas by shortening hemlines about eight inches above the knees. After she took some evening classes in design construction and pattern making, she expanded her line from short chemises to include smock tops, sleeveless tunic dresses with pleated skirts, and Shetland tweed cardigan dresses, all in the miniskirt length.

The influence of "swinging London," however, did not hit America as quickly as it did France and Italy. In Milan, Rome, and Paris, young couture designers discovered new avenues for innovation from the anti-establishment looks of the street-scene youth. Yves Saint Laurent created a furor at Dior in 1960 when he launched his versions of youthful, street-inspired clothing, which included a jacket of crocodile skin trimmed with mink that was modeled on the motorcycle leather jacket worn by Marlon Brando in *The Wild One*.

In the debate over who originated the miniskirt, Paris couturier André Courréges claimed that distinction because he officially presented versions in his 1962 collection. Besides Quant's and Courréges's designs, one of the overlooked previews of the miniskirt was the beach cover-up. (Figure 5-4.) In January 1961, *Vogue* ran a spread of these "leggy little dresses" with photos that showed thigh-high hemlines.[5] Shot on city streets instead of a beach, the photos—and dresses—would have resembled daytime styles in any catalog or fashion magazine of 1968.

Most of the European fashion innovations, though, only minimally impacted the broader American ready-to-wear

Cotton for play looks right, feels right, is right. It's as sunny as the sun that made it grow, as fresh as the rain and the dew that watered it, as dependable as the earth that nourished it. Cotton is of the outdoors for the outdoors. Cotton is to romp in—cool, light, comfortable, spirited! For smart America at play, cotton is a natural. **National Cotton Council, Memphis—New York—Los Angeles.** 100% cotton beach cover-up by Brigance for Sinclair

for daytime playtime cotton is a natural

Figure 5-4. One of the predecessors to the miniskirt was the beach cover-up. Designed as resortwear dresses rather than the traditional bathrobe wrap, these new versions of cover-ups forecast styles of the thigh-high miniskirt of the late 1960s. Ad 1961.

market in the early 1960s. According to Jane Mulvagh, the problem with the couture industry from a business perspective was that innovative designers such as Saint Laurent "failed to court the buyers and press by gently evolving a line collection by collection, offering them a taste of styles to come while maintaining a popular silhouette for a few seasons."[6] This business model had ensured great success for Dior, Balenciaga, and Chanel. Even when the couturiers' stylistic innovations were reported in the fashion press, without an interested—or comprehending—ready-to-wear and retail market in America, the new looks did not inspire change.

The Youth Explosion of the Midsixties

America was jolted out of its fifties conformity and complacency with the violent turmoil of 1963. On the evening television newscasts, millions watched in horror as police dogs tore into peace marchers in Birmingham, Alabama. TV reports showed the smoldering rubble of a Southern church where four little girls had been killed by a segregationist's bomb. Buddhist monks were photographed burning themselves to death in Saigon streets to protest the repressive regime supported by the U.S. Then, JFK was assassinated and the nation collectively grieved during the live telecast of the funeral.

Change was suddenly palpable all across America. Young people especially began to challenge the ways of government and a social order that had led to such a state of disarray and disruption in the national landscape. They had new causes and new perspectives about their generation. They were more socially and politically aware than had been their parents as teens. College campuses sprouted community service organizations in which student volunteers addressed local issues of illiteracy, health care, and poverty. Many young people joined the newly formed Peace Corps in an effort to stem the spread of Communism in third world countries. Busloads of freedom riders went into the South to effect desegregation with voter registration drives.

These young people also wanted to look different from their parents. They rejected the sixties versions of the fifteen-year-old New Look, but the fashion industry was slow to respond to their demand for something fresh and unique. In the 1963 Americana edition of *Vogue*, this dichotomy is clearly documented in the fashion spreads featuring the "beat of American clothes." Fashions "go like '63," exclaimed the editors in a hip vernacular, "gear to the raciest new beat of the era . . . dances that have it, the people who're with it; the clothes that never miss it."[7] Across a dozen pages of photos are depicted young people wildly dancing the wobble, the madison, or the bossa nova. Yet the fashion models shown with

the dancers wear belted chemises, Chanel suits, and A Line coats, most all completely accessorized with hats, gloves, pumps, and sedate costume jewelry. Even by the fall of that year, an editorial invoked the ghost of Dior with its description of the requisite "tiny waist and rounded hips" for the current silhouette.[8]

In spite of the fashion dictates of traditional couture and its dependent ready-to-wear industry, American young people began to respond to the British invasion of mod styles. They found the short skirts and "far out" accessories they wanted in the European-style boutiques that opened by the dozens in New York, Chicago, Los Angeles, and San Francisco. The first of these youth styles to impact America was the schoolgirl look. Hemlines now moved above the knee, and big, loose-fitting sweaters, vests, or belted menswear shirts completed the outfits. Little straightline shifts, some with empire waistlines, were also popular silhouettes of this look and were worn with textured or vividly colored hosiery. The schoolgirl style contrasted sharply with the other avenue of young women's clothing, the mondaine look. The former was more for a high school or collegiate ingénue, the latter was for the traditional young married woman. Both of these looks ran parallel in American fashion during 1963 and 1964, despite the innovative directions taken by the boutique designers and even some couturiers. (Figure 5-5.)

By 1964 the youth scene in Europe was receiving considerable coverage in the American press. *Vogue* wrote about the "new rush of Bright Young People in Britain": "The girl of the hour has a fresh, burnished enthusiasm; her vitality is felt on both sides of the ocean, and London is filled with these young women, their right-up-to-the-minute look, their passion for doing things, their absolute talent for fun."[9] That year, the Beatles performed on American TV before an audience of tens of millions when they appeared on the *Ed Sullivan Show*. Discothéques opened in U.S. cities and towns all across America and attracted swarms of young people with the music of the Beatles, Rolling Stones, Herman's Hermits, and other British-invasion pop groups. These new kinds of dance clubs with their loud music and flashing lights replaced the urban coffeehouses and beer cellars of the beatniks as the latest anti-establishment haunts of the young. The second wave of the baby boom (1955–64) would expand this cultural phenomenon into a nationwide disco craze in the following decade.

In August 1964, *Vogue* reported on the fashions that were "fresh on the discothéque scene," including "dresses with the barest of knees, flicked by short walking skirts."[10] Besides knee-baring dresses, *Vogue* also previewed a new type of pants on the youth scene. "Riding low on the hips and flared below the knees," flamenco pants foretold the coming of the ubiquitous bell-bottom silhouette.[11]

From the couturiers came subtleties and extremes in the midsixties. Givenchy dressed Audrey Hepburn in his 1964 fall collection to be photographed by *Vogue*. "The smashing days of Givenchy," commented the editors, presented "a feeling of taller, narrower proportions—hats high, covering high top-knots; long legs, small midriffs, pretty legs—exquisite clothes to wear and wear."[12] Along with Balenciaga and Chanel, Givenchy was an advocate of the traditional young misses look. On the other hand, Pierre Cardin offered dresses that exemplified the schoolgirl look. "The perfect young shape . . . absolutely simple, touching the figure here and there," observed *Vogue*.[13] Meanwhile, from Courréges came a futuristic "space-age" collection, featuring suits, dresses, and trousers that seemed sculpted rather than sewn. The clean, hard-edge lines of Courréges's fashion futurism defined the sophisticated avant-garde look of the midsixties. (Figure 5-6.) The little white boots that accessorized Courréges's space-age runway models sparked the go-go boot fad that swept America.

Variations of the futuristic look combined the clean line architecture of the garments with visual elements from modern art. Motifs from Pop art, such as Andy Warhol's soup can prints, Op art, with its flat, geometric patterns, and Kinetic art, with its dynamic motion, were all incorporated into virtually every category of clothing. (Figure 5-7.) In 1965 Yves Saint Laurent applied the heavy black lines and primary colors of a Piet Mondrian rectangle painting to a simple chemise that became one of the most copied styles of the year.

American designer Rudi Gernreich blasted onto the fashion stage in 1964 with a topless bathing suit, the monokini, that actually sold in the thousands. The following year his experiments with lingerie led to the development of the No-Bra bra. (See chapter 7.) The sheer, unconstructed bra allowed him to design dresses and tops without the usual darts and seams at the bustline. Gernreich's special influence in fashion was the exposure of as much of the body as possible. However, his transparent blouses and dramatic cutouts and cutaways were translated by cautious American ready-to-wear makers into simple cropped tops or diminutive mesh insets. (Figure 5-8.)

As more flesh was displayed and hemlines moved up the thigh, a health and fitness craze ensued for women of all ages who wanted to dress younger. *Vogue* prophesied that "for this moment . . . for this era . . . the line of soft fabric flowing against a clean, taut line of body is the line of today . . . the strength of the body showing through transparent clothes is the strength of fashion."[14]

After being largely ignored for almost twenty years, Hollywood once again began to influence American fashions and style. (Figure 5-9.) Sensuous, luxurious interpretations of Renaissance dresses for eveningwear were derived from *The*

Big sweater handknit of wool-mohair-other fiber in checkerboard pattern: blue, yellow, cranberry, olive, teal, pink, white, black, beige, mint, 15.00
Little shortskirt, Bermuda length, in camel or oxford grey wool flannel, 25.00
At all Lord & Taylor stores

Korell in Orlon*
(If you are 5'5" or under, only a Korell fits like a Korell)

Designed and cut to your proportions, your figure. No costly iterations that ruin the look and the line. Plaid group for fall in 50% Orlon® acrylic and 50% rayon. Left, slim dress in red/grey or green/grey. Sizes 10+ to 20+. About $15. Center, step-in sheath in red/green or blue/green. Sizes 12+ to 22+. About $15. Right, three-piece suit in red/blue or green/blue. Sizes 10+ to 20+. About $23.At SAKS 34th STREET, NEW YORK; Mabley & Carew, Cincinnati, O.; The Union Co., Columbus, O.; Himelhoch's, Detroit, Mich.; Strawbridge & Clothier, Philadelphia, Pa.; Julleff's, Washington, D.C.; and fine stores on facing page. Korell Company, 1350 Broadway, N. Y. 18.

Figure 5-5. Fashions for American young women of the early 1960s followed two parallel paths. First was the schoolgirl look, with hemlines above the knee and loose-fitting tops. Second was the young miss look worn by traditional married women with all the accouterments of the New Look. Lord and Taylor ad 1963, Korell ad 1964.

Figure 5-6. The futuristic look of American fashions in the midsixties was inspired by the 1964 space-age collection from Courréges.

Agony and the Ecstasy (1965). *Dr. Zhivago* (1965) boosted sales of fur coats, capes, hats, gloves, and muffs. The makeup worn by Elizabeth Taylor in *Cleopatra* (1963) revolutionized the cosmetic industry and opened the door for the painted face of the midsixties. In addition, the exoticism of ancient Egyptian and Near Eastern costumes from *Cleopatra* and *Lawrence of Arabia* (1962) inspired the "Sheherazaderie" and "desertique" styles of caftans, turbans, and balloon-legged chalwar trousers. (Figure 5-10.) Although *Vogue* asserted that this "exoticism and eroticism" was "deliciously translated in the modern idiom of at-home clothes, clothes for la vie privée,"[15] many elements of the look would be appropriated for the streetwear of counterculture groups. Ankle bracelets, toe rings, and slave bracelets (finger rings attached by tiny chains to metal bracelets) became anti-establishment accessories.

Counterculture and the Late Sixties

Throughout the midsixties, President Lyndon Johnson worked tirelessly to build his Great Society programs for America. His ideas included a war on poverty to educate and provide job skills for every American. He maneuvered Medicare and the most sweeping civil rights legislation since Reconstruction through a reluctant Congress. At the same time, he also committed more and more American soldiers to the quagmire of Vietnam.

Student protests against the war began as early as 1965 and quickly spread to campuses all across the country. The American people began to listen to their youngsters, and the tide of public opinion turned against military involvement in Southeast Asia. The Vietnam War was a key hot-button issue in the election of 1968. A protest at the Democratic convention in Chicago turned violent, and Americans watched net-

There's a **L**ady in the house!

1964

There is only one Arnel.
It's the Celanese way
to cruise along
without a care.

1966

THE INGENUITY OF COTTON

1966

Off to the soft life—with Hertz and Orlon

DUPONT

1966

I. MAGNIN & CO

silk from France
for the swing-in
designed by
Jean Louis exclusively
for us

1967

Figure 5-7. Graphic patterns and design elements from the Pop, Op, and Kinetic art movements complemented the clean, futuristic lines of styles from the midsixties.

Figure 5-8. American ready-to-wear makers responded to the revealing cutaway, cutout, and sheer styles created by London and Paris designers with tamer cropped tops or minimal insets of mesh. Ads 1965.

work broadcasts in shock as their teenage children were beaten by police in riot gear. As a consequence of the war and negative public opinion against the Johnson administration, the Republicans recaptured the White House. No single figure of the 1960s brought the idea of the "Establishment" into focus like Richard Nixon. For law-and-order conservatives, it was about time; for most of America's youth, almost nothing could have been more polarizing.

The youthquake especially took center stage in America during the second half of the decade. The sociopolitical movements and activities of subcultures kept parents, teachers, politicians, and fashion designers constantly guessing.

Young people were asked in a song by Scott McKenzie, "Are you going to San Francisco?" and told that, if so, to be sure to wear some flowers in their hair. When the flower children arrived there, they often migrated to the Haight-Ashbury area to "turn on, tune in, drop out," as Timothy Leary had recommended. They became hippies—a label derived from the word "hip," meaning "aware." *Vogue* explored some of the

contrasts of the hippies' ideals with those of the Establishment and concluded:

> About morality, concerning motivation, ideals, and one's own actions, the hippie offers to the [Establishment's] code, best described in practice by the term expedience, this alternative: "Get your own head straight first." About ethics, concerning one's reactions in worldly situations and one's reaction in interactions, to the [Establishment's] controlling code of consistency, the expected at almost any cost, the hippie answers: "Let every human being do his own thing."[16]

During the 1967 "summer of love," hippies indulged in doing their own thing by dancing in the parks and streets, communing with nature, exploring new sexual experiences, and experimenting with recreational drugs. That year the Beatles sang, "All you need is love," and the Rolling Stones released their album *Flowers*. The look of the flower children was a myriad of unique and self-styled images: pattern-mixed gypsy costumes; ethnic garments from Africa and Asia; bell-bottom jeans and fringed leather vests; monochromatic military sur-

Figure 5-9. Influences from Hollywood once again were felt in the American fashion industry during the midsixties. The movie *Cleopatra* inspired exotic makeup and Near Eastern styles of clothing and textile prints. *The Agony and the Ecstasy* provided a source for romantic dresses of silk, velvet, and other luxurious fabrics. Dan Millstein ad 1963, Silk Association ad 1965.

Figure 5-10. Hollywood's costume films of the midsixties such as *Cleopatra* and *Lawrence of Arabia* inspired exotic eveningwear to be worn mostly for home entertaining. By the late 1960s, numerous varieties of Eastern garments, textiles, trimmings, and accessories were adapted to streetwear by counterculture groups. Vanity Fair ad 1967, Chester Weinberg ad 1968.

Figure 5-11. By the late 1960s, hemlines were ubiquitously thigh-high. The freedom and simplicity of the contemporary silhouette, coupled with the new directions of groovy accessories, conclusively ended the long-running influence of the New Look. Ads 1968–69.

plus; thrift-shop castoffs; tie-dyed anything; flower-printed everything. Yves Saint Laurent found inspiration from the colorful look of the hippies and presented gypsy-print shifts and headkerchiefs in his 1968 Paris collections.

But even thrift-store clothes—not to mention rent, groceries, and pot—cost money. Some hippies sold tie-dyed T-shirts, handmade peasant blouses, bead jewelry, or flower-embroidered jeans for income. Many others collected together into communes and became self-sufficient away from the demands of society and other tentacles of the Establishment.

As a subculture, the hippie movement was social drama, but narrow and short lived. For mainstream, Main Street youth, the hippie philosophy of "do your own thing" was only selectively applied. As for the look of the flower children, most Americans preferred less dramatic alternatives. For men, Eastern influences included the Nehru-collar jacket, with the occasional short paisley scarf or, more daringly, love beads or a jeweled pendant around the neck. However, there were no complete masculine wardrobe conversions to the theatrical Sergeant Pepper costumes. For women, the hemlines were ubiquitously thigh-high. Prints were bold and colors vivid

with unorthodox combinations of pink and orange or purple and red. (Figure 5-11 and color plate 21.)

The young styles looked fresh and contemporary, with no vestiges of the New Look left. The groovy new miniskirt silhouettes seemed especially modern when photographed on the model of the day, Leslie Hornby, better known as Twiggy. Even though few women past their teens had Twiggy's ninety-pound figure and her long, slender legs, women still wanted, and wore, all the permutations of the mini, including the fingertip-length micromini. (Color plate 22.)

Bell-bottom hiphuggers likewise were best suited to the slim, teenage figure. The low-rise waistband cut across the hips with a visual emphasis similar to the middy of the 1950s, except now, the ideal was narrow, boyish hips rather than the full, rounded contours of the New Look. With such an exclusive requirement, hiphuggers paired with skinny-rib or other knit tops quickly became the casual youth look with mass appeal. (Color plate 23.)

This redefinition of feminine beauty included new applications of cosmetics and completely different hairstyles. As mentioned above, the movie *Cleopatra* had changed the ideals of makeup. Multicolored eye shadows were now blended over a wider area around the eyes. Glitter and sequins were applied to add sparkle in the flashing lights of discothéques. Frosted and metallic colors of lipstick and nail polish projected a futuristic look. Hippies liberally applied body paint depicting flowers, ankhs, peace symbols, and antiestablishment slogans. The TV variety show *Laugh-In* featured young "sock-it-to-me" dancers wearing bikinis and painted head to toe with similar graffiti.

Hairstyles also were modernized in the sixties. The bouffant bubble cut worn by Jackie Kennedy was popular with women across a wide range of ages. By mid-decade, the geometric wedge cuts of Vidal Sassoon better complemented the space-age and youthful British mod fashions. As the free-flowing look of the flower children became more widely publicized in the mass media, young women opted for unstyled, straight hair. Many girls ironed their tresses to simulate the looks of Cher or *Vogue*'s premier model, Verushka. Men grew their hair long, and electric hair dryer sales soared while hat sales plummeted. The hit musical *Hair* toured the country in 1968. "Give me down to there, hair!, shoulder-length or longer." Young blacks, men and women, grew natural Afros rather than chemically straightening their hair as had their parents and grandparents.

New emphasis on ethnicity in America went far beyond the haircuts and hippie adaptations of ethnic clothing. From the successes of the civil rights movement of the late fifties and early sixties, the African American experience evolved into a new pride and self-awareness. At the 1968 Mexico City

Figure 5-12. For many young women of the late 1960s, fashions and styles of the counterculture were antithetical to their disillusioned mood. The preppie look reflected a backlash of traditionalism. Ads 1969.

Vivid contrast
in a black
and white
gala midi,
a **MIGNON**
design by
Dorothy Farbo
and in the
silken power
of the
Oldsmobile
TORONADO,
official car
of **HEMISFAIR'68®**
in San Antonio.

It's wool   mark of the world's best

PURE VIRGIN WOOL

Don Sophisticates proves that fashions in wool can go to any length: hi classes—as Jane Justin accomplishes, a marvelous midi length dress with great finesse. The spark of genius here: wool knitted by **Lebanon**, applauded for its naturally crease-resistant fiber and its wonderful way with color. Jewel-toned plaid midi has a matching, wear as you wish shawl.

The American Way With Wool

HER LONG COACHMAN COAT FROM OUR BILL BLASS TRIBOUT COLLECT

F R O S T   B R O S.

1968

1968

1969

Figure 5-13. Costumes created for the hit movie *Bonnie and Clyde* inspired fashion designers to experiment with lower hemlines in the late sixties. The midi extended to midcalf and the maxi dropped to the ankles. However, women generally rejected the looks.

Olympics, black champions raised their fists overhead during the awards ceremony as a demonstration of black power. That same year, the slogan "Black is beautiful" first appeared in the mass media. Many blacks expressed their African heritage by wearing loose-fitting tunics called dashikis, wrap-around dresses, and headwraps. Some of these garments were made from hand-loomed fabrics woven with African patterns, and others were sewn from kente cloth printed with brightly colored tribal motifs. Boutiques and mail order businesses operated by black entrepreneurs supplied these specialized garments to their niche market and advertised their goods in publications such as *Essence* and *Ebony*. Beauty products such as the Flori Roberts line were formulated specifically for African Americans and distributed to upscale department stores nationwide.

The social changes, the impact of the youthquake, the restlessness and turmoil that have come to symbolize the revolutionary sixties reached a crescendo in the final two years of the decade. Peace demonstrations and a change of administrations had not brought an end to the Vietnam War. In 1968, young, idealistic Bobby Kennedy was assassinated in California after a triumphal primary win there in his bid for the presidency. That same year, Nobel Peace Prize–winner Martin

Luther King Jr. was assassinated in Memphis, where he had gone to continue his work toward civil rights. Desegregation pressed inexorably forward in the South, but in northern cities, ghetto riots erupted in reaction to police actions and de facto segregation.

The last two years of the decade also saw momentous achievements. The first Strategic Arms Limitation Talks were conducted with the Soviet Union. In July 1969, the lunar module *Eagle* landed on the moon and Neil Armstrong made his "one small step for man, one giant leap for mankind." The following month, three hundred thousand young people gathered for the three-day Woodstock music festival near Bethel, New York, and forever set the image of the counterculture generation in the nation's psyche.

Fashions of the closing years of the decade continued to run on parallel courses of futurism, the counterculture, urban ethnicity, and sexual exhibitionism. One reaction to all the diversity of looks, lifestyles, and attitudes was a broad-based return of the preppie look. (Figure 5-12.) Many young people became disillusioned with the confusing results of the dramatic changes of the decade. Consequently, in a backlash of traditionalism preppie clothing became a hallmark of those young people who wished to distance themselves from groups associated with the counterculture. Their look was simplistic, conformist, and comfortably familiar. Wardrobe staples including plain turtlenecks with pleated schoolgirl skirts, alligator logos on dresses with longer hemlines, button-down shirts, cableknit pullovers, knee socks, Pilgrim buckle shoes, and penny loafers. These were the core clothing lines of Penney's and Sears, certainly not boutique fashions.

Hollywood also became a key influence in the last years of the decade. In 1967, the movie *Bonnie and Clyde* kindled an interest in costumes of the thirties, especially the longer hemlines. Designers responded with the midi at midcalf and the maxi to the ankles. (Figure 5-13.) Although the longer skirts provided designers with fun and interesting new challenges, women largely rejected the looks. To appease women who liked the leggy look of the miniskirt, designers even tried versions of the midi that buttoned or zipped up the front and could be worn open to midthigh. But women would have none of it. Only the maxi coat had any moderate success, primarily in northern climates where miniskirts offered little warmth against winter's blasts.

Another historical costume style that gained wide appeal at the end of the sixties was the flapper look. (Figure 5-14.) In 1966 an exhibition in Paris called Les Années '25 featured art deco graphics, paintings, and decorative arts of the 1920s. Soon afterward, museums in America coordinated similar shows and produced catalogs, books, and posters on art deco. Fashion designers adapted the 1920s dropped waistline to the modern-day chemise, or extended loose-fitting overblouses, sweaters, and cardigans over the hips to simulate the look. Even versions of the cloche were revived at a time when hats were seldom worn by young people anymore.

At the conclusion of the 1960s, Americans were divided on many fronts, not the least of which included fashion and personal style. The counterculture generation had coined the slogan "Do your own thing," which manifested itself in looks as diverse as those of the hippies, urban ethnics, and suburban preppies.

The "Me Decade" Begins

On January 1, 1970, most Americans genuinely felt that a significant change had occurred with the rollover of the calendar. Perhaps it was mostly a fundamental feeling of relief that the turbulent sixties were over. People wanted to start anew, to build on the lessons of the previous decade, but to do so in a less radical, volatile way. Unfortunately, though, reality soon dashed these hopes. Too much of the discontent of the sixties persisted well into the early seventies, and some turmoil even intensified.

The Vietnam War dragged on as Nixon sent troops into

Figure 5-14. Exhibits of art deco posters, paintings, and decorative arts renewed public interest in styles of the 1920s and influenced a fashion revivalism of the flapper look. Robinson's ad 1968, Enka ad 1969.

Figure 5-15. Hemlines of the early seventies reflected the "schizophrenia" of fashion and the confusion of styles. Ads 1970–71.

JORDAN MARSH
NEW ENGLAND'S LARGEST STORE

Ungaro of Paris interprets the soft look of the seventies in a kaleidoscopic sheer wool print bound in black. One from a collection now in the Jordan Marsh Designers' Shop, Boston.

Mini

Jacobson's
Michigan

Our Young Signature collection presents...
soft **Ban-Lon** scarf print knit of Du Pont nylon. From Collectors Items®
by ANNE FOGARTY. Beige with white, 4 to 14 sizes. 65.00

Kneelength

VALENTINO

Our very own perfection of a reproduction here—the epoch-making midi costume, coat split to reveal the tiny dress beneath. White with brown. In Contempora, Third Floor Lord & Taylor, New York alone.

Midi

very Saks Fifth Avenue

Maxi

neighboring Cambodia that spring. Campus demonstrations against this action led to student killings by militia in Ohio and by law enforcement agents in Mississippi. Feminists marked the fiftieth anniversary of the Nineteenth Amendment, which granted women the right to vote, with highly publicized advocacy campaigns. Minorities continued to confront racism in public forums and would soon face school-busing hostilities in northern cities. Homosexuals celebrated the first anniversary of the Stonewall riot that launched the gay activist movement.

The seventies also brought about a mass introspection by Americans. Hippie communes disbanded, and former flower children moved into mainstream society. College students of the seventies enrolled in business programs rather than the humanities. Idealism was defeated at the polls in 1972 when Richard Nixon won a landslide victory over George McGovern. "What's in it for me?" became the philosophic doctrine of the era.

The look of the "me generation" initially evolved as an amalgamation of the antifashion styles of the sixties. "To understand seventies style," wrote fashion historian Valerie Steele, "one must recognize that fashion was not in fashion." [17] The dictates of Paris ceased to be the governing factor. For example, that great historical determinant of fashion, the hemline, was all over the place in 1970. (Figure 5-15.) *Vogue* suggested at the time, "Let's blow away forever

Figure 5-16. The short-lived hot pants of the early seventies differed from sportswear short shorts in their tailored detailing and designer fabrics. Ads 1971.

any worry about exactly what length is right. There are no rules. Let's relax, wear whatever length—or as many lengths—as we want. Let's have fun . . . experiment. Be happy." [18] In 1975 Georgina Howell noted this confusion of styles with a chapter called "The Uncertain Seventies" in her book *In Vogue.* For the 1991 revision the chapter was tellingly changed to "The Schizophrenic Seventies." Without strict guidance from Paris, fashion journalists had to extrapolate trends, predictions, and views from a wider source base, including high-society "A lists," Hollywood and television costumers, and apparel makers from the emerging garment centers of Spain, Germany, and Asia. Fashion reports in magazines read more like descriptive catalog copy, without so much "in" and "out" hyperbole as in the past.

Despite *Vogue*'s recommendation to wear whatever length of hemline made readers happy, the editors seemed to be enthused by the fashion industry's second try at the midi. As had couturiers in the early 1920s, designers of the early 1970s persisted in trying to lower hemlines despite resistance from consumers. Younger women still liked to reveal their shapely legs; older women felt dowdy and looked matronly in such long lengths. To most designers, though, it was time for a new look. The mini seemed dated and inextricably linked to the

sixties. Ready-to-wear makers mass produced new versions of the midi, even though the style had failed to sell when introduced two years earlier. Fashion ads and editorials in issue after issue of *Vogue* throughout 1970 depicted the midcalf length on dresses and skirts. Even *Vogue*'s pattern department reproduced styles of the midi length.

Instead of taking to the midi, young women responded to an even shorter, more revealing garment that came to be known as hot pants, a label coined by *Women's Wear Daily.* (Figure 5-16.) Essentially, they were simply short shorts made of designer fabrics and other upscale materials such as suede and lamé. Introduced in European collections of 1970, the style became popular the following year in America. A *Vogue* photo spread in 1971 featured the new short outfits made of linen, rayon, and Ban-Lon. "You haven't worn shorts into town yet?" asked the editors. "There's never been a season when shorts . . . looked so absolutely correct and adorable." [19] Even so, the hot pants phenomenon was short lived. Perhaps because the look became associated with prostitutes, the style faded quickly.

With the dawning of the 1970s emerged a renewed, vital feminism rooted in women's social issues of the preceding decade. More than a million women had bought Betty

Figure 5-17. Marketers and advertisers recognized the emerging economic influence of feminists in the early seventies and crafted messages targeting this segment of consumers. Left ad 1970, right ad 1974.

Friedan's *Feminine Mystique* in the 1960s and reexamined their lives in light of the questions she posed. In 1966 the National Organization for Women was founded, and in 1969 the Women's Equity Action League was formed. The efforts of these and other feminist organizations in political, economic, and social arenas raised the nation's consciousness on women's issues. As a result, greater numbers of women sought college degrees and senior-level positions in business. Entrenched barriers at universities and in the workplace began to ease. Marketers and advertisers took notice and tailored their messages to this emerging powerhouse consumer segment. (Figure 5-17.)

One of these barriers that rapidly disappeared in the early seventies was the taboo against women's fashion pants in corporate and formal social settings. Although versions of fashion trousers for women had been acceptable for certain activities since the nineteenth century, such as equestrian events or bicycling excursions, and female factory workers had worn work pants since the First World War, policies against women in pants remained in place for most offices and formal social occasions until about 1970. However, as the renewed voice of American feminism began to be heard nationwide, and as an ever-increasing number of women joined the work force, such policies were viewed as sexist and inappropriate. As the barriers came down, women by the millions bought the new styles of pantsuits for work and pant sets for the theater, ballrooms, and even proms. (Figure 5-18.) Initially these pant ensembles were softly constructed and designed with silhouettes that were decidedly feminine. By mid-decade women's pantsuits began to more closely resemble the business suits of their male counterparts. The blazer

became the single most popular garment for women's business attire of the 1970s. By the end of the decade, designers even began to appropriate versions of the old banded-collar styles of men's dress shirts for women's corporate wardrobes.

Despite the great success of the pantsuit, the style was not universally worn. Traditional dresses, suits, and separates were the standards for the great majority of women. One way that manufacturers could achieve an updated look for a traditional silhouette was with a modern textile print or pattern. In the early 1970s, a variety of trends was widely promoted by ready-to-wear makers and retailers. (Figure 5-19.) Boldly colored and patterned designs from Italian textile makers continued to dominate both couture and ready-to-wear fashions. (Color plate 25.) Prints of reptile skins were applied to almost everything from accessories to complete outfits. Young people especially liked the snakeskin patterns on clothing that fit like a second skin, such as nylon tank tops, spandex tube tops, and clingy knit halter dresses. From the influence of the gypsy looks of hippies came a more orchestrated, commercialized interest in folk art patterns. Prints of folklorica textile patterns and motifs appeared in most fashion magazines and catalogs throughout the seventies, especially on dirndl skirts, vests, and knitwear. For most mainstream clothing, though, the most distinctive textile print variations of the early seventies were pattern mixing and pattern-on-pattern designs. Unlike the thrift-store look of the sixties, these boldly mixed patterns were carefully color-coordinated for separates collections. Ready-to-wear manufacturers produced color schemes that worked with each garment over several seasons to encourage multiple and repeat sales. For instance, a group of spring skirts, pants, and blouses might be produced in a solid sky blue as well as in

Figure 5-18. By the early 1970s the last taboos against women's fashion pants faded. Corporate and formal-occasion rules were eased as more and more women chose the new styles of pant sets and pantsuits as an alternative to the mini or maxi dress. Ads 1970.

a mixed pattern of sky-blue motifs. The following season a collection of different patterns in the same sky blue would encourage consumers to match new items to the solid skirt or blouse they had bought a couple of months earlier.

After the style storms of the sixties and the confused looks of the early seventies, this mundane codification of clothing became the calm that large segments of American women wanted. Exaggerations and extremes such as the punk look or the Japanese Big Look were fun to see in the fashion magazines, but consumers avoided such challenges to their wardrobes. Instead, American fashion of the midseventies was determined by "the new sophistication in the putting-together of pieces," according to *Vogue*.[20]

Even cosmetics became subdued, with an emphasis on natural looks. Lip gloss in subtle colors and only the slightest hints of blush and eye shadow were the preference for daytime. Exemplifying the all-American face of the seventies was Revlon model Lauren Hutton. (Figure 5-20.) Compared to the baby-doll look of Twiggy or the gothic features of Penelope

Figure 5-19. Commercialized textile patterns provided ready-to-wear manufacturers with options for new looks even though silhouettes had not changed. Four key trends of the early seventies were reptile-skin prints, Tartar folk art motifs, pattern mixing, and pattern-on-pattern designs. Ads 1970.

Tree, Hutton projected a beauty of ideal proportions. Her eyes were heavy lidded, overarched by fine brows. Her lips were full without a pouty or bee-stung protrusion. Her cheekbones were well defined and her nose unobtrusive. Her one flaw, the gap in her front teeth, was usually filled by a prosthesis or by photo touch-up. *Vogue* said of her in 1975, "The straight shining hair; the easy confidence . . . that look of total naturalness, total simplicity, of glamour that slips on as easily as jeans. It's more effective than all the razzle-dazzle in the world."[21] Like the idealized features of the Gibson Girl seventy-five years earlier, Hutton's beauty was itself a standard of the era.

Most of the codified looks and clothes, however, were not the style of the young. Although there was no second youthquake in the 1970s, children born in the second half of the baby boom moved into their teens and twenties during this decade. The sexual revolution of the 1960s reached full flower with this generation in the early seventies, and sexual exhibitionism became a key factor for their wardrobe choices. The mini and micromini remained popular through mid-decade. Both men and women wore shirts opened several buttons at the throat to display firm pecs or cleavage. Jeans became skintight and were sometimes worn with thong styles of underwear or without underwear to avoid telltale pantylines. Brooke Shields writhed around in a TV commercial and confessed that nothing came between her and her Calvin Klein jeans. A proper fit required wearers to lie down to zip or but-

Figure 5-20. Model Lauren Hutton exemplified the all-American beauty of the 1970s. Her natural features were striking without being exaggerated. Ad 1973.

ton up their jeans. Similarly, elephant bell-bottoms were especially expressive of sexuality with their low-rise waistband and five-inch fly topped by a three-inch-wide leather belt. Young people wore a "spray-painted" fit around the hips and thighs that emphasized the contours of the buttocks and crotch. The exaggerated bell-bottoms had to completely cover the feet and drag the ground, even at the cost of frayed hems.

Other conspicuous extremes in American fashions of the seventies included (for women and men) high-heel platform shoes, shoulder-wide lapels, long collar points, enormously wide pants legs, and all forms of denim embellished with appliques, beading, embroidery, and leather patches. In a 2000 retrospective review of the 1970s, *People Magazine* declared that in the transition from the sixties to the seventies "fashion went from mod to mortifying."[22]

One inspiration for the looks that young people adopted originated with the stars of pop music. "Glam" or "glitter rock" burst onto the American music scene in 1972 when David Bowie released his album *The Rise and Fall of Ziggy Stardust and the Spiders from Mars*. The theme of the album was transformations, which Bowie demonstrated at his live concerts all through the 1970s. In an extravagant display, Bowie dyed his spiked hair bright red, applied heavy cosmetics and glitter

Figure 5-21. American designers worked within a narrow range of possibilities for their mainstream ready-to-wear markets. In the midseventies, revivalisms of hip interest were introduced as a new silhouette. Ads 1976.

Figure 5-22. French designers, led by Yves Saint Laurent, dazzled the fashion world with innovative and exciting new looks. Yet most Paris modes failed to connect with American consumers, so ready-to-wear makers seldom adapted the styles for mass production. One exception was Saint Laurent's Russian peasant collections of 1976–77, which influenced the hemlines and layered looks of the late seventies. Ads 1977.

paint to his face, and donned glitzy costumes for each performance. At the same time, Mick Jagger and Elton John created similar stage personas with lavish, theatrical costumes, makeup, hairstyles, and props for their concert tours. The androgyny of these and other rock stars became one of the most publicized antiestablishment looks of the 1970s.

Another influence on youth looks was the African American "flash" or "funk" style. It was an emulation of the James Brown style featuring silk jerseys, Italian shirts, often with ruffles, black turtlenecks, tight pants, leather jackets or dusters, and half-boots with chunky high heels and platform soles. The so-called blaxploitation films like *Shaft* (1971) and *Superfly* (1972) presented these looks to a broad-based stratum of young people.

As the second half of the decade began, a narrow but highly visible segment of urban youth evolved a dramatic new self-expression called the punk look. Punk rock groups such as the Sex Pistols and the Ramones gathered substantial followings, especially among teenagers who felt disillusioned by family life, school, and a failed economy. In Britain the punk look had emerged as a style of revolt—or as many felt, a

revolting style. Clothes were slashed or ripped and then pinned together with safety pins. T-shirts and jackets were imprinted with swastikas, obscene words, pornographic images, and cultist symbols. Garments were embellished with chains, metal studs, tampons, and just about anything that could create shock value. The punks were originally called the "plastic peculiars" because they wore plastic, rubber, Lurex, and leather in colors and textures that had been discarded by traditional fashion and upholstery businesses. Tribal haircuts included mohawks, rooster's combs, and spiked crests of all sizes and colors. Body piercing was extended from the earlobes to the nose and lips. The punks were the first counterculture group to wear several earrings in each ear. Tattoos large and small were applied to most any part of the body.

In America, the iconoclasm of British punks was diluted and mixed with elements of the funky styles of African American culture and the androgyny of glam rock. Not until the 1990s did body piercing and tattooing become a widely pursued trend of young people in the U.S.

From Ennui to the Search for Novelty

American ready-to-wear success stories such as those of Calvin Klein, Geoffrey Beene, Bill Blass, Oscar de la Renta, Ralph Lauren, and Halston were the result of designers understanding the American taste of the time. *Vogue* credited these designers with creating clothing that showcased "the American Look at its best"—styles based primarily on an "ease and simplicity of the silhouette."[23] Inevitably, though, designers faced redundancy and creative ennui in having to produce collection after collection of basic blazers, pant sets, shirtdresses, and T-shirts. Yet, to stay in business, this was the challenge each of them confronted from their competition.

One way that American designers found to express their creativity was in marketing the image of their labels—and themselves as noteworthy personalities. Logos, initials, and signatures went from tags inside the garments to embroidered, appliqued, printed, woven, or riveted elements on most any external surface. At the height of the disco era, designer labels on jeans were acceptable by doormen for admission to clubs, whereas the same five-pocket style with a Wrangler or Levi's label would be turned away. Halston, Calvin Klein, and Ralph Lauren were often photographed in their ads. Media budgets were substantially increased to out-brand the competition. Journalists were given easy access to the designers for

Figure 5-23. The Russian peasant collections of 1976–77 by Yves Saint Laurent created a sensation with the layered cossack look. French and American designers immediately launched their own versions of long skirts, soft jackets and tops, and bulky wraps of all kinds. Ads 1977.

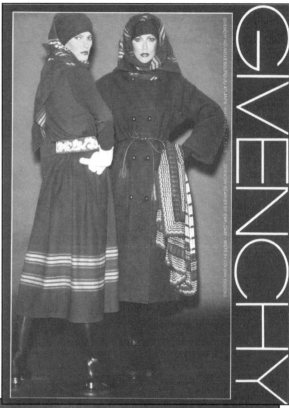

Figure 5-24. The Japanese Big Look was not a commercial success in America. U.S. designers selectively translated the silhouette into oversized basic garments, but with the new fitness boom in America, women did not want to conceal the figures that they had worked so hard to achieve. Ads 1975.

interviews and photos. Public relations departments issued avalanches of news releases and publicity photos. Wherever the paparazzi might be, designers were sure to make a smiling entrance and exit.

This is not to say that American designers were stagnant and unwilling to experiment during the midseventies. In fact, the innovative looks that were being produced by the French and Japanese often inspired American designers to attempt translations of those styles for the U.S. market. Consumers responded well to subtle changes so long as they were kept simple. One such new look of the mid-decade was a revivalism of hip interest from the fifties. "Everyone has discovered hips!" declared *Vogue* in its 1976 Paris report.[24] But the "hip-bound, hip-swathed, and hip-wrapped" sarongs and big bows of the French collections were too exaggerated for the American market. Instead, U.S. designers adapted simplified hip-interest silhouettes that were just different enough to look fresh and new, and yet still work with most women's wardrobes. (Figure 5-21.)

Paris collections of the second half of the seventies were also marked by their search for novelty. Yves Saint Laurent was the preeminent designer of the era. His collections reflected the schizophrenia of the time with the ease of his shirt-jacket dressing and Chanel-like suits on the same runway as his lavish, theatrical costumes for evening. In the 1976–77 collections, Saint Laurent dazzled the fashion world with his Russian peasant looks. (Figure 5-22.) *Vogue*'s editors were ecstatic about the drama of the styles: "Yves Saint Laurent presented his new fall collection—his small-waisted, big-skirted 'rich peasants' in lamé and furs and passementeried wools—and knocked the town on its ear. It was frontpage news in *The New York Times*, it was compared to the Dior New Look, it was called a revolution." The assortment of silk bow blouses, collarless jackets, midcalf skirts, and layered vests, shawls, and scarves was proclaimed to be the "romance that shook the world."[25]

The impact of Saint Laurent's cossack collections on American designers was significant. By 1977, most ready-to-wear makers and retailers were promoting their versions of the layered look made in fabrics and folk art prints more suited to American tastes. (Figure 5-23 and color plate 26.) One of the reasons for the success of the look, according to *Vogue*, was that "it raised the curtain on a whole new area of day-into-easy-evening dressing—and a lot of women are going to wish themselves into it."[26] Versatility was a key factor in fashion choices of the American woman. The variety of layered garments coupled with an almost infinite assortment of accessories provided women the opportunity to dress creatively, unlike with the repertoire of codified ready-to-wear separates. The layered look was so well received that Holly-

1975

1976

1977

wood used it to help define the contemporary characters portrayed by Diane Keaton in the movies *Annie Hall* (1977) and *Manhattan* (1979).

In addition to the excitement from Saint Laurent's collections, Paris fashion enjoyed the avant-garde innovations from the Japanese school. In the early seventies, designers such as Kenzo and Miyake began to make a name for themselves by creating Big Look clothing based on traditional loose-fitting garments native to Japan. As they explored creative perspectives of clothing and the human form, they began to generate controversy. They ignored established methods of fabric cutting and garment construction, preferring instead to experiment with draping and fit. Tops were inverted to be worn as bottoms, and pants were cut with one leg at the knee and the other at the ankle. They also found inspiration in the slashed and shredded clothing typical of the punk look.

Initially, American designers attempted to translate the Japanese Big Look concepts into simpler, more wearable silhouettes. (Figure 5-24.) For the most part, though, the Big Look was not successful. Fitness had become a significant part of the me decade, and women did not want clothing that concealed the slim figures they had worked so hard to achieve.

Figure 5-25. In 1972 Richard Nixon made an epochal visit to China and began the normalization of relationships that had ceased with the Communist takeover in 1949. Soon afterward, designers began to incorporate Chinese motifs and silhouettes into their collections.

THE BACKDROP

Jardine's streamlined, cascading-back dinner and disco dress with jacket, dramatized by Jack Fuller in black acetate/rayon crepe. S-M sizes, $105. Young Designer Collections, 84. Imposter jewels from the Joseph Maxer collection. Fashion Jewelry, 16. Charles Jourdan rhinestoned shoes, $118. Designer Shoes, 158. To order, call toll-free (800) 228-2055 any time.

Robinson's California

Calvin Klein. It's glamour taken to a grand extreme. So, so light in diamond foulard silk and rayon lame metallic. 4-10. The tunic. $360. The pant. $220. Innovators in selected stores. CALL 1-800-228-2044 TO ORDER.

Bullock's

Downtown • Pasadena • Westwood • Santa Ana • Sherman Oaks • Lakewood • Del Amo
La Habra • Northridge • South Coast Plaza • San Diego • West Covina • Century City • Phoenix • Scottsdale

You supply the backdrop. John Anthony provides the elegance, in rich deep mauve. The back. Bare for a fla revelation. The skirt. On the rise for a stunning show of leg. All one long shimmer of silk charmeuse for intense

Higbe

BASILE

The captivating camisole...here, beautifully bared for dancing, with a petal skirt responding to your every move in electric tints on spaced floral silk gauze. From our bewitching Basile collection in Pacesetter on Six, State Street; also Water Tower Place, Chicago Sandal by Shoe Biz from our Shoe Salon

Marshall Field & Company
There's nothing like it back home.

Calvin Klein Jeans

Figure 5-26. The disco phenomenon swept American pop culture when the movie *Saturday Night Fever* was released in 1977. American ready-to-wear makers responded with mass productions of pencil-slim pants and dresses of every shimmering, sparkling style. Ads 1978–79.

ALICE MAYNARD

THE WOMAN'S SHOP

55 WEST 42ND STREET, NEW YORK

EMBROIDERED LINEN GOWN

Plate 1. Edwardian S-bend silhouette 1902.

CHENEY SILKS

THE variety of designs and colors in which these beautiful silks are offered, make them particularly desirable for the development of the new fashions.

Spring and Summer styles again favor the extensive use of lightweight silks, especially

"Shower-Proof" Foulards

because of their many attractive colors and recognized durability.

Cheney Silks offer a choice of over five hundred different patterns in printed dress silks, including many multicolor prints and border designs.

They include "Shower-Proof" Foulards, Dress Silks of all kinds, Florentines, Decorative Silks, Upholstery Goods, Velours, Ribbons, Cravats, Velvet Ribbons, Spun Silk Yarns, Reeled Silks, etc.

CHENEY BROTHERS

Silk Manufacturers

4th Ave. and 18th Street, New York

Plate 2. Revival of the narrow, columnar directoire style 1912.

Plate 3. Massive Edwardian hats from A. D. Burgesser. Detail of ad 1909.

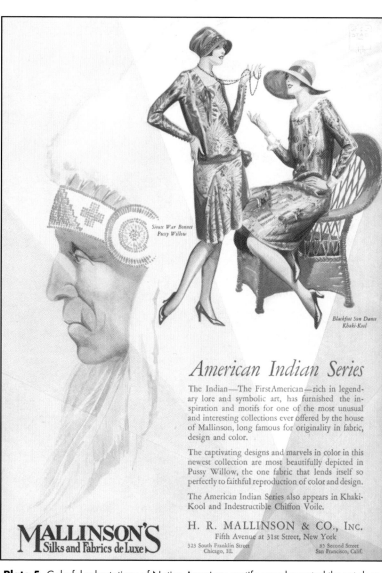

The *Chiffons* & *Printed Silks*

Paris is now wearing··

Practical only if guarded from two enemies

THE Longchamps track is brilliant now with smart women wearing the new creations of the Paris couturiers.

Everywhere are printed silks and chiffons, the newest versions of silk crepe—a bewildering variety of lovely fabrics in fascinating colors!

Such delicate fabrics, such exquisite colors *are practical only if guarded from two enemies.*

The first danger is rubbing with cake soap. Rubbing destroys the rich, soft sheen of silks and chiffons.

The other menace is the destructive alkali contained in so many soaps—regardless of whether they are flakes, chips or cakes. Alkali fades colors and weakens the sensitive silken fibres—may cut their life in half.

With Lux you avoid these destructive foes of silks and chiffons.

The rich, bubbling Lux suds cleanse without harmful rubbing. The tissue-thin Lux diamonds contain no harmful alkali. Any fabric that is safe in water alone Lux leaves bright and unfaded, as beautiful as new. Lever Bros. Co., Cambridge, Mass.

LUX

Plate 4. Vividly hued art deco prints 1927.

Blonde, brunette, or titian . . . there are certain Jantzen colors best suited to your type. Once you've chosen yours, 'tis a simple matter to complete your ensemble . . . robe, cap, belt, shoes . . . for beach parade.

Then, when cool waters beckon, cast aside your robe and enjoy the full pleasure of swimming in a Jantzen. Tightly knitted from the strongest long-fibred wool, a Jantzen fits you perfectly, permits such freedom for swimming that you scarcely know its on you! Smart, too, in appearance, with its trim, youthful lines.

See the new models at your favorite store . . . the Twosome, Sun-suit, Speed-suit. Conveniently buttonless in sizes to 42; unbreakable rubber button on larger sizes. Specially packed in color harmony sets for each type. Gay hues, pastel shades, or stripes. Color-fast; being literally dyed-in-the-wool. Your weight is your size. Jantzen Knitting Mills, Portland, Oregon; Vancouver, Canada; Sydney, Australia.

Jantzen

The suit that changed bathing to swimming

JANTZEN KNITTING MILLS, DEPT. 67, PORTLAND, OREGON.

Plate 6. Jantzen's sleek, one-piece swimsuits "changed bathing to swimming," avowed ads in 1929.

Sioux War Bonnet
Pussy Willow

Blackfoot Sun Dance
Khaki-Kool

American Indian Series

The Indian—The First American—rich in legendary lore and symbolic art, has furnished the inspiration and motifs for one of the most unusual and interesting collections ever offered by the house of Mallinson, long famous for originality in fabric, design and color.

The captivating designs and marvels in color in this newest collection are most beautifully depicted in Pussy Willow, the one fabric that lends itself so perfectly to faithful reproduction of color and design.

The American Indian Series also appears in Khaki-Kool and Indestructible Chiffon Voile.

MALLINSON'S
Silks and Fabrics de Luxe

H. R. MALLINSON & CO., INC.
Fifth Avenue at 31st Street, New York
323 South Franklin Street   85 Second Street
Chicago, Ill.   San Francisco, Calif.

Plate 5. Colorful adaptations of Native American motifs complemented the art deco patterns used for textiles and accessories in the twenties. Ad 1928.

Plate 7. The hard-edged geometry of art deco design gave classic shoe styles a vital modernity in the twenties. Detail of ad 1927.

SHEER WOOLENS GO SOUTH

The distinguished quality of Forstmann Woolens is perfectly expressed in the important, sheer weight woolens for mid-winter and spring. Their clinging textures and soft, delicate shades are utterly charming. They are indispensable for the one-piece dress, the dressmaker suit, the lounging, or beach pajama for the woman going south . . . on a cruise . . . or merely staying at home. They tailor marvelously, and resist the ravages of hasty packing. All smart shops are showing them.

FORSTMANN WOOLENS

FORSTMANN WOOLEN CO., PASSAIC, N. J. SALES HEADQUARTERS, JULIUS FORSTMANN CORP., 200 MADISON AVE., NEW YORK

Color Plate 8. The ideal silhouette of the 1930s was tall and slender with an emphasis on the bust, hips, and natural waistline. Ad 1932.

Color Plate 9. With the optimism of Roosevelt's New Deal came a renewed delight in vibrant color and bold prints in fashion. Ad 1935.

Color Plate 10. By the end of the thirties, skirts were short, waists cinched, and shoulders squared. Ad 1939.

Color Plate 11. Exaggerated angles and striking color added drama to simple, little hats of the Depression era. Detail of Gabar ad 1937.

Plate 12. Under the strict guidelines by the U.S. War Production Board, the dress silhouette of the Second World War was narrowed, simplified, and shortened to the knees. Ad 1943.

Plate 13. Trousers for women became more widely acceptable during World War II. Ad 1945.

Plate 14. Brow-tilted hats and snood of World War II. Details of ads 1942–44.

Plate 15. The ultrafeminine New Look featured long skirts, cinched waists, and rounded hips. Ad 1949.

Plate 16. New Look ensembles were made complete with an abundance of head to toe accessories. Ad 1953.

Modess.... *because*

DISCOVERY! DISCOVERY! FEMININE FABRIC!
sheerest luxury.... perfected protection
make Modess your discovery this month

Plate 17. Adaptations of Dior's H Line silhouette molded the waistline and hips and pushed up the bosom. Ad 1957.

Plate 18. The middy featured a snugly contoured bodice and a dropped waistline at the hips. Ad 1955.

Plate 19. Strands of beads re-mained the favorite jewelry adornment of the New Look era. Ad 1955.

Plate 20. Adaptations of exotic Asian jewelry were often inspired by Holly-wood. Ad 1956.

Switched-on!

Fluid knits of Antron®

DOMANI does the coat and dress duo with beautiful flow and fantastic glow. The result: switched-on fashion pulsing with brilliant color. And no wonder. It's knitted jersey of 88% textured Antron® nylon / 12% Du Pont nylon. By Domani Knits, a division of Puritan Fashions Corp. Mao-collar coat and dress with short set-in sleeves. Pink or lime, 8-16. Club-collar coat and dress with short set-in sleeves. Turquoise or gray-pink, 10-18. Each, under $70. (Slightly higher in the West.) At the stores listed on opposite page.

DU PONT

Better things for better living...through chemistry

Plate 21. Miniskirts and matching coats in psychedelic prints 1968.

Now the Levi's Fit fits you.

The low rise. The lean legs. The fabulous fabrics. Everything you ever liked about men's Levi's® are now in Levi's for Gals. Only the proportions have been changed. They're a little wider at the hips. A bit narrower at the waist. In all, you can choose from over 200 pairs of Levi's for Gals (many of them Sta-Prest,® most of them fortified with Fortrel polyester). Plus Jamaica shorts, an outrageous A-line jeans skirt, a chambray work shirt, and an authentic Levi's jeans jacket. **LEVI'S** Levi's for Gals. Try a pair on for size.

Levi's for Gals

Plate 23. Low-rise bell bottoms and denim shirt by Levi's 1969.

This is all me and then some.

ME+PLUS™

The way I like to look now is Long. One Long Line of pure, undeniable smash. I get what I want in these supple wool doubleknits from Catalina. Smashing lanky pants in linear plaids, long-bodied tunic that turns into a great dress. And more. All me and more. That's why they're called ME+PLUS. **ME+PLUS WOOL KNIT TOGETHERS FROM CATALINA.**

The Woolmark is your assurance of quality in Pure Virgin Wool

Plate 22. Micromini and tunic pantsuit from Catalina 1969.

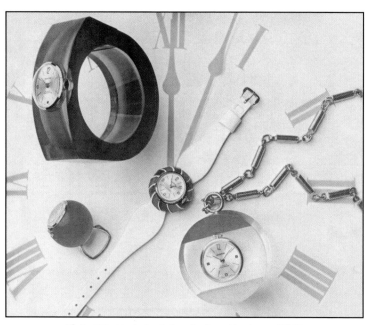

Plate 24. Mod plastic jewelry from Vendrome 1967.

Plate 25. Seventies print drama from Léonard 1972.

Plate 26. The layered look of the mid-seventies provided women with options for wardrobe versatility. Ad 1974.

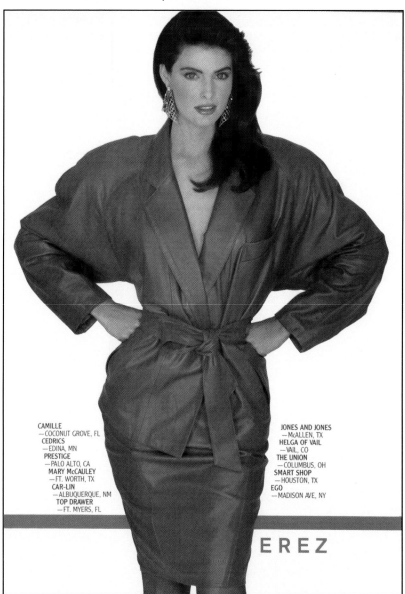

CAMILLE
—COCONUT GROVE, FL
CEDRICS
—EDINA, MN
PRESTIGE
—PALO ALTO, CA
MARY McCAULEY
—FT. WORTH, TX
CAR-LIN
—ALBUQUERQUE, NM
TOP DRAWER
—FT. MYERS, FL

JONES AND JONES
—McALLEN, TX
HELGA OF VAIL
—VAIL, CO
THE UNION
—COLUMBUS, OH
SMART SHOP
—HOUSTON, TX
EGO
—MADISON AVE, NY

EREZ

Plate 27. The sculpted body look of eighties fashion with enormous shoulders and slim skirt. Ad 1987.

Plate 28. Romantique modes such as flounced skirts, ruffled collars, and bow-front blouses were an alternative to the severity of power suits. Ad 1980.

Plate 29. Glamazon sex appeal in advertising 1992.

Plate 30. Sophisticated city shorts and long-line jacket by Jaeger 1992.

Plate 31. Retro-sixties look from Bebe 1996.

Plate 32. Pop Art trompe l'oeil print chemise 1997.

Unlike the radical Big Look modes from the Japanese, more traditional Asian silhouettes and motifs became a significant trend throughout the later seventies. In 1972 Richard Nixon made an epochal visit to the People's Republic of China, which began a normalization of diplomatic and economic relationships that had ceased when the Communists took over in 1949. Almost immediately fashion designers and interior decorators incorporated visual elements from Chinese culture into their work. (Figure 5-25.) Saint Laurent made some forays into the Chinese look early on but then rolled out an entire collection of Oriental-inspired designs in 1978. Two years later he launched his fragrance Opium and licensed the bamboo logo for use on bedding and linens.

The Opium name also represented the state of drugs, sex, and the self-absorption of modern society at the time. The one scene where all of this most notoriously came together was in the disco—seventies style. An editor of *People* recalled: "We just couldn't resist the big-beat dance craze—not after we got our first glimpse of John Travolta's moves in that Trojan horse of the disco army, 1977's all-conquering *Saturday Night Fever*. Originally the province of gays and blacks, disco's pounding beat had rug cutters of all ages doing the hustle after *Fever* ran its course: both its star and its Bee Gees–driven soundtrack won over the masses."[27] The disco phenomenon profoundly affected fashions of the late 1970s. Since the disco was not solely the domain of the very young, as had been the discothéques of the sixties, ready-to-wear makers had a broader market for which to mass produce the easy, new looks of eveningwear. (Figure 5-26.) Even for those partiers who did not crowd into Studio 54, or their hometown version of the infamous New York club, the sound and fury of disco fever blasted away at most every roller skating rink, college frat house, high school prom, and neighborhood bar throughout the country. Everyone wanted to dress the part even if they were not Saturday night regulars. "Everybody's dancing!" exclaimed *Vogue*. "And when you're dancing you want leggy, racy, narrow clothes. . . . The idea: dressing that shows a lot of body."[28] The disco was the last bastion of the thigh-high miniskirt, which had finally passed from women's wardrobes around 1975. Pencil-slim pants and painted-on jeans— branded with a designer's label, of course—were topped with big tunics that slid off shoulders or shirts that were opened two, maybe three buttons at the neck. Anything that glimmered, shimmered, and shined was appropriate for the nightlife. Accessories sparkled and moved. Shoes were strappy and satiny with the spikiest heels. Even underwear became shiny when Gossard introduced its collection called the Glossies. Everyone had fun dressing up and celebrating the party as the decade spun to its conclusion.

Conclusion

The origins of the American youthquake of the 1960s lay in the consumer-driven fifties. For the first time in history, marketers directly targeted teenagers, rather than their parents. TV programs and movies depicted the growing purchasing power of teenagers, which included their own clothing styles. Adolescents of the 1950s achieved a self-awareness that previous generations had not. Even in the 1920s, the youth-oriented pop culture revolved around collegiate young people rather than grade-school youngsters. In addition, the sixties opened with a great deal of attention focused on the youngest president ever elected to that office, John F. Kennedy, and his fashion-conscious wife, Jackie. Their personal style was young and fresh after the dowdy Eisenhower years.

Despite the lingering prevalence of the New Look style for women's clothing, ready-to-wear makers began responding to the demands of America's youth. Beginning in the late fifties, teens sought out their unique looks from specialty boutiques that introduced the vivacious mod styles from swinging England. Paris ceased to dictate a unified single look as designers tried to grasp the new emphasis on youth and compete with the emerging dominance of London. Skirts that had been at the knees in 1960 became thigh high by mid-decade. Space-age collections popularized the go-go boot. Counterculture groups expressed themselves with antiestablishment looks that ready-to-wear makers translated into tailored bell-bottom pants and wildly patterned tops and dresses.

Youth obsession continued into the early 1970s as the Vietnam War dragged on and social unrest remained rampant. The styles of the sixties were infused with fresh looks from revivals, especially 1930s styles in the form of midis and maxis, and from global influences such as Asian costumes and motifs following Nixon's visit to China.

As the U.S. approached its bicentennial, though, fashions changed to meet the needs of career-focused young people as much of America's youth went to work or business college. Hemlines dropped, and the miniskirt became obsolete. A revitalized women's movement dismantled barriers in the workplace, making possible the pantsuit as acceptable business attire. The sexual revolution also matured as the teenybopper discothéque scene of the sixties evolved into a sexually charged disco fever.

To meet the demands of an increasingly fragmented market, many ready-to-wear makers of the 1970s had to specialize by producing limited categories of apparel. Advertisers, too, narrowed their messages to better target the many moods of these diverse consumer groups, whether the career woman or college student by day or the disco queen by night.

6

THE SYBARITIC EIGHTIES AND THE
FIN DE SIÈCLE

By December 1979, the "me decade" had evolved into the cynical seventies as one journalist labeled the times. Americans had witnessed the scandals of Watergate and the resignation of Richard Nixon. The Vietnam War was lost, and American soldiers returned to a nation of mixed feelings of welcome, indifference, and shame. Embargoes by a coalition of oil-producing nations had wreaked havoc on the most powerful economy in the world. Interest rates shot up to over 20 percent, and a recession caused widespread unemployment. U.S. citizens were held as hostages by religious fanatics in the Middle East.

Also during the seventies, the two segments of baby boomers (1946–53 and 1954–64) had sought divergent but parallel paths of self-fulfillment. Most of those in the former group had turned thirty and began to focus on money. The latter group enjoyed their teens and twenties in the disco era of drugs, sex, and rock-and-roll indulgence. The paths of both of these groups would converge and segue into the social and status rituals of the 1980s. The yuppie (young urban professional) was born. "You can have it all," suggested a beer slogan of the eighties. "Greed is good," declared a character in the movie *Wall Street* (1987).

After the excesses and disappointments of the 1970s, most Americans desperately longed for a change in the new decade ahead. Despite the personal popularity of Jimmy Carter, his administration's foreign and domestic policies were widely regarded as failures. In the presidential election of 1980, Ronald Reagan asked the American people, "Are you better off today than you were four years ago?" Voters answered by sending to the White House the most ultraconservative chief executive in seventy-five years.

Style in a New Gilded Age

Glamour in the White House had been conspicuously absent during much of the 1970s. None of the First Families of this decade—the Nixons, the Fords, and the Carters—were extravagant or exhibitionistic in their social personae. By dramatic contrast, the Reagans were veterans of Hollywood who understood the effectiveness of image and style. The president's public appearances were carefully choreographed by political handlers and savvy marketing teams, not unlike the studio crews Reagan had known as an actor. Fashion was a key component of the image. Calvin Klein remarked that everyone on Seventh Avenue now expected "that glamour would be back and we'd be doing glam evening dresses to show it off . . . because the Reagans are Californian and California is pretty showy."[1] Reagan's nicknames included "the Celluloid President," "the Great Manipulator," and "the Great Communicator." But this self-assured style was exactly what Americans needed at the time. The Reagan campaign slogans of a new "morning in America" conveyed a hope and promise that the country had not felt since the idealized days of Kennedy's Camelot.

The Reagan policies for economic recovery favored the wealthy without apology. Tax cuts, deregulation, and heavy deficit spending were implemented to enrich the upper-income classes. The theory was that the wealthy would then invest in productive enterprises, thus creating millions of new jobs and economic growth. Although Reaganomics gradually led to an economic recovery, the trickle down of wealth to the middle and lower economic strata did not occur. Meanwhile, though, the era became a new Gilded Age, which like its counterpart of the 1880s fostered opulence, ostentation, and exhibitionism amongst the nouveau rich. The Reagan social court sparkled with stars from Hollywood and the glitterati from among America's elite.

The First Lady, Nancy Reagan, was ideally suited to the role of hostess for this carnival. Thin, a standard size eight, and fashion conscious, Mrs. Reagan exuded glamour and style. Among her first controversies with the American public was her solicitation from her friends of "donations" of new china for the White House, featuring a pattern edged in her favorite color, red. Almost simultaneously, she was widely criticized for accepting "loans" of original designer fashions and accessories from couturiers such as Galanos and Adolfo. Even so, her preoccupation with image—her husband's first, her own second—set the tone for all the Reagan social secretaries and press managers. Consequently, the public image was one of wealth, privilege, and glamour.

Besides the "A-list" society of the Reagan court, rock and royalty were two other representations of wealth and glamour constantly featured in American mass media. The wedding of Lady Diana Spencer to Britain's Charles, Prince of Wales, was one of the most watched televised events of the decade, reaching a worldwide audience of 750 million people. All through the eighties, Diana was constantly scrutinized and photographed by the media. The world watched with fascination as her hairstyles and wardrobes changed year after year. Friends and peers with whom she socialized were assessed by the press for style worthiness and image compatibility.

Similarly, wealth and exhibitionism were intricately linked to the stars of the rock-and-roll music industry. Madonna's song *Material Girl* became an anthem of the era. The videos of MTV (Music Television Network) telecast an endless array

of images of pop stars that were eagerly copied by hordes of teens. Legitimate newscasts featured reports on the fashions and personal styles of attendees at music, movie, and popularity awards ceremonies. The 1980s television program *Lifestyles of the Rich and Famous* provided a voyeuristic glimpse at the extravagance that many of rock and roll's royalty enjoyed.

One other contributing source to the affluent image of the new Gilded Age in America was network television programming. Prime-time soaps such as *Dallas* and *Dynasty* featured casts of beautiful people whose wardrobes were theatrically extravagant. The sumptuous fabrics, jewel-tone colors, and perfectly coordinated accessories of the costumes were what most Americans imagined the super-rich always wore.

During the eighties all the new images of wealth and glamour inspired fashion designers to extraordinary excesses, most particularly the European couturiers. American ready-to-wear makers, on the other hand, were more low-key but still adopted many of the lavish fashion elements in clothing that projected the sophisticated images of *Dynasty*, Buckingham Palace, and the White House. (Figure 6-1.) The rich look

Figure 6-1. Opulence, extravagance, and exhibitionism hallmarked formal attire in the 1980s. Influenced by the glamour of the Hollywood couple in the White House, by the mass media's obsession with rock and royalty, and by the fantasies of TV prime-time soaps, affluent women were encouraged to flaunt their wealth and status. Ads 1981.

would run continually throughout the 1980s, resurfacing as big looks, narrow looks, bouffant looks, and a dozen other variations. However, unlike with the female protagonists of *Dallas* and *Dynasty* or women of the courts of Britain and Washington, mainstream Americans, even the affluent, reserved such looks for high social events. In daytime, weddings and charity functions might warrant the exuberance of lace and silk with pearls or subtle touches of diamonds. Only evening theater performances, dinner parties, balls, and art gallery openings called for the flaunting of full, ostentatious regalia.

Pluralism and Witticism

When not in dazzling formal attire, most American women opted for any number of looks that suited their personal styles. Never before in American fashion history had there been such a pluralism of clothing types. To scan through issues of fashion magazines, trade papers, and retail catalogs of the era for a finite look or consistent theme is bewildering to a researcher. In the January 1980 issue of *Vogue*, the editors advised readers that the key to dressing now was versatility: "What's true of all clothes [today]: they provide options, they work and keep working, time after time, season after season. Not in a random, hit-or-miss way, but by design—giving you look after look, each one finished, polished."[2] Such an abundance of choice reflected the status and the diverse needs and demands of American women in the 1980s. (Figure 6-2.)

So much choice was not only the great opportunity but also the great dilemma that women faced during the last quarter of the twentieth century. In 1980 Blythe Babyak wrote of modern women: "We demand more. Try harder to be superwomen—first rate career women, tennis players, hostesses, friends, mothers, and wives. We tend to feel guilty if we don't do it all, and do it marvelously."[3]

The increasingly diverse lifestyle options that women of the eighties enjoyed also provided equally as many business options for fashion makers. One of the biggest trends for women in the 1980s, the fitness boom, had emerged in the midseventies and evolved into a national obsession by the beginning of the eighties. More than half of all baby boomers were now past thirty, and many turned forty at mid-decade. The quest of the youthquake generation to hold back signs of aging manifested itself in a cult of thinness and health. Consumers spent billions of dollars on fitness club memberships, fitness classes, fitness books and videotapes, physical training equipment, processed health foods, and vitamins. Television networks produced morning workout programs sponsored by these businesses. The fashion industry responded with new

Figure 6-2. American women of the 1980s faced more choices than at any other time in U.S. history. In response to their needs, fashions of the era provided broad options to suit most every lifestyle. Detail of a 1983 ad.

types of activewear that not only functioned well on the Nautilus machines or jogging trails but also looked flattering and attractive. (Figure 6-3.) Observed *Vogue* in 1982, "Women are putting a lot of thought into what they wear for working out. . . . The result: a whole new 'gym chic'—more polished, more carefully put together than ever before."[4] For her best-selling workout tapes, Jane Fonda was filmed in various bodysuits, leotards, headbands, and leg warmers. Vibrant colors and prints of spandex clothing replaced gray sweats and white terrycloth in gym lockers. In cities all over the country women strode to work in their power suits and specially engineered athletic shoes—with high heels tucked away in their tote bags for the office. Fashion magazines regularly featured segments on health, exercise, and workout clothing for the active woman.

European designers reacted to the American fitness phenomenon with collections of body-conscious fashions that reflected the new, svelte profile of women. Azzedine Alaia created mermaid gowns of acetate knit that clung to every contour of the body. At Chanel, Karl Lagerfeld reinvented the Chanel suit to have a sharper silhouette, and redefined the little black dress with a softer, formfitting look. Jean-Paul Gaultier strapped women into three-piece ensembles comprised of a black satin bra, velvet corset, and lace skirt. Christian Lacroix's strapless pouf dresses cinched the waist-

line and exaggerated the hips. Issey Miyake even went to the edge with a plastic molded bustier that featured a navel indentation and nipple protrusions as might be evident in a spandex bodysuit.

The witticisms of European designers, though, appealed to only a narrow segment of women in the U.S. As had been the case with the avant-garde styles of Yves Saint Laurent and Kenzo in the 1970s, European fashions were fun to look at in the fashion magazines, but for the most part were not wearable outside of select circles.

Even American designers were largely impervious to the costume dramas from Paris and Milan. Instead, they focused on what they knew American women needed to wear for their contemporary lifestyles. In 1980, *Vogue* recognized that women were multifaceted and needed a complementary wardrobe: "You function on many levels every day. You need clothes that do the same. Clothes you can reach for any morning, knowing they'll make you feel attractive, appropriate, not 'trendy' but 'in style.'"[5] At the time, "in style" could mean a host of different things. Many ready-to-wear makers emphasized two significant changes at the start of the decade. First, jackets were given a longer, leaner look from the traditional blazer and bolero silhouettes of the seventies. The fingertip-length jacket became especially popular and was made in seasonless fabrics for wearing year round. (Figure 6-4.) The

Figure 6-3. The fitness boom that had emerged in the 1970s evolved into a national craze with baby boomers in the eighties. Instead of gray gym sweats, fashion-conscious women worked out in spandex body suits, leggings, tights, and accessories, all coordinated in vivid colors and prints. Details of ads 1982–83.

Figure 6-4. New for 1980 was the longer line of jackets. The look was a fresh alternative to the traditional blazer and bolero styles of the seventies.

bolero became more prevalent as a stylistic variation for jacket-dresses. The blazer, by now a permanent fixture in most every woman's wardrobe, achieved newness with color and texture. Ready-to-wear makers expanded color palettes for jackets from the ubiquitous navy, black, and charcoal to include vibrant jewel tones of sapphire, emerald, ruby, and topaz.

A second change was a renewed emphasis on the chemise. (Figure 6-5.) Although the silhouette had remained a wardrobe staple throughout the seventies, the popularity of coordinates and separates had diminished the appeal of plain dresses. However, the chemise worked particularly well for the woman of the eighties on two fronts. It was a dressy, feminine alternative to the power suit in the office, even with shoulder pads. The look also served as a day-into-night garment for women who rushed from the office to a cocktail party or dinner engagement. A renewed interest in lots of accessories allowed women

The Black Chemise: A Dress of Captivating Simplicity.

From Pierre Cardin...the quiet drama of black wool crepe. And the elegant shape of the chemise. A silhouette that flatters... as it falls liquid-smooth and light from bold, strong shoulders, *then stops...just below the knee. More than just a dress—a statement!—of grace and restraint. Piped in black, for sizes 4 to 14. $178. Spordress Collections— where we are all the things you are.*

Figure 6-5. New versions of the chemise were introduced in the early eighties as a more feminine alternative to the power suit. In addition, the silhouette provided easy day-into-evening options for busy career women. Saks ad 1980, Dalton Sport ad 1983.

Figure 6-6. The power suit of the early 1980s was derived from the look of corporate menswear. Even when made of soft fabrics such as tweed or wool crepe, the silhouette was tailored and controlled. O'Neil's ad 1980, Salvatore Ferragamo ad 1983.

to achieve different looks each time the basic dress was worn. For the ready-to-wear maker, the simplicity of the chemise had innumerable possibilities with hemlines, shoulderlines, and sleeves. Seasonless fabrics such as wool crepes or rayon and other synthetics eased production burdens. For example, a long-sleeved chemise could easily be made into a sleeveless version for the next season with only minor alterations to pattern cutting and no change in fabric.

In 1977, John Molloy had published a fashion guide for career women titled *Dress for Success*. The influence of the book on American ready-to-wear became especially apparent in the 1980s with the proliferation of women's power suits. Apparel advertisers played up the theme of dressing for success with photos of models holding briefcases or talking on the phone in corporate settings. Ad copy reinforced the image of the career woman. Some of the headlines in ready-to-wear suit ads from one 1981 edition of *Vogue* included:

> "Evan-Picone. Clothes that work."
> "Crickateer tailored woman."
> "Austin Hill. As smart as the woman who wears it."
> "Techtonically David Hayes."[6]

The power suit did not so much copy men's suit styles as it emulated the power-broking masculine look. A tailored feel was characteristic of the power suit, even when made of soft tweeds, supersuedes, and wool crepes. Jackets were paired with pleated pants or narrow skirts and sometimes a menswear vest to replicate the feel of a corporate men's suit. (Figure 6-6.) Feminizing elements such as the bow blouse or ruffles at the collar and cuffs softened the menswear look.

One of the most significant influences on the American power-suit look came from Italy. Giorgio Armani had begun to experiment with a new freedom in his men's suit designs of the late 1970s. He began to "deconstruct" suit jackets by removing stiff interlinings and paddings. Armani wanted his clothes to draw attention to the well-proportioned masculine body. He added tactile appeal by using fluid fabrics such as cashmere and silk/wool blends. In 1979 he introduced drape-cut jackets for women that were inspired by his menswear collections. Women found that the sexy elegance that men had enjoyed with Armani suits could be theirs with his power-suit variations for women.

The luxury and sexiness of Italian clothing had great appeal to American women as a countermeasure to the severity of many styles from U.S. makers. (Figure 6-7.) The Italian spirit, as Joan Juliet Buck wrote for *Vogue* in 1981, had inspired "clothes with the character of our times." Key to this character and the times was "a generosity of style": "Racy, crisp, very modern, the appeal of the best Italian clothes, today, is in the style; it's also in the sensibility behind it. What women respond to: dressing that transcends season and categories, with the comfort of sportswear, with an attention to detail inspired by menswear. They're clothes

Figure 6-7. The luxury and sexiness of Italian fashions especially appealed to American women in the eighties. Ad 1981.

with personality."[7] Italian designers had successfully struck a chord with American women, who especially delighted in comfortable clothes "with personality" that complemented their own lifestyles.

Vogue's roster of the most important names in Italian fashion was led by Armani, whose clothing exemplified "a subtle and sensuous modern style." The Missonis created knits that were "lighthearted, unpretentious, and absolutely right for the way women live now." Aldo Ferrante focused on "fabric and the silhouette." Former architect Gianfranco Ferré incorporated the clean lines and purity of modern buildings into his designs. Mario Valentino, Roberto Gucci, and the Fendis produced superlative leather fashions and accessories.[8]

Another antidote to the severity of American power suits and the masculinity of sportswear in the early eighties was a revival of romantique modes. (Figure 6-8 and color plate 28.) Laura Ashley had maintained a consistency in her Victoriana motifs since the late sixties. Cutting-edge designers such as Valentino and Yves Saint Laurent appropriated historical costume elements for modern interpretations in their collections.

Ralph Lauren added little paisley cravats and watch fobs to his preppie looks and lace trimmings to velvet suits. Hair ornaments, copies of period jewelry, and delicate lace collars and cuffs all added finishing touches of romanticism. Princess Diana's much publicized, photographed, and televised wedding in July 1981 further fueled a desire in many women for a touch of frou-frou femininity in their wardrobes and, perhaps, lifestyles. Not only was Diana's wedding gown an apotheosis of gathers, puffs, ruffles, bows, and lace, but her bridal trousseau also featured puffed sleeves, lace fichus, and befeathered hats in soft, warm palettes of salmon, pink, and peach.

Gimmicks and Exaggerations of the Mideighties

In the American corporate culture black became the chic color of the decade in northeastern business circles. (Southerners and westerners continued to prefer colorful clothing and often remarked that the streets of New York looked as if the entire city were in mourning.) Black was also much more functional in maneuvering through the sooty urban sidewalks during fall and winter workdays in northern climates. Beyond the banal practicality of the color, though, European couturiers viewed black as fresh and chic, evoking new attitudes for the wearer in the 1980s. Japanese designers explored combinations of black fabrics in shades that had been cooled with blue tints or warmed with tinges of red. For avant-garde French designers, the preponderance of the color harkened back to the bohemian beatniks and bikers of the fifties. The romantique revivalists, especially Anne Demeulemeister, felt that black evoked the decadent essence of the nineteenth-century poets and artists.

By the mideighties, the continued current of androgyny reached new levels of ambiguity in clothing and marketing. The theatricality that hallmarked androgyny in the seventies—men with makeup and glam clothing or women in men's attire and accessories—evolved into a vague, unisex look in the 1980s. Ads many times depicted male and female models with nearly identical facial types and hairstyles. Even the leading proponent of the androgynous look for more than a decade, David Bowie, now opted for a natural look that emphasized the feminine mannequinesque bone structure of his face. His

female counterpart, singer Annie Lennox of the Eurythmics, could have been his twin with her spiked hair, strong cheekbones, and narrow eyes. Such cultural icons as rock-and-roll stars "coolly jumbled all our safe ideas about gender," wrote novelist Anne Rice at the time.[9] Fashion designers likewise jumbled the conventional gender demarcations with their loose, bulky clothing, especially casualwear, that even denied a feminine or masculine cut of the silhouettes. Colors, textile patterns, and fabrics were equally subject to gender bending by ready-to-wear makers. (Figure 6-9.)

Where the differentiation of the female form became most apparent was in the sculpted body fashions of the mideighties. Shoulder interest and padding returned with a vengeance. Wide, sculptural belts at small waistlines and slim skirts—usually short—created a curvilinear contrast with the shoulders. (Figure 6-10 and color plate 27.) The big news in all the fashion magazines of 1985 was the new fitted silhouette. Wrote *Vogue*'s editors: "This is a year of newly shaped and fitted clothes, day, night, across the board. . . . With a shape that starts right at the shoulder—a shoulder defined by cut or by padding, never exaggerated, but strong enough to set up a different look, to set up a different attitude. And you'll see a small waist, held or belted; a gentle roundness over the

Figure 6-8. In reaction to the masculine severity of power suits and dress-for-success clothing, many American women added romantic styles and accessories to their wardrobes for a touch of femininity. Ads 1980.

hips."[10] Softer fabrications such as wool jersey and cashmere knits that contoured the hips and thighs of the figure in motion added to the sexy, sculpted body look.

The sculpted look also took shape in more architectural silhouettes, especially in garments constructed of leather or stiff fabrics like satin and taffeta. Vivienne Westwood's leather corsets compressed women's breasts into Tudor-style cleavages that were reminiscent of Dior's 1954 H Line collection. Jean-Paul Gaultier dressed women in girdle dresses tightly laced up the back or in snugly fitting "two cornetti" dresses that featured exaggerated fabric cones over the breasts. Fetishism, sexual fantasies, and erotic exhibitionism populated the sculpted body collections of the couturiers. Even in mainstream American magazines, images of taboo sex games more frequently appeared in fashion ads. (Figure 6-11.)

A derivative of the sculpted body look was the little cocktail dress of the mideighties. By 1985 eveningwear variations included thigh-high, bell-shaped, and bouffant dresses that were given added dimension with multiple layers of crinolines or were sculpted with bustle treatments, overskirts, tiers, or swags of drapery. (Figure 6-12.) These whimsical little dresses were clearly designed to be worn at events that did not involve much sitting, such as cocktail mixers and art gallery openings. In 1986, French couturier Christian Lacroix took the little cocktail dress to an even more capricious silhouette with his bubble or pouf dress. The bubble-style skirt had made its debut in the late 1950s, but the proportions then were long, heavy, and cumbersome. Lacroix created airy meringues of fabric that seemed to float about the wearer. Sleeveless bodices were sculpted into formfitting corsets. The international fashion

Figure 6-9. The androgynous looks of the 1980s reflected the emergence of clothing that was largely unisex in cut, color, and fit. Ads for these styles often depicted male and female models with nearly identical facial types and hairstyles. Details of ads 1985.

1985

GIORGIO ARMANI

1986

1987

Figure 6-10. The new fitted silhouettes of the mideighties were achieved by sculpted garment construction. Padded shoulders were offset by small waistlines cinched by large, sculptural belts. Skirts were usually short and narrow.

press was so delighted with the wit of Lacroix's little dresses that it awarded him the Golden Thimble that year.

Revivalisms and the New Ideal Body

As the decade edged toward its conclusion, a sense of nostalgia rippled through the country. A feeling prevailed that the high-flying times were at an end. Daily news headlines were disturbing. President Reagan ended his second term amidst the Iran-contra scandal, where armaments had been sold to the Iranians in exchange for help in freeing American hostages held in Lebanon. A frightening epidemic that became known as AIDS swept the land in the 1980s, and still no cure was imminent. Crack cocaine abuse was rampant in low-income urban communities. Statistics on rising crime rates were alarming. The top 1 percent of the upper-income bracket had grown immensely richer from Reagan's economic policies, yet the homeless situation had reached an alarming proportion. A sobering crash of the stock market in October 1987 halted bull-market enthusiasm and set the stage for a prolonged recession.

In eras of socioeconomic crisis and anxiety, a nation's peo-

Figure 6-11. Fashions that seemed to display fetishism and sexual exhibitionism were featured in designers' collections all through the mideighties. Advertising even became less inhibited about depicting taboo sex games. Detail of 1983 ad.

ple often will look to their past as an imagined time of simpler, easier solutions to the complexities of contemporary problems. In the late 1980s, cable television networks were launched with program schedules filled with the innocuous sitcoms and game shows of the fifties and sixties. Movies such as *The Big Chill* presented introspective modern characters accompanied by music from their youths twenty years earlier. Bookstores abounded with new biographies and history books about recent eras. Middle-aged baby boomers avidly collected toys, china, decorative arts, furniture, and other ephemera from their childhoods. Thrift shops evolved into vintage clothing stores with high-priced used clothing and accessories from bygone years.

Fashion designers, too, stepped back from the modernity and excesses of the mideighties and found that their customers had an interest in revivalisms of the 1940s and 1950s. (Figure 6-13.) "Look back with glamour," *Vogue* suggested in 1987. "The newest—and newsiest—young designers don't focus on skirts and sweaters, they fall for fifties chic, Audrey Hepburn nights." For example, Christopher Morgenstern revived the

Givenchy's rhinestone cocktail dress. In black rayon and cupra velvet, and silk satin jacquard, by Moreau and Bucol. Photographed at the Musée National du Château de Versailles et Des Trianons, Versailles.

Saks Fifth Avenue

1985

CAROLINA HERRERA

POUFF POSITIVE

Get set for the 150 proof pouff: one heady shakeup of shape stirred over you, as the secret ingredient. What intoxication it is. A coupling of back baring cling, dashed with taffeta swing. Navy and white to conquer the night. Silk crepe and taffeta. 1,930.00. The 28 Shop®, State Street, Water Tower Place, and San Antonio.

Marshall Field's

1987

THAT AYRES LOOK VICTOR COSTA

RECIPIENT OF THE 1987 AYRES LOOK AWARD

L.S. Ayres + co

Indianapolis   Cincinnati

1987

Figure 6-12. The sculpted body look extended into eveningwear with variations of short cocktail dresses. Some were shaped by multiple layers of crinolines, and others were sculpted by the addition of tiers or swags of drapery.

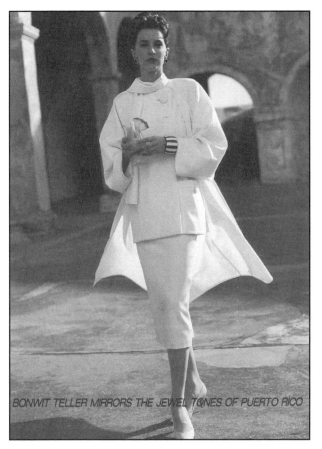

BONWIT TELLER MIRRORS THE JEWEL TONES OF PUERTO RICO

N A N C Y
J O H N S O N
LORD & TAYLOR

Figure 6-13. World events and domestic socioeconomic issues at the end of the eighties generated ripples of nostalgia in America. Fashion designers responded with revivalisms of styles from the 1940s and 1950s. Ads 1987.

styling of the 1950s sheath made famous by Grace Kelly, admitting that his clothing was specifically designed "with a sense of history."[11] Hemlines of many styles dropped below the knee, some even to midcalf. Long shirtdresses with big circle skirts evoked images of *I Love Lucy*. Accessory makers revived the oversized proportions and burnt colorations of costume jewelry, scarves, and leather goods from the 1940s and 1950s. Hats even enjoyed a comeback.

Another revivalism of the late eighties that swept across the country was the Western theme. Not since the heyday of Western television shows in the 1950s had Western motifs been so popular in mainstream fashion. Fifties TV programs such as *Gunsmoke*, *Bonanza*, and *Maverick* along with scores of Western-themed movies had glamorized the mystique and mythologies of the American West. At that time, everything from cowboy hats, boots, and leather vests to cowgirl suede

skirts and gingham prairie dresses was replicated. The revivalism of the late 1980s, however, focused much less on accurate duplication of historical costumes than on interpreting elements of Western style. *Vogue* defined "how the West was worn" in 1989: "Western wear may be indigenous to America, but it's the Europeans who take the look and run with it. Down the runways of Europe sashay an assortment of cowboys and Indians as designers engage in a range war of unabashed camp."[12] Interpretations of the cowboy look presented by the Europeans included Gaultier's bib overalls with chaps and Byblos's fitted vest, fringed skirt, and sombrero. American designers added "ranch dressing" garments to their collections that were more wearable than the novelty looks from Europe. (Figure 6-14.) J. Crew offered gauntlet gloves with leather fringe from elbow to fingertip. Melody Danielson's elbow-length evening gloves were embroidered with buglebead cacti

Figure 6-14. Revivalisms of the late eighties also included Western-themed styles such as fringed jackets, cowboy hats, boots, and shoulder-yoke shirts. Ads 1989.

and trimmed with red silk fringe. Ralph Lauren produced Navaho blanket sweaters and suede pants stitched with broad strips of leather. Western shirts with contrasting shoulder yokes, often embroidered or beaded, were adapted from country-western music shows and made of silk or dyed suede. Elaborately tooled leather cowboy boots were everywhere from the sidewalks of New York to the riverwalks in Paris.

Despite these fun revivalisms of the late 1980s, most American ready-to-wear makers continued to concentrate on apparel for working women. By the end of the 1980s, more than 50 percent of women in the U.S. were employed outside of the home. Suits and dresses were still the preferred corporate look of the decade, although a few companies had begun to modify dress codes to include options for "business casual" attire. Fashion ads that depicted women in professional business settings continued to be standard marketing iconography of the time. (Figure 6-15.)

In the late 1980s, one noteworthy anomaly occurred in fashion. The beauty ideal shifted, albeit just for a short while. Instead of the traditionally tall, emaciated figure of the ballerina as the fashionable ideal, a new type of model emerged.

Full breasts and rounded but slender hips and thighs were suddenly the desired look. "Breasts are big, breasts are back, breasts are boffo," exclaimed a writer for *Vogue* in 1989.[13] (Figure 6-16.) Supermodels Cindy Crawford, Claudia Schiffer, Naomi Campbell, and Elle McPherson posed in all sorts of décolleté clothing, leaning forward with shoulders pushed together to emphasize their cleavage. These "glamazons" were not photographed only in the fantasy sex clothing by Lacroix or Gaultier, they more often modeled American ready-to-wear apparel, giving classic styles a whole different look. The curvaceous model was suddenly on the runways, in the fashion magazine editorials, and in all the apparel catalogs of the time. Not since the S-bend corset of the Edwardian era had women of these proportions been idolized by the fashion industry.

Two sources are credited with the glamazon phenomenon. First was the media saturation of images of Madonna in various stages of undress. Her ample cleavage figured prominently in many of her video and stage costumes. Second was the 1988 release of the movie *Dangerous Liaisons*, which featured Glenn Close, Michelle Pfeiffer, and Uma Thurman

Figure 6-15. By the end of the 1980s more than 50 percent of American women were employed outside of the home. Ready-to-wear makers continued to produce variations of the power suit, and advertisers continued to depict the working woman in professional occupations. Ad 1989.

wearing eighteenth-century-style costumes with revealing, plunging necklines. "Décolletage hasn't been as fashionable—or as dramatic—since the eighteenth century," wrote *Vogue* editor Polly Mellen.[14] Whatever the timing and taste of the era that inspired this new ideal of beauty, the look was pervasive for a few years into the midnineties, when super-thin would return as the preferred fashion profile.

Whereas the new, sexy ideals of feminine beauty invited fashion designs that flattered and accentuated shapely contours, many teenagers of the late 1980s opted for the opposite—a more concealing, antifashion look. Inspired by hip-hop music of the inner city and grunge rock and roll from white suburbia, their clothing style was big, baggy, and bulky. Size two girls wrapped themselves in extra-large sweaters, oversized T-shirts, and similar shapeless tops. Jeans were likewise worn several sizes too large—they sometimes were called

Figure 6-16. For a few years at the end of the 1980s into the early 1990s, the full-figured woman became the ideal beauty of fashion. Supermodels had large breasts, rounded hips, and shapely legs. Details of ads 1989.

"fifties" for their size fifty waist—and required a constant struggle to keep up. Young men let the waistbands of their oversized pants ride down upon the hips, revealing vividly patterned boxer shorts and designer-label briefs that fit snugly on the waist. Ironically, the styles preferred by many American teens of the time were heirs of the Big Look from the Japanese more than a decade earlier. Both the big, baggy street look and the leggy, full-figured glamazon look of the supermodels would extend well into the 1990s. (Color plate 29.)

The Democracy of Fashion in the 1990s

The opening of the nineties did not herald the kind of optimism for change that had occurred ten years earlier. In 1980, the demarcation of eras seemed strikingly clear as the seventies were happily left behind and the sixties were even more distant in time. In 1990, though, George H. Bush began his third year as president, and to most Americans, his administration was just a continuation of the Reagan era. The Persian Gulf crisis was only in the brewing stages. The momentous fall of Communism and its consequences— the removal of the Berlin Wall, the democratization of Eastern bloc countries, the emergence of independent republics from the Soviet Union— had been an ongoing process throughout the eighties and seemed anticlimactic by 1990. The impact of technology on the lives of ordinary Americans had been gradual and significant, from ATMs to VCRs to PCs, so that the dynamics of technological change remained a constant. Reports of rampant drug abuse and crime were still featured daily on network and local television news. AIDS continued to kill, with no cure on the horizon. The economic downturn had not deterred a preoccupation with making money and pursuing the good life.

On the threshold of the nineties, fashion remained pluralistic, and it became even more balkanized into tribes of style as the decade progressed. In the January 1990 issue, *Vogue*'s editors broadly covered all the diverse bases with tentative general predictions: "This is the new era of femininity in dress—of jackets with softer shoulders, of curvy tailoring, of a fluidity in skirts. Of dresses that show the body without grabbing it. Of lace and chiffon and untucked shirts over soft shorts. Gone is the need to prove a sociological truth through everything one wears."[15] But predicting styles—even generally—that everyone might expect to be wearing became an increasingly difficult challenge not only for fashion pundits but even more so for designers.

The pluralism of the era was especially evident in the designs of traditional suits and dresses for the workplace. Ready-to-wear makers responded to the continued market demand with endless variations on eighties themes, and retailers ran volumes of advertising to promote the new lines of the same styles. The subtle difference was that women began to explore individualism within the confines of their workplace wardrobes: greater variety of skirt lengths and widths, pleated and plain-front trousers, maybe one longline jacket, possibly a pair of city shorts, and enough accessories to change each outfit into several new looks season after season. "The body and the clothes of the nineties are based on the freedom of the individual spirit," asserted Karl Lagerfeld in 1990.[16] Christian Lacroix echoed the call for individuality. "The danger of the future is uniformity," Lacroix cautioned. "In the nineties we have to affirm individuality and personality."[17] For designers, the issue was what to offer American women that was wearable and yet provided options for this individualism.

One answer from Lagerfeld was to reinvent the Chanel suit. (Figure 6-17.) Although Coco had been dead for twenty years, the Chanel enterprise continued to produce couture versions of the impeccably tailored suit that had made the house famous. During the sixties and seventies, the look had become synonymous with matrons of age fifty-plus. That changed in 1983 when Lagerfeld left Chloe to join the Chanel salon. Throughout the eighties he explored ways of deconstructing the legendary Chanel look. Sales soared to a billion dollars a year by 1990, and the median age of customers dropped to the thirties. "The Chanel look today is a kind of collage, an assemblage, and Lagerfeld puts it together with a changing and spontaneous hand," wrote Jane Kramer for *Vogue*. "To reinvent the Chanel look, Lagerfeld had to deconstruct the symbols: the pearl ropes, the chain and leather-threaded belts."[18] The Chanel suit was suddenly chic again and worked as well in adaptations by ready-to-wear makers that included trousers, city shorts, or miniskirts as with the traditional knee-length skirt. Individuality was now possible with the new Chanel look. When model Jerry Hall wore her classic red tweed Chanel suit, she accessorized the look traditionally with a fancy handbag and lots of jewelry. Designer Inés de la Fressange, on the other hand, wore the same red suit over a Fruit of the Loom T-shirt.

Another option for women to express their wardrobe individuality were the tailored city shorts. (Figure 6-18 and color plate 30.) "Shorts have never looked this chic before," reported *Vogue* in 1990. "Carefully tailored and paired with a jacket . . . the shorts of the '90s have come a long way since hot pants; they're sophisticated rather than vulgar."[19] The new silhouettes of city shorts were designed with pleats, cuffs, welt pockets, brass buttons, and other similar construction elements that were usually reserved for tailored suit trousers. Luxury fabrics for city shorts included linen, silk, wool crepe, and rayon. City shorts were most often a component of suit separates collections that also included matching jackets, cardigans, and vests.

One of the first revivalisms of the decade was the adaptation of Pop and Op art motifs from the 1960s. These bold graphics, shapes, and colors were a relief from the glitz and glitter of the eighties. (Figure 6-19 and color plate 32.) Gianni Versace even appropriated the visual cliché of Andy Warhol's print of Marilyn Monroe in acid colors for the fabric of some of his designs. These retro styles were but a prelude to the riptide of revivalisms that would run as a powerful current all through the 1990s.

Meanwhile, in the realm of couture, grandiose chaos reigned. European designers entered into the nineties with fashion collections that were astonishingly unwearable. Leather bondage looks, pinstriped suits with Jackson Pollack paint splashes, biker ensembles, clashing plaids, fringed lampshade hats, underwear on the outside, and a host of revivalisms ranging from sixteenth-century farthingale gowns through seventies punk denim hallmarked the couture shows of 1990 and 1991. Such outrageousness prompted many in the fashion press to wonder if the leadership of Parisian couture was at last dead. (Many fashion aficionados felt that true couture actually had died in 1968 when Balenciaga retired and closed his salon.) "Creating chaos out of order is the essence of change," wrote Melissa Richards in *Key Moments in Fashion*. "This is why so often couture houses show such mad and exaggerated clothes on the runway."[20] Couture fashion shows have always been about showmanship, even when Charles Worth unveiled

Figure 6-17. The Chanel look was deconstructed and repeatedly reinterpreted by Karl Lagerfeld throughout the 1990s. Adaptations of the Chanel suit by ready-to-wear makers provided American women with acceptable alternatives to the more theatrical costumes from Parisian couturiers. Ads 1990–91.

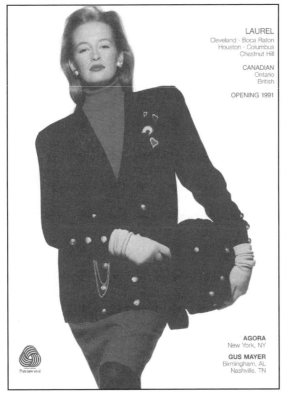

LAUREL
Cleveland · Boca Raton
Houston · Columbus
Chestnut Hill

CANADIAN
Ontario
British

OPENING 1991

AGORA
New York, NY

GUS MAYER
Birmingham, AL
Nashville, TN

JAEGER
For the Jaeger store nearest you, call 1-800-7-JAEGER

Figure 6-18. City shorts became a popular variation of women's business suits in the early 1990s. Tailored styles featured sophisticated construction elements and luxury fabrics. Saks Jandel ad (detail) 1990, Laurèl ad 1991.

his collections a century earlier. By the 1990s, though, these premieres were viewed by *Vogue* as "the theatre of the absurd."[21] Couture at the end of the twentieth century was high art and drama, the means of expression for the designer. The real business of fashion was ready-to-wear. Couture was also the publicity engine that drove the multibillion-dollar licensing industry for scarves, handbags, belts, luggage, lingerie, hosiery, bed linens, interior decorative accessories, and oceans of fragrance.

Hence, fashions on the runways of Paris, Milan, and London in the nineties could not have been more dissimilar to sidewalk fashions in America. For most fin de siècle women in the U.S., the transition of their personal and career lifestyles from the eighties into the nineties had been without the need to search for a new fashion identity each year. Theirs was a sense of ease and comfort, not high style and fashion drama. The American formula was simple enough, despite the seeming lack of glamour. As *Vogue* noted in 1990: "Americans are, in many ways, beyond

style. While some might argue that Americans are beneath style, or behind style, or styleless, the pleasant truth is that we have something else on our minds besides making an impression. It's as if our sense of sight were replaced by a sense of comfort. . . . We know that the way we feel is more important than the way we look."[22] Designers like Ralph Lauren, Geoffrey Beene, and Calvin Klein instinctively understood this and steered clear of the antics that European designers displayed on their runways. "I think women are naturally attracted to what looks easy," affirmed Lauren.[23]

Part of that sense of comfort included an attitude about personal style that was perpetuated by the mass media, especially advertising. Ralph Lauren successfully parlayed the image of his country gentry clothing into a lifestyle aspiration through marketing. His advertising campaigns conveyed to viewers that they too could easily possess this comfortable, classic look with Polo clothing and RL signature sheets, home furnishings, and decorative accessories. At the other end of the personal-

Figure 6-19. As a relief from the glitz and glitter of the eighties, designers revived motifs from Op and Pop art for one of the decade's first revivalisms. Ads 1990–91.

style spectrum, Calvin Klein's marketing bespoke a natural sensuality and sexuality through the use of numerous depictions of nude (or seminude) female and male models in his fragrance, jeans, and underwear ads. Just as Ralph Lauren's tweed jackets could make his customers feel like gentry, so too could Calvin Klein's underwear make his customers feel as sexy as the models in Bruce Weber's photographs.

Despite branding and image-marketing successes, American designers still suffered from stylistic uncertainty in the nineties, although less traumatically than did their counterparts in Europe. For example, dress hemlines were all up and down the leg. "Never has a decade been so indecisive about fashion," complained a *Vogue* editor in 1996, "and nowhere was that more obvious than in the zigzagging of hemlines."[24] (Figure 6-20.) In that year designers featured style after style of thigh-high dresses concurrently with knee-length and ankle-length versions. By mid-decade, though, hemlines had generally settled in at about knee level, although variations still

commonly ranged from the upper thigh to just above the ankle.

As a break from the monotony of producing simplistic collections of sportswear and separates, some American designers revived the biker look in the early nineties. (Figure 6-21.) "Marlon Brando meets Madonna," declared *Vogue*, "as black leather combines with fishnet, rap jewelry, pearls and soft skirts for a sexy new look."[25] Rather than adopting the full costume look, many American women cherry-picked a biker jacket or leather skirt to spice up their wardrobes. In a reverse influence, European designers responded to the American biker looks with styles that were more camp than fashion. Versace paired studded black leather jackets with short pleated silk skirts. Lagerfeld draped quilted leather jackets over leather bustiers and ankle-length silk skirts of mint candy pastels. Montana created leather jumpers, bodysuits, and straight skirts to go with his biker jackets. Yves Saint Laurent put black biker's boots and motorcycle chain jewelry with his sequined gowns.

Grunge, Cyberstyle, and Menswear

The first unique fashion style of the 1990s was the grunge look. (Figure 6-22.) The pop phenomenon originated in the dilapidated rock clubs of Seattle as a reaction to the elitist eighties. The affluence of Microsoft and Boeing employees was a conspicuous contrast to the mostly working-class population of the region. The hobo-chic clothing of grungemania had its "roots in urban bohemianism and in slacker-era schleppiness," wrote Grace Coddington in 1992. "Wary of the prissy pretension that reigned unchecked, frustrated students and minimum-wage slaves banded together and created a lifestyle, ever cynical and utilitarian, that more accurately reflected their conditions."[26] The look was a new take on layering: ratty sweaters, old flannel shirts, long johns, baggy corduroy trousers, ripped jeans, baseball caps, knit hats, and clunky work boots or Dr. Marten's as key footgear. The common denominator was the plaid flannel shirt (sometimes with the sleeves roughly cut off at the shoulders) worn layered over rock-tour T-shirts and floral-patterned dresses or just tied around the shoulders or waist. Bands like Pearl Jam and Nirvana perpetuated the grunge look to nationwide audiences through their music videos, television appearances, and concerts.

American fashion designers responded with upscale grunge clothing such as Ralph Lauren's three-hundred-dollar plaid jacket shirts and Antonio Beecroft's five-hundred-dollar sweaters replete with built-in dropped stitches and holes. Trendy European designers opted into the look, with similar styles they called "groonge." However, the American mass market did not buy the look and retailers ended up with major markdowns on tattered jeans, flannel shirts, and distressed T-shirts. Consequently, the trend passed quickly, leaving designers without any tangible signposts for the future.

Following the demise of grunge, though, some designers briefly experimented with a spiritual or monastic look in 1993. Calvin Klein offered black maxi-length priest's coats and shapeless Amish jackets, both accessorized with wide-brimmed Shaker-style hats. Gaultier spoofed the hasidic look, complete with curly side locks on the models. Donna Karan covered her runway models in crosses.

Simultaneously with the American black-on-black penitent looks, European collections included Galliano's exuberant ball gowns for Givenchy, Prada's minimalist suits and skirts, Lacroix's corset dresses, and even a run at neopunk from Versace. "What an identity crisis! Who did we want to be?" wondered *Vogue*.[27]

By mid-decade, fashion designers found inspiration from the much-hyped new technologies. The Internet was becoming better known to consumers as service providers hooked up businesses and households to the World Wide Web. Cyber-

Talbots

Talbots is the classics

Figure 6-20. During the 1990s, uncertainty on trends for silhouettes, especially hemlines, was pervasive from virtually all designers. Ads 1991.

Figure 6-21. A reintroduction of the 1950s biker look was one of the more popular revivalisms of the early nineties. Details of Calvin Klein ads 1991–92.

Bring your own attitude.

COMPANY
ELLEN TRACY

Figure 6-22. Grunge was the first unique fashion style of the 1990s. The hobo-chic look featured layers of clothing including ratty sweaters, old flannel shirts, long johns, ripped jeans, and heavy boots. Ads 1993.

Figure 6-23. Cyberstyle stemmed from the combination of street looks from biker and punk revivals with technovision influences from computers and technology. Left, detail of Ralph Lauren ad 1994, right, detail of Ellen Tracy ad 1995.

style was actually a merging of street styles, including the biker revival, punk revival, and the tribal collections from Helmut Lang, Jean-Paul Gaultier, and Anna Sui. Like futuristic costumes from *Blade Runner* or the Mad Max movies, designs featured metal breastplates, body armor, and CD-ROMs or hard-drive chips for ornamentation. Garments were constructed of technofabrics made of neoprene, polyurethane, nylon, and rubber. *Vogue* noted that this "future chic . . . was not the work of a Hollywood costumer but a glimpse at fashion for the coming millennium."[28] Translated into mainstream ready-to-wear versions, the technovision look featured minimalist clothing made of black and silver leather, accented with metal details, quilting, slashing, or laces. (Figure 6-23.)

Mainstream American fashions also revisited the menswear suit for the new career woman of the midnineties. Unlike dressing for success with the power suit of the eighties, the menswear look of the nineties skipped back a decade for influences of the sharp lines and feminine silhouettes of the seventies. (Figure 6-24.) *Vogue* noted that "from Paris's trendy Les Halles neighborhood to New York's Madison Avenue, women are trading in grunge and minimalism for a decidedly polished and tailored look that combines the timeless, sleek cut of a masculine pantsuit circa 1975 with the hard-edged,

flash-in-your-face stance of a Helmut Newton photograph and the gusto, but not the shoulder pads, of the eighties working woman." The updated menswear look was complemented by the "forceful femininity of high stiletto heels, and the polish of smooth hair, lined eyes, and really red lips."[29]

This revisit of menswear looks reflected the strong undercurrent of revivalisms that had continually surfaced season after season in the nineties. By mid-decade *Vogue* had reported on revivalisms each year:

1990: "The fifties movie-star look is back."

1991: "From music and movies to art and fashion, the past has invaded the future."

1992: "Two simplified silhouettes: one that follows the loose line of the thirties, another with the spare flare of the seventies."

1993: "When they weren't deconstructing clothes, designers were pillaging the past."

1994: "The three periods I'm concentrating on," said Lacroix, "are 1980, 1800, and 1944 in postwar France."

1995: "At the recent spring collections, the entire twentieth century paraded down runways as designers poached looks from every decade."[30]

Such interests in the fashions of recent decades, or even distant centuries, would continue to prevail with designers, both in Europe and America, throughout the nineties. (Color plate 31.) For many designers, tapping into the past sparked creativity with new experiences that ranged from obsolete garment construction to working with vintage fabrics.

In addition, social events and pop culture often inspired a designer. As had been the case since the 1930s, for example, Hollywood frequently influenced fashion with its period movies. Empire waistlines reappeared in dresses of the late 1990s following the release of *Emma*. Isaac Mizrahi presented versions of Dior's New Look from *Evita*. The J. Peterman catalog featured hobble-skirt dresses influenced by the costumes of *Titanic*. Similarly, the much-publicized death of a celebrity often prompted a public awareness of a time and place in history. In 1996 the estate auction of Jackie Kennedy Onassis generated a renewed interest in Camelot, and replicas of her jewelry and accessories were mass produced. In 1998, the glitz of the early eighties resurfaced in fashion designs when Princess Diana's gowns were sold at a benefit auction.

Coming Full Circle

In the second half of the nineties, ideals of beauty reverted to the ultrathin. Instead of the busty, curvaceous glamazons of the late eighties and early nineties, boyish waifs appeared by the score on runways and fashion magazine covers. Kate Moss was the first among equals from the new stable of thin, angular, androgynous models. (Figure 6-25.) At only five-foot-seven she seemed an unlikely candidate for supermodel status. Her eyes were too far apart, and she often photographed as wall-eyed. She was so thin that she repeatedly had to deny to the press that she suffered from anorexia. Nevertheless, *Vogue* noted that her "unadorned beauty and slight frame gave her instant name recognition."[31] She was featured on six *Vogue* covers and in dozens of Calvin Klein ads by the end of the decade.

As a look, androgyny had never ceased to be a constant in the nineties, both on the streets and in marketing. Styles such as grunge, technominimalism, corporate suiting, and revivals of the hippie sixties and punk seventies all lent themselves to unisex clothing, accessories, and hairstyles. One variation on this theme that was unique to the 1990s was a brief experiment with the heroin-addict look at mid-decade. Both male and female models sported unkempt hair, ashen skin, dark circles around the eyes, and emaciated bodies. The antibeauty results were startling and got plenty of attention when presented on runways and in advertising. (Figure 6-26.)

Yet, it all became too much by the end of the decade. As early as 1996 *Vogue* had been alarmed by the fact that "the

Figure 6-24. In the midnineties designers revisited the menswear styles of the 1970s and 1980s in part as a reaction to the unconstructed styles of grunge and slip dresses. Working women welcomed the tailored, polished look. Famous Barr ad 1994, Saks Fifth Avenue ad (detail)1996.

Figure 6-25. By the midnineties, ideals of beauty had reverted to the ultrathin. At only five-foot-seven, Kate Moss seemed an unlikely candidate for supermodel. She was featured on six *Vogue* covers and in dozens of Calvin Klein ads by the end of the decade. Detail of Calvin Klein ad 1995.

nineties have already spawned so many looks at such breakneck speed."[32] A year earlier, Gianni Versace had avowed, "There's been too much confusion in our work. . . . It got to a point where designers could have just put a blanket over a woman's head and called it fashion."[33] The result, reported the fashion press, was a backlash of conservatism in fashion and style. In 1998 Grace Coddington wrote about the end of the era: "The nineties as we see them now are about a less constructed, more personal look—which women, not surprisingly, support. . . . The idea that one dictated look fits all is anathema to modern women, who value diversity and who pride themselves on assembling a unique look. Savvy designers have gotten the message."[34] In actuality, though, that sense of moderation, personal style, and versatility had always been there. Despite the range afield into fun, experimental styles and revivalisms, American designers had never abandoned the production of simple, easy clothing. For instance, for the fall 1999 edition of *Vogue*, the editors selected "185 great day looks" that were predicted to take modern American women into the twenty-first century. Among the highlights were basic pants and skirts paired with easy tops, the simple chemise, tailored coats, and any number of moderate revival silhouettes— exactly what women had been buying all decade long.

As a final note on the 1990s, one might wonder what revival of the decade could appear on runways and in store windows and Internet catalogs fifteen or twenty years hence. What look that was powerfully unique to the 1990s would be

Figure 6-26. Androgynous looks and clothing persisted throughout the 1990s. One unique variation for the era was the heroin-addict look, which featured emaciated models with unkempt hair, ashen skin, and circles around the eyes. Details of ads 1996–97.

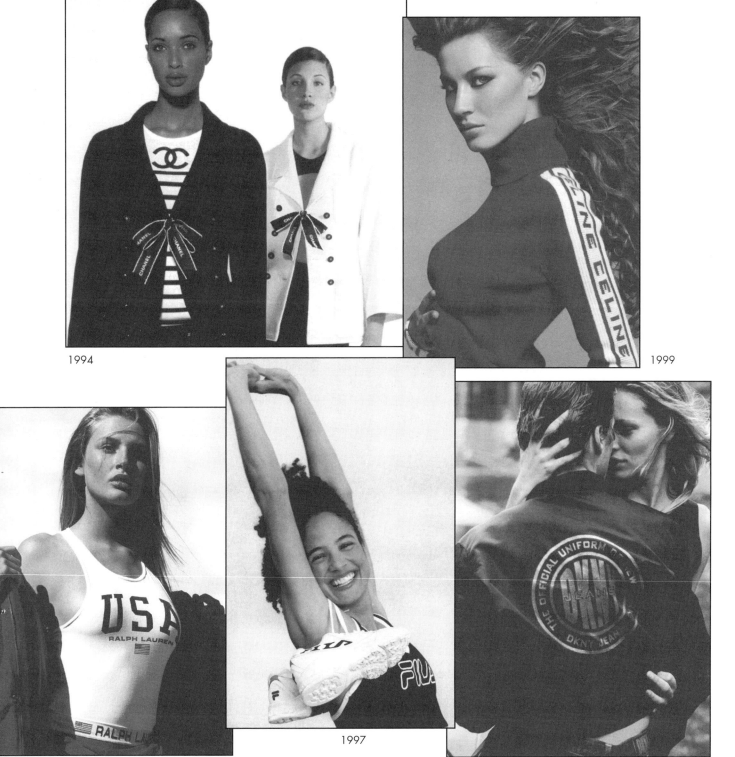

1994

1999

1996

1997

1998

Figure 6-27. Throughout the 1990s, casual sportswear with designers'
logos was a hallmark of American style. Mass production and mass marketing
of logo apparel fostered a sense of continuity and tribalism with consumers.

worthy of revisiting? Grunge? Monastic? Cyberstyle? Or if not unique, then what was pervasive, besides endless revivalisms? In scanning through more than ten thousand pages of fashion ads and editorials of *Vogue* from the 1990s, a reader would notice that the truly American look of ease, comfort, and personal style, year after year, was achieved with logo sportswear. The branded label that had first moved from the inside of clothing to the outside decades earlier had became an identity of personal style for many Americans in the nineties. (Figure 6-27.) "Anything emblazoned with a logo is a best seller," mused *Vogue* in 1995.[35] It could also represent continuity amidst all the rapid fluctuations of looks. Few consumers could escape owning at least a signature T-shirt at some time in the nineties, due to mass production and a proliferation of outlet malls and Web-site discounters. For some people, images created by marketing were the sole governing factor in choosing to wear that logo. Ralph Lauren's polo rider conveyed a country gentry feel, while the CK of Calvin Klein represented sensuality and sexuality. The DKNY acronym for Donna Karan New York bespoke a casual yet sophisticated urban style. Tommy Hilfiger was ubiquitously middle America. And for those who could afford the symbols of upscale lifestyles, the linked double C's of Chanel, the tête-bêche F's from Fendi, and the D&G emblems of Dolce and Gabbana were worn as quiet exhibitionism of an affluent status. Just as league jerseys or college colors demonstrated the sports fan's allegiance to a favorite team, the signatures and graphics of fashion designers' logos were tribal markings that most all Americans recognized. Perhaps the look will be headlined as retro-tribalism in the ads or editorials of some distant future edition of *Vogue*.

Conclusion

American culture of the 1980s has often been compared to the Gilded Age of a century earlier. Both were eras of great disparity between the haves and have-nots. The affluent un-abashedly displayed their good fortune through ostentation and exhibitionism, particularly in their dress. Following high-profile examples in the Reagan White House and entertainment industries, American women of means indulged in opulence and glamour. For the middle classes, ready-to-wear makers provided affordable simulations of the sumptuous looks from Paris and Milan. Smart advertising projected the image of high style, encouraging the masses to aspire to look like the rich and famous, even if only briefly at a community garden party or family wedding.

Unlike in the nineteenth century, though, women of the 1980s more often than not earned their own money. To compete for the high salaries against the established boy's clubs of big business, women "dressed for success" in tailored power suits. Big shoulders and menswear details prevailed in the designs of women's suits. Occasionally, however, to remind men, and perhaps themselves, of their femininity, many working women also opted for the chic, ultrafeminine styles of the fluid chemise, the sculpted dress, or any number of New Look revivalisms from the fifties.

By the 1990s, ever-greater fashion pluralism came to dominate the fashion landscape. Women sought ways to express their individualism with fashion. Ready-to-wear makers increasingly specialized to meet the needs of this new fashion democracy. For marketers, that meant a focus on image branding—from the classic, gentrified look of Ralph Lauren to the projection of feminine sensuality with Calvin Klein clothing. Logos also served to affirm a woman's personal style, ranging from sporty and casual with Polo and Fila to exclusive and elite with Chanel and Fendi.

Culture clashes in the 1990s included grunge, biker styles, and new wave cyberpunk. The androgynous look of the young that had emerged in the eighties also continued throughout the 1990s. Revivalisms likewise repeatedly recurred in forms that newly mixed elements of distant styles with technofabrics and accouterments of the Technology Age.

7

THE BARE ESSENTIALS: LINGERIE AND SWIMWEAR

Fashion historians have written volumes on the evolution of underwear, tracing its origins back to the very earliest civilizations. To ancient peoples utilitarian underwear provided additional warmth or served as a foundation for the attachment of outer clothing. In some cases, creating sexual allure seems to have been the purpose of undergarments, such as the corsets of Minoan women, which cinched the waist and supported the bare breasts.

By the Christian era, however, the concept of clothing itself took on significance quite different from that of ancient societies. Biblical texts told of the loss of innocence of the first man and woman, whose nakedness was clothed with coats of skins from the hand of God. To early church fathers, the nakedness of pagan peoples was perceived as loss of innocence, surrendered to wanton sensuality. In its relentless attempts to deny the eroticism of the naked flesh, the Christian social order ultimately required that virtually every part of the body be concealed by clothing. By the beginning of the Dark Ages, attire for all classes covered the entire body except for the face and hands. To the medieval Christian, then, layers of undergarments—camisoles, chemises, petticoats, hosiery, and undergirdles—served as an extra measure of modesty and virtue.

Despite persistent admonitions from the church down through the centuries, many variations of underwear were designed to project sexuality by exaggerated contortions and distortions of the human figure. As a result, the actual garments themselves became viewed as highly erotic. After all, underwear touched the most intimate parts of the body. In addition, only the closest of relations—spouse, parent, doctor, servant, or lover—would be permitted to see a woman in her underwear. As the variety and sophistication of intimate gar-

ments developed, sexual provocateurs and prostitutes capitalized on this mystique with exhibitionism of underwear costumes as a device of enticement. Anne Hollander suggested in her book *Seeing through Clothes* that "the hint of depravity, the legacy of centuries of taboo, had given an element of strong erotic importance to the existence of women's underpants rather than to their absence."[1] By the 1890s a voyeuristic glimpse of a woman's underwear was the appeal of the licentious can-can dance, which was so shocking that it was soon banned even in Paris.

Such long traditions of modesty and sexual prudery collided headlong on many fronts with the entrepreneurial objectives of the Industrial Revolution in the nineteenth century. During the second half of the 1800s, new manufacturing technologies rapidly led to more advanced principles of mass production and mass distribution of goods, including ready-made intimate apparel. Everything from store displays to print advertising required special consideration in marketing the new styles of unmentionables. Although advertisers had to work within the restrictions of obscenity laws, they did not have to conform to standards of taste and decorum.

To illustrate their products in advertisements, two solutions were possible for underwear makers. First was a pedantic representation of the garments solely as products. Corsets were featured as hollow shapes, and soft goods such as drawers, petticoats, or chemises were depicted flat or folded. But this approach could be confusing since it failed to convey a sense of shape, proportion, and fashion style. An alternative was the depiction of the garment on a human figure, which was more daring, especially when photography was used. (See Figure 2-1.) By the beginning of the twentieth century, though, ads for intimate apparel readily depicted undressed models in naturalistic poses and private settings such as the boudoir. Careful presentation of imagery in advertising, though, remained the constant challenge for intimate apparel marketers. Even at the end of the twentieth century, a negative backlash was possible with the wrong image or ad message, which Calvin Klein discovered when he was sued in 1995 for the sexually charged depictions of teenage models in some of his underwear ads.[2]

Nevertheless, as the Victorian era closed, unmentionables had been mentioned often in all forms of advertising. Depictions of women wearing lingerie and corsets were commonly featured in mass-circulation magazines, retail catalogs, and direct mail pieces, as well as in public places on posters, billboards, and trolley cards. The imagery became so common that even the society periodicals of the nineteenth century, including *Vogue*, accepted ads for intimate apparel.

Corsetry

As a specialized garment, the corset has been in use since ancient times. Minoan figurines from Crete that date to about 1500 BC represent young women with flounced skirts tightly cinched at the waist by a decorative corset. Artifacts from ancient Egyptian, Persian, Greek, and Roman sites also illustrate versions of the laced-up corset that were sometimes worn as part of ritualistic or formal costumes. During the Middle Ages, though, corsets were not worn by women in the Christian West until the Crusades, when the lavishly decorative girdle was introduced from the East. Since the garment had been worn by women of rank in the Mongol, Turkish, and Arabian courts, European nobility readily adopted the exotic fashion. By the beginning of the fourteenth century, the laced-up girdle had evolved into a full bodice of intricately worked leather panels and fine linen. Women of wealthy mercantile families asserted their status by imitating the styles from royal courts and helped spread the fashion of corsetry throughout cities and towns all across Europe. In subsequent centuries, the corset was modified into the front-lacing girdlestead of the fifteenth century, the two-panel underbodice called a *corps* (France) or "pair of bodies" (England) of the sixteenth century, the bust-compressing stomacher of the seventeenth and eighteenth centuries, and finally the contorting, hourglass-shaped version of the Victorian era.

Over the past 150 years much has been written on the evils of corsetry. As early as the mid-1800s, women's groups began to advocate dress reform with special emphasis on the elimination of the corset. The call for a ban on the corset was wholly supported by physicians for medical reasons, the clergy for moralistic reasons, and a considerable number of the male population who thought the fashion was excessive. In 1870, Dr.

George Napheys complained in his book *Physical Life of Woman* that due to the constricting corset, "many women are forced to neglect their duties to their ownselves that so many thousands walk the streets of our great cities, living martyrs....We refer to the foolish and injurious pressure which is exerted on the lower part of the chest and the abdomen by tight corset, belts, and bands to support the under clothing: in other words, *tight lacing*."[3] Various suggestions have been proposed in answer to this concern expressed by Dr. Napheys—and the generations of men who have since objected to the peculiarity of corsetry. Some social theorists have maintained that, despite their protests, the restricting corset was actually devised by men to keep women subdued and in the home. Others argued that the corset provided visible evidence of class separation, since women who were trussed up in tightly laced corsets were unable to endure the exertion of physical labor.

One of the more common explanations for the endurance of the corset has been that of sex appeal. The hourglass figure suggested feminine sexuality and implied fertility by the illusion of broader hips and larger bosoms. Havelock Ellis even suggested that the tightly laced waistline "advertises the alluring bosom by keeping it in constant and manifest movement."[4] This wasp-waist silhouette was not peculiar just to the Victorian era, though. In the 1930s, Mae West exemplified the quintessential hourglass profile with cinched-waist corsets and tight, sheath-style dresses. Fifty years later, Madonna achieved similar results with corsetry, only she wore her intimate apparel on the outside of her stage costumes.

A part of this endeavor for sex appeal included the attempt to preserve the illusion of youth by artificially creating the hips and waistline of a young woman. Decade after decade, the marketing efforts of corset makers especially focused on this message in their advertising. In the early twenties, for example, the Gossard Corset Company sent a direct mail piece to customers asserting that "a woman who has carried naturally small hips and thighs past the age of thirty is rare indeed."[5]

During some eras, though, such as the 1910s, 1920s, and 1970s, sex appeal was not at all enhanced by corsetry. Indeed, the fashion silhouettes of these decades were usually far from appealing to men. The straightline hobble-skirt styles of the teens, the boxy flapper chemise of the twenties, and the menswear suits of the seventies utterly denied feminine curves. Instead, corsets and girdles were actually reengineered to produce the columnar or boyish profiles of the time.

Hence, the most prevalent explanation for the continued success of the corset has been that of changing fashion. As mentioned in the examples above, in some instances, the corset was redesigned to reinforce the prevailing fashion trends. In other instances the corset itself defined the fashion silhouette, as with the S-bend Edwardian styles or the contrived ultrafemininity of Dior's New Look during the post–World War II years.

Once the profile of the fashionable figure had been determined by the trends of the day, the corset manufacturers shifted into high marketing gear to produce innumerable specialized styles. Particularly from the 1890s forward, corset makers expanded their lines to include dozens of styles specially constructed for golfing, bicycling, dancing, and other strenuous activities. In addition, specialized corsets were designed for social occasions that required lengthy periods of sitting, such as the theater and garden teas. By the midteens, corset makers were producing so many specialized styles that *Vogue* complained of this "seeming madness": "To golf in an evening corset is now but little less unspeakable than to golf in an evening gown. The tailored costume, the riding habit, the negligee, each must be worn over its own especial model. Only the robe de nuit is exempt, and who can say how long it may enjoy its unique position."[6] That women accepted this "madness" of so many specialized corsets was a delight to makers, who perpetuated the notion through mass marketing and advertising.

From the S-bend Corset to the New Millennium Bustier

By the end of the nineteenth century, ready-made corsets were among the most heavily advertised consumer goods in America, rivaling patent medicines, soaps, and processed foods. As with most mass-produced merchandise at the time, the corset had benefited from the rapid advances of manufacturing technologies and expanding retail distribution. Whereas a custom-designed corset could cost more than thirty dollars, mass-produced versions were profitably retailed at only one to three dollars. Instead of the ivory or whalebone stays and fine silk brocades used in made-to-order models, mass-produced corsets were constructed of less-durable celluloid or iron wiring that rusted when wet. Cheaper grades of cotton or even buckram were steam molded over the supports into standardized proportions that were often ill-fitting and even injurious with prolonged wear.

Nevertheless, mass production of corsets, coupled with a burgeoning ready-to-wear industry, brought fashion to the American masses. Fashion mass marketing through advertising and magazine editorials reached a broad socioeconomic spectrum of women consumers. Fashion news was dispatched almost instantaneously coast-to-coast. Within a single season of stylistic changes, mass distributors such as Sears, Roebuck, and Company had affordable versions in their stores and mail-order catalogs.

The first dramatic fashion change of the twentieth century occurred in 1900 when French designer Mme. Gaches-

Figure 7-1. In 1900 the S-bend corset was introduced as a healthful alternative to the Victorian hourglass model. The exaggerated shape and fit were so radical and fresh that the new styles defined the silhouette of fashions all through the Edwardian era. Ad 1902.

Figure 7-2. The long, narrow silhouette of the directoire hobble-skirt fashions required a new style of corset to replace the curvaceous S-bend models. A slender, girlish figure now became the ideal. Corsets extended in a compressed, longer line over the hips, reaching to midthigh in some designs. Gardner ad 1909, Schwartz ad 1910.

Sarraute introduced a completely reengineered corset. Instead of the indented, curved front of the Victorian styles, the French "health corset" had a straight-line busk that pushed back the hips and forced the bosom forward into an exaggerated S-bend silhouette. (Figure 7-1.) The design was originally intended to relieve the pressures exerted on the internal organs by the hourglass-shaped corset. Instead, the French model caused stress on the spine, lower back, shoulders, and hip joints.

Even so, the fashion look was innovative, fresh, and exciting. Although clothing styles did not appreciably change from those of the late 1890s, silhouettes were modified to follow the contours of the new feminine form. Shirtwaists and dresses developed a straight-line dropped front. Skirts were gathered, tucked, or pleated at the back waistline to better drape and conceal the rear edges of the corset. Despite the exaggerated kangaroo posture and the physical discomfort caused by the S-bend corset, the style would remain popular throughout the decade.

In 1908, Parisian couturier Paul Poiret introduced a dramatic challenge to the S-bend profile with his columnar interpretations of the directoire style. The silhouette was completely different from the look of Edwardian modes. Not

only was the waistline shifted to just under the bust, but also the narrow dress contoured the hips and thighs. To achieve the fluid draping of the shortened, slim skirt, Poiret had a new corset designed to replace the S-bend model. (Figure 7-2.) A slender, girlish figure now became the ideal. The redesigned corset was upright and extended well over the hips, reaching to midthigh in some versions. By the early 1910s the Poiret hobble skirt and the upright corset were universal. Ads by corset makers promised to produce the "fashionable low bust, the long hip and back, the altogether straight effect which stands for the final word in Parisian fashions."[7]

Soon after the outbreak of World War I, the narrow hobble skirt disappeared for more practical fuller lines. As an increasing number of women joined in the war effort by volunteering services or working outside the home, the demand for comfort and ease of movement in clothing influenced fashion silhouettes. Corset makers, too, responded to women's demands and produced models with lighter stays and construction. (Figure 7-3.) *Vogue* said of the new corset designs in 1918 that "it is not necessary to hold a figure in close restraint in order to secure perfection of line, as the construction of the corset, not the boning, produced this effect without confining the body."[8]

Once women had become accustomed to the ease and comfort of the lighter, reduced models, the way was paved for complete freedom from the corset in the 1920s. As early as 1922, a *Printers' Ink* editorial noted that corset marketers were scrambling to "sell the corsetry idea" in their advertising because "a considerable number of young American women [had decided] that wearing corsets is not just 'the thing,' judged by the Paris standard."[9] Soon after World War I, that Paris standard had begun its evolution toward the loose, dropped-waist chemise with hemlines that would eventually rise to the knees within a few years. Feminine curves were suddenly unfashionable. Nor were the garter snaps of the corset needed anymore, since young women rolled their stockings down over banded garters just above the knee.

Consequently, corset makers had to redesign their models to provide women with the contours of a bustless, hipless, boyish figure. Modern corsetry styles now compressed rather than shaped or supported the figure—exactly what was called for to simulate the thin, teenage figure of the flapper. (Figure 7-4.) In addition, marketing messages focused on the youth-oriented culture of the Jazz and Gin Age. A sampling of copy headlines in corset ads read:

"For all women who want to keep young." (1921)

"Are yours the lines of youthful flexibility?" (1922)

"Now for a girlish figure as lovely as your smile." (1923)

"Youthful grace of figure." (1924)[10]

For older women who attempted to join the flappers in abandoning the corset, a *Vogue* editorial in 1925 warned that "the middle-aged spread . . . is not conducive to narrow hips and that boyish line at the back." Bluntly the editors advised that "for some women, heroic measures are necessary, and a real corset, well cut, well boned, quite long, and as determined as pink brocade can be, is the only thing that will restore its erring wearer to the straight and narrow way."[11]

The straight and narrow way, however, ended more abruptly than it began. Suddenly, at the end of 1929, Parisian fashion collections presented a radically new silhouette. The curvaceous female figure returned in full force. Dress styles emphasized the natural waistline and full, rounded hips and bust. The favored materials of the new fashions of the 1930s included clingy knits, silks, and rayons. This meant that corsets could not be bulky or constructed with hard edges and ridges that would show through the fluid fabrics and slim lines.

During the late twenties, corset makers began experimenting with new fibers and finishes for foundation garments. Elasticized yarns were successfully woven into panels of narrow widths and short lengths that then could be constructed into corsets and brassieres. By the beginning of the thirties,

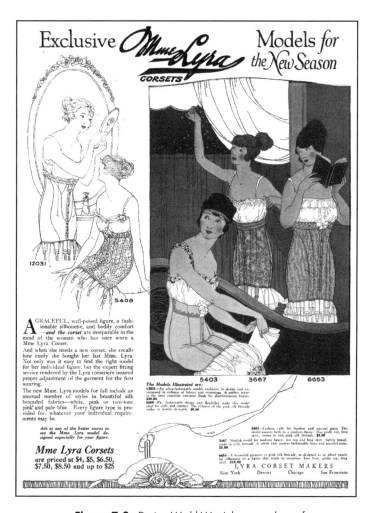

Figure 7-3. During World War I, huge numbers of women joined the war effort by working outside the home or volunteering for wartime services. As a result, they needed greater ease and comfort in clothing styles. Corset makers responded by designing models with lighter boning and construction. Ad 1918.

advances in knitting technologies made possible the spinning of different elasticized strands that could be circular knitted into a seamless tube. Corsetry was revolutionized. "Hips and derrières are no longer put in their place by girdles with dozens of stays," reported *Vogue* with delight in 1933. "The new girdles of two-way stretch fabric and fashioned elastic give support without any rigidity or riding up."[12] One-piece bodysuit corsets and girdles now were manufactured without laces and hooks. Styles could easily be made that were cut away for the new backless or halter-style evening gowns and yet still provided shape and support. The use of innovative fabrics and simplified construction techniques allowed foundation garment makers to mass produce the lightest-weight versions in corsetry history. "Tipping the scales at no more than a few ounces apiece, these foundations are actually pounds lighter than the whalebone birdcages of yesterday," noted *Vogue*.[13] By mid-decade, rust-proof zippers were introduced to eliminate the disheveling process of squeezing into the tubular models. (Figure 7-5.)

As for the new marketing messages from the makers of

foundation garments, the emphasis was on the curvaceous silhouette. For younger women that could mean enhancements of the bust and rear if needed. "Curves...curves...curves!" declared the headline in one ad from 1931. For older women, that meant maintaining the illusionary reduction of inches from the waist, hips, and thighs. "Summer exposure, with every curve controlled," promised a Vassarette ad in 1937.[14]

Although Parisian collections of 1939 began to show a dramatic shift in silhouette, World War II erupted and shut down the couture export business before the new trend could make its way into the ready-to-wear circuits of America and Britain. Instead, as the 1940s opened, manufacturers of foundation garments encountered many of the same shortages and restrictions on materials as all other fashion industries. Reserves of Dutch, Belgian, and French laces, Italian brocades, German dyes, and domestic silks and synthetics soon dried up. Substitutions such as fabric blends or lower grades of materials were used for consumer products. The amount of rubber that was used in elasticized yarns was severely reduced by the War Production Board.

Figure 7-4. Corsets of the 1920s compressed rather than shaped or supported the figure to simulate the fashionable boyish silhouette of the flapper. Warner's ad 1923, Modart ad 1927.

Women understood the necessity of sacrifices for the duration but could not help complaining about the poor quality of the austerity foundation garments. *Vogue* did its part for propaganda in 1943 by publishing a report on the new constructions of wartime corsetry. "All rumors to the contrary," the editors avowed, "the new corsets bend when you bend, stoop when you stoop, move when you move, stretch when you stretch and adjust themselves perfectly to busy, active lives."[15] Corset marketers likewise changed the messages and imagery of their advertising to emphasize flexibility in their new designs. Illustrations often depicted women gyrating in such wildly active poses that no consumer could miss the point. (Figure 7-6.)

After the deprivations and austerity of the war years American women were ready for a total fashion makeover from the foundations outward. In 1947, Christian Dior swept the fashion world with the debut of his New Look collection. The silhouettes were ultrafeminine with cinched waists, full hips and bustlines, and head-to-toe accessories. Underneath it all were foundation garments that negated almost thirty years

1932

Figure 7-5. Advances in fiber and knitting technologies in the 1930s led to a revolution in corsetry. Instead of stays and laces, circular-knitted tubes of elasticized yarns provided smooth lines and substantial support. By mid-decade, the introduction of the zipper eliminated the process of squeezing into tight foundation garments.

1935

1935

1937

Figure 7-6. During World War II the War Production Board severely limited the nonmilitary use of rubber, silk, and many other materials used in manufacturing foundation garments. Advertising efforts focused on the flexibility and comfort of the new corset designs made with substitution materials. Ad 1943.

of development toward comfort, ease, and flexibility. Instead, constricting stays, tight laces, and long lines resurfaced in corsetry, even for young, slender women. (Figure 7-7.) A *Vogue* editorial noted in 1948 that the "new American figure" featured "the smallest waistline in captivity...and a smooth, round line at the hips."[16] To help women achieve this new figure, some corsets included attached bras and extended to midthigh in a single piece. Even girdles were redesigned for longer lines that reached from the rib cage to the thighs. With wartime rationing at an end, pure silk and satin brocades combined with elasticized rayon or nylon added just the right touches of femininity and configuring support for the New Look.

From 1948 into the early 1960s, Dior's New Look dominated American ready-to-wear fashions. The woman's ideal profile of the time, wrote fashion historian Christina Probert, was "aggressively female rather than softly feminine."[17] Throughout those years, this theme of an emphatically feminine (or female) silhouette recurred in fashion editorials and advertising copy. "Because the waist is exaggeratedly small, the bosom must be rounded, the hips decidedly out-curved," wrote a *Vogue* editor five years after Dior's first showing.[18]

Figure 7-7. After years of wartime deprivations and austerity, women responded enthusiastically to Christian Dior's New Look collection of 1947. To achieve the radically different silhouette of cinched waist, rounded hips, and full bustline, corset makers reverted to constricting stays, tight laces, and longline designs. The New Look continued to be the dominant silhouette through the fifties and well into the early sixties. Flexees ad 1948, Formfit ad 1953.

Finally, by the midsixties, a revolution of society, pop culture, and fashion ended the New Look reign, and with it, the types of corsetry that defined the silhouette. Natural contours and curves were the order of the day, smoothed and controlled by new, light, elastic fabrics. As clothing became briefer, so did foundation garments. (Figure 7-8.) Configuring, controlling corsetry as a defining fashion necessity had reached the end. Young women abandoned foundation garments altogether, even if obesity was a concern. Huge numbers of women over the age of thirty responded to the youthquake of the era by assiduously dieting and exercising to preserve the appearance of slim, young figures. In addition, pantyhose and panties were made with control-top panels of strong, synthetic textiles that provided comfortable support without the need for girdles or other controlling undergarments.

As the 1970s progressed mass-media advertising of corsets and girdles diminished precipitously. Department stores relegated girdles, long-line bras, and similar figure-control lingerie to the back of intimate apparel areas for the shopping comfort of the older female customers who still preferred these items. In reviewing a 1975 DuPont study on "what happened to the girdle," Elizabeth Ewing concluded, "Wearing a girdle was until recent years 'almost a legal requirement.' Everyone did. Now, given the choice by casual dress and tights [pantyhose], by the 'go natural' lifestyles and relaxed social standards, women en mass decided no."[19]

In an ironic twist of fashion, though, corsetry evolved from an undergarment to an exogarment in the last quarter of the century. From the late seventies through the eighties and into the new millennium, the external corset continued to be a favorite revivalism of avant-garde fashion designers such as Yves Saint Laurent, Claude Montana, Jean-Paul Gaultier, and Thierry Mugler. (Figure 7-9.) As with styles from centuries past, modern versions of the external corset were covered in all sorts of fabrics or constructed of contemporary materials that now included an array of molded plastics, synthetic fibers, and technotextiles.

Bust Supporters to Wonderbras

During the late nineteenth century, categories and designs of intimate apparel became increasingly diverse and specialized. The modern-day bra, for example, evolved from basic camisole-like undergarments that were worn more for protection and modesty than for support. (Figure 7-10.) The French brassiere originated in the 1880s when couturiers and dressmakers began sewing wire or fabric cups into the bodices of décolleté gowns to fit over the breasts and secure the bustline just above the topmost edge of the corset. Until the 1910s, though, most women wore simple corset liners, chemise-like

Figure 7-8. Foundation garments of the 1960s were designed to provide smooth, natural contours. Ad 1965.

bust supporters, or camisole brassieres made of silk, silk blends, linen, or cotton. Many times quilted padding or additional lining was added to enhance the dimensions of the bustline for a more shapely hourglass silhouette.

In 1914, Mary Phelps Jacobs patented a new brassiere design for the American market. Her pattern featured a bilateral construction between the breasts with a tab at the bottom that fastened to the corset. Two narrow straps fitted over the shoulders, and the segmented panels for the breasts were held in place by straps that tied under the arms in the back. The innovative design was comfortable, easy to wear, and provided a four-point secured support at the shoulders and under each arm. Jacobs later sold the patent for her bra pattern to Warner's for a mere fifteen hundred dollars.[20]

By the late 1920s, two major advances were made in bra designs. First was the paring down of the garment from the longline camisole style that fit over the entire upper torso to the briefer bandeau versions encasing only the bust. Second was the introduction of elasticized fabrics in the construction of the new bra styles. Combined, these two developments in bra engineering provided "an upward *converging* support" and

SAINT LAURENT
rive gauche

CLAUDE MONTANA
GHINEA

BETSEY BUNKY NINI – New York, NY / BLOOMINGDALE'S – New York, NY
JIMMY'S – Brooklyn, NY / MARTHA – New York, NY – Palm Beach, FL
RUTH SHAW – Baltimore, MD

1983

1995

NORDSTROM

1998

Figure 7-9. By the last quarter of the century, the corset had evolved from a defining undergarment to an external design element.

a "perfect contour" of the bosom, as a 1928 ad claimed.[21]

As the fashions of the 1930s returned to a curvaceous, feminine silhouette, bra designs evolved into the cup models that are the standard today. "Cup the bust into smart, subtle, natural curves," invited the copy of a 1931 ad.[22] Fabrics such as silk jersey added to the softer, rounded bustline. In 1935, Warner's solved the fit issue when it introduced alphabet cup sizes that became the industry standard that is still used today.

Following the unbridled sweep of Dior's New Look in the late forties, and especially throughout the 1950s, the bra became a figure-enhancing, fashion-defining construction. "The bra that helps you bridge the gap between the silhouette nature gave you and the silhouette fashion demands," promised a 1948 ad.[23] As with most foundation garments of the Dior era, hard-edged engineering of the bra created the artifice that delineated the bustline. Sweater girls Lana Turner, Jayne Mansfield, and Anita Ekberg became famous for their quintessential torpedo bras. This fashionable look was so prevalent that when the Barbie doll was first produced in 1959, her bustline was sculpted as two concentric projections to create the New Look silhouette rather than the contours of a natural bosom. Fashion historian Melissa Richards said of these whirlpool-stitched bras, "The cantileverage and weapon-like silhouette make it apparent that the designers of aircraft and bras were men living out very Freudian and aggressive fantasies with universal appeal."[24]

The antithesis of this intimate apparel constructionism emerged in styles of the 1960s. The fashion silhouette was now defined by the natural contours of the body rather than by the contrived distortions of the New Look. Clothing designs were the briefest since antiquity, with micro-minis on every American street and bikini swimwear on American beaches becoming common. From the 1960s forward, bras more naturally contoured the breasts. Rudi Gernreich's No-Bra bra of 1965, for example, had no cup construction at all, relying instead on the sheer nylon spandex fabric as support. In addition, bras of the sixties were more enticingly embellished with feminine touches of lace, satin rosettes, and ribbons. Intimate apparel advertising featured sexy images and sex-sell messages instead of the usual product poses that had been the repeated norm since the 1800s. By the end of the century, many lingerie ads and catalogs featured such provocative photography that conservative groups objected to them as softcore pornography. But the marketing of sex and lingerie continued to realize explosive sales and industry growth. For instance, the sex-sell marketing of Victoria's Secret was a phenomenon of 1980s retailing. The Wonderbra became a best-seller of the midnineties by promising most every woman a full, rounded cleavage irrespective of bust size. Even traditional bra makers joined the progressive competition. In 1995

Maidenform introduced the new Satin Seduction Bra with ads that asked, "What's your lingerie doing for you?"[25]

Long Johns to Panty Thongs

Throughout the entire twentieth century, intimate apparel in all its many forms has comprised a substantial portion of the American woman's wardrobe. In addition to the corsets, girdles, and bras discussed above, other categories of intimate apparel have included hosiery, garters, daywear (slips, petticoats, teddies, camisoles, tap pants), sleepwear, and underpants. For most of these lingerie items, the evolution of their silhouettes has been subtle. Changes in hemlines, widths, weights, fabrics, and ornamentation have been consistent with fashion trends of the time. With two exceptions—hosiery and underpants—technology has not significantly affected the design of these intimate garments the way it did corsetry and the bra.

The development of hosiery was inextricably linked to advances in technology. Although woolen socks and leggings were worn by northern European tribes in ancient times, the production of these garments was labor intensive, requiring hours of hand knitting. By the Middle Ages, the separate components of the sock and the military legging were combined to produce handknitted one-piece tights for men. Despite the convenience and comfort of one-piece hosiery, women were restricted to individual stockings with garters since, according to Anne Hollander, "the separation of women's legs, even by a single layer of fabric, was thought for many centuries to be obscene and unholy."[26] During the sixteenth century Londoner William Lee invented a loom for machine-knitted hosiery and commercially produced the first silk stockings. By the late nineteenth century, advances in machine-knitting technologies made possible the mass production of fine-gauge cotton and silk hosiery with reinforced heels and toes as well as flawless seams down the back. Even with mass production, though, silk was an expensive material for hosiery. Experiments with synthetics such as rayon were not successful, since knitted synthetic yarns lost their shape and bagged. Finally, in 1940, DuPont introduced hosiery made of a sheer, "indestructible" nylon yarn. Affordable and durable, nylon hose replaced silk stockings almost overnight. The next technological innovation in hosiery was the development of seamless stockings in the midfifties. Soon afterwards, fashion trends of the 1960s led to the creation of colorful and patterned tights to be worn with the leggy looks of miniskirts. Almost immediately, hosiery manufacturers adapted the knitting machinery to produce sheer nylon versions of the fashion tights, and the mass production of pantyhose was launched.

Women's underpants, likewise, evolved dramatically from

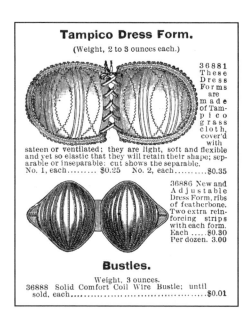

Tampico Dress Form.

(Weight, 2 to 3 ounces each.)

36881 These Dress Forms are made of Tampico grass cloth, cover'd with sateen or ventilated; they are light, soft and flexible and yet so elastic that they will retain their shape; separable or inseparable: cut shows the separable.
No. 1, each......... $0.25   No. 2, each.........$0.35

36886 New and Adjustable Dress Form, ribs of featherbone. Two extra reinforcing strips with each form.
Each $0.30
Per dozen. 3.00

Bustles.

Weight, 3 ounces.
36888 Solid Comfort Coil Wire Bustle; until sold, each...$0.01

1895

PATENTED DEC 5TH 1899.

KABO BUST PERFECTOR

May be worn over any corset and prove invaluable to the modiste, in that it creates a superbly correct bust and masks every imperfection, including those very annoying hollows about the collar bone; worn without a corset, it is the perfection of shirt waist distenders, and is fine for those desiring bust support with freedom at waist-line.

No. 1 Coutel, white, drab, black, $1.00
No. 2 Batiste, white, black, and
  high colors,   -   -   -   -   1.50
No. 3 Satin, all colors,   -   -   2.50
No. 4 Ventilated, net, white,   -   1.00
No. 5 Linen, tan, for bathing,   1.00
Sizes 18 to 30; order one size larger than corset worn. Weight 3 to 5 ounces.
At all corset departments, or
388 BROADWAY

THE GARDNER BUST SUPPORT

An indispensable article of dress when a shirt waist is worn and for golf, tennis, and other out-door sports its advantages are manifest.

1900   1902

A PERFECT FIGURE FOR EVERY WOMAN

Model No. 12, Price **$1.50**

THE A. P. BRASSIERE DIRECTOIRE

1909

DeBevoise Brassière

Styles for every figure and occasion fifty cents to ten dollars on sale at all good stores

Guaranteed the BEST in fit and effect

1915 Style Book free on request

CHAS. R. DeBevoise Co.
1270-F Broadway
New York City

DeBevoise

(Pronounced "debb-e-voice")

Style 1606
"Decollete"

1915

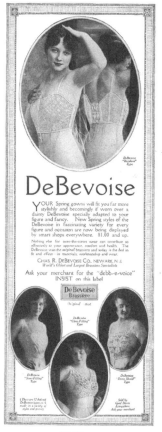

DeBevoise

YOUR Spring gowns will fit you far more stylishly and becomingly if worn over a dainty DeBevoise specially adapted to your figure and fancy.   New Spring styles of the DeBevoise in fascinating variety for every figure and occasion are now being displayed by smart shops everywhere. $1.00 and up.

Nothing else for over-the-corset wear can contribute so effectively to your appearance, comfort and health. The DeBevoise was the original brassiere and today is the best in fit and effect—in materials, workmanship and wear.

CHAS. R. DeBevoise CO., NEWARK, N. J.
World's Oldest and Largest Brassiere Specialists

Ask your merchant for the "debb-e-voice"
INSIST on this label

DeBevoise Brassière

1918

DeBevoise

Brassieres that Beautify

TURN over the fashion pages—see the slim-bodied modes! How imperative that your frocks this season be fitted over DeBevoise Brassieres!

Say "Debb-E-Voice" at your favorite corset department. See the new styles in booklet we will send free on request.

Made, Labeled, and Guaranteed by
CHAS. R. DeBEVOISE CO., Newark, N. J.
World's Oldest and Largest Brassiere Manufacturers

DeBevoise Brassière
ORIGINAL - BEST

1921

Figure 7-10. Prior to the First World War, various predecessors of the modern-day bra included chemise-type bust supporters and camisole brassieres. In 1914 the first American design for the bra was patented. During the 1920s, the bra was pared down to a bandeau style. In the thirties, alphabet cup sizes were introduced. Following Dior's 1947 launch of the New Look, bras became rigidly constructed foundation garments that defined the exaggerated feminine silhouette of the era. From the sexual revolution of the 1960s forward, bras and other lingerie were specifically marketed as sexually alluring apparel.

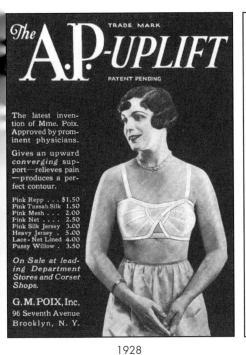

The A.P.-UPLIFT

TRADE MARK

PATENT PENDING

The latest invention of Mme. Poix. Approved by prominent physicians.

Gives an upward *converging* support—relieves pain—produces a perfect contour.

Pink Repp . . . $1.50
Pink Tussah Silk 1.50
Pink Mesh . . . 2.00
Pink Net 2.50
Pink Silk Jersey 3.00
Heavy Jersey . . 5.00
Lace - Net Lined 4.00
Pussy Willow . 3.50

On Sale at leading Department Stores and Corset Shops.

G. M. POIX, Inc.
96 Seventh Avenue
Brooklyn, N. Y.

1928

CUP-FORM
PATENTED

Brassière *by Model*

Curves..Curves..Curves!

Cup-form's soft, silken inner cups—cup the bust into smart subtle natural curves. Cup-form reduces an over-developed bust, adds charm and appeal to an under-developed bust and gives stylish comforting support. There is a Cup-form for every figure from the narrow bandeau to the full width brassiere.

Model Brassiere Co.
DEPT. 18
London   Paris
Empire State Building
Fifth Avenue at 34th St., New York, N. Y.
E. & S. CURRIE, LTD., 50 YORK ST., TORONTO, CAN.

No Other Brassiere Cups the Bust like Cup-Form. IT'S PATENTED

Illustrated—1138 of silk jersey, pink, white and black, $2.50. Others $1.00 to $5.00 at all leading stores. Write for illustrated style booklet.

COPYRIGHTED 1931, M. B. CO., INC.

1931

AGAIN...
STITCHING
ALONE
DOES IT!

for LOVELY
ROUNDED
UPLIFT
SUPPORT

"INTER-LUDE"
REG. U.S. PAT. OFF.   PAT. APP. FOR

To accomplish a lovely classic roundness of contour, Maiden Form creates "Inter-Lude" brassieres which—by semi-circular stitching—give firm uplift support, with a slight separation between the breasts. Made in simple bandeau style or with 2-, 4-, or 6-inch band for diaphragm control. At all leading stores — $1.00 to $5.00.

Send for free Foundation Booklet VO
Maiden Form
Brassiere Co., Inc.,
New York, N.Y.

Maiden Form
BRASSIERES
GIRDLES GARTER BELTS

LOOK FOR THIS TRADE-MARK ON

"There's a Maiden Form for Every Type of Figure"

1935

Alene

the **bra** that helps you bridge the gap between the silhouette nature gave you . . . and the silhouette fashion demands

1948

Inner Circle lifts the just-ordinary figure—out-of-the-ordinary! This artful bra is designed especially to glorify the average and average-full A, B or C cup ...with idealized curves and permanent uplift. And, thanks to the patented Dura-form cup, Inner Circle gives you more than uplift—*uplong!* (Keeps its shape, and yours... after many, many wearings and washings.) Join the millions who have discovered that THE SECRET'S IN THE CIRCLE!

get into the PETER PAN *inner Circle*

regular
strapless
plunging
longline

Peter Pan Foundations, Inc., 389 Fifth Ave., New York 16

1953

The Olga Plus: Pretty No-Seam Smoothness

THE PRETTIEST SHOULDER LOOK SINCE THE BRA BEGAN

Show-Off Shoulder* Olga's innovative Secret Hug* stretch lace bra. Now in a no-seam style for almost every figure. It keeps its adjustable straps a secret. Smoothes, hides hardware. Peeks prettily through your see-through tops. By Olga, so you know the bra fits comfortably. Keeps its shape and yours, beautifully. Softcup 32-38 BC. 7.50. Lightly shaped 32-38 ABC, 9.00. Padded 32-38 AB. 9.50.

behind every OLGA *there really is an Olga*

For where-to-buy call toll-free 800-447-4700
In Illinois call 800-322-4400

1977

"Satin Seduction" Bra from Maidenform. (What's your lingerie doing for you?)

MAIDENFORM

1995

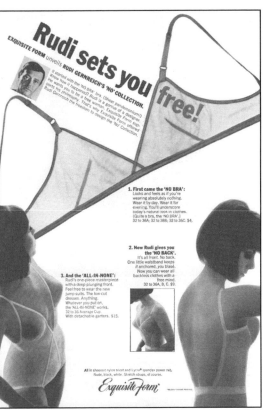

EXQUISITE FORM *unveils* RUDI GERNREICH'S 'NO' COLLECTION.

Rudi sets you free!

It started with the 'NO BRA' bra. (Sheer pandemonium!) Please how it helped Rudi (it's a piece of a designer). He wants you to be a free woman. Exquisite Form pads his philosophy. That's why Exquisite Form offered Rudi Gernreich the freedom to design the 'No' Collection.

1. **First came the 'NO BRA':** Looks and feels as if you're wearing absolutely nothing. Wear it by day. Wear it for evening. You'll underscore today's natural look in clothes. (Quite a bra, the 'NO BRA'.) 32 to 36A; 32 to 38B; 32 to 36C. $4.

2. **New Rudi gives you the 'NO BACK'.** It's all front. No back. One little waistband keeps it anchored, you blasé. Now you can wear all backless clothes with a free mind. 32 to 36A, B, C. $9.

3. **And the 'ALL-IN-NONE':** Rudi's one-piece masterpiece with a deep plunging front. Feel free to wear the new jump suits. The low-cut dresses. Anything. Whatever you put on, the 'ALL-IN-NONE' works. 32 to 36 Average Cup. With detachable garters. $15.

All in sheerest nylon tricot and Lycra® spandex power net. Nude, black, white. Stretch straps, of course.

Exquisite Form®

1965

—155—

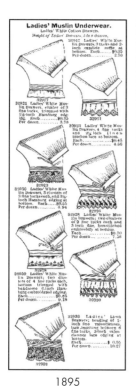

1895

1897

ITALIAN SILK UNDERWEAR

The Lingerie that is loose, yet close-fitting

Made in every Undergarment that a well-dressed woman wears

1902

1907

1913

1917

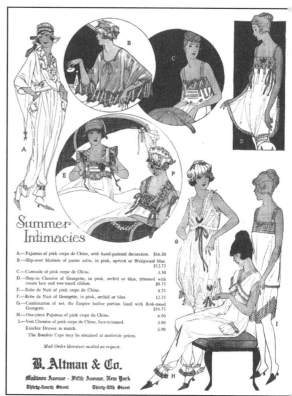

1919

Figure 7-11. The evolution of women's underpants is far more dramatic than with most other categories of intimate apparel, such as petticoats or sleepwear. By the beginning of World War I, the Victorian union suit and long drawers were replaced by versions of the briefer camiknickers and short bloomers. These styles continued to be pared down to that of the flapper's step-in. The skintight panty briefs of the 1930s became the model for skants, bikinis, and eventually the thong.

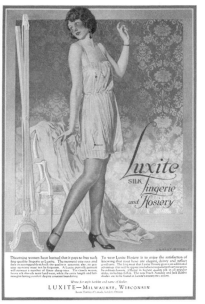

1924

1927

1935

1937

1943

1977

1985

their nineteenth-century origins. (Figure 7-11.) The Victorian styles of women's drawers were wide-legged pantalets that varied in length from midcalf to the ankle. Even the simplest versions were usually embellished at the hems with ruffles or decorative trim. Ready-to-wear models shown in the 1895 Montgomery Ward catalog featured Hamburg edging, embroidery, or Valenciennes lace trim. Drawstrings were sewn into the waistband or at the back to secure the garment in place before fitting the corset over it.

In the 1880s, American knitting mills began mass production of the combination or union suit—so-called not because it was made by labor unions but because the knit tops and bottom drawers were united into one piece. Made of ribbed cotton jersey for transitional seasons or wool jersey for winter, the union suit was plainly functional with only the slightest hint of feminine embellishment in the form of scalloped collars. Versions of the union suit, still referred to as long johns, continue to be produced even today, especially for residents of northern climates and winter sports enthusiasts.

By the 1910s, hobble-skirt hemlines had edged upward toward the tops of the ankles. Bulky, long drawers and union suits were inappropriate for the narrow, shorter skirts of the era. Instead, lighter and briefer camiknickers were introduced from France, along with the upright corset. As hemlines continued to rise during the late teens and especially into the twenties, styles of underpants were continually redesigned into ever-briefer cuts. A *Vogue* editor cautioned in 1925 that for modern fashions, "one's lingerie simply must seem altogether nonexistent, with nothing to break the knife silhouette…or to show about or below the brief space that intervenes between a low neckline and a high hemline."[27] Yet intimate apparel makers were hard-pressed to keep pace with the rapid rise of the hemlines of the twenties. In 1926 *Vogue* warned the flapper that "although the smart world has become accustomed to seeing practically all of a stocking, it still considers the bloomer an intimate garment and conceals even its smallest edges."[28]

Within a couple of years of the high point at which hemlines had peaked, skirt lengths plummeted almost to the ankle as the Great Depression settled in. Despite covering much more skin than did the styles of the flapper, fashions of the thirties were far more formfitting. Even the baggy tap pants and short step-in bloomers of the twenties were too bulky for the clingy dresses and fluid skirts of the Depression era. "You can't bluff much about your figure under the merciless clothes of today," observed a *Vogue* editorial on intimate apparel in 1933.[29] Panties and bras became softly constructed and were made of various patented elasticized yarns. Underwear fit like a second skin. "Not a bulge or a bump to mar your silhouette," promised the copy in a Vanity Fair Skintite panties ad of

1935.[30] By the midthirties underwear styles for both women and men were influenced by the new brief models of swimwear from Europe. Although the waistband was still above the navel, the leg openings of the panty brief were cut in an arc to rise from the crotch to the hip joint. The brief served as a template for most all variations of panties for the rest of the century. Beginning in the late thirties skants were introduced, featuring very high-cut leg openings and a lower rise to the waistband. By the 1960s, the bikini swimsuit had influenced panty styles and coincided with the cut of the new low-rise jeans and pants. In the seventies, when skintight jeans were worn to the discos, thong versions of the panty became mainstream, since the open, stringed back eliminated any telltale panty line across the rear and hips. By the eighties, the design of the French-cut panty pushed the waistband back up to the natural waistline and the rise of the leg openings was nearly as high. As with the bra and other types of lingerie, manufacturers of the last quarter of the century marketed panty styles that were designed primarily for their sexual allure. Modern versions of panties run the gamut of silhouettes from the briefest thong to knock-offs of menswear boxers. Most every style comes in a myriad of fabrics, colors, textures, and prints.

Swimwear

Swimming is an unnatural activity for human beings. Unlike most all other animals, we are not born with an instinct for swimming. However, ancient peoples who settled along seacoasts, lakeshores, and riverfronts had to learn to swim for gathering food and for simple survival. From this necessity, recreational swimming would have developed, both as an activity for individuals and as a group social practice.

In many ancient civilizations, communal swimming and, later, bathing rituals were an integral part of society. Many of the public bathhouses of Greece and Rome were palatial complexes with heated pools and sophisticated plumbing systems. Despite the fact that early Christian leaders viewed the bathhouses as dens of orgies and had them closed, recreational swimming continued to be enjoyed by those peoples who lived along waterways and shorelines. In addition, ancient salt-water resorts or spas built around mineral springs remained operational for the benefits of hydrotherapy, although visitors were now segregated by sex, and everyone bathed fully clothed. The most famous of these spas in the West is at Bath, England, and has been in continual use since Roman times.

By the nineteenth century, a growing middle class in Europe and America began to enjoy vacation time at beaches and resorts with the convenience and efficiency of the expanding network of railroads. "Taking the waters" at a seashore meant wading out into the shallows buoyed by a floating canopy to prevent sunburn and to shield against prying eyes. Not until the mid-1800s did special forms of attire develop for public bathing. Even then, bathing costumes still closely resembled street clothing. A high-necked, fitted bodice was worn with a full, ankle-length skirt over voluminous bloomers. Heavy black stockings, canvas shoes, and a broad-brimmed hat completed the ensemble. Most bathing costumes were made of stiff taffeta in black, navy, or plum, although wool was frequently used in climates where waters were chilly even in summer. When wet, such outfits were terrible weight burdens, and drownings were common for the unwary.

Nevertheless, as more and more women began to request bathing costumes from their dressmakers, fashion styling diverged from daytime modes. By the the beginning of the twentieth century, bathing suits had become lighter, with shorter overskirts and bloomers. Bodices were daringly sleeveless, some with décolleté necklines. (Figure 7-12.) Hats were still a must for women in public, but the swim styles became more functional, designed as rubberized turbans and caps. Nautical motifs such as sailor's collars and brass buttons were combined with sea-theme fabric prints or embroidered anchors, ropes, and ships. During the Edwardian period, the components of the bathing suit did not change, although the S-bend silhouette was applied, with its pigeon-breast bodices and overskirts gathered at the back.

Despite the proliferation of seaside resorts and lake retreats during the last quarter of the nineteenth century, though, the market for swimwear remained narrow. Retailers saw no great demand for the outfits, so only a few ready-to-wear makers attempted any mass production of swimwear. In the 1895 spring and summer edition of Montgomery Ward's catalog, hundreds of specialized garments were listed, including clothing specifically for dentists, barbers, and cooks, but not one item of swimwear. *Vogue*'s pattern department did not feature a swimwear model until 1907.

By the 1910s three significant social changes had occurred in America that helped broaden the appeal of recreational

A Sun Bath, or a bath in the ocean, is good, if it doesn't result in blistering the skin, but even then the pain may be relieved and the evil effects overcome by the use of

Salva=cea,

(TRADE MARK)

the new CURATIVE LUBRICANT, the most marvellous medical discovery of the age in its effect upon all skin troubles. Under its influence STRAINED or OVERWORKED MUSCLES, CHAFINGS, or any SORENESS or STIFFNESS, the BITES and STINGS of INSECTS, BURNS, BRUISES lose their pain immediately, and even obstinate diseases—as ECZEMA and SALT RHEUM, etc.—are cured.

Two sizes, 25 and 50 cents per box.   At Druggists, or by mail.

THE BRANDRETH COMPANY, 274 Canal Street, New York.

"USE IVORY SOAP—IT FLOATS!"

"One morning, last summer, at a Michigan resort, a party of girls went down to the lake in their bathing suits for the purpose of washing their hair. Each carried the necessary articles, including a cake of soap. One had a cake of _____'s soap; another, a cake of _____ soap. Several other varieties were represented.

The place selected was near the pier, and the implements for washing the hair were placed in the interstices of the logs supporting the pier. During the process of washing, the _____'s soap girl lost her soap and in the effort to recover it, the _____ soap girl lost hers, too. The girl with the Ivory Soap thereupon threw it far out into the lake, swam after it and, holding it aloft, cried: 'Use Ivory Soap—it floats!'

In the end, all three girls used Ivory Soap—they had to!"

—Extract from a Letter

Again we ask: Even if Ivory Soap were no better than other soaps, does not the fact that *it floats* make it better?

Figure 7-12. Victorian bathing suits included an overdress, bloomers, opaque hosiery, shoes and hats. Stylistically the ensemble would change in detailing and embellishment, but the components would remain until around 1920. Salva-cea ad 1895, Ivory ad 1909.

swimming for women. First, Henry Ford had made the Model T affordable to the masses beginning with its production in 1908, and in a short time, automobile excursions and vacations to the seaside or local lake resorts were enjoyed by wider socioeconomic classes. Second, the styling of the bathing suit, with its knee-length skirt and sleeveless bodice, had been a familiar image in the mass media and on public beaches for almost twenty years by this time, so the stigma of immodesty had diminished considerably. Third, a new self-image of sex appeal was experienced by young women in this decade. Movies showed them how modern feminine sensuality looked and the effect it had on men when adroitly applied. Advertising, too, did its part to promote feminine sex appeal in the 1910s with campaigns such as the Woodbury soap ads that illustrated young couples embracing beneath the caption "a skin you love to touch." Consequently, young women experimented with sexual display by donning skimpy bathing suits and inviting the gazes of men on public beaches.

As a result of these social shifts, the market for bathing suits suddenly burgeoned, and ready-to-wear makers responded with stylish costumes that were chic and affordable. (Figure 7-13.) *Vogue* advised in 1915 that "in the annual social contest with the wild waves, the smart bathing suit is ever half the battle."[31] For the most part, though, until 1920 the components of women's bathing suits changed very little from the Victorian ensembles of the 1890s. In 1917, a *Vogue* editorial differentiated between the "beach butterfly," whose resort fashions were "for the sole benefit of passersby," and the bather, whose swimwear styles had changed "not so much."[32] All bathing costumes still featured the overdress, bloomers or some type of pantalets, opaque hosiery, shoes, and hat. The preferred fabric was still silk taffeta or satin.

In 1915, a new development in knitting technology was about to change the look and fit of swimwear for both women and men. That year Danish immigrant Carl Jantzen invented a specialized machine that produced lightweight elasticized knits that held their shape even when wet. Originally the new knits were intended to be used in the production of winter sweaters, scarves, and gloves. But when a friend who was a rower heard about the new ribknits, he persuaded Jantzen to design some athletic sportswear for his team. The skintight, stretch suits were an immediate success. In 1920, Jantzen

Figure 7-13. Although the components of women's bathing suits had not changed since the 1890s, ready-to-wear makers mass produced chic and affordable variations for the modern woman of the 1910s. Franklin Simon ad 1915, Macy's ad 1917.

1922

1925

1929

introduced swimwear versions of his rower's suits that "changed bathing to swimming," as their advertising slogan proclaimed. (Figure 7-14 and color plate 6.) The most daring versions were the one-piece suits that only the most confident flapper would risk wearing. "A Jantzen suit fits you perfectly," asserted the copy in an ad, "and permits such freedom for swimming that you scarcely know it's on you."[33]

However, not all manufacturers converted productions to the skintight knit styles, and not all young women rushed out to buy the new modes. The 1922 Bonwit Teller ad shown here depicts two versions of the knit suit at the bottom of the page, while the feature photo illustrates the standard styles that had been the model for thirty years. Even into the early 1920s, women who wore a one-piece knit swimsuit on some public beaches could be arrested for indecency.[34] Nevertheless, *Vogue* noted the sudden change in swimsuit styling and cautioned readers in a 1922 editorial:

> Gone are the days when one could be negligent in the matter of the bathing suit, and the shrunken flannels or shiny mohair, sailor-collared suits were taken from the trunk each season and used as long as they would last. Today the bathing suit must not only be of excellent material, but it must also be very well cut and most carefully finished to the veriest detail, and, above all things, it must achieve smartness.[35]

Figure 7-14. In 1920, Jantzen introduced the ribknit swimsuit that "changed bathing to swimming." Despite the innovative silhouette and immediate success, the transition away from the Victorian overskirt and bloomers was slow. By the end of the twenties, though, the formfitting knit styles prevailed.

As the 1920s progressed, swimwear followed the lines of dresses and rose to shorter lengths up the leg. Tentative cutouts and open-back styles, called crab-backs, appeared on beaches frequented by the more fashionable set. Hosiery, shoes, and even hats ceased to a prerequisite of the swimsuit ensemble.

The evolution of swimwear in the 1930s continued the trend toward brevity and more exposure of skin. (Figure 7-15.) "They're briefer and tighter, these new suits," wrote a *Vogue* editor in 1932. "So much briefer and tighter that they make your old ones seem to hang long and limp. And so much tighter that they make the others feel as though they flopped about you in the wind." [36] Variations included backless halter styles, maillots with cutaway sides, and strappy suspender modes. Pant legs continued to rise until by mid-decade they aligned with the crotch. For men, the topless brief style was introduced from Europe in 1933. Within a couple of years, the leg openings of some women's models were cut with similar arcs rising above the crotch to fully expose all of the thigh.

Figure 7-15. Swimwear styles of the 1930s continued the trend toward brevity and tighter fits. By middecade the men's brief had been introduced from Europe.

1931

1935

1937

Most women, though, preferred the longer line or even the modesty skirt styles. Also in the late thirties, the first two-piece styles fully opened the midriff all around the torso. Ironically, even though more skin was shown and the formfitting knit fabrics were very revealing on women and men, American swimwear styles were all designed with high waistlines to always cover the navel. This peculiar social more would go unchallenged by designers until after World War II.

With the interruption of fashion influences from Europe during the war years, American fashion makers took center stage. California ready-to-wear manufacturers especially moved into the limelight during the 1940s, led by the West Coast sportswear makers such as Cole, White Stag, and Koret. However, swimwear designs of the era did not present any notable innovation. The fashion news of each season centered on color palettes, fabrics, and prints rather than innovation of silhouette.

The next leap in swimwear design occurred after the war and once again came from France. When Paris designer Louis Réard planned to launch a radical new swimsuit in 1946, he wanted to generate as much publicity as possible. He achieved this partially by calling the style the bikini, named for one of the nuclear test site islands then in the news. The scant, two-piece set actually received more debate and condemnation than the bomb tests had generated. For American ready-to-wear manufacturers, though, the issue was moot since the look was too scandalous to be taken seriously. The most daring cut that women had accepted in a two-piece swimsuit was the halter or bandeau with a midriff bottom. (Figure 7-16.)

Swimwear designs of the forties, fifties, and even into the early sixties followed existing silhouettes that had mostly evolved in the 1930s. In fact, by the midfifties, *Vogue* reported that swimwear had become more of a "state of dress, not of undress."[37] The more popular styles of swimwear included the skirted maillot, which concealed a lot of physical anomalies. In keeping with the ultrafeminine look of daytime fashions in the Dior era, swimwear styles also included the cinched-waist profile and a constructed bustline. Swimwear ads of the time more often than not depicted women on the beach fully accessorized with earrings, bracelets, hair ornaments, hats, scarves, sunglasses, matching beach bags, and cover-ups.

By the 1960s, the bikini became identified with the youth-quake generation through beach-scene movies and pop music. Although Rudi Gernreich titillated the fashion press with his topless swimsuit in 1964, the style was not even remotely considered by ready-to-wear makers, let alone the mass market of American women. In the seventies and eighties, versions of the bikini were pared down to ever-briefer dimensions that culminated in the string bikini, with its triangular patches for the breasts, crotch, and buttocks literally held together by

Figure 7-16. The next leap in the evolution of swimwear design came in 1946 when French designer Louis Réard launched the bikini. American women, though, refused to wear the radical new look, preferring to keep their navels covered with high-waist bottoms. Cole ad 1943, Surf Togs ad 1947.

glamorize your curves in SeaMolds

Show a more glamorous you...charm beach companions...wear SeaMolds for superlative figure flattery!

Visible in every line...Flexees personalized fit! Shapely bras, hip-sleeking lastique panties!

Variety unlimited...fabulous fabrics ...fashions for every figure; priced for every purse; $12.95 to $22.95

flexees.

AT BETTER STORES or WRITE FLEXEES, Inc.
417 FIFTH AVENUE, NEW YORK 16, N.Y.

1954

Figure 7-17. From the 1950s forward, swimwear designs continued to be pared down for more exposure of skin. In the 1960s the bikini became more widely accepted due in part to the youthquake of the baby boomers and their beach movies and music. In the seventies and eighties versions of the bikini became ever briefer, ultimately culminating in the thong styles of the 1990s.

in love with life in a *Catalina*

1965

1979

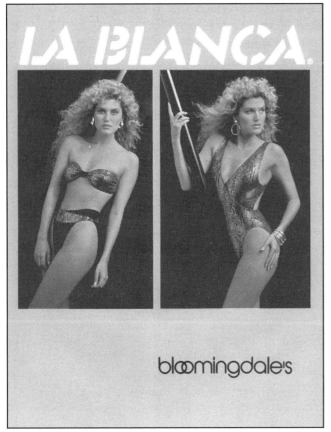

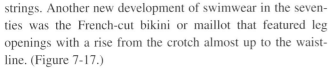

1988

1995

1997

strings. Another new development of swimwear in the seventies was the French-cut bikini or maillot that featured leg openings with a rise from the crotch almost up to the waistline. (Figure 7-17.)

Although nude beaches had become increasingly accepted in certain regions during the 1990s, most American women were reluctant to go that far in public. Still, the thong bottom became widely popular with young women, especially for the college ritual of spring break in Florida. In an ironic, full-circle of style, some swimsuit silhouettes of the late nineties were cut on the patterns of designs of the 1920s. Instead of knits, though, Lycra blends provided the favored second-skin fit. From the thirties, the maillot with a longer pant leg was also revived and promoted to the aging baby boomers as a flattering alternative for women with fuller hips. Similarly, the tankini featured a bikini bottom with a cropped tank top made of skintight spandex and resembled workout sports clothing of the early eighties. Even though more skin was covered with these revival styles, some were made of a new fabric that allowed all-over sun tanning and yet still retained its concealing opacity.

For the American beach-going woman at the end of the century, the swimsuit had evolved to its most extreme possibilities. In the 1999 swimsuit edition of *Vogue*, every style featured was a revival of past innovation, right down to sixties mod prints from 007 spy-theme movies. Even the editorial homage to the sun-worshipper at poolside or surfside could have applied to the "beach butterfly" of 1917: "Let's hear it for the girl. The all-American queen of the beach-club scene.... So perfect is she, she can show up, in her open top roadster, naturally, with nothing save her suit swinging from her wrist in a tiny coordinating bag."[38] The two challenges ahead for swimwear makers of the new millennium are further reductionism—perhaps even another run at complete elimination like Gernreich's topless attempt in the sixties—or yet more adaptations and revivalisms.

Conclusion

The bare essentials of underwear and swimwear for the most part have been marketed and promoted independently of outer clothing. Catalogers and retailers separate these categories of garments into sections unto themselves despite their integral links to the modes of the time. With that in mind, the principal forms of underwear and swimwear are described in this separate chapter for a clearer view of their technological and stylistic evolution across the past hundred years.

Despite clothing reform movements and dire warnings from physicians, Victorian women refused to abandon their corsets. When the S-bend model was introduced in 1900, women were delighted with the fresh silhouette it provided, even though the design did not live up to its intent as a healthful alternative to the indented hourglass corsets of the previous century. When fashions of the 1910s became upright and columnar, corsets were made longer, fitting well over the hips to ensure a proper longline look. In the 1920s, young women discarded the corset, but most others needed foundation garments that could simulate the youthful, trim figure of the flap-

per. In the thirties, corsets were important in shaping the female form with curves. By the fifties, the cinched-waist corset returned, some with rigid boning and constricting laces not seen in decades.

Through it all, corset makers adjusted their technologies and marketing strategies to meet consumer demands. New engineering of corsets, combined with advances in textile production, contorted the female form into the S-bend of the Edwardian era, compacted the hips in the 1910s, compressed the buttocks in the 1920s, and cinched the waists in the 1950s. Images and copywriting in advertising targeted women with the message of the day—youthful and slim in the 1920s, curvaceous in the 1930s, practical and comfortable during the two World Wars, and ultrafeminine in the 1950s.

Bras similarly underwent reengineering from the camisole-type bust supporters at the beginning of the 1900s to the articulated cup forms with alphabet sizing in the 1930s. For drawers and union suits, reduction was necessary as hemlines began to rise and clothing narrowed in the 1910s, ultimately culminating in the barest skant panty of the 1930s.

As the bra and panty were reengineered and cut ever briefer, so too were swimwear styles. The heavy overskirts and knee-length bloomers or drawers began to be recut and reduced along the lines of men's styles in the late 1910s. Through the 1920s women's swimwear became formfitting and briefer, with knit tank-style tops and thigh-high leg openings in the 1930s. The midriff was exposed with two-piece suits that evolved into the first bikini swimwear immediately after the Second World War. Well into the 1960s, though, American women, resisted further exposure of skin beyond the styles that had emerged in the thirties, especially the bikini. With the sixties youthquake and the sexual revolution of the time, women more readily accepted the bikini in its more reduced forms. By the beginning of the new millennium, swimsuits on public beaches might range from the miniscule thong, with as much flesh bared as legally permissible, to revivals of tank suits reminiscent of the flapper era.

8

ACCESSORIES: HATS, SHOES, AND JEWELRY

Hats

Ladies' hat designs of the late nineteenth and early twentieth centuries were largely governed by women's coiffures. The Victorian notion that a woman's hair is her glory pervaded all socioeconomic classes. Married women and single girls of marrying age piled their tresses atop their heads in all manner of knots and twists, some even enhancing the volume with attachments of false hair. Consequently, hat styles were created with an airy, light construction, while maintaining the Victorian penchant for fussiness. A profusion of feathers, netting, lace, ribbons, or similar lightweight materials crowned most millinery styles, often completely obscuring any profile of the actual hat itself.

During the first decade of the twentieth century, the S-bend silhouette was accentuated by hats that projected forward over the brow. Excessive ornamentation was reduced as the scale of headwear steadily increased year by year. By the end of the Edwardian period, hats had expanded to enormous dimensions and were laden with piles of plumes, bouquets of silk flowers, huge bows, entire birds, and swathes of draped fabric. (Color plate 3.) In 1907 *Vogue* observed that "the future elegance in

HATS — TOQUES — BONNETS
STREET, CARRIAGE AND RECEPTION
DRESSES
RIDING HABITS — TAILOR GOWNS
IMPORTERS OF THE FASSO CORSET
B. ALTMAN & CO.
18TH—19TH STREETS—SIXTH AVENUE, NEW YORK

(A.) 1893

(B.) 1896

(C.) 1903

Lord & Taylor

Broadway and Twentieth Street,   New York

(D.) 1909

(E.) 1911

vogue" for hats was "in size colossal."[1] Two years later, a *Vogue* editorial credited the camera for many of the oversized millinery styles of the day. That is, Parisian and New York hat designers would have seen thousands of photos of exotic peoples and their native costumes as published in travel and geographic periodicals. "It would not be the first time that milliners have gone to 'fur and furrin parts' for their inspiration," concluded *Vogue*.[2] Among those influences from distant cultures was the huge "peach basket" hat that simulated styles of Congo natives. Similarly, the yard-wide "merry widow" hats resembled those worn by Javanese plantation workers, and the effusive eveningwear turban designs were possibly influenced by Japanese peasant headgear. Exaggerated proportions of millinery remained popular until the start of World War I, when

(F.) 1914

(G.) 1914

(H.) 1919

(l.) 1918

such extravagances were not only impractical, but were regarded as unpatriotic in light of shortages and rationing.

Nonetheless, milliners were highly inventive with hat styles of the war years. In 1918, *Vogue* noted that "no fruit or flower is too strange, no material too unexpected, whether tinted parchment, kid or metal, to trim the new hats."[3] Silhouettes of hat designs underwent a significant transformation during the First World War. The mammoth widths of Edwardian creations were dramatically reduced in scale to perch atop the new bobbed or closely cropped hairstyles. Drama was created by the sharp angles at which the hats were worn, and even more so by the extreme verticality of feathers or fabric and silk ornaments. By the end of the war, hat silhouettes were still vertical, but the look was achieved more by higher crowns than by extensions of trimmings.

The most singular look that characterized the 1920s was the flapper's cloche. Although hat styles were as varied as they had ever been, "this hat like a medieval helmet," as *Vogue* described the close-fitting cloche in 1922, became the most ubiquitous style of the era.[4] As more women bobbed or shingled their hair they needed a hat that would stay on without

hat pins or straps. Versions of the cloche ranged from simple felt or velvet models that were worn loosely and casually to dressy versions decorated with art deco motifs and Jazz Age trimmings.

The cloche continued to be so popular that the look transcended the considerable changes in dress and suit silhouettes of the early 1930s. After a couple of years of sameness, though, women increasingly sought greater variety in their hat styles. "The millinery gods give you all the liberty in the world," commented *Vogue* at the time. "You can have no brim. You can have a medium brim. You can have an enormously wide brim. Take your choice."[5] Among the new looks of 1932 was the shepherdess hat, which was close fitting with a small brim that could be flipped up on any one side for a variety of looks. Simplicity was very much the order of the day in the early 1930s. Soft, simple shapes such as toques, canotiers, and tambourine berets complemented the smooth, curvaceous silhouettes of dresses and suits. Newness was created by the exaggerated angles at which the simple little hats were worn. "Down in front and up at the side or back," recommended *Vogue* in 1932.[6] (Color plate 11.) For Schiaparelli, "down in front" meant pushing her hats so far over the brow that *Vogue* referred to the look as "nose-diving."[7]

By the end of the 1930s, two new looks for hats began to emerge as key trends. First was a verticality not unlike that of the designs of the First World War. "Hats are made tall by bright quills and wings and ribbons," noted *Vogue* in 1938.[8] Second was the binding up of hair with scarves, netting, and wide ribbons attached to hats. In 1939 the bound look included the thickly crocheted or plaited netting of the snood, which could be worn with or without a hat. "Snoods are a landslide, snoods are a sensation," effervesced *Vogue*, "and practically every feminine head in the country has worn one of some variety."[9]

In 1940 imports of Parisian millinery were cut off when Germany occupied France and closed its borders. American designers then looked to their roots for inspiration and innovative ideas. Familiar models such as the Gibson Girl boater, the swagger fedora of the early thirties, and the miniature doll's hats of the late teens were revived and embellished with new patterns of netting, veils, and trimmings. Other influences came from Britain, including the Winston Churchill bowler, the bobbie's helmet, and the Cardinal Wolsey beret. Styles such as the bowler and doll's hats were "definitely not for the unselfconfident," warned *Vogue* in 1941.[10] Just as the cloche is inextricably associated with fashions of the Roaring Twenties, the vertical hat thrust forward onto the forehead is the look most associated with Second World War millinery. (Color plate 14.)

With the launch of Dior's New Look in 1947, an emphasis

Bluebird Hats — Paris Inspired

(J.) 1921

(K.) 1924

KNOX

WITH the return to vogue of the sailor hat, Knox again proves its claim as style leader. The fame of Knox sailor hats has long been abroad in the land, and the new designs now showing, while modestly priced, fully measure up to the Knox reputation.

KNOX HAT COMPANY

(L.) 1924

(M.) 1928

MALLORY
Hats of Quality since 1823
392 FIFTH AVENUE ~ NEW YORK

(N.) 1928

(O.) 1932

A SAILOR OF CRÊPE-MAT STRAW. FOLDED CROWN, 2-TONE QUILL, CONTRASTING RIBBON TRIM. $18.50.

PAILLE DE SPORTS STRAW — TRIMMED WITH RIBBON COCADE ON LEFT SIDE BACK. $8.50.

Hats of Tomorrow Today!

Knox hats for Spring are charmingly out of the beaten style path. And although they are new and lovely enough to turn any feminine head, they possess that much talked about Knox wearability—a very rare combination that makes them a doubly delightful investment. More good news! Knox hats, in all the new Spring colors, now start at $8.50.

THE KNOX HAT CO.,
711 FIFTH AVENUE, NEW YORK

THE SAILOR GOES BOLERO! WOVEN OF LUMINOUS ST. TROPEZ STRAW, BELTING RIBBON TRIM. $12.50.

KNOX

(P.) 1932

NEW YORKER

FIVE HUNDRED

SCALLAWAG

(Q.) 1935

KNOX THEME SONGS FOR SPRING!

Cruise & Travel
IN 3 EDITIONS

1 CRUISE & TRAVEL I. Knox Felt or Panama $8.75.
2 CRUISE & TRAVEL II. Knox Felt $8.75, Toyo or Baku $12.75.
3 CRUISE & TRAVEL III. Knox Felt $8.75.

*Voyageur**
IN 3 EDITIONS

1 VOYAGEUR I. In Felt $12.75.
2 VOYAGEUR II. Felt, Toyo, Mont Blanc Braid or Baku $12.75.
3 VOYAGEUR III. Felt $12.75, Toyo or Baku $15.00.

*Registered

CASA KNOX, MEXICO CITY, MEXICO • MITCHELL & MITCHELL, SANTIAGO, CHILE
CHAS. BIRKS & CO., LTD., ADELAIDE, AUSTRALIA

KNOX THE HATTER
5th Avenue at 40th Street, New York City

(R.) 1937

(S.) 1937

on an abundance of accessories dominated American fashions. In addition to the fundamental requirements of hats, shoes, and handbags, the full head-to-toe regalia of accessories became indispensable for the fashionable woman's total ensemble: gloves, jewelry, handkerchiefs, scarves, belts and even parasols. Every category of accessory had new importance, and fashion designers, editors, and modistes focused on each with critical emphasis. Wrote a *Vogue* editor in 1948: "A good silhouette is either over-all, or not at all. It's the shadow you cast—your irrevocable and complete shape. Some women in buying a hat, forget this; but if you want to look all of a piece, you can't isolate your head as an unrelated thing to be dressed and adorned independently."[11] Given this assessment, it is easy to understand the enormous variety of hat styles that were produced season after season from the late forties through the fifties. The indomitable influence of the New Look would be shaken off only with the fashion revolutions of the 1960s. Many of the hat styles of the 1950s that milliners designed had actually originated in the thirties and forties.

North? South?
Your Hats— Bendel Originals

(T.) 1941

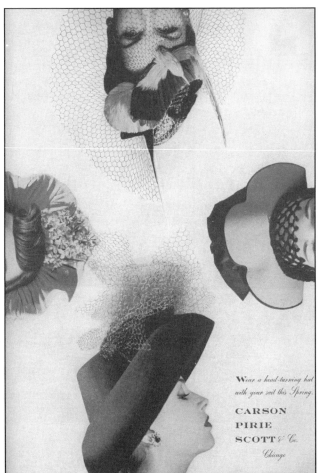

(U.) 1941

(V.) 1943

Innumerable versions of the conical coolie, the broad mushroom cap, the high-crowned toque, the voluminous turban, and the wide-brimmed fedora reappeared in hat shops and fashion magazines almost every year throughout the decade. To keep the revivals fresh, designers were innovative in construction materials and trimmings. For example, the skullcaps of the early thirties were translated into sleek sheath hats made of finely layered feathers. Similarly, the straw coolie hats of the early 1940s were revamped with felt or delicate crepe veneers and accented with beading or tassels.

As the 1960s dawned, hairstyles began to have an impact on hat designs. Exuberant bouffant coifs themselves became a crowning accessory, and women began to discard their hats in favor of the beehive or bubble cut. One compromise that was

(W.) 1944

(X.) 1944

(Y.) 1945

(Z.) 1948

Germaine Montabert

711 Fifth Avenue, New York 22, N.Y.

(AA.) 1950

Hattie

(BB.) 1951

(CC.) 1951

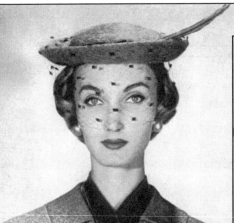

(DD.) 1954

(EE.) 1954

—175—

(FF.) 1961

(GG.) 1964

(HH.) 1966

(II.) 1971

made popular by First Lady Jacqueline Kennedy was Oleg Cassini's little pillbox hat that easily could perch atop the heavily teased and lacquered hairstyles of the time.

With the British invasion of mod looks in the midsixties, American hat designs reflected the street-scene styles of swinging London mixed with the space-age silhouettes from designers like Courréges. Unisex hat models such as the Nureyev cap (named for the ballet dancer Rudolph Nureyev, who brought the style from Russia) were worn by both young men and women with no gender differentiation of fabric, color, or shape. The round-domed British Bobbie's helmet, revived from the 1940s, had a futuristic look of high-tech space helmets when created in white leather or smooth syn-

thetic fabrics. At the end of the decade, hats became an anti-establishment statement for many young people when decorated with psychedelic flowers, antiwar slogans, or beaded and befeathered hatbands. Styles included tweed or leather news-boy caps, Mao (Tse-tung) caps, cowboy hats, floppy leather or suede fedoras, and all varieties of military hats and caps.

By the early 1970s, millinery was no longer the critical component of a woman's ensemble that it had been with the New Look. Choosing just the right hat for just the right dress or suit silhouette was an exercise for fashion magazine editors and runway show stylists. Women tended to wear hats only for special occasions such as weddings and Easter Sunday or as the weather dictated. In case of the latter, hat choices might

(JJ.) 1972

(KK.) 1977

(LL.) 1983

be more of a universal style like a beret or a fedora that worked easily with a number of coats, jackets, and suits.

Instead of hats, many young women of the early seventies opted for colorful scarves tied tightly around the head in various knots. The look had been made popular on TV by the Rhoda character on the *Mary Tyler Moore Show*.

Television programming similarly influenced fashion hat styles in the early 1980s. The prime-time soaps *Dynasty* and *Dallas* featured wealthy characters whose lavish costume ensembles often included perfectly coordinated hats and lots of accessories. The American public came to think that this was a true reflection of how all very rich women dressed every day.

By the end of the century, casual comfort was the governing criterion for most women's wardrobe choices. Apparel makers and retailers emphasized personal style in their marketing efforts, to which women responded enthusiastically. Businesses and schools began to implement casual-attire policies. Even churches were receptive to congregations that dressed down from the traditional Sunday best. Such democratization of fashion did not provide much opportunity or need for hats beyond utilitarian purposes.

(MM.) 1998

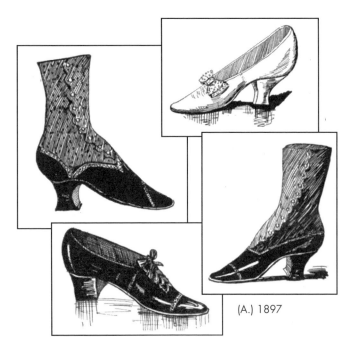

(A.) 1897

(B.) 1899

(C.) 1902

Shoes

American shoe manufacturing had developed highly efficient production and distribution methods by the 1890s. Season after season a vast array of affordable styles was mass produced with the latest modes of heel and toe shapes and current trends in topstitching, decoration, ornamentation, colors, and materials. One 1895 ad for a retailer claimed to offer more than one hundred styles of ladies' shoes priced at three dollars or less per pair.[12] In an 1897 editorial, *Vogue* asserted that mass-production footwear manufacturers had "brought shoemaking to a high state of beauty and perfection, and introduced every device possible for comfort and elegance."[13]

Standardization was a chief factor in the success of quality shoe manufacturing in America. For example, the heels and the uppers on high-top street shoes were mostly all designed with the same height. This made possible standardization of parts, materials, and assembly, irrespective of final decoration or color. One simple shoe model, for instance, could be converted into a dozen different styles by simply adding jet beads, perforated ornamentation, or contrasting appliques.

By the first decade of the twentieth century, shoe manufacturers had their mass-production processes down to an exact science. Style varieties could be implemented more readily than even a decade earlier. Consumers began to demand and expect greater variety of shoe and heel shapes as well as decoration. The shoe as a fashion accessory became much more important as hemlines began to rise at the end of the Edwardian period.

One of the first innovative changes in shoe silhouettes was the introduction of the Cuban heel following the Spanish-American War. The beveled slant at the back and the wide, lower construction created a fresh new look that complemented the more casual mode of the shirtwaist and skirt outfits.

With the dawning of the new century also came a nostalgia for all things colonial in America. Revivals of Pilgrim shoes with their large silver or brass buckles were translated into numerous modern variations. Similarly, bold, eighteenth-century shoe colors such as turquoise, emerald, crimson, and ochre were also popular with Edwardian women for day and evening pumps.

Conservatism was forced upon the shoe industry during the teens when materials shortages and production restrictions were in effect. High-top street shoes once again became some-

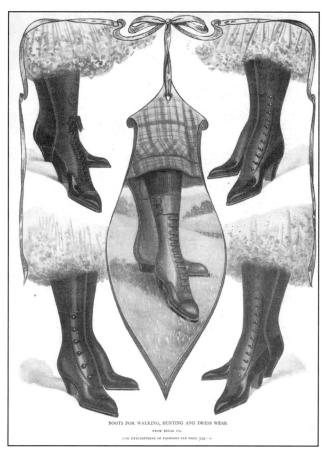

BOOTS FOR WALKING, HUNTING AND DRESS WEAR
FROM REGAL CO.
FOR DESCRIPTIONS OF FASHIONS SEE PAGE 524—A

(D.) 1907

EDWARD HAYES

Custom Foot Wear for Ladies

Creator of Distinctive Styles for Street and Evening Wear

We make footwear to order in its strictest sense. We match gowns in any material—the same obedience to individual taste as a dressmaker gives to your gown.

Pat. June 25, 1907

9 West 29th St., NEW YORK

Pat. June 25, 1907

Call or write Dept. V. for Illustrated Catalogue

(E.) 1908

Individuality
—to lead rather than follow the Fashion— has attracted to us the custom of the most fastidious.

JACK'S
Short Vamp Shoes *for* Street *and* Evening Wear

give to the Arch of the Foot Perfect Support and are more handsome in appearance than any other Footwear.

SNUG FITTING STREET PUMPS
Style No. 9017

Hand Welt, Cuban Heel, Non-Slipping Pumps, executed in Black Romaine Silk Cloth, Patent Colt, Dull Kid, various shades of Buckskin, Velooze (velvet), Satin and other materials.

Five Dollars the Pair

OUR NEW SPRING SHOWING comprises many beautiful models at $5.00 to $9.00 the pair.
We carry a complete line of "Onyx" SILK and LISLE HOSIERY in all shades and qualities.
WE CAN SERVE YOU BY MAIL as perfectly as in person. Write for our NEW CATALOG H, and self-measurement blank.

JACK'S SHORT VAMP SHOE SHOP
495 SIXTH AVENUE, NEW YORK
Tel. Mad. Sq. 7054   Between 29th and 30th Sts.

(F.) 1911

DULL KID or PATENT LEATHER, dull top, button, turn sole, Spanish heel $4.50

PATENT VAMP or DULL CALF VAMP, gray buckskin quarters, leather piping $4.98

SATIN PUMP, turn sole, 2 in. Louis XV heel, all colors $3.00
Silk Hosiery to match 95c and $1.50.
Silk Hosiery dyed to match color of gown from sample $2.00.

PATENT COLT, CIRCULAR FOX, MAT KID, short vamp, 2½ inch Louis XV heel, turn sole, button or lace $3.98

Also in black vici kid, button or lace and tan calf button.

Send for Catalogue V of New Fall and Winter Models

SATIN PUMP with rosette, Cuban heel, extra straps, all colors $2.35

L. M. HIRSCH SAMPLE SHOE CO.
404-406 Sixth Avenue Bet. 24th and 25th Streets New York

(G.) 1914

Come, give your feet to

Keds

(H.) 1917

Franklin Simon & Co.

Fifth Avenue, 37th and 38th Sts., New York

Women's Fall and Winter Shoes

EXCLUSIVE STYLES IN
BOOTS, OXFORDS and PUMPS

(I.) 1918

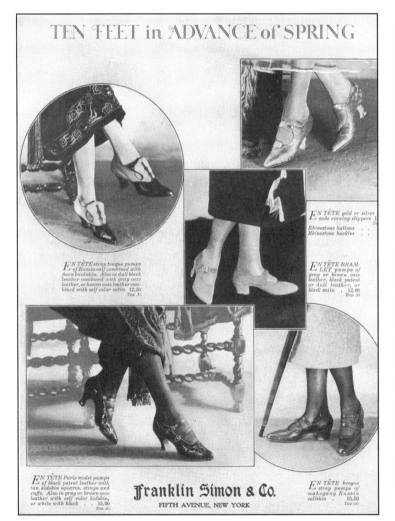

TEN FEET in ADVANCE of SPRING

EN TÊTE strap tongue pumps
of Russia calf combined with
fawn buckskin. Also in dull black
leather combined with gray ooze
leather, black patent or henna ooze
leather, or henna ooze leather combined with self color satin. 12.50
Tax .50

EN TÊTE gold or silver
ooze evening slippers 1
Rhinestone buttons
Rhinestone buckles

EN TÊTE BRAM-
LEY pumps of
gray or brown ooze
leather, black patent
or dull leather, or
black satin . 12.00
Tax .50

EN TÊTE Paris model pumps
of black patent leather with
tan kidskin squares, straps and
cuffs. Also in gray or brown ooze
leather with self color kidskin,
or white with black . . 15.00
Tax .50

EN TÊTE brogue
strap pumps of
mahogany Russia
calfskin . 10.50
Tax .50

Franklin Simon & Co.

FIFTH AVENUE, NEW YORK

(J.) 1921

"AMBASSADOR"
Patent Leather with
Apricot (light tan) top.
Bow to match

Famous Shoes for Women
and Young Women

Most
Styles **$7**⁵⁰

AUTHENTIC
MODES IN

AMERICA'S
BEST KNOWN MAKE

QUEEN QUALITY offers
smart shoes in styles
approved by leaders of
fashion the world over
— PLUS comfort and
enduring character —
a new measure of shoe
satisfaction within the
price range of every
woman.

NEW
STYLE BOOKLET
MAILED FREE
ON REQUEST

"SOCIETY"
A smart one-eyelet tie, of
BLACK SATIN, with wood
"spike" Louis heel and
flexible sole

"ROANOKE"
A new QUEEN QUALITY
pump of MAPLE BROWN
KID, with flexible sole
and wood Cuban heel

"RADIANT"
A three-strap street mod-
el of VASSAR BROWN
KID; welt sole; Cuban
rubber-top heel

Queen Quality

(K.) 1924

what standardized and were limited to a maximum height of eight and a half inches. In addition, since chemicals used in dyes were needed for the war efforts, shoes were manufactured only in black, tan, gray, or white.[14]

Despite the ever-increasing rise of the hemline, the look of the Victorian high-button boot persisted into the early 1920s, especially with the wide appeal of spats. By 1924, though, skirt lengths were nearing the knee, so that spats looked dated and interrupted the long line of the leg that the flapper wanted. Just as the straightline chemise became the silhouette of choice for women during the Jazz Age, so too was the Louis-heel shoe part of the flapper uniform. "The shoe in profile will be much the same," observed *Vogue* in 1924; choice, instead, came from "the material rather than the line, [which] runs through the whole shoe mode."[15] Colors and materials of shoes were more widely varied than ever before, including traditional textiles like satin and brocade in every hue, new synthetics such as rayon and acetate, and jewel-tone tinted leathers. Shoe designers were inspired by the art deco movement and combined materials to fashion geometric appliques and sculpted patterns in the moderne look. (Color plate 7.)

The most dramatic changes in shoe silhouettes since the eccentricities of the seventeenth century occurred during the 1930s. As women tightened their purse strings during the Depression, shoe designers, manufacturers, and retailers devised all sorts of new shoe types to tempt the fashion-conscious consumer. Heels ranged from wide, flat Cubans to high, spindly spikes. Pumps, flats, sandals, mules, open-toes, sling-backs, and ankle-straps were but a few of the many innovative cuts designed during the thirties. In addition, avant-garde wedges and platforms were introduced from the resort playgrounds of the fashionably rich. Thick, cork-soled Lido shoes were first featured in *Vogue* in 1937.[16]

After becoming accustomed to such a vast variety of affordable shoe styles, American women found that the austerity restrictions of World War II required significant adjustments. *Vogue* advised readers in 1943 that their one allotted leather pair should be "comfortable, versatile, handsome...so simple you can't weary of them." On the other hand, suggested the editor, fabric shoes were unrestricted and provided "a way to indulge a whim of color, a mite less conservatism."[17] Ironically, despite the War Production Board restrictions of so many materials, platform shoes became a favorite trend and continued in popularity even after the war.

In the fall of 1947, Christian Dior's New Look revolutionized women's fashions from head to toe. The simplistic utility

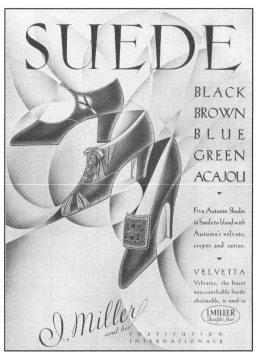

(L.) 1928

(M.) 1932

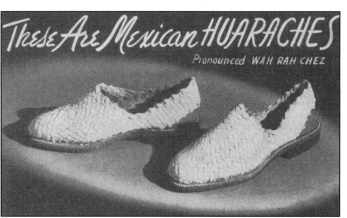

(N.) 1938

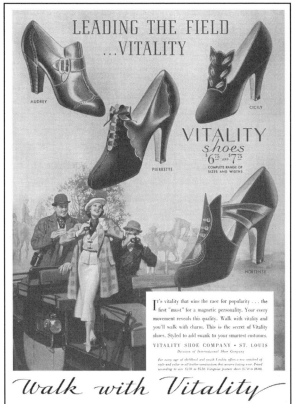

(O.) 1937

(P.) 1939

shoes and the heavy platforms of the war years were happily discarded for totally different styles. A fashion editor advised that the right shoes were key to the New Look. "It is the shoe with a certain amount of heel, enough to give the feeling of delicacy, to lengthen the line from the hem to the floor." [18] Narrow, pointed, and rigidly structured, the new shoe styles complemented the cinched, fitted silhouette of the New Look all through the late forties and entire fifties. The stiletto pump with its thin, four-inch heel was introduced from Italy in 1950, and became an instant hit. In the second half of the fifties, though, heels moderated into a midheight of two to two and five-eighths inches with pencil-thin contours as dramatically curved as the corseted waistline of the time. The slender, mid-heeled profile was the prevalent model through the early 1960s.

During the late 1950s, the fashion looks that would become known as the mod style of the sixties began to emerge in the boutiques of London and some couture salons in Paris and Rome. Clean, brief lines hallmarked the new miniskirts, little pullovers, and chemises. All elements of the New Look were discarded—including the sleek pumps with their slender heels and pointed toes. Instead, shoe styles were modeled on wide work boots and orthopedic granny heels as sharp contrast to the contrived delicacy of fifties trends. From the street

scenes of swinging London the look was appropriated by American shoe makers for mass production in the sixties. The new shoe profiles, explained an ad in 1968, featured "broader toes, higher stacked heels and vigorous tongues." [19]

The single most important footwear trend of the 1960s, though, was the boot. As early as 1963 fashion editorials and runway shows presented boots of every style, from little ankle models to thigh-high riding boots. In 1965 the white go-go boot fad swept America on the crest of the youthquake. A pop record by Nancy Sinatra titled *These Boots Are Made for Walkin'* even became a chart hit the following year.

Boots continued to be the important fashion accessory into the early 1970s. Young women still preferred the long, leggy silhouette created by the miniskirt, and the boot had become an established complement to the look. In 1971 hot pants became an extension of the miniskirt and new styles of boots were introduced, including lace-ups, colorful suedes, and distressed pieced-leather designs.

The seventies also saw a revival of the platform shoe—this time for men as well as women. "Now everyone, whatever age or wage, wears elevated shoes," noted *Vogue* in 1972. [20] Unlike the styles of the forties, the new designs sometimes reached amazingly exaggerated proportions. Soles could be as thick as five inches, with accompanying heels towering at eight inches.

(Q.) 1941

(R.) 1941

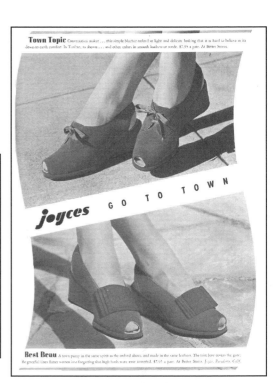

(S.) 1943

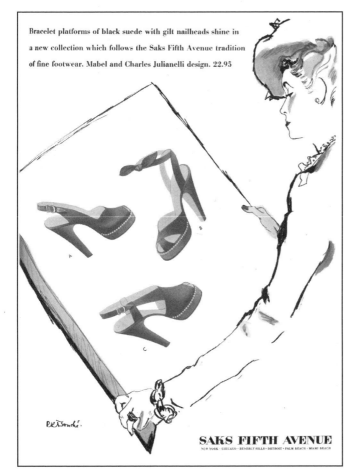

Bracelet platforms of black suede with gilt nailheads shine in a new collection which follows the Saks Fifth Avenue tradition of fine footwear. Mabel and Charles Julianelli design. 22.95

SAKS FIFTH AVENUE

(T.) 1945

c.h. baker *Strato-clog*

—*too smart for words*

(U.) 1945

(V.) 1948

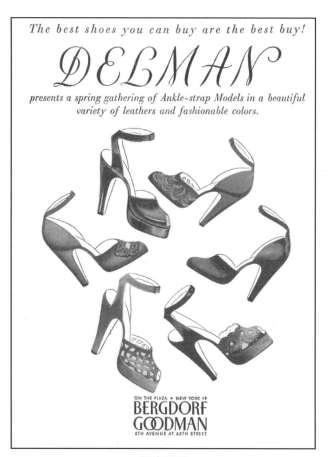

(W.) 1948

(X.) 1951

New-age materials were incorporated into the new platforms, including Lucite, vinyl, synthetic rubber, and aluminum. Most mainstream platform shoes, though, followed traditional models such as gillies, oxfords, and pumps with moderate one-half- to one-inch soles and heels at about three inches. Even tennis shoes were made in platform varieties.

As the platform faded from fashion in the midseventies, no new wave of innovative shoe styles or designs filled the vacuum. Hemlines dropped across the board, keeping boots in hot demand. By the beginning of the 1980s, revivalisms so affected hemlines that any sense of a specific trend was nearly impossible to discern. Mini to maxi lengths appeared simultaneously on runways and on American streets year after year through to the end of the century. The eclecticism of fashions meant an equally varied use of accessories—especially shoes. Every conceivable style of footwear was also revived, although not necessarily to achieve a period-costume look. The delicate pumps of the New Look were worn with jeans as easily as with a Lagerfeld suit. Platforms revivals were worn as readily with an ankle-length skirt as with a power pantsuit. In the end, fashion—and shoes—was a matter of personal style.

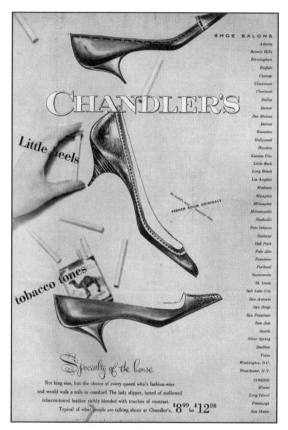

Not king size, but the choice of every queen who's fashion-wise and would walk a mile in comfort! The lady slipper, lasted of mellowed tobacco-toned leather richly blended with touches of contrast. Typical of what people are talking about at Chandler's. $8.99 to $12.98

(Y.) 1956

(Z.) 1956

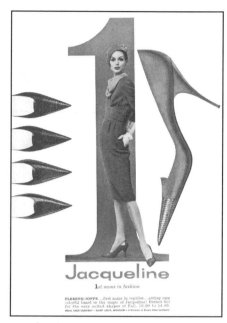

(AA.) 1961

(BB.) 1961

Simonetta of Paris designed them. B.F.Goodrich makes them. And you'll love them! They're Bootinos —the newest, most beautiful bootwear ever. In three intriguing heights: a sassy low top, a dashing medium and a regal high. All in glove-soft Vynarich —the luxurious grained vinyl that's completely waterproof. And all are warm-lined with deep, soft pile. So if you don't mind looking glamorous—slip into Bootinos! Where? Where else but at the finest stores you know.

(CC.) 1963

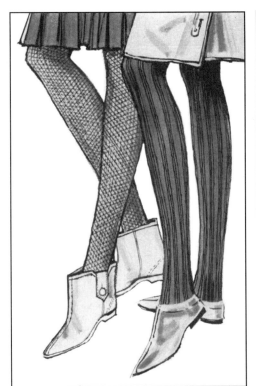

(DD.) 1963

900 FRANCS?

WATERPROOF
BOOTINOS
From B.F.Goodrich

(EE.) 1965

Evins' now-frontier look
in napped Corfam

Feel free...you're in Corfam

(GG.) 1968

(FF.) 1966

The YOU *shoe*

California
COBBLERS

(HH.) 1968

You're about to
fall in love with a heel.

They're more than shoes. They're Hush Puppies

(II.) 1972

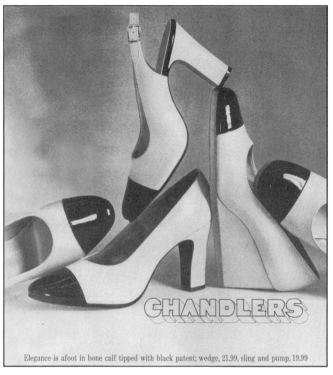

Elegance is afoot in bone calf tipped with black patent; wedge, 21.99, sling and pump, 19.99

(JJ.) 1974

Boot panache
HERBERT LEVINE
footnotes fall fashion with
glove soft knee-high boots—
sets the riding boot on a high
stacked heel—the Russian dancer's
low on a flat.

Neiman-Marcus Dallas · Houston · Fort Worth · Bal Harbour · Atlanta · St. Louis

(KK.) 1974

JACQUES COHEN

Jacques Cohen· Ltd.,   1370 Avenue of the Americas, New York, N.Y. 10019

(LL.) 1977

(MM.) 1978

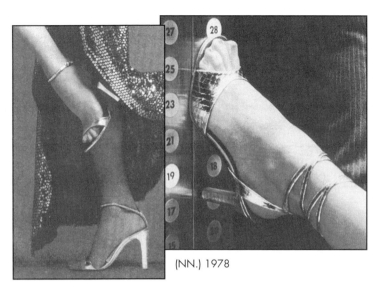

(NN.) 1978

(OO.) 19

SHOW

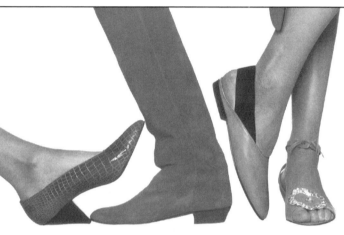

THE WORLD

YOUR SHOES

FROM ITALY

(PP.) 1988

CAPARROS

AVAILABLE AT THE BROADWAY, EMPORIUM, BROADWAY SOUTH WEST

"ABSENCE DOES NOT MAKE THE HEART GROW FONDER, BUT IT SURE HEATS UP THE BLOOD." ELIZABETH ASHLEY.

M BRUNO MAGLI SMART SHOES. SMART STYLE.

the SHOE

The stiletto gives the season its proper perspective

Sleek. Soaring. And streamlined of detail.

(QQ.) 1992

(RR.) 1995

VIA SPIGA VS STUDIO PAOLO
765 Madison Avenue · 212 - 988 - 4877 · Also at Tootsies, Dallas

VIA SPIGA VS STUDIO PAOLO
765 Madison Avenue · 212 - 988 - 4877 · Also at Tootsies, Dallas

(SS.) 1997

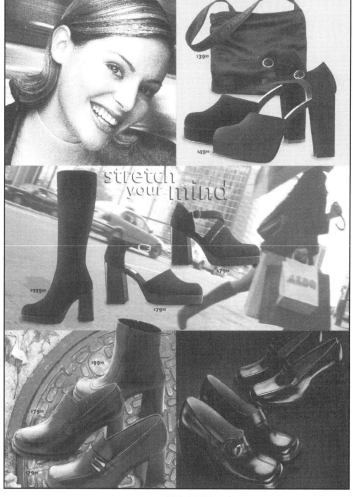

stretch your mind

(TT.) 1997

(A.) 1900

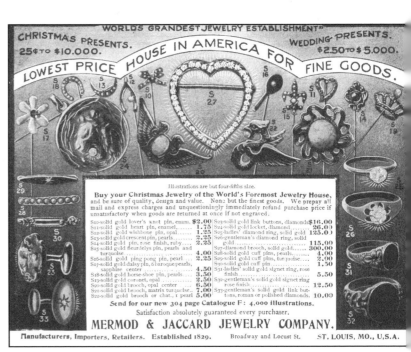

(B.) 1902

Jewelry

Since before the dawn of civilization, women and men have adorned themselves with all sorts of personal ornamentation that served no more function than decoration. Excavations of twenty-five-thousand-year-old Paleolithic sites have yielded finely carved bone pins and drilled stone necklace beads. Over succeeding centuries, civilizations developed distinct artistic styles and motifs that craftsmen applied to the decoration of jewelry. Design elements such as the stylized Egyptian scarab or the straight-nosed profile of Apollo so differentiated jewelry styles of the ancient world that they are recognized and copied even today.

By the beginning of the twentieth century, most all categories of jewelry were being mass produced in America as efficiently as soap or boxed cereal. In fact, retail costs of jewelry were determined more by materials than by design or craftsmanship. For instance, an art nouveau dragonfly brooch could be cast in solid gold with ruby stones affixed into the wings for a retail price of a thousand dollars. The same mold could be used for a white-metal version (alloy of tin, zinc, and other base metals) with cut-glass stones that sold for one dollar.

For the upper-class Edwardian woman, choosing jewelry for her different wardrobe changes was cause for serious thought. Said *Vogue* in 1909, "The well-dressed woman must now decide with especial discrimination what precious stones and metals are particularly appropriate for her several daily costumes." [21] For instance, the editor insisted, silver jewelry should never be worn past noon and diamonds should never be worn before evening. Even beyond the types of stones or metal, women were advised on choosing the correct style of jewelry with equal discrimination. "To wear jewels appropriately is an art by which the mistress of it adds distinction to her costume," avowed a *Vogue* editor in 1914. "Original jewelry must be carefully selected and worn only with certain costumes." [22] It was a question of taste, the editor suggested. For example, a novelty gold Buddha pendant dangling from a chain about one's neck as ornamentation might offend those of Asian nationalities.

Stylistically, American jewelry has had far fewer distinctive modes than those of hats or shoes. Indeed, as mentioned

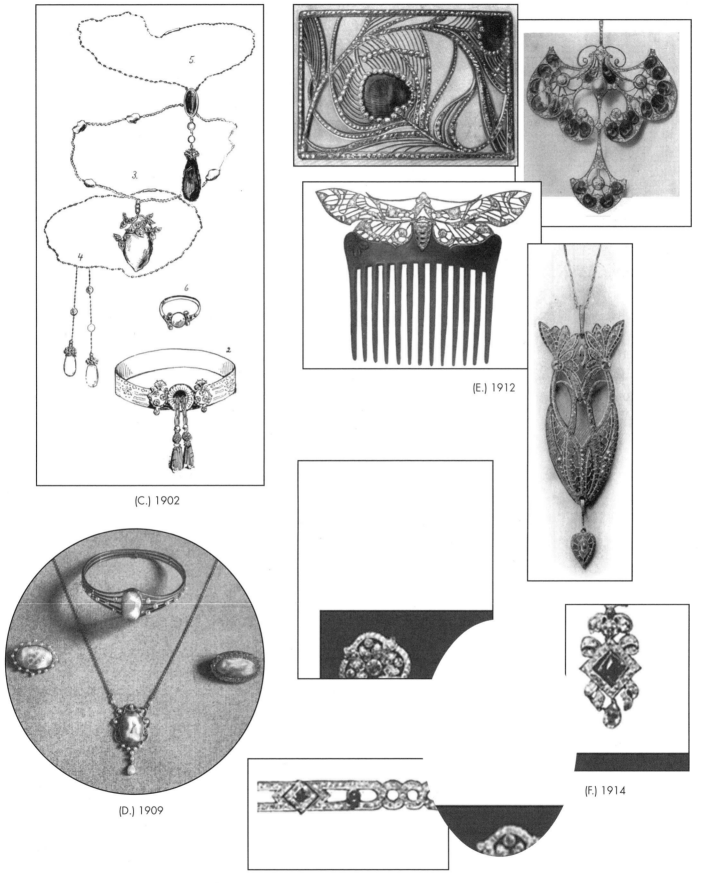

(C.) 1902

(E.) 1912

(D.) 1909

(F.) 1914

(G.) 1924

(H.) 1924

above, some recurring motifs are more than two thousand years old. However, two distinct art movements of the first quarter of the twentieth century particularly translated well into jewelry designs. By 1900 the art nouveau style had dominated everything from architecture and decorative arts to fashion and jewelry for almost a decade. The sinuous, swirling lines and stylized organic elements that characterized art nouveau were easily applied to earrings, bracelets, necklaces, brooches, hat pins, hair combs, and most all other small accessories. The motifs and design elements that distinguished art nouveau would continue to be popular even into the 1910s.

Concurrent with art nouveau designs were the traditional Victorian styles that the more conservative Edwardian ladies preferred. Smaller in scale than art nouveau pieces, the overly busy versions of representational floral and fauna motifs or sentimental hearts and initials remained favorites well into the 1940s.

Soon after World War I, a second significant art movement

began to emerge that would universally influence jewelry design for decades. Inspired by the streamlined, geometric lines of Machine Age technologies coupled with the vivid color palettes of the Cubist and Fauve painters, art deco was born. "The new art in jeweled ornamentation is marked by brilliance in massing of color, a decided avoidance of ostentation and a new note of slenderness," noted *Vogue* in 1921.[23]

In most instances, fashion editorials focused on the designs and makers of fine jewelry or on the social conventions of what jewelry to wear and when. However, in the 1920s Chanel changed all that. With great aplomb she would mix rare gems with an abundance of costume jewelry to wear with most any outfit that suited her at the moment, from casual sportswear to evening gowns. In addition, her salon fashion models were heaped with numerous necklaces and bracelets for their appearance at openings. In 1927 a fashion editor wrote that Chanel's costume jewelry made "no effort to supplant real jewels in elegance, and in this very quality lies their chic."[24]

In addition to rare and important pieces our customers will find a notable collection of gifts suitable for Christmas.

Right : vanity case, diamond, emerald and sapphire jewelry on mother of pearl.

Below : Bracelet with a large emerald, jewelry of round and odd cut diamonds.

MAUBOUSSIN

EXHIBIT NOW IN THEIR ESTABLISHMENT

330. PARK AVENUE. NEW YORK

THE LATEST CREATIONS IN JEWELRY LATELY
RECEIVED FROM THE MAIN BRANCH

1.3. RUE DE CHOISEUL . PARIS

ESTABLISHED IN 1827

(I.) 1927

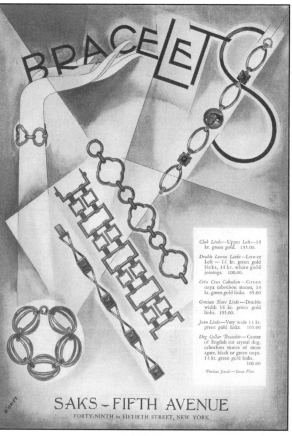

BRACELETS

Club Links—Upper Left—14 kt. green gold. 135.00.

Double Lenoa Links—Lower Left—14 kt. green gold links, 14 kt. white gold joinings. 100.00.

Criss Cross Cabochon—Green onyx cabochon stones, 14 kt. green gold links. 65.00.

Grecian Slave Links—Double width 14 kt. green gold links. 195.00.

Juno Links—Very wide 14 kt. green gold links. 165.00.

Dog Collar Bracelets—Center of English cut crystal dog, cabochon stones of moss agate, black or green onyx. 14 kt. green gold links. 100.00.

Precious Jewels—Street Floor

SAKS – FIFTH AVENUE

FORTY-NINTH to FIFTIETH STREET, NEW YORK

(J.) 1926

OREUM

THE LAST WHISPER IN PARIS NOVELTY JEWELRY

68 CHAUSSÉE D'ANTIN - PARIS

(K.) 1928

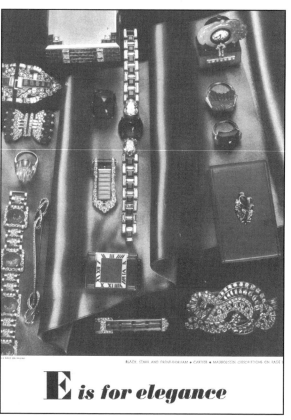

BLACK, STARR AND FROST-GORHAM • CARTIER • MAUBOUSSIN (DESCRIPTIONS ON PAGE

E *is for elegance*

(L.) 1933

(M.) 1934

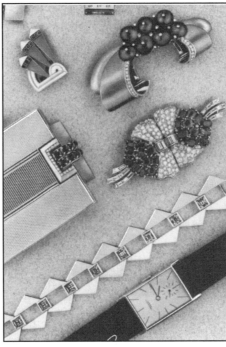

(N.) 1937

(O.) 1937

The art deco style, or moderne as it was commonly called at the time, dominated jewelry designs of the Depression era as well. Instead of glittering, flashy stones—real or costume—moderne jewelry was more simple and pure in form. New types of plastics such as colorful Bakelite were molded in crisp, linear shapes that were fashioned into high-style jewelry for distribution to the cost-conscious masses.

During World War II, jewelry makers were confronted with material shortages yet again. Japanese pearls were no longer imported. The multicolored crystals from Czechoslovakia and Rumania that simulated gemstones were unavailable due to Nazi occupation of those countries. Precious metals needed for the war effort were in short supply, and white-metal production for consumer use was frozen on October 1, 1942. In response to the shortages, *Vogue* suggested that women could readily find "charming and often inexpensive antique pieces" from pawnshops and antiques stores.[25]

When materials were available for jewelry production, makers tried to meet market demands for designs with military emblems or patriotic motifs. And any piece of jewelry with red, white, and blue beads, stones, or enamels was popular.

As the war concluded, costume-jewelry makers resumed their mass-production lines for eager consumers who were swept up in the New Look demand for accessories. "Good costume jewels," noted *Vogue*, "often have the design and workmanship of the real thing."[26] Major production firms such as Trifari and Monet emerged from the war years with national

(P.) 1941

(Q.) 1941

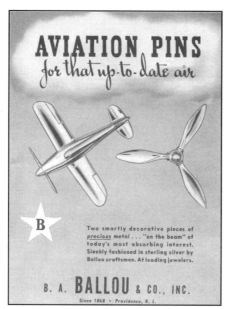

(R.) 1942

(S.) 1943

(T.) 1944

marketing campaigns for their costume jewelry lines, and are still the leading branded manufacturers today. Although the variety of costume jewelry was vast in the New Look era, designs did not reflect any exceptional innovations. At one end of the spectrum were simple strands of beads while at the other end were adaptations of exotic Asian styles, often inspired by Hollywood movies. (Color plates 19 and 20.)

In 1953 Schiaparelli attempted to break the monotonous traditionalism of jewelry styles with two unconventional approaches to wearing earrings. First were her duplex earrings that featured a coordinated set with one clipped onto the top of

the ear at the hairline and the other onto the earlobe. A more startling look was the over-the-ear hoops, which were about the size of wire-thin bracelets and were worn looped over the ears.[27] By and large, though, the most nontraditional look that women of the time would attempt was the revival of the Chanel abundance of costume jewelry, inspired by the designer's return to Paris in 1954. *Vogue* heralded the look of numerous bangle bracelets at the wrist and bold hoop earrings as a "musical accompaniment" to fashion.[28]

In the 1960s, jewelry took a radical departure from the predictable conservatism of the fifties. As a balance to shorter

(U.) 1945

(V.) 1948

(W.) 1951

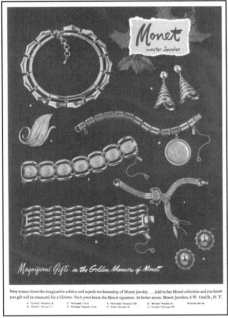

(X.) 1953

(Y.) 1952

(Z.) 1954

and briefer clothing, jewelry became enormous. Earrings became so large that women had to adjust head movements so as to avoid losing the heavy pieces or injuring their ears. Necklaces, bracelets, and rings became massive sculptures. Colors, patterns, and shapes were inspired by the Pop, Op, and Kinetic art movements of the time. (Color plate 24.) Anti-establishment symbols such as the Egyptian ankh, peace sign, doves, and horoscope sunsigns were popular with both women and men. Flower children opted for handmade jewelry

of braided leather or brightly colored yarns, accented with beads and feathers. Fashion jewelry for men even extended to mass-produced beaded necklaces for their Nehru-collar jackets or puka-shell chokers for the beach.

In the 1970s, art deco jewelry became immensely popular again. "At the same time that authentic Art Deco is being collected, it is also becoming a big influence on current costume jewelry, often with beautiful results," observed *Vogue* in 1972.[29] Art deco jewelry pieces were smaller, lighter, and

(AA.) 1956

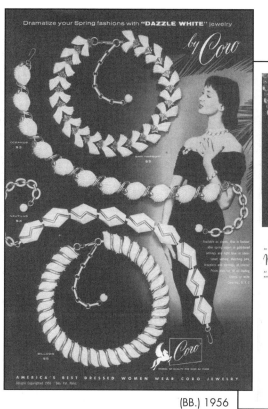

(BB.) 1956

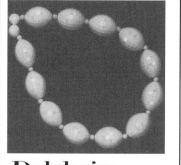

Dalsheim
high fashion faceted ovals

High-polished
lucite jewels . . .
light as the
proverbial feather . . .
in the beautiful
new spring and
summer shades of
white, coral, turquoise,
yellow, blue and pink.
Necklace, bracelet,
earrings, each $2*

*plus tax

at fine stores everywhere, or write:
DALSHEIM ACCESSORIES, Inc., 389 Fifth Ave., New York City

(CC.) 1956

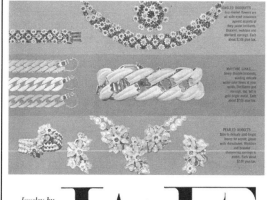

Jewelry by **LERU** *the luxury look*

originated by america's foremost craftsmen   available at fine stores everywhere

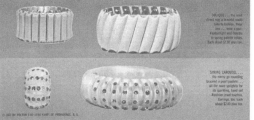

(DD.) 1957

(EE.) 1961

ICE EXOTIQUE!
Great fashion gesture
of the splendid Orientale:
Tidal pearl necklace with
jewelled clasp $22.00.
Pins from $8.50 to $13.50.
Earrings $11.00...others from $6.50.
Adjustable ring $9.00.

Eisenberg Ice

Eisenberg Jewelry, 22 West Madison Street, Chicago
14 East 38th Street, New York
Authentic only when trademarked Eisenberg • Eisenberg Designs Copyrighted
Costume by Burke-Amey

(FF.) 1965

(GG.) 1966

Trifari
unveils
JEWELS OF INDIA

DIANE LOVE for TRIFARI

(II.) 1972

From Our New Collection

Diamond and eighteen karat gold jewelry: A *Earrings,* $625.
B *Pins, may be worn singly or as a pair,* $1,375. *each pin.* C *Pin,* $1,600.
D *Ring,* $795. E *Bracelet,* $1,275. *Bangle bracelets:* F $1,000. G $1,200.
Of polished eighteen karat gold: H $495. I $550. **TIFFANY & CO.**

NEW YORK FIFTH AVE. AND 57TH ST.

ATLANTA PHIPPS PLAZA · CHICAGO 715 NORTH MICHIGAN AVE. · HOUSTON THE HOUSTON GALLERIA · SAN FRANCISCO 252 GRANT AVE. · BEVERLY HILLS 9502 WILSHIRE BLVD.

American Express · BankAmericard

(JJ.) 1972

Medieval belt and pendant crafted by

ACCESSOCRAFT

389 Fifth Avenue, New York, N.Y. 10016
Bloomingdale's, Burdine's, Marshall Field, I. Magnin Co.

(HH.) 1971

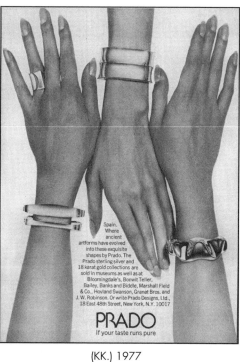

Spain. Where ancient artforms have evolved into these exquisite shapes by Prado. The Prado sterling silver and 18 karat gold collections are sold in museums as well as at Bloomingdale's, Bonwit Teller, Bailey, Banks and Biddle, Marshall Field & Co., Hovland Swanson, Granat Bros. and J. W. Robinson. Or write Prado Designs, Ltd., 18 East 48th Street, New York, N.Y. 10017

PRADO
If your taste runs pure

(KK.) 1977

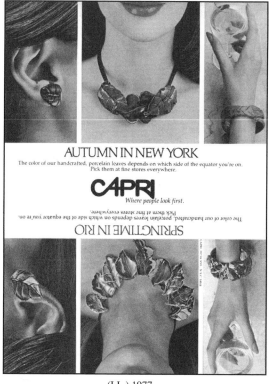

AUTUMN IN NEW YORK

The color of our handcrafted, porcelain leaves depends on which side of the equator you're on.
Pick them at fine stores everywhere.

CAPRI
Where people look first.

(LL.) 1977

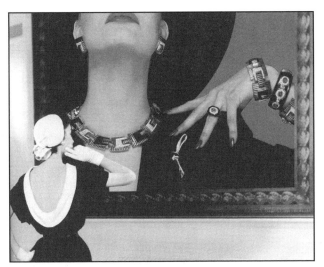

(MM.) 1986

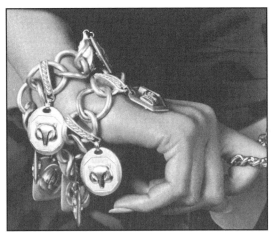

(NN.) 1986

(OO.) 1988

(PP.) 1997

more versatile than the mod styles of a few years earlier. In addition, the familiar styles and motifs of art deco jewelry became so popular in part because of a wave of nostalgia in America following the tumult of the sixties.

Jewelry styles of the seventies were also influenced by two major cultural events. First was President Richard Nixon's trip to China in 1973. Almost immediately Asian motifs, symbols, and imagery became all the rage in everything from home decorative accessories to fashion. Jewelry made of jade, lacquer, and carved cinnabar offered a fresh departure from traditional Western styles. Inexpensive simulations were mass produced and broadly distributed even to discount retailers. The second cultural event that influenced jewelry design was the year-long celebration of America's bicentennial in 1976. Red, white, and blue were the fashion colors of the season. Jewelry makers responded with the primary colors on everything. Designs of flags, stars, and other patriotic motifs were created in the full range of traditional to interpretive variations. Even styles that had been produced during the World Wars were reintroduced in keeping with the nation's sense of history and nostalgia.

The seventies closed with the disco craze. Ironically, instead of shimmering, glittering jewelry becoming a must-have for disco divas, accessories were kept to a minimum to avoid interference with the dance gyrations of the hustle or the bump. One of the enduring images of jewelry from the disco era is that of the heavy gold chains worn by men to focus attention on hairy chests or well-developed pecs.

During the last two decades of the century, jewelry designs followed the conservative, traditional paths reminiscent of the fifties. Simplicity was the hallmark for jewelry adornment by

First Lady Nancy Reagan. First Lady Barbara Bush inspired a renewed interest in oversized bead necklaces like those worn by TV moms of the 1950s. First Lady Hillary Clinton continued the trend of understated elegance with her favorite pearl earrings and necklaces.

Mass-production jewelry makers recycled period designs to keep pace with the many ready-to-wear revivals. In addition, logos moved from inside garments to the outside and eventually onto accessories. The Anne Klein lion's head, the Chanel tête bêche C's, and the horseshoe A of Etienne Aigner are but a few examples of logos that appeared in numerous variations of costume jewelry.

In the early nineties, the youth look called grunge revived body piercing from the 1970s punk movement. Silver studs were inserted through tongues, lips, and noses; hoops pierced navels, eyebrows, and the entire edge of the ear from top to lobe. Even more mainstream consumers opted for multiple pierced earrings, which would be worn in combinations of hoops and studs or tiered hoops.

Conclusion

Accessories have always provided a woman with the greatest opportunity for individuality and self-expression even within the confines of fashion dictates and social etiquette. Across the decades she may have been compelled to don the S-bend dress, the dropped-waist chemise, the wartime utility suit, the mod miniskirt, or the broad-shouldered power suit, but she had far wider choices of hats, shoes, and jewelry. For instance, many Edwardian women preferred the narrow toque to the more fashionable, yard-wide spread of a mushroom-cap hat; tall women of the fifties eschewed stiletto heels despite the New Look; and not all yuppies of the 1980s opted for the exhibitionism of oversized gold and gemstone jewelry.

The technologies of mass production that developed in the nineteenth century became refined and efficient enough to expand beyond standardized commodity clothing and include hats, shoes, and jewelry. Manufacturers of these products kept a finger on the pulse of fashion and could quickly supply the styles consumers demanded for trends of the day. For example, the elements that defined key design movements such as art nouveau and art deco were easily adapted to mass-produced accessories. Accessory makers were also on the cutting edge of experimentation with new materials like plastics in the thirties, nylon and other synthetics in the forties and fifties, and techno materials in the nineties.

Advertising not only created product and brand awareness for accessory manufacturers, but also provided their customers with style guides to how to wear their products—Depression-era hats cocked to the side or headwear of the Second World War angled forward onto the brow; shoes with spats in 1922 but without in 1924; glittering art deco jewelry for the Jazz Age but simplified moderne looks in plastic a decade later.

In tandem, fashion style, mass production, and advertising broadened the market for accessory makers and provided women with multiple options to feel fashionable and to express their individuality with the personality of a hat, the distinction of a shoe style or color, or the personal adornment of jewelry.

NOTES

PREFACE

1. Edna Woolman Chase, "Best-dressed Women and Why," *Vogue*, February 1, 1938, 145.
2. Caroline Milbank, *New York Fashion* (New York: Harry N. Abrams, 1996), 172.
3. Jane Mulvagh, *Vogue: History of Twentieth Century Fashion* (London: Viking, 1988), 181.

CHAPTER 1

1. Amy Janello and Brennon Jones, *The American Magazine* (New York: Harry N. Abrams, 1991), 12.
2. Patricia Kery, *Great Magazine Covers of the World* (New York: Abbeville, 1982), 24.
3. Magazine Publishers of America ad: *Adweek*, October 20, 1997, 43.
4. Ann Marie Kerwin, "Recast Seven Sisters Still Seek Points of Difference," *Advertising Age*, April 6, 1998, 10.
5. Anon., "Fashions for August," *Harper's New Monthly Magazine*, August 1864, 415–416; Charles Dickens, "Our Mutual Friend," ibid., 380–98; William Thackeray, "Denis Duval," ibid., 358–71; Anon., "The Lost Lamb," ibid., 408; Anon., "Editor's Drawer," ibid., 409–14; W. Winwood Reade, "A Club Man in Africa," ibid., 281–92; Anon., "The Military Hospitals at Fortress Monroe," ibid., 306–22; Anon.,"Treatment of the Apparently Drowned," ibid., 377–79.
6. The second *a* was added to the title in 1929.
7. Sarah Hale, "Editor's Table," *Godey's Lady's Book*, April 1849, 296.
8. Ibid., January 1849, 64.
9. Jessica Daves, *Ready-Made Miracle* (New York: G. P. Putnam's Sons, 1967), 168.
10. Emmeline Raymond, "House-work," *Harper's Bazar*, September 6, 1879, 566.
11. Anon., "New York Fashions," *Harper's Bazar*, September 18, 1869, 595.
12. Jenny Croly, "The Fashions," *Godey's Lady's Book*, December 1888, 501.
13. Anon., "New York Fashions; Ready Made Costumes," *Harper's Bazar*, June 12, 1875, 379.
14. Ibid.
15. Paul Nystrom, *Economics of Fashion* (New York: Ronald, 1928), 38–43.
16. Ibid., 55–83.
17. Frank Rowsome, *They Laughed When I Sat Down* (New York: Bonanza, 1959), 23.
18. Richard Ohmann, *Selling Culture* (London: Verso, 1996), 25.
19. *Vogue* ad: *Cosmopolitan*, February 1893, 19.
20. *Vogue* ad: *Life*, December 29, 1898, 557.
21. Caroline Seebohm, *The Man Who Was Vogue* (New York: Viking, 1982), 33.
22. Josephine Redding, "Vogue's Weekly Pattern," *Vogue,* July 20, 1899, 48.
23. Ibid., "Business Notices," November 16, 1899, ii.
24. Charles Zingg, "'Vogue,' the Fashion Journal," *Printers' Ink*, October 19, 1904, 16.
25. Ibid., 15, 17.
26. *Vogue* ad: *Vogue,* February 5, 1903, 184.
27. Seebohm, 31, 38.
28. Chase, "Fifty Years of Vogue," *Vogue,* November 15, 1943, 109.
29. Marie Harrison, "Noblesse Oblige," *Vogue,* March 15, 1911, 68.
30. Ibid., "S and X," 13.
31. Seebohm, 79.
32. Ibid., 76.
33. Ibid., 90.

CHAPTER 2

1. Mark Sullivan, *Our Times: The United States 1900–1925* (New York: Charles Scribner's Sons, 1927), 26.
2. Nystrom, 16.
3. George Napheys, *Physical Life of Woman* (Philadelphia: George MacClean, 1870), 281.
4. Elizabeth Ewing, *History of Twentieth Century Fashion* (New York: Charles Scribner's Sons, 1974), 9.
5. Aube de Siecle, "Paris," *Vogue,* February 13, 1902, 128.
6. Ibid., July 10, 1902, 58.
7. Ibid., 39, 58.
8. Ewing, *History of Twentieth Century Fashion,* 6.
9. Susan Meyer, *America's Great Illustrators* (New York: Galahad, 1987), 211.
10. Marie Harrison, "Vogue's Weekly Pattern," *Vogue,* October 25, 1900, 272.
11. Ibid., "Paris," October 17, 1907, 538.
12. Ibid., "What She Wears," December 17, 1908, 1028.
13. Ibid., "Afternoon Gowning at the Horse Show," November 27, 1909, 903.
14. Ibid., "What She Wears," October 2, 1909, 500.
15. Edward Bok, "What Paris Says Will Be Correct," *Ladies' Home Journal,* September 15, 1910, 3.
16. Lou Eleanor Colby, "The Color Question in Clothes," *Ladies' Home Journal,* September 15, 1910, 22.
17. Anna Westermann, "Can America Originate Its Own Fashions?" *Ladies' Home Journal,* September 1909, 11, 81.
18. Bok, "The Editor's Personal Page," *Ladies' Home Journal,* January 1910, 1.
19. Nystrom, 181.
20. Chase, "The Paris Openings," September 15, 1914, 27–29.
21. Emily Post, "Where Fashionables and Fashion Met," December 1, 1914, 37.
22. Chase, "Paris in the Busyness of Midseason," February 1, 1915, 22.
23. Ibid., "Paris Plays Patience," June 15, 1915, 26.
24. Ibid., "Costumes," September 1, 1918, 62.
25. Betty Wales ad: *Vogue,* September 1, 1918, 9.
26. "Appropriate attire," Star Skirt ad: *Vogue,* November 1, 1918, 102; "The

most beautiful," Pelgram and Myer ad: September 1, 1918, *Vogue,* 110; "Authorized," John Wanamaker ad: *Vogue,* October 15, 1918, 7; "War conservation," John Wanamaker ad:*Vogue,* April 15, 1918, 7. 27.Finck ad: *Literary Digest*, October 12, 1918, 77.

CHAPTER 3

1. John Irving Romer, "President Coolidge Pays Advertising Its Highest Tribute," *Printers' Ink*, November 4, 1926, 196.
2. Chase, "Chanel Attains Chic by Avoiding Extremes," October 15, 1921, 42.
3. Ibid., "The Parisienne Covers Her Frock with Glory," April 15, 1920, 74.
4. Ibid., "Frocks for the Better Half of a Paris Day," 142.
5. Ibid., 59.
6. Ibid., "The Spring Mode Adds Glories to Paris Nights," 62.
7. Ibid., 63.
8. Ibid., "Paris Issues Its Ultimatum for Winter," October 15, 1921, 36.
9. Ibid., "A Summary of the New Mode," 110.
10. Ibid., "What Smart New York Women Consider Chic," July 15, 1923, 50–51.
11. Nystrom, 388.
12. Ibid., "The Problem of the Straight Silhouette: Fitting the Flat Back to the Full Figure," November 15, 1923, 128.
13. Ibid., "Paris Holds the Mirror Up to Fashion," April 15, 1924, 48.
14. Bruce Bliven, "Flapper Jane," *New Republic*, September 9, 1925, 65.
15. Georgina Howell, *In Vogue: Seventy-five Years of Style* (London: Condé Nast, 1991), 16.
16. Malcolm Keir, "Women in Industry," in *Men's Ideas/Women's Realities*, ed. Louise Michele Newman (New York: Pergamon, 1985), 292.
17. Nystrom, 405.
18. Daves, 43.
19. Charles Zingg, "The Siegel-Cooper Company," *Printers' Ink*, September 7, 1904, 10; "A Store for Women Advertised by a Woman," ibid, 14–15; "New York's Newest Store," ibid, 19.
20. Chase, "The Amazing Tale of the New York Shops," May 1, 1926, 62.
21. Ibid., "Seen in the Shops," April 15, 1920, 94.
22. Edward Underwood, "Eighteen—the Most Dangerous Age for Girls," *Physical Culture*, December 1928, 119.
23. Patricia Warner, "Clothing as a Barrier: American Women in the Olympics 1900–1920," *Dress*, 1997, 61.
24. Chase, "Paris Holds the Mirror Up to Fashion," *Vogue,* April 15, 1924, 118.
25. Ibid., "Correct Clothes for the Country," October 1, 1921, 74.
26. Philip Kennedy, "Foreign Exports—Quantities and Values," in *Statistical Abstract of the United States, 1919* (Washington, D.C.: Government Printing Office, 1920), 508; O. P. Hopkins, "Exports of United States Merchandise by Commodity Group and Articles," in *Statistical Abstract of the United States, 1929* (Washington, D.C.: Government Printing Office, 1929), 516.
27. Chase, "The Grandes Maisons Take a Sporting Chance," May 15, 1922, 38.
28. Ibid., "Paris Holds the Mirror Up to Fashion," April 15, 1924, 118.
29. Mulvagh, *Vogue: History of Twentieth Century Fashion*, 52.
30. Bliven, 65.
31. Alastair Duncan, *Art Deco* (London: Thames and Hudson, 1988), 8.
32. Nystrom, 185.
33. Dan Klein, *All Colour Book of Art Deco* (London: Octopus, 1974), 4.
34. Nystrom, 185–86.
35. Chase, "The Modernistic Influence Spreads over French Wall-Papers,"

May 1, 1926, 90; "Imported Fabrics Use Modern Designs and Colourings," ibid., 91.
36. Ibid., "Vogue's-Eye View of the Mode," September 14, 1929, 75.
37. Romer, "Anent Women's Styles," *Printers' Ink*, November 7, 1929, 211.
38. Milbank, 98; Mulvagh, *Vogue: History of Twentieth Century Fashion*, 89.
39. Chase, "Whispers to a Girl with Nothing a Year," May 10, 1930, 95.
40. Ibid., "Chic," May 10, 1930, 87; "Practicality by Day," 90; "Unlimited Smartness," 89; "Accessories," 94; "Wise Economy," 92.
41. Frederick Lewis Allen, *Only Yesterday* (New York: Harper and Brothers, 1931), 348.
42. Chase, "Vogue's-Eye View of the Mode," February 15, 1930, 57.
43. Ibid., "Black Steps to the Front," October 1, 1933, 27.
44. Ibid., "Follies of 1932," August 1, 1932, 43, 65.
45. Ibid., "Vogue's Eye View of the Mode," June 1, 1933, 23.
46. Ibid., "Those Silly Hats from Paris," June 1, 1933, 50.
47. Ibid., "Shoulders Have a Special Interest," September 1, 1932, 77.
48. Mulvagh, *Vogue: History of Twentieth Century Fashion*, 123.
49. Margit Mayer, "Hollywood Sets the Trends," in *Icons of Fashion of the Twentieth Century*, ed. Gerda Buxbaum (Munich: Prestel Verlag, 1999), 54.
50. Judith Cameron, *The Art of Gone with the Wind* (New York: Prentice Hall, 1989), 160; Gerald and Harriet Gardner, *PictorialHistory of Gone with the Wind* (New York: Bonanza, 1983), 111.
51. Daves, 112.
52. Chase, "What about Pants? Where? When?" June 15, 1936, 39.
53. Ibid., "Slacks and Skirts for Country Living," April 15, 1939, 51.
54. Ibid., "New York Couture," April 15, 1933, 33.
55. Ibid., "Best Dressed Women—and Why," February 1, 1938, 87.
56. Ibid., "New York Couture," April 15, 1933, 34.
57. Ibid., 96.
58. Ibid.
59. Ibid.
60. Ibid.
61. Ibid.
62. Ibid.
63. Ibid.
64. Ibid., 34.
65. Ibid., 96.
66. Ibid., "Best Dressed Women—and Why," February 1, 1938, 87.
67. Ibid., "Vogue's-Eye View of the World of Tomorrow," February 1, 1939, 59.
68. Ibid., "Hoop Skirts to Hobble Skirts at the Paris Openings," September 1, 1939, 45.
69. Ibid., "These Are the Key Silhouettes in Paris; These Are the New Corsets to Build Them," September 1, 1939, 62–63.
70. Ibid., "What America Imported from the Paris Openings," October 1, 1939, 51.
71. Ibid.

CHAPTER 4

1. Elsa Schiaparelli, "Needles and Guns," *Vogue,* September 1, 1940, 57.
2. Ibid.
3. Thomas Bailey, *The American Pageant* 4th ed. (Lexington, Mass.: D. C. Heath, 1971), 906.
4. Chase, "Paris Presents: Narrower and Narrower Silhouettes for Day," March 15, 1940, 53.
5. Ibid., "Paris Presents: Prints America Loves," March 15, 1940, 69.
6. Ibid., "Vogue's-Eye View of Paris Collection in War-Time," March 1, 1940, 49.

7. Schiaparelli, 57.

8. Seebohm, 349.

9. Chase, "American Collections," September 1, 1940, p. 49.

10. Wilhela Cushman, "New York Fall Collections," *Ladies' Home Journal,* November 1940, 21.

11. Henry Luce, ed., "American Designers," *Life,* May 8, 1944, 63.

12. Ibid., "New Styles from Paris and New York," August 16, 1943, 42.

13. Milbank, 165.

14. Luce, "American Designers," 66.

15. Daves, 118.

16. Dale McConathy, "Mainbocher," in *American Fashion,* ed. Sarah Tomerlin Lee (New York: Fashion Institute of Technology, 1975), 128.

17. Chase, "Fashion in America Now," February 1, 1942, 50.

18. Ibid., 123.

19. Ibid., "It Narrows Down to This," September 1, 1943, 75.

20. Ibid., "Shoe-String Silhouette," February 1, 1943, 58.

21. Mulvagh, *Vogue: History of Twentieth Century Fashion,* 169.

22. Chase, "Paris Fashions," October 15, 1944, 100.

23. Ibid., "Basques, Buckrum, Sleeve-Business," September 1, 1945, 122.

24. Ibid., "Paris Collections, Autumn 1945," October 15, 1945, 99.

25. Howell, 113.

26. Chase, "People Are Talking About . . . in Fashion," November 1, 1947, 145.

27. Ibid., "The Half Century," January 1950, 93.

28. Ibid., "Fashion Changes," September 1, 1947, 169.

29. Ibid., 188.

30. Howell, 113.

31. William Chafe, *The Paradox of Change: American Women in the Twentieth Century* (New York: Oxford University Press, 1991), 187.

32. Carol Hymowitz and Michaele Weissman, "Don't Steal a Job from a Man," in *A History of Women in America* (New York: Bantam, 1978), 313–14.

33. Jensen, Oliver, *The Revolt of American Women* (New York: Harcourt Brace, 1952), 114.

34. Frances Ilg, "The Three 'I's' of Parenthood," *Vogue,* August 1, 1950, 75; Victoria Ferguson, "A Child's Reputation," *Vogue,* March 1, 1950, 185; Nancy Ross, "The Fine Art of Being a Stepmother," *Vogue,* April 15, 1950, 74; Jessica Daves, ed., "Wonderful 'Average' Woman," *Vogue,* March 15, 1950, 125.

35. Daves, "Vogue's Eye View, 1954: A Different Kind of Woman," January 1954, 89.

36. Betty Friedan, *The Feminine Mystique,* rev. ed. (New York: Laurel), 18.

37. Cecil Beaton, "Audrey Hepburn," *Vogue,* November 1, 1954, 129.

38. Chase, "New Fashions Chosen with a Man in Mind," March 1, 1948, front cover, 181–82.

39. Anne Fogarty, *Wife Dressing* (New York: Julian Messner, 1959), 10, 160.

40. Peter Jennings and Todd Brewster, "Mass Markets, 1953–1961," in *The Century* (New York: Doubleday, 1998), 326.

41. Chase, "1950 Body Line," January 1950, 114.

42. Ibid., "Paris Tendencies," March 1, 1950, 124.

43. Ibid., "There Goes an American," February 1, 1950, 126.

44. Milbank, 175.

45. Mulvagh, *Vogue: History of Twentieth Century Fashion,* 187.

46. Daves, "The Position of the Waistline in America," *Vogue,* February 1, 1952, 163. (Column from the *New Yorker,* September 22, 1951, reproduced in *Vogue.*)

47. Ibid., "The Middy-Line Dress," February 1, 1952, 165.

48. Ibid., "Italy, Collections Bubbling with Ideas," March 15, 1953, 76.

49. Geigy Chemical ad (Lyle and Scott sweater): *Vogue,* November 15, 1954, 61.

50. Valerie Steele, *Fifty Years of Fashion: New Look to Now* (New Haven, Conn.: Yale University Press, 1997), 28.

51. Daves, "Chanel Changes—in Perennial Chanel Red," *Vogue,* January 1955, 118.

52. Daves, "The Tunic Smock," September 1, 1958, 191.

53. Ibid., "Summer Uniform, 90 Days on a Trapeze," June 1958, 73.

CHAPTER 5

1. Daves, "Beige, What Makes It Go like '60," January 1, 1960, 116.

2. Ibid., "Mrs. Kennedy's New Evening Choices," February 1, 1961, 137.

3. Ibid., "Vogue's Eye View of a Look," August 1, 1961, 55.

4. Ewing, *History of Twentieth Century Fashion,* 179.

5. Daves, "U.S. Sun-Flash—Short Wave from Australia," January 1961, 120–21.

6. Mulvagh, *Vogue: History of Twentieth Century Fashion,* 263.

7. Daves, "The Special Beat of American Clothes," February 1, 1963, 101.

8. Ibid., "Balenciaga," October 15, 1963, 70.

9. Diana Vreeland, ed., "From Britain: the Dash of Bold Bright Tweeds in Narrow Coats, Spanking Suits," *Vogue,* September 15, 1964, 162.

10. Ibid., "Disc-erino Dressing," August 1, 1964, 70.

11. Ibid., "The Fashion for Pants at Night," June 1964, 114.

12. Ibid., "Givenchy/Hepburn," November 1, 1964, 147.

13. Ibid., "Cardin, the Bias Idea," April 15, 1965, 97.

14. Ibid., "Vogue's Eye View: The Body Bulletin," April 1, 1965, 113.

15. Ibid., "Sheherazaderie," April 15, 1965, 101.

16. Kurt Von Meier, "Love, Mysticism, and the Hippies," *Vogue,* November 15, 1967, 85.

17. Steele, 79.

18. Vreeland, "Vogue's Eye View," March 15, 1970, 41.

19. Ibid., "You . . . the Girl for Shorts," June 1971, 124.

20. Mirabella, "The American Look," *Vogue,* September 1975, 228.

21. Ibid., "Big Time," September 1975, 245.

22. Eric Levin, "If Looks Could Kill," *People, Special Collector's Edition,* 2000, 114.

23. Mirabella, "The American Look," September 1975, 228.

24. Ibid., "Paris Looks," January 1976, 74.

25. Ibid., "Fashion Now," October 1976, 205.

26. Ibid., 207.

27. Levin, 117.

28. Mirabella, "Disco Style," February 1978, 188–91.

CHAPTER 6

1. Mulvagh, *Vogue: History of Twentieth Century Fashion,* 347.

2. Mirabella, "Fashion: The New Options," January 1980, 120.

3. Blythe Babyak, "Trade-Offs, the Deals You Make with Life," *Vogue,* January 1980, 126.

4. Mirabella, "Vogue's View, Dressing Up for Working Out," April 1982, 255.

5. Ibid., "Day In and Day Out, the Looks That Work for You," September 1980, 487.

6. Evan-Picone ad: *Vogue,* September 1981, 152; Crickateer ad: ibid., 480; Austin Hill ad: ibid., 336; David Hayes ad: ibid., 81.

7. Joan Juliet Buck, "Italian Spirit," *Vogue,* October 1981, 297.

8. Mirabella, "The Names," October 1981, 329–33.

9. Anne Rice, "Bowie," *Vogue,* November 1983, 434.

10. Mirabella, "Fall '85, the Season Takes Shape," September 1985, 611.

11. Ibid., "Vogue's View," March 1987, 388–90.

12. Anna Wintour, ed., "How the West Is Worn," *Vogue,* March 1989, 113.

13. Cynthia Heimel, "Why the Bust Boom Now?" *Vogue,* March 1989, 520.

14. Polly Mellen, "Beauty and the Breast," *Vogue,* March 1989, 518.

15. Wintour, "Vogue Point of View," January 1990, 145.

16. Grace Coddington, "Predictions 1990," *Vogue,* January 1990, 148.

17. Katherine Betts, "The Best and Worst Looks of the '90s," *Vogue,* January 1996, 124.

18. Jane Kramer, "The Chanel Obsession," *Vogue,* September 1991, 515–18.

19. Jenny Capitain, "The New Short Story," *Vogue,* April 1990, 354–56.

20. Melissa Richards, "Anti-Fashion and Punk Couture," in *Key Moments in Fashion: The Evolution of Style,* ed. Mike Evans (London: Octopus, 1999), 150.

21. Suzy Menkes, "The Couture Controversy," *Vogue,* October 1991, 263.

22. Shirley Lord, "Images," *Vogue,* September 1990, 311.

23. Coddington, "Predictions 1990," January 1990, 150.

24. Betts, "The Best and Worst Looks of the '90s," January 1996, 120.

25. Coddington, "Wild at Heart," *Vogue,* September 1991, 485.

26. Ibid., "Grunge and Glory," December 1992, 260.

27. Betts, "The Best and Worst Looks of the '90s," 126.

28. Janet Siroto, "Future Chic," *Vogue,* March 1994, 164.

29. Betts, "Fashion's New Woman: Strong and Sexy," May 1994, 235.

30. Laurie Schechter, "View," *Vogue,* November 1990, 121; Herbert Muschamp, "Now and Then," *Vogue,* January 1991, 186; Katherine Betts, "Paris Couture, Time for Change," *Vogue,* October 1992, 271; Katherine Betts, "Vogue's View," *Vogue,* July 1993, 47; Andre Leon Talley, The Couture Journals," *Vogue,* March 1994, 356; Katherine Betts, "Vogue's View," *Vogue,* January 1995, 53.

31. Camilla Nickerson, "The Übermodels," *Vogue,* November 1999, 434.

32. Betts, "The Best and Worst Looks of the '90s," 120.

33. Betts, "Vogue's View, Fall '95: the Uptown Aesthetic," July 1995, 45.

34. Coddington, "Summing Up the '90s," July 1998, 85.

35. Betts, "Vogue's View," March 1995, 202.

CHAPTER 7

1. Anne Hollander, *Seeing through Clothes,* rev. ed. (New York: Avon, 1980), 133.

2. Lisa Lockwood, "Calvin Klein Withdraws Controversial Ad Campaign," *Women's Wear Daily,* August 29, 1995, 2.

3. Napheys, 280–81.

4. Havelock Ellis, *Man and Woman* (Boston: Houghton Mifflin, 1929), 56.

5. C. M. Harrison, "Quit Corsets? Flappers' Ban Brings New Kind of Advertising," *Printers' Ink,* April 27, 1922, 86.

6. Chase, "The New Corsets Are Straight and Supple," August 15, 1917, 61.

7. Lyra ad: *Vogue,* March 15, 1912, 107.

8. Chase, "The Importance of Being Correctly Corseted," February 1, 1918, 63.

9. Harrison, 85.

10. Jackson ad: *Vogue,* November 1, 1921, 116; N. Practical Front ad: *Vogue,* November 15, 1922, 112; N. Practical Front ad: *Vogue,* March 15, 1923, 28; C/B ad: *Vogue,* February 1, 1924, 104.

11. Chase, "The Straight and Narrow Way," February 15, 1925, 100.

12. Ibid., "New Facts in Figures," June 15, 1933, 53.

13. Ibid., "Summer Weights," June 15, 1937, 70.

14. Cupform ad: *Vogue,* May 1, 1931, 113; Vassarette ad: *Vogue,* May 15, 1937, 114.

15. Chase, "Corsets Still Stretch," March 1, 1943, 70.

16. Ibid., "Foundations of the New Line," February 15, 1948, 125.

17. Christina Probert, *Lingerie in Vogue since 1910* (New York: Abbeville, 1981), 54.

18. Daves, "Plotting the Quick Curve," April 15, 1952, 105.

19. Elizabeth Ewing, *Dress and Undress* (New York: Drama, 1978), 173.

20. Charles Panati, *Panati's Extraordinary Origins of Everyday Things,* rev. ed. (New York: Perennial Library, 1989), 341.

21. G. M. Poix ad: *Vogue,* January 15, 1928, 131.

22. Model Brassiere ad: *Vogue,* May 1, 1931, 113.

23. Alene Bra ad: *Vogue,* February 15, 1948, 60.

24. Melissa Richards, "The Birth of the Bra," in *Key Moments in Fashion,* ed. Mike Evans (London: Octopus, 1999), 25.

25. Maidenform ad: *Vogue,* March 1995, 197.

26. Hollander, 132.

27. Chase, "The Narrow Way," February 15, 1925, 108.

28. Ibid., "Vogue's-Eye View of the Mode," April 15, 1926, 79.

29. Ibid.,"New Facts in Figure," June 15, 1933, 53.

30. Vanity Fair ad: October 1, 1935, 26.

31. Chase, "Seen in the Shops," June 1, 1915, 57.

32. Ibid., "In the Name of Neptune," June 1, 1917, 92.

33. Jantzen ad: *Vogue,* June 22, 1929, 15.

34. Ralph Andrist, ed., *The American Heritage History of the 1920s and 1930s* (New York: Bonanza, 1987), 63.

35. Chase, "Seen in the Shops," June 1, 1922, 77.

36. Chase, "Wet or Dry," July 1, 1932, 36.

37. Daves, "Covered: The 1954 Bathing Suit," May 1, 1954, 107.

38. Lauren DuPont, "Last Look," *Vogue,* May 1999, 342.

CHAPTER 8

1. Harrison, "What She Wears," September 19, 1907, 330.

2. Ibid., "Curious Coincidences of Hat Styles," August 19, 1909, 205.

3. Chase, "The Hats That Bloom in Paris," February 15, 1918, 27.

4. Ibid., "Ribbons and Feathers Appear in High Places," March 1, 1922, 35.

5. Ibid., "Bonnets, Berets, Brims," *Vogue,* August 15, 1933, 33.

6. Ibid., "Down in Front and Up at the Side or Back," September 15, 1932, 58.

7. Ibid., "Schiaparelli's New Silhouette," September 1, 1935, 65.

8. Ibid., "Paris Openings," September 1, 1938, 55.

9. Ibid., "Hat Story—Success Story," November 1, 1939, 50.

10. Ibid., "Under Your Hat," January 1, 1941, 38

11. Ibid., "Hat and Silhouette," March 1, 1948, 213.

12. M. S. Karl ad: *Vogue,* December 25, 1895, xiii.

13. Redding, "Shoes," June 17, 1897, vi.

14. Chase, "Spring Puts Its Best Footwear Forward," April 15, 1918, 60.

15. Ibid., "The Chic American Shoe," April 15, 1924, 57.

16. Ibid., "Figures in the News," December 1, 1937, 87.

17. Ibid., "In Good Standing," July 1, 1943, 60–61.

18. Ibid., "The Shoe the Key," March 1, 1948, 189.

19. Chandler's ad: *Vogue,* September 1, 1968, 209.

20. Mirabella, "Vogue Observations," August 1, 1972, 35.

21. Harrison, "Smart Fads in Jewelry," October 30, 1909, 731.

22. Chase, "Within the Jewel Box," November 15, 1914, 58, 60.

23. Ibid., "Slender Jewels of a New Brilliance," July 1, 1921, 69.

24. Ibid., "Imitation Stones Are Featured by Chanel in New Evening Jewellery," December 1, 1927, 95.

25. Ibid., "Rumour about Jewelry," February 1, 1943, 115.

26. Ibid., "Jewels Make the Costume," April 1, 1945, 123.

27. Ibid., "Paris—the Breath of World Fashion," March 15, 1953, 65.

28. Ibid., "In with a Bangle—Big Bold Earrings, Hoop Bracelets," March 15, 1953, 117.

29. Mirabella, "Vogue Boutique," October 1, 1972, 91.

ILLUSTRATIONS

CHAPTER 1

Figure 1-1: *Godey's Lady's Book*, January 1849, inset following 72; October 1888, inset following iv.

Figure 1-2: *Harper's Bazar* covers, November 23, 1867; August 14, 1875; February 23, 1884.

Figure 1-3: *Ladies' Home Journal* covers, January 1895, May 1896, March 1899.

Figure 1-4: *Harper's Bazar*, June 6, 1878, 439.

Figure 1-5: Pages from 1895 Montgomery Ward catalog.

Figure 1-6: *Cosmopolitan*, February 1893, 19.

Figure 1-7: *Vogue* covers, March 25, 1893; May 27, 1893; February 18, 1893; February 25, 1893.

Figure 1-8: *Vogue*, Nov. 16, 1899, vii.

Figure 1-9: *Vogue* covers: A. March 15, 1912; B. June 1, 1913; C. April 15, 1914; D. July 1, 1914; E. July 1, 1915; F. June 1, 1915; G. April 15, 1915; H. March 1, 1915; I. April 15, 1916; J. April 1, 1916; K. June 1, 1917; L. April 1, 1917; M. October 1, 1917; N. March 15, 1918; O. June 15, 1918; P. May 1, 1918; Q. July 1, 1918; R. March 15, 1919; S. March 1, 1919; T. July 1, 1919; U. October 15, 1919; V. April 1, 1920; W. February 15, 1920; X. December 15, 1920; Y. January 1, 1920.

CHAPTER 2

Figure 2-1: Pansy and R and G ads: *Vogue*, November 22, 1894, 337, 339.

Figure 2-2: Gardner ad: *Vogue*, October 25, 1900, back cover.

Figure 2-3: Morrison ad: *Vogue*, October 2, 1901, xiii.

Figure 2-4: Keiser ad: *Vogue*, February 5, 1903, 169.

Figure 2-5: Fullaytar and Keen ad: *Vogue*, February 13, 1902, 123; Oatman ad: *Vogue*, May 7, 1903, 680.

Figure 2-6: F. W. Read cartoon: *Life*, January 9, 1896, 25; Felix Carmen poem, *Life*, February 13, 1896, 113.

Figure 2-7: Gibson Girl illustrations: *Ladies' Home Journal*, October 1902, 7.

Figure 2-8: Viyella ad: *Vogue*, November 27, 1902, 768; Hannis and Jenkins ad: *Vogue*, November 27, 1902, 783; "The King" and Forsythe ads: *Vogue*, April 10, 1902, 316.

Figure 2-9: Binner ad: *Vogue*, August 19, 1909, 242.

Figure 2-10: Franklin Simon ad: *Vogue*, July 15, 1909, 58; Stern Brothers ad: *Vogue*, May 15, 1910, 4.

Figure 2-11: "Foolish Fashion," *Vogue*, February 11, 1909, 226.

Figure 2-12: Reiling and Schoen ad: *Vogue*, March 15, 1911, 113; Bergdorf and Goodman ad: *Vogue*, March 15, 1912, 101.

Figure 2-13: "New York Fashions Are Adjudged Smart," *Vogue*, December 1, 1914, 38, 39.

Figure 2-14: Franklin Simon ad: *Vogue*, June 15, 1915, 3; Lord and Taylor ad: *Vogue*, June 1, 1915, 5; B. Altman ad: *Vogue*, February 1, 1915, 11.

Figure 2-15: Chas. A. Stevens ad: *Vogue*, April 15, 1918, 6.

Figure 2-16: Bonwit Teller ad: *Vogue*, April 15, 1918, 4; Finck ad: *Literary Digest*, October 12, 1918, 77; Robbins and Myers ad: *Literary Digest*, February 8, 1919, 136.

CHAPTER 3

Figure 3-1: Macy's ad: *Vogue*, April 15, 1920, 9; Rosemary Dresses ad: *Vogue*, April 15, 1920, 44–45.

Figure 3-2: Sidney Blumenthal ad: *Vogue*, August 1, 1920, 1; Champot ad: *Vogue*, January 1, 1920, 92.

Figure 3-3: Bonwit Teller ad: *Vogue*, March 1, 1923, 5; Blackshire ad: *Vogue*, February 1, 1924, 12.

Figure 3-4: Best ad: *Vogue*, September 15, 1925, 5; Hubrite ad: *Vogue*, June 15, 1925, 118.

Figure 3-5: Ann Fish Illustration, "Paint and Powder Philosophy": *Vogue*, February 15, 1921, 41; Harley Stivers illustrution, detail of Vanity Fair ad: *Vogue*, November 15, 1926, 4; John Held Jr. illustration, detail of Vanity Fair ad: *Vogue*, April 15, 1926, 4.

Figure 3-6: Wilkin and Adler ad: *Vogue*, March 1, 1922, 114; Amsterdam ad: *Vogue*, July 15, 1923, 86; E. J. Wile ad: *Vogue*, March 15, 1923, 129.

Figure 3-7: Golflex ad: *Vogue*, January 1, 1923, 183; Jersey Silk Mills ad: *Vogue*, June 1, 1922, 7.

Figure 3-8: United States Lines ad: *Literary Digest*, September 14, 1929, 63; Wesson Oil ad: *Literary Digest*, 1928*; General Electric ad: *Literary Digest*, May 18, 1929*; Listerine ad: *Country Life*, August 1925, 97; Marmon ad: *Literary Digest*, November 9, 1929*; International Silver ad: *Good Housekeeping*, September 1929*; Victor Red Seal ad: *Literary Digest*, January 28, 1928*; Martex ad: *Ladies' Home Journal*, May 1929, 196.

Figure 3-9: Wilkin and Adler (Golflex) ad: *Vogue*, October 15, 1925, 15; Howlett and Hockmeyer (Waterside Corduroy) ad: *Vogue*, October 15, 1925, 139; Stewart ad: *Vogue*, May 1, 1926, 4; Lord and Taylor ad: *Vogue*, May 1, 1926, 11; Mrs. Franklin ad: *Vogue*, November 1, 1927, 130; Mangone ad: *Vogue*, January 1, 1927, 14; Bergdorf Goodman ad: *Vogue*, January 1, 1927, 102; Haas Brothers ad: *Vogue*, April 1, 1928, 135; Bonwit Teller ad: *Vogue*, June 1, 1928, 5; I. J. Rubin ad: *Vogue*, July 15, 1928, 94.

Figure 3-10: Bedeli: ad: *Vogue*, December 21, 1929, 9.

Figure 3-11: Déjà ad: *Vogue*, December 22, 1930, 6; Jeunesse ad: *Vogue*, November 1, 1931, 17; Lastex ad: *Vogue*, March 1, 1933, 2.

Figure 3-12: Talon ads: *Vogue*, September 1, 1932, 29; *Esquire*, December 1935, 197; Crown Zipper ad: *Vogue*, September 15, 1938, 16.

Figure 3-13: Franklin Simon ad: *Vogue*, November 1, 1931, 5; Lord and Taylor ad: *Vogue*, December 1, 1933, 6.

Figure 3-14: Jeanne Barrie ad: *Vogue*, May 1, 1936, 8; L. S. Ayres ad: *Vogue*, April 15, 1936, 29; Carolyn ad: *Vogue*, May 1, 1936, 25.

Figure 3-15: Coca-Cola ad: *Vogue*, September 15, 1934, 107; Velveteen ad: *Vogue*, August 15, 1936, 6.

Figure 3-16: Skinner's Silks ad: *Vogue*, May 1, 1931, 18; Johnson, Stephens, and Shinkle ad: *Vogue*, March 1, 1938, 38c; Princess Pat ad: *Vogue*, May 15, 1931, 117.

Figure 3-17: Snyder ad: *Vogue*, May 1, 1936, 116; Kay Christy ad: *Vogue*, December 15, 1937, 98; E. B. Myers ad: *Vogue*, December 15, 1937, 101.

Figure 3-18: Cotton Textiles ad: *Vogue*, January 4, 1930, 12; Mrs. Franklin ad: *Vogue*, January 1, 1931, 82; Best ad: *Vogue*, January 1, 1934, 3; I. Magnin ad: *Vogue*, April 15, 1939, 9.

Figure 3-19: Bergdorf Goodman ad: *Vogue*, February 1, 1938, 3; Lord and Taylor ad: *Vogue*, February 1, 1938, 5.

Figure 3-20: Hattie Carnegie ad: *Vogue*, January 15, 1931, 96; Sally Milgrim ad: *Vogue*, October 1, 1932, 98; Peggy Hoyt ad: *Vogue*, September 1, 1932, 92; Mrs. Franklin ad: *Vogue*, September 1, 1932, 96; Frances Clyne ad: *Vogue*, April 1, 1933, 84; Jessie Franklin Turner ad: *Vogue*, December 1, 1933, 100; Jay-Thorpe ad: *Vogue*, April 15, 1933, 9; Henri Bendel ad: *Vogue*, March 1, 1934, 113.

Figure 3-21: Fred A. Block ad: *Vogue*, February 1, 1939, 130; Franklin Simon ad: *Vogue*, November 1, 1939, 106.

Figure 3-22: International Silk Guild ad: *Vogue*, October 1, 1939, 8; Bergdorf Goodman ad: *Vogue*, October 15, 1939, 1.

*Ads from tearsheet collection; additional information not available.

CHAPTER 4

Figure 4-1: Lord and Taylor ad: *Vogue,* June 1, 1940, 5; Peck and Peck ad: *Vogue,* January 15, 1940, 89; Toujours ad: *Vogue,* January 15, 1940, 21; Bonwit Teller ad: *Vogue,* January 1, 1941, 7.

Figure 4-2: NBC ad: *Vogue,* September 1, 1941, 124.

Figure 4-3: Germaine Monteil ad: *Vogue,* February 1, 1940, 13; Nettie Rosenstein ad: *Vogue,* February 1, 1940, 17; Bonwit Teller (Wragge) ad: *Vogue,* February 1, 1940, 3; Bonwit Teller (Traina-Norell) ad: *Vogue,* October 1, 1941, 5; Adele Simpson ad: *Vogue,* September 15, 1942, 23; Bonwit Teller (Potter) ad: *Vogue,* May 15, 1942, 1; Lilli Ann ad: *Vogue,* August 1, 1944, 29.

Figure 4-4: I. Magnin ad: *Vogue,* May 1, 1942, 1; Frances Dexter ad: *Vogue,* August 15, 1942, 98; Best ad: *Vogue,* May 1, 1943, 94; Handmacher ad: *Vogue,* May 1, 1944, 43.

Figure 4-5: Tish-U-Knit ad: *Vogue,* August 15, 1940, 141; Caerlee ad: *Vogue,* April 1, 1941, 48.

Figure 4-6: Carolyn ad: *Vogue,* September 1, 1945, 75; McKettrick ad: *Vogue,* September 1, 1945, 80; Dayton ad: *Vogue,* September 15, 1945, 36; Lindner Coy ad: *Vogue,* August 15, 1945, 15; Paul Sachs ad: *Vogue,* August 15, 1945, 75; Lilli Ann ad: *Vogue,* August 1, 1945, 20.

Figure 4-7: Stern's ad: *Vogue,* November 1, 1947, 21; May ad: *Vogue,* September 15, 1948, 24; Montaldo's ad: *Vogue,* August 1, 1948, 26.

Figure 4-8: Jack Herzog ad: *Vogue,* November 1, 1947, 50; Adele Simpson ad: *Vogue,* September 15, 1948, 49.

Figure 4-9: Nan Duskin ad: *Vogue,* October 1, 1947, 44; SportLeigh ad: *Vogue,* October 1, 1948, 92.

Figure 4-10: Jordan Marsh ad: *Vogue,* August 15, 1950, 23; Lord and Taylor ad: *Vogue,* March 15, 1954, 46; Oleg Cassini ad: *Vogue,* February 1, 1959, 70.

Figure 4-11: Mynette ad: *Vogue,* April 1, 1950, 32; Harzfeld's ad: *Vogue,* February 1, 1950, 31.

Figure 4-12: David Levine ad: *Vogue,* September 1, 1950, 58; William Block ad: *Vogue,* September 1, 1950, 63; Broadway ad: *Vogue,* February 1, 1950, 29.

Figure 4-13: John Wanamaker ad: *Vogue,* April 1, 1951, 33; Swansdown ad: *Vogue,* August 15, 1951, 25.

Figure 4-14: Carson Pirie Scott ad: *Vogue,* January 1953, 91; Lanz ad: *Vogue,* April 1, 1955, 37.

Figure 4-15: Peck and Peck ad: *Vogue,* February 1, 1956, 111; Mollie Parnis ad: *Vogue,* February 1, 1954, 79; Geigy Chemical ad: *Vogue,* November 15, 1954, 61; Marjorie Michael ad: *Vogue,* November 15, 1955, 49; Saks Fifth Avenue ad: *Vogue,* December 1955, 7.

Figure 4-16: Mission Valley ad: *Vogue,* November 15, 1955, 58; Chemstrand Nylon ad: *Vogue,* November 1, 1954, 48.

Figure 4-17: I. Magnin ad: *Vogue,* October 1, 1958, 27.

Figure 4-18: Tricosa ad: *Vogue,* September 1, 1958, 160; Neiman Marcus ad: *Vogue,* September 1, 1958, 57.

Figure 4-19: Cadillac ad: *Vogue,* February 1, 1956, 17; Marshall Field's ad: *Vogue,* March 1, 1957, 97.

Figure 4-20: Avisco ad: *Vogue,* August 15, 1958, 25.

CHAPTER 5

Figure 5-1: Camay ad: *Seventeen,* November 1952, 7; Jantzen ad: *Seventeen,* November 1952, 19; Formfit ad: *Seventeen,* November 1952, 120; Kotex ad: *Seventeen,* November 1952, 122; Chicago Skates ad: *Seventeen,* November 1952, 142; Listerine ad: *Life,* April 12, 1954, 159; Bell Telephone ad: *Woman's Home Companion,* December 1955, 20.

Figure 5-2: Toni Hunt ad: *Vogue,* July 1960, 31; DuPont ad: *Vogue,* July 1960, 33; Glenhaven ad: *Vogue,* April 1, 1960, 34; Himelhoch's ad: *Vogue,* September 15, 1960, 89.

Figure 5-3: Oleg Cassini ad: *Vogue,* February 1, 1961, 4.

Figure 5-4: National Cotton Council ad: *Vogue,* December 1961, 67.

Figure 5-5: Lord and Taylor ad: *Vogue,* August 1, 1963, 7; Korell ad: *Vogue,* September 1, 1964, 123.

Figure 5-6: Samuel Robert ad: *Vogue,* December 1964, 94; Thayer ad: *Vogue,* August 15, 1965, 47; LA Sport ad: *Vogue,* October 1, 1965, 20.

Figure 5-7: Lady Manhattan ad: *Vogue,* December 1964, 125; Celanese Arnel ad: *Vogue,* November 15, 1966, 87; DuPont ad: *Vogue,* January 15, 1966, 23; National Cotton Council ad: *Vogue,* April 15, 1966, 16; I. Magnin ad: *Vogue,* August 15, 1967, 7.

Figure 5-8: Saks Fifth Avenue ad: *Vogue,* January 15, 1965, 9; Robert Sloan ad: *Vogue,* April 15, 1965, 8.

Figure 5-9: Dan Millstein ad: *Vogue,* August 1, 1963, 27; Silk Association ad: *Vogue,* October 1, 1965, 58.

Figure 5-10: Vanity Fair ad: *Vogue,* April 1, 1967, 97; Chester Weinberg ad: *Vogue,* September 1, 1968, 15.

Figure 5-11: Cotton Institute ad: *Vogue,* May 1968, 96; Old England ad: *Vogue,* May 1968, 91; Avondale ad: *Vogue,* January 15, 1968, 31.

Figure 5-12: Valley Set ad: *Vogue,* September 1, 1969, 206; David Crystal ad: *Vogue,* September 1, 1969, 164.

Figure 5-13: Frost Brothers ad: *Vogue,* April 1, 1968, 19; Wool Council ad: *Vogue,* April 1, 1968, 76; John Wanamaker ad: *Vogue,* September 1, 1969, 205.

Figure 5-14: Robinson's ad: *Vogue,* May 1968, 47; Enka ad: April 1, 1969, 143.

Figure 5-15: Jordan Marsh ad: *Vogue,* March 1, 1970, 8; Jacobson's ad: *Vogue,* May 1970, 18; Lord and Taylor ad: *Vogue,* March 15, 1970, 9; Saks Fifth Avenue ad: *Vogue,* April 15, 1971, 10.

Figure 5-16: Bonnie Doon ad: *Vogue,* August 15, 1971, 30; Superskins ad: *Vogue,* September 1, 1971, 178.

Figure 5-17: Virginia Slims ads: *Vogue,* October 15, 1970, back cover; November 1974, 145.

Figure 5-18: Adele Martin ad: *Vogue,* November 1, 1970, 50; Hudson's ad: *Vogue,* September 1, 1970, 109; Sacony ad: *Vogue,* August 15, 1970, 37.

Figure 5-19: Lord and Taylor ad: *Vogue,* March 1, 1970, 11; Malcolm Starr ad: *Vogue,* May 1970, 10; Valentino ad: *Vogue,* October 1, 1970, 46; Paganne ad: *Vogue,* November 1, 1970, 12.

Figure 5-20: Ultima II ad: *Vogue,* August 1973, 8.

Figure 5-21: Robert-David Morton ad: *Vogue,* April 1976, 89; Avon ad: *Vogue,* October 1976, 161.

Figure 5-22: Saint Laurent ads: *Vogue,* March 1977, 50, 52, 55.

Figure 5-23: Higbee's ad: *Vogue,* September 1977, 82–83; Givenchy ad: *Vogue,* October 1977, 57.

Figure 5-24: Beaunit ad: *Vogue,* September 1975, 165; Bonwit Teller ad: *Vogue,* October 1975, 7.

Figure 5-25: Liberty House ad: *Vogue,* December 1975, 24; Saint Laurent ad: *Vogue,* September 1976, 119; Adele Simpson ad: *Vogue,* February 1977, 75.

Figure 5-26: Robinson's ad: *Vogue,* August 1978, 51; Bullock's ad: *Vogue,* September 1979, 323; Higbee's ad: *Vogue,* September 1978, 135; Marshall Field's ad: *Vogue,* April 1979, 7; Calvin Klein ad: *Vogue,* April 1979, 53.

CHAPTER 6

Figure 6-1: Fiandaca ad: *Vogue,* April 1981, 228; Balliet's ad: *Vogue,* September 1981, 164; Léonard ad (detail): *Vogue,* September 1981, 254.

Figure 6-2: Ron Chereskin ad (detail): *Vogue,* September 1983, 175.

Figure 6-3: Danskin ad (detail): *Vogue*, September 1982, 375; Vantage ad (detail): *Vogue*, August 1983, 95.

Figure 6-4: Marshall Field's ad: *Vogue*, May 1980, 7.

Figure 6-5: Saks Fifth Avenue ad: *Vogue*, September 1980, 27; Dalton Sport ad (detail): *Vogue*, November 1983, 318.

Figure 6-6: O'Neil's ad: *Vogue*, September 1980, 315; Salvatore Ferragamo ad (detail): *Vogue*, August 1983, 104.

Figure 6-7: I. Magnin ad: *Vogue*, October 1981, 26–27.

Figure 6-8: Lily Simon ad (detail): *Vogue*, September 1980, 197; Ralph Lauren ad (detail): *Vogue*, September 1980, 105.

Figure 6-9: Jean-Paul Gaultier checks ad (detail): *Vogue*, February 1985, 157; Perry Ellis sportswear ad (detail): *Vogue*, March 1985, 9; Calvin Klein denim ad (detail): *Vogue*, December 1985, 271.

Figure 6-10: Giorgio Armani ad (detail): *Vogue*, August 1985, 79; Woodward and Lothrop ad: *Vogue*, March 1986, 46; Rich's ad: *Vogue*, September 1987, 265.

Figure 6-11: North Beach Leather ad (detail): *Vogue*, September 1983, 147.

Figure 6-12: Saks Fifth Avenue ad (detail): *Vogue*, September 1985, 85; Marshall Field's ad: *Vogue*, February 1987, 7; L. S. Ayres ad: *Vogue*, September 1987, 202.

Figure 6-13: Nancy Johnson ad (detail): *Vogue*, August 1987, 122; Bonwit Teller ad: *Vogue*, February 1987, 109.

Figure 6-14: Ivey's ad: *Vogue*, August 1989, 104; Guess ad: *Vogue*, September 1989, 93.

Figure 6-15: St. Gillian ad: *Vogue*, March 1989, 141.

Figure 6-16: Alberta Ferretti ad (detail): *Vogue*, March 1989, 258; Patrick Kelly ad (detail): *Vogue*, March 1989, 35.

Figure 6-17: Jaeger ad (detail): *Vogue*, January 1990, 49; Laurél (detail): *Vogue*, July 1990, 102; Chanel ad (detail): *Vogue*, March 1991, 333.

Figure 6-18: Saks Jandel ad (detail): *Vogue*, November 1990, 50; Laurel ad (detail): *Vogue*, April 1991, 195.

Figure 6-19: Caché ad (detail): *Vogue*, March 1991, 45; Escada ad: *Vogue*, September 1991, 86; Nordstrom ad: *Vogue*, April 1990, 2.

Figure 6-20: Talbots ad (detail): *Vogue*, September 1991, 265; Round the Clock ad (detail): *Vogue*, September 1991, 281.

Figure 6-21: Calvin Klein ads (details): *Vogue*, November 1991, 227; February 1992, 176.

Figure 6-22: Neiman Marcus ad: *Vogue*, April 1993, 102; Ellen Tracy ad (detail): *Vogue*, August 1993, 28.

Figure 6-23: Ralph Lauren ad (detail): *Vogue*, September 1994, 69; Ellen Tracy ad (detail): *Vogue*, September 1995, 29.

Figure 6-24: Famous Barr ad (detail): *Vogue*, September 1994, 323; Saks Fifth Avenue ad (detail): *Vogue*, September 1996, 8.

Figure 6-25: Calvin Klein ad (detail): *Vogue*, March 1995, 337.

Figure 6-26: Gucci ad (detail): *Vogue*, September 1996, 171; Chanel ad (detail): *Vogue*, March 1997, 185; Alberta Ferretti ad (detail): *Vogue*, April 1997, 161.

Figure 6-27: Chanel ad (detail): *Vogue*, March 1994, 119; Celine ad (detail): *Vogue*, August 1999, 31; DKNY ad (detail): *Vogue*, April 1998, 212; Fila ad (detail): *Vogue*, April 1997, 144; Ralph Lauren ad (detail): *Vogue*, September 1996, 1.

CHAPTER 7

Figure 7-1: Redfern ad: *Vogue*, April 17, 1902, xl.

Figure 7-2: Gardner ad: *Vogue*, October 2, 1909, 488; Schwartz ad: *Vogue*, May 15, 1910, 51.

Figure 7-3: Lyra ad: *Vogue*, September 1, 1918, 25.

Figure 7-4: Warner's ad: *Vogue*, March 1, 1923, 113; Modart ad: *Vogue*, February 15, 1927, 117.

Figure 7-5: Vassarette ad: *Vogue*, November 15, 1933, 87; Stein ad: *Vogue*, September 15, 1935, 126; Munsingwear ad: *Vogue*, February 1, 1935, 91; Hookless Fastener ad: *Vogue*, May 15, 1937, 23.

Figure 7-6: Carter's ad: *Vogue*, April 15, 1943, 15.

Figure 7-7: Flexees ad: *Vogue*, February 15, 1948, 45; Formfit: *Vogue*, November 1, 1953, 175.

Figure 7-8: Formfit ad: *Vogue*, March 15, 1965, 47.

Figure 7-9: Saint Laurent ad: *Vogue*, March 1977, 51; Claude Montana ad (detail): *Vogue*, September 1983, 448; Saks Fifth Avenue ad (detail): *Vogue*, March 1995, 107; Nordstrom ad: *Vogue*, March 1998, 2.

Figure 7-10: Dress forms from 1895 Montgomery Ward catalog #57, 311; Bust Perfector ad: *Vogue*, March 22, 1900, vi; Gardner ad: *Vogue*, November, 27, 1902, 765; G. M. Poix ad (detail): *Vogue*, October 2, 1909, 530; DeBevoise ad: *Vogue*, March 1, 1915, 109; DeBevoise ad: *Vogue*, April 15, 1918, 94; DeBevoise ad: *Vogue*, October 1, 1921, 138; G. M. Poix ad: *Vogue*, January 15, 1928, 131; Model ad: *Vogue*, May 1, 1931, 113; Maidenform ad: *Vogue*, October 1, 1935, 25; Alene ad: *Vogue*, February 15, 1948, 60; Peter Pan ad: *Vogue*, November 1, 1953, 70; Exquisite Form ad: *Vogue*, April 15, 1965, 23; Olga ad: *Vogue*, September 1977, 231; Maidenform ad (detail): *Vogue*, March 1995, 197.

Figure 7-11: Women's drawers from 1895 Montgomery Ward catalog #57, 284; Oneita ad: *Vogue*, October 7, 1897, vii; Italian Silk ad: *Vogue*, November 27, 1902, 785; Olmstead ad (detail): *Vogue*, September 12, 1907, 362; Best ad: *Vogue*, November 15, 1913, 87; M. Wilber Dyer ad: *Vogue*, September 15, 1917, 104; B. Altman ad: *Vogue*, May 1, 1919, 11; Luxite ad: *Vogue*, May 1, 1924, 17; Van Raalte ad: *Vogue*, November, 15, 1927, 37; Vanity Fair ad: *Vogue*, October 1, 1935, 26; Kleinert's ad: *Vogue*, June 15, 1937, 86; Kayser ad: *Vogue*, June 15, 1943, 56–57; Ban Lon ad: *Vogue*, May 1977, 88; Maidenform ad (detail): *Vogue*, March 1985, 135.

Figure 7-12: Salva-cea ad: *Vogue*, July 11, 1895, back cover; Ivory ad: *Cosmopolitan*, August 1909, 104.

Figure 7-13: Franklin Simon ad: *Vogue*, June 1, 1915, 1; Macy's ad: *Vogue*, June 1, 1917, 4.

Figure 7-14: Bonwit Teller ad: *Vogue*, June 1, 1922, 5; Best ad: *Vogue*, June 15, 1925, 3; Abercrombie and Fitch ad: *Vogue*, June 22, 1929, 11.

Figure 7-15: Jantzen ad: *Vogue*, January 1, 1931, 80; Burdine's ad: *Vogue*, January 15, 1935, 5; Jantzen ad: *Vogue*, May 15, 1937, 20.

Figure 7-16: Cole ad: *Vogue*, June 15, 1943, 9; Surf Togs ad: *Vogue*, May 15, 1947, 26.

Figure 7-17: Flexees ad: *Vogue*, May 1, 1954, 50; Catalina ad: *Vogue*, May 1965, 113; Hawaiian Tropic ad (detail): *Vogue*, March 1979, 128; Bloomingdale's ad (detail): *Vogue*, January 1988, 65; Guess ad (detail): *Vogue*, January 1995, 13; Gucci ad (detail): display poster, 1997.

CHAPTER 8

Hats: (A.) B. Altman ad (detail): *Vogue*, February 25, 1893, back cover; (B.) *Vogue* (detail): November 5, 1896, 293; (C.) Phipps and Atchison ad: *Vogue*, May 7, 1903, 660; (D.) Lord and Taylor ad: *Vogue*, August 19, 1909, 241; (E.) L. F. Castle ad: *Vogue*, March 15, 1911, 11; (F.) C. M. Phipps ad: *Vogue*, September 1, 1914, 99; (G.) Fisk ad: *Vogue*, September 1, 1914, 108; (H.) B. Altman ad (detail): *Vogue*, March 15, 1919, 9; (I.) *Vogue* (detail): February 15, 1918, 29; (J.) Bluebird ad (detail): *Vogue*, September 15, 1921, 118; (K.) Dobb's ad (detail): *Vogue*, January 1, 1924, 77; (L.) Knox ad: *Vogue*, April 15, 1924, 34; (M.) Dobb's ad (detail): *Vogue*, April 1, 1928, 103; (N.) Mallory ad: *Vogue*, April 1, 1928, 16; (O.) Stetson ad (detail): *Vogue*, August 1, 1932, 64; (P.) Knox ad: *Vogue*, February 1, 1932, 8; (Q.) Dobb's ad (detail): *Vogue*, September 1, 1935, 2; (R.) Knox ad (detail): *Vogue*, January 15, 1937, 113; (S.) Marshall Field's ad (detail):

Vogue, October 1, 1937, 13; Henri Bendel ad (detail): *Vogue*, September 1, 1937, 9; Marshall Field's ad (detail), *Vogue*, September 1, 1937, 13; (T.) Henri Bendel ad: *Vogue*, January 1, 1941, 9; (U.) Carson Pirie Scott ad: *Vogue*, March 1, 1941, 13; (V.) Dunlap ad: *Vogue*, September 15, 1943, 161; (W.) Dobb's ad (detail): *Vogue*, September 15, 1944, 82; (X.) Holmes ad (detail): *Vogue*, September 15, 1944, 27; Adrian ad (detail): September 15, 1944, 29; (Y.) Dobb's Hats ad: *Vogue*, August 15, 1945, 35; Lilly Dache ad: *Vogue*, February 15, 1945, 135; (Z.) Dunlap ad: *Vogue*, April 1, 1948, 30; (AA.) Germaine Montabert ad: *Vogue*, September 15, 1950, 211; (BB.) Hattie Carnegie ad (detail): *Vogue*, February 15, 1951, 17; (CC.) Himelhoch's ad (detail): *Vogue*, February 15, 1951, 15; (DD.) Alice Stewart ad (detail): *Vogue*, November 1, 1954, 49; (EE.) Clockwise top to bottom, Bonwit Teller ad (detail): *Vogue*, September 15, 1954, 5; Forstmann ad (detail): *Vogue*, September 15, 1954, inside cover; Brigance ad (detail): May 1, 1954, 21; DuPont ad (detail): *Vogue*, September 15, 1954, 34; Handmacher ad (detail): *Vogue*, September 15, 1954, 14; (FF.) Cover Girl ad (detail): *Vogue*, April 1, 1961, 22; (GG.) Romia ad (detail): *Vogue*, September 1, 1964, 79; Couture Specialties ad (detail): *Vogue*, September 1, 1964, 104; DuPont ad (detail): *Vogue*, September 1, 1964, 107; (HH.) Carriage Corner ad (detail): *Vogue*, September 1, 1966, 34; (II.) Echo ad (detail): *Vogue*, November 1, 1971, 53; (JJ.) Celanese ad (detail): *Vogue*, March 1, 1972, 63; Joseph Stein ad (details): *Vogue*, February 1, 1972, 22, 23; (KK.) Elizabeth Arden ad (detail): *Vogue*, February 1977, 105; (LL.) Hanes ad (detail): *Vogue*, September 1983, 319. (MM.) Ellen Tracy ad (detail): *Vogue*, October 1998, 33; Elizabeth Arden ad (detail): *Vogue*, March 1998, 163.

Shoes: (A.) *Vogue* (detail): June 17, 1897, vi; (B.) Francis O'Neill ad: *Vogue*, November 16, 1899, ix; (C.) Jantzen ad (detail): *Vogue*, May 8, 1902, 482; (D.) Royal ad: *Vogue*, October 17, 1907, 537; (E.) Edward Hayes ad: *Vogue*, April 16, 1908, 517; (F.) Jack's ad (detail): *Vogue*, March 11, 1911, 75; (G.) L. M. Hirsch ad (detail): *Vogue*, October 15, 1914, 126; (H.) Keds ad (detail): *Vogue*, July 1, 1917, 80; (I.) Franklin Simon ad (detail): *Vogue*, October 15, 1918, 3; (J.) Franklin Simon ad: *Vogue*, February 15, 1921, 3; (K.) Queen ad: *Vogue*, February 15, 1925, 127; (L.) I. Miller ad: *Vogue*, February 15, 1928, 16; (M.) Queen ad: *Vogue*, September 1, 1932, 25; (N.) Old Mexico ad: *Vogue*, May 15, 1938, 45; (O.) Vitality ad: *Vogue*, September 1, 1937, 44a; (P.) Joyce ad: *Vogue*, April 1, 1939, 41; (Q.) Joyces ad (detail): *Vogue*, May 1, 1941, 9; (R.) Bergdorf Goodman ad (detail): *Vogue*, October 1, 1941, 2; (S.) Joyces Shoe ad: *Vogue*, January 15, 1943, 17; (T.) Saks Fifth Avenue ad: *Vogue*, February 15, 1945, 7; (U.) C. H. Baker ad: *Vogue*, October 15, 1945, 35; (V.) Fortunet ad (detail): *Vogue*, April 1, 1948, 30; (W.) Bergdorf Goodman ad (detail): *Vogue*, April 1, 1948, 1; (X.) Troylings ad (detail): *Vogue*, September 15, 1951, 81; (Y.) Chandlers ad: *Vogue*, August 15, 1956, 61; (Z.) Cotillion ad: *Vogue*, March 1, 1956, 189; (AA.) Wohl ad: *Vogue*, September 1, 1961, 94; (BB.) I. Miller ad: *Vogue*, February 1, 1961, 117; (CC.) B. F. Goodrich ad: *Vogue*, October 15, 1963, 62; (DD.) Bonnie Doon ad (detail): *Vogue*, August 1, 1963, 137; (EE.) Bootinos ad: *Vogue*, August 15, 1965, 56; (FF.) Revelations ad (detail): *Vogue*, November 1, 1966, 117; (GG.) DuPont ad (detail): *Vogue*, August 15, 1968, 39; (HH.) California Cobbler's ad: *Vogue*, August 15, 1968, 16; (II.) Hush Puppies ad: *Vogue*, September 1, 1972, 158; Saks Fifth Avenue ad (detail): February 1, 1972, 9; (JJ.) Chandlers ad: *Vogue*, March 1974, 65; (KK.) Neiman Marcus ad: *Vogue*, August 1974, 4; (LL.) Jacques Cohen ad: *Vogue*, March 1977, 64; (MM.) Famolare ad (detail): *Vogue*, August 1978, 135; (NN.) Smyth Brothers ad (detail): *Vogue*, February 1978, 90; Burlington ad (detail): March 1979, 111; (OO.) Evan Picone ad (detail): *Vogue*, September 1983, 275; (PP.) Italian Shoe Center ad (detail): *Vogue*, October 1988, 149–52; (QQ.) Caparros ad: *Vogue*, September 1992, 202;

Bruno Magli ad: *Vogue*, September 1992, 170; (RR.) Saks Fifth Avenue ad (detail): *Vogue*, March 1995, 116; (SS.) Studio Paolo ad (detail): *Vogue*, September 1997, 89–92; (TT.) Aldo ad (detail): *Vogue*, September 1997, 506.

Jewelry: (A.) Frederic's ad: *Vogue*, October 25, 1900, viii; (B.) Mermod and Jaccard ad: *Vogue*, November 27, 1902, 790; (C.) *Vogue* (detail): April 10, 1902, 336; (D.) *Vogue* (detail): October 30, 1909, 731; (E.) *Vogue* (detail): November 15, 1912, 60, 102; (F.) *Vogue* (detail): November 15, 1914, 58; (G.) *Vogue* (detail): May 15, 1924, 71, 79; (H.) Cecla ad (detail): *Vogue*, February 1, 1924, 89; (I.) Mauboussin ad: *Vogue*, December 1, 1927, 144; J. E. Caldwell ad (detail): 123; (J.) Saks ad: *Vogue*, August 1, 1926, 28; (K.) Oreum ad: *Vogue*, July 15, 1928, 32; (L.) *Vogue* (detail), December 1, 1933, 53; (M.) Cecla ad: *Vogue*, December 1, 1934, 33; (N.) Trabert and Hoeffer ad (detail): *Vogue*, December 1, 1937, 152; (O.) Black Star and Frost Gorham ad (detail): *Vogue*, October 1, 1937, 132; (P.) Eisenberg ad (detail): *Vogue*, September 1, 1941, 19; (Q.) Trabert and Hoeffer ad: *Vogue*, December 1, 1941, 129; (R.) Ballou ad: *Vogue*, April 15, 1942, 109; (S.) Mossalone ad: *Vogue*, March 1, 1943, 102; (T.) Chen Yu ad (detail): *Vogue*, September 1, 1944, 9; (U.) Eisenberg ad: *Vogue*, April 1, 1945, 29; (V.) Hughes ad (detail): *Vogue*, March 1, 1948, 87; (W.) Bergère ad: *Vogue*, October 15, 1951, 8; (X.) Monet ad: *Vogue*, November 15, 1953, 15; (Y.) Coro ad: *Vogue*, April 1, 1952, 11; (Z.) Castlecliff ad: *Vogue*, December 1954, 177; (AA.) Clarke ad (detail): *Vogue*, September 15, 1956, 64; (BB.) Coro ad: *Vogue*, March 1, 1956, 55; Marcel Boucher ad: *Vogue*, October 1, 1956, 36; (CC.) Dalsheim ad: *Vogue*, March 1, 1956, 180; (DD.) Leru ad: *Vogue*, March 15, 1957, 22–23; (EE.) Richelieu ad: *Vogue*, September 15, 1961, 121; (FF.) Eisenberg ad: *Vogue*, October 1, 1965, 55; Trifari ad: 133; (GG.) Celanese ad (details): *Vogue*, May 1966, 60-61; DuPont ad: June 1966, 27; (HH.) Accessocraft ad: *Vogue*, June 1971, 54; (II.) Trifari ad (detail): *Vogue*, November 1, 1972, 79; (JJ.) Tiffany ad: *Vogue*, November 1, 1972, 4; (KK.) Prado ad: *Vogue*, March 1977, 119; (LL.) Capri ad: *Vogue*, August 1977, 89; (MM.) Christian Dior ad (detail): *Vogue*, October 1986, 125; (NN.) Monet ad (detail): *Vogue*, October 1986, 154; (OO.) Silver Information Center ad (detail): *Vogue*, October 1988, 113; (P.) Anne Klein ad (detail): *Vogue*, September 1997, 303.

COLOR PLATES

Color plate 18: Vicara ad: *Vogue,* September 1, 1955, 20.

Color plate 19: Coro ad: *Vogue,* January 1955, 67.

Color plate 20: Marcel Boucher ad: *Vogue,* October 1, 1956, 36.

Color plate 21: DuPont ad: *Vogue,* April 1, 1968, 95.

Color plate 22: Catalina ad: *Vogue,* October 1, 1969, 121.

Color plate 23: Levi's ad: *Vogue,* April 1, 1969, 122.

Color plate 24: Vendrome ad: *Vogue,* April 15, 1967, 39.

Color plate 25: Bergdorf Goodman ads: *Vogue,* March 15, 1972, 1; *Vogue,* December 1972, 32.

Color plate 26: Jaeger ad: *Vogue,* October 1974, 175.

Color plate 27: Erez ad: *Vogue,* September 1987, 383.

Color plate 28: Frederick and Nelson ad: *Vogue,* September 1980, 107.

Color plate 29: Capezio ad: *Vogue,* March 1992, 57.

Color plate 30: Jaeger ad (detail): *Vogue,* March 1992, 38.

Color plate 31: Bebe ad: *Vogue,* April 1996, 113.

Color plate 32: Nicole Miller ad: *Vogue,* March 1997, 47.

BIBLIOGRAPHY

FASHION: GENERAL

Baclawski, Karen. *The Guide to Historic Costume.* New York: Drama, 1995.

Bailey, Adrian. *The Passion for Fashion: Three Centuries of Changing Styles,* Limpsfield, U.K.: Dragon's World, 1988.

Baines, Barbara. *Fashion Revivals from the Elizabethan Age to the Present Day.* London: B. T. Batsford, 1981.

Barfoot, Audrey. *Discovering Costume.* London: University of London Press, 1959.

Batterberry, Michael, and Ariane Batterberry. *Mirror, Mirror: A Social History of Fashion.* New York: Holt, Rinehart, and Winston, 1977.

Black, J. Anderson, and Madge Garland. *A History of Fashion.* New York: William Morrow, 1981.

Blanc, Charles. *Art in Ornament and Dress.* Detroit: Tower, 1971.

Boucher, Francois. *A History of Costume in the West.* London: Thames and Hudson, 1967.

Braun-Ronsdorf, Margarete. *Mirror of Fashion: A History of European Costume, 1789–1929.* New York: McGraw-Hill, 1964.

Calasibetta, Charlotte. *Essential Terms of Fashion.* New York: Fairchild, 1986.

Carter, Ernestine. *The Changing World of Fashion.* New York: Putnam's, 1977.

Cassin-Scott, Jack. *The Illustrated Encyclopedia of Costume and Fashion from 1066 to the Present.* London: Studio Vista, 1998.

Coleman, Elizabeth. *Changing Fashions, 1800–1970.* Brooklyn, N.Y.: Brooklyn Museum, 1972.

Contini, Mila. *Fashion from Ancient Egypt to the Present Day.* New York: Odyssey, 1965.

Cosgrave, Bronwyn. *The Complete History of Costume and Fashion from Ancient Egypt to the Present Day.* New York: Checkmark, 2000.

Cremers-Van de Does, Eline. *The Agony of Fashion.* Trans. Leo Van Witsen. Poole, U.K.: Blandford, 1980.

Cunnington, Phillis. *Costume in Pictures.* London: Herbert, 1981.

———. *The History of Underclothes.* London: Michael Joseph, 1951.

Davenport, Millia. *The Book of Costume.* New York: Crown, 1948.

Editors of *American Fabrics and Fashions Magazine. Encyclopedia of Textiles.* 3rd ed. Englewood Cliffs, N.J.: Prentice-Hall, 1980.

Ewing, Elizabeth. *Everyday Dress, 1650–1900.* London: B. T. Batsford, 1984.

Flugel, J. C. *The Psychology of Clothes.* London: Hogarth, 1950.

Ginsburg, Madeleine. *The Hat: Trends and Traditions.* Hauppage, N.Y.: Barron's Educational, 1990.

Gorsline, Douglas. *What People Wore.* New York: Viking, 1952.

Grass, Milton. *History of Hosiery: From the Piloi of Ancient Greece to the Nylons of Modern America.* New York: Fairchild, 1955.

Hill, Margot, and Peter Bucknell. *The Evolution of Fashion: Pattern and Cut from 1066–1930.* London: B. T. Batsford, 1967.

Hollander, Anne. *Seeing through Clothes.* Rev. ed. New York: Avon, 1980.

Keyes, Jean. *A History of Women's Hairstyles, 1500–1965.* London: Methuen, 1967.

Koda, Harold. *Extreme Beauty: The Body Transformed.* New York: Metropolitan Museum of Art, 2001.

Kybalova, Ludmila. *The Pictorial Encyclopedia of Fashion.* Trans. Claudia Rosoux. London: Hamlyn, 1968.

Laver, James. *A Concise History of Costume and Fashion.* London: Thames and Hudson, 1979.

———. *Costume and Fashion.* London: Thames and Hudson, 1995.

———. *Modesty in Dress.* London: Heinemann, 1969.

Lester, Katherine, and Rose Kerr. *Historic Costume.* Peoria, Ill.: Charles A. Bennett, 1977.

Lurie, Alison. *The Language of Clothes.* New York: Henry Holt, 2000.

McDowell, Colin. *Hats: Status, Style, and Glamour.* New York: Rizzoli, 1992.

Moore, Doris. *Fashion through Fashion Plates, 1771–1970.* New York: Clarkson Potter, 1971.

Nunn, Joan. *Fashion in Costume, 1200–1980.* New York: Schocken, 1984.

Parsons, Frank. *The Psychology of Dress.* Garden City, N.Y.: Doubleday and Page, 1921.

Peacock, John. *The Chronicle of Western Fashion from Ancient Times to the Present Day.* New York: Harry N. Abrams, 1991.

———. *Costume, 1066–1966: A Complete Guide to English Costume Design and History.* London: Thames and Hudson, 1992.

Ribeiro, Aileen. *Dress and Morality.* New York: Holmes and Meier, 1986.

Ribeiro, Aileen, and Valerie Cumming. *The Visual History of Costume.* London: B. T. Batsford, 1989.

Robinson, Julian. *Body Packaging: A Guide to Human Sexual Display.* Los Angeles: Elysium Growth, 1988.

Ruby, Jennifer. *Costume in Context: Underwear.* London: B. T. Batsford, 1996.

Rudofsky, Bernard. *Are Clothes Modern?* Chicago: Paul Theobald, 1947.

Russell, Douglas. *Costume History and Style.* Englewood Cliffs, N.J.: Prentice-Hall, 1983.

Schnurnberger, Lynn. *Let There Be Clothes: 40,000 Years of Fashion.* New York: Workman, 1991.

Selbie, Robert. *The Anatomy of Costume.* New York: Crescent, 1977.

Shover, Edna. *Art in Costume Design.* Springfield, Mass.: Milton Bradley, 1920.

Sichel, Marion. *History of Women's Costume.* London: Batsford Academic and Educational, 1984.

Squire, Geoffrey. *Dress and Society, 1560–1970*. New York: Viking, 1974.

Steele, Valerie. *Men and Women: Dressing the Part*. Washington, D.C.: Smithsonian Institution, 1989.

Tilke, Max. *Costume Patterns and Designs*. New York: Frederick A. Praeger, 1957.

Tortora, Phyllis and Keith Eubank. *Survey of Historic Costume*. New York: Fairchild, 1998.

Wheeler, R. E. M. *Costume, 1558–1933*. London: Lancaster House, 1934.

Wilcox, Turner. *Dictionary of Costume*. New York: Charles Scribner's Sons, 1969.

———. *Five Centuries of American Costume*. New York: Charles Scribner's Sons, 1963.

———. *The Mode in Footwear*. New York: Charles Scribner's Sons, 1958.

———. *The Mode in Furs*. New York: Charles Scribner's Sons, 1951.

———. *The Mode in Hats and Dresses*. New York: Charles Scribner's Sons, 1945.

Wykes-Joyce, Max. *Cosmetics and Adornment*. New York: Philosophical Library, 1961.

Yarwood, Doreen. *The Encyclopedia of World Costume*. New York: Bonanza, 1978.

———. *Fashion in the Western World, 1500–1990*. New York: Drama, 1992.

FASHION: NINETEENTH CENTURY

Armstrong, Nancy. *Victorian Jewelry*. New York: Macmillan, 1976.

Bryk, Nancy, ed. *American Dress Pattern Catalogs, 1873–1909*. New York: Dover, 1988.

Buck, Anne. *Victorian Costume and Costume Accessories*. New York: Thomas Nelson, 1961.

Byrde, Penelope. *Nineteenth-Century Fashion*. London: B. T. Batsford, 1992.

Calthrop, Dion C. *English Dress from Victoria to George V*. London: Chapman and Hall, 1934.

Cashen, Marilynn. *A Moment in Time: Images of Victorian Fashions from the Mid-1800s*. South Plainfield, N.J.: MAC Publications, 1992.

Cunnington, Cecil. *English Women's Clothing in the Nineteenth Century*. New York: Dover, 1990.

Cunnington, Phillis. *Costumes for Births, Marriages, and Deaths*. New York: Barnes and Noble, 1972.

———. *Handbook of English Costume in the Nineteenth Century*. London: Faber and Faber, 1970.

Dalrymple, Priscilla. *American Victorian Costume in Early Photographs*. New York: Dover, 1991.

Emmet, Boris. *Montgomery Ward Catalogue and Buyer's Guide*. New York: Dover, 1969.

Foster, Vanda. *A Visual History of Costume in the Nineteenth Century*. London: B. T. Batsford, 1982.

Gere, Charlotte. *European and American Jewellery, 1830–1914*. London: Heinemann, 1975.

Gernsheim, Alison. *Victorian and Edwardian Fashion*. New York: Dover, 1981.

Goldthorpe, Caroline. *From Queen to Empress: Victorian Dress, 1837–1877*. New York: Metropolitan Museum of Art, 1988.

Harris, Kristina. *Victorian and Edwardian Fashions for Women, 1840–1919*. Atglen, Pa. Schiffer, 1995.

Holland, Vyvyan. *Hand Coloured Fashion Plates 1770–1899*. London: B. T. Batsford, 1955.

Kerr, Rose. *One Hundred Years of Costumes in America*. Worcester, Mass.: Davis, 1981.

Laver, James. *Fashion and Fashion Plates 1800–1900*. London: King Penguin, 1943.

———. *Victoriana*. New York: Hawthorne, 1967.

———. *Victorian Vista*. Boston: Houghton Mifflin, 1955.

Levitt, Sarah. *Victorians Unbuttoned*. Boston: Allen and Unwin, 1986.

McClellan, Elisabeth. *History of American Costume 1607–1870*. New York: Tudor, 1969.

Montebello, Philippe de, et al. *The Imperial Style: Fashions of the Hapsburg Era*. New York: Metropolitan Museum of Art, 1980.

Norris, Herbert. *Nineteenth-Century Costume and Fashion*. Mineola, N.Y.: Dover, 1999.

Olian, Joanne. *Children's Fashions, 1860–1912*. New York: Dover, 1993.

Perrot, Philippe. *Fashioning the Bourgeoisie: A History of Clothing in the Nineteenth Century*. Trans. Richard Bienvenu. Princeton, N.J.: Princeton University Press, 1987.

Ruby, Jennifer. *Costume in Context: The Victorians*. London: B. T. Batsford, 1994.

Sichel, Marion, *Costume Reference: Victorians*. Vol. 6. New York: Chelsea House, 1986.

Summers, Leigh. *Bound to Please: A History of the Victorian Corset*. New York: Oxford University Press, 2001.

Thieme, Otto, et al. *With Grace and Favor: Victorian and Edwardian Fashion in America*. Cincinnati: Cincinnati Art Museum, 1993.

Tozer, Jane, and Sarah Levitt. *Fabric of Society: A Century of People and Their Clothes, 1770–1870*. Manchester, U.K.: Laura Ashley, 1983.

Walkley, Christina. *Dressed to Impress, 1840–1914*. London: B. T. Batsford, 1989.

Worrell, Estelle. *American Costume 1840–1920*. Harrisburg, Pa.: Stackpole, 1979.

FASHION: 1900–1919

Brooke, Iris. *English Costume 1900–1950*. London: Methuen, 1951.

Laver, James. *Edwardian Promenade*. Boston: Houghton Mifflin, 1958.

Mackrell, Alice. *Paul Poiret*. New York: Holmes and Meier, 1990.

Ruby, Jennifer. *Costume in Context: The Edwardians and the First World War*. London: B. T. Batsford, 1988.

Sichel, Marion. *Costume Reference: Edwardians*. Vol. 7. New York: Chelsea House, 1978.

FASHION: 1920–1939

Battersby, Martin. *Art Deco Fashion: French Designers, 1908–1925*. New York: St. Martin's Press, 1974.

Garland, Madge, et al. *Fashion, 1900–1939*. London: Idea, 1975.

Gutner, Howard. *Gowns by Adrian: The MGM Years, 1928–1941*. New York: Harry N. Abrams, 2001.

Hall, Carolyn. *The Thirties in Vogue*. New York: Harmony, 1985.

———. *The Twenties in Vogue*. New York: Harmony, 1983.

Hunt, Marsha. *The Way We Were: Styles of the 1930s and '40s*. Fallbrook, Calif.: Fallbrook, 1993.

Lussier, Suzanne. *Art Deco Fashion*. New York: Bulfinch, 2003.

Maeder, Edward. *Hollywood and History: Costume Design in Film*.

London: Thames and Hudson, 1987.

Martin, Richard. *Cubism and Fashion*. New Haven, Conn.: Yale University Press, 1999.

Martin, Richard, and Harold Koda. *Splash! A History of Swimwear*. New York: Rizzoli, 1990.

Olian, Joanne. *Authentic French Fashions of the Twenties*. New York: Dover, 1990.

Peacock, John. *Fashion Sourcebooks: The 1920s*. New York: Thames and Hudson, 1997.

———. *Fashion Sourcebooks: The 1930s*. New York: Thames and Hudson, 1997.

Ruby, Jennifer. *Costume in Context: The 1920s and 1930s*. London: B. T. Batsford, 1988.

Sichel, Marion. *Costume Reference: 1918–1939*. Vol. 8. Boston: Plays, 1978.

FASHION: 1940–1959

Dorner, Jane. *Fashion in the Forties and Fifties*. New Rochelle, N.Y.: Arlington House, 1975.

Drake, Nicholas. *The Fifties in Vogue*. New York: Henry Holt, 1987.

Hall, Carolyn. *The Forties in Vogue*. New York: Harmony, 1985.

Maeder, Edward. *Salvatore Ferragamo: Art of the Shoe, 1896–1960*. New York: Rizzoli, 1992.

Martin, Richard. *Charles James*. New York: Universe, 1999.

Muir, Robin. *Clifford Coffin: Photographs from Vogue, 1945 to 1955*. New York: Stewart, Tabori, and Chang, 1997.

Peacock, John. *Fashion Sourcebooks: The 1940s*. New York: Thames and Hudson, 1998.

———. *Fashion Sourcebooks: The 1950s*. New York: Thames and Hudson, 1997.

Ruby, Jennifer. *Costume in Context, 1930–1945*. London: B. T. Batsford, 1995.

Sichel, Marion. *Costume Reference, 1939–1950*. Vol. 9. London: B. T. Batsford, 1987.

FASHION: 1960–1979

Cassini, Oleg. *A Thousand Days of Magic: Dressing Jacqueline Kennedy for the White House*. New York: Rizzoli, 1995.

Drake, Nicholas, ed. *The Sixties: A Decade in Vogue*. New York: Prentice-Hall, 1988.

Lobenthal, Joel. *Radical Rags: Fashions of the Sixties*. New York: Abbeville, 1990.

Moffitt, Peggy. *The Rudi Gernreich Book*. New York: Rizzoli, 1991.

Mulvaney, Jay. *Jackie: The Clothes of Camelot*. New York: St. Martin's Press, 2001.

Peacock, John. *Fashion Sourcebooks: The 1960s*. New York: Thames and Hudson, 1998.

———. *Fashion Sourcebooks: The 1970s*. New York: Thames and Hudson, 1997.

Ruby, Jennifer. *Costume in Context: The 1960s and 1970s*. London: B. T. Batsford, 1989.

FASHION: 1980–PRESENT

Baudot, Francois. *Christian Lacroix*. New York: Universe, 1997.

Berch, Bettina. *Radical by Design*. New York: E. P. Dutton, 1988.

Cassini, Oleg. *In My Own Fashion: An Autobiography*. New York: Simon and Schuster, 1987.

Coleridge, Nicholas. *The Fashion Conspiracy*. London: Heinemann,

1989.

Deloffre, Claude, ed. *Thierry Mugler: Fashion, Fetish, Fantasy*. Los Angeles: General, 1998.

Fujii, Satoru, ed. *Vision: George Stavrinos*. Tokyo: Tokyo Designers Gakuin College, 1984.

Gan, Stephen. *Visionaire's Fashion 2000: Designers at the Turn of the Millennium*. New York: Universe, 1997.

———. *Visionaire's Fashion 2001: Designers of the New Avant-Garde*. New York: Universe, 1999.

Greenwood, Kathryn, and Mary Murphy. *Fashion Innovation and Marketing*. New York: Macmillan, 1978.

Hemphill, Christopher. *Antonio's Girls*. New York: Congreve, 1982.

McDermott, Catherine. *Street Style: British Design in the Eighties*. New York: Rizzoli, 1987.

McDowell, Colin. *Fashion Today*. New York: Phaidon, 2000.

McRobbie, Angela. *British Fashion Design: Rag Trade or Image Industry?* London: Routledge, 1998.

———. *In the Culture Society: Art, Fashion, and Popular Music*. London: Routledge, 1999.

Oldham, Todd. *Todd Oldham: Without Boundaries*. New York: Rizzoli, 1997.

Peacock, John. *Fashion Sourcebooks: The 1980s*. New York: Thames and Hudson, 1998.

Pelle, Marie-Paul. *Valentino: Thirty Years of Magic*. New York: Abbeville, 1991.

Polhemus, Ted. *Street Style: From Sidewalk to Catwalk*. London: Thames and Hudson, 1994.

———. *Style Surfing: What to Wear in the Third Millennium*. New York: Thames and Hudson, 1996.

Steele, Valerie. *Red Dress*. New York: Rizzoli, 2001.

Strong, Roy. *Gianni Versace: Do Not Disturb*. New York: Abbeville, 1996.

Versace, Gianni. *Rock and Royalty*. New York: Abbeville, 1996.

———. *Signatures*. New York: Abbeville, 1992.

Wilcox, Claire. *Radical Fashion*. London: Victoria and Albert Museum, 2001.

FASHION: GENERAL TWENTIETH CENTURY

Agins, Teri. *The End of Fashion: The Mass Marketing of the Clothing Business*. New York: William Morrow, 1999.

Angeloglou, Maggie. *A History of Make-up*. London: Macmillan, 1965.

Ball, Joanne. *The Art of Fashion Accessories: A Twentieth Century Retrospective*. Atglen, Pa.: Schiffer, 1993.

Barnard, Malcolm. *Fashion as Communication*. London: Routledge, 1996.

Baudot, Francois. *Elsa Schiaparelli*. New York: Universe, 1997.

———. *Fashion: The Twentieth Century*. New York: Universe, 1999.

Benson, Elaine, and John Esten. *Unmentionables: A Brief History of Underwear*. New York: Simon and Schuster, 1996.

Bianchino, Gloria, et al., ed. *Italian Fashion: The Origins of High Fashion and Knitwear*. Vol. 1. New York: Rizzoli, 1980.

Bond, David. *Glamour in Fashion*. London: Guinness, 1992.

Bonner, Paul, ed. *The World in Vogue*. New York: Viking, 1963.

Bosker, Gideon, and Lena Lencek. *Making Waves: Swimsuits and the Undressing of America*. San Francisco: Chronicle, 1988.

Breward, Christopher. *The Culture of Fashion*. Manchester, U.K.:

Manchester University Press, 1995.

Brown, Marcia. *Unsigned Beauties of Costume Jewelry.* Paducah, Ky.: Collector, 2000.

Bullis, Douglas. *California Fashion Designers.* Layton, Utah: Gibbs M. Smith, 1987.

Bure, Gilles de. *Gruau.* Paris: Editions Herscher, 1989.

Butazzi, Grazie, and Alessandra Molfino, eds. *Italian Fashion: From Anti-fashion to Stylism.* Vol. 2. New York: Rizzoli, 1987.

Buttolph, Angela, et al. *The Fashion Book.* London: Phaidon, 1998.

Buxbaum, Gerda, ed. *Icons of Fashion of the Twentieth Century.* Munich: Prestel Verlag, 1999.

Carter, Ernestine. *The Changing World of Fashion.* New York: G. P. Putnam's Sons, 1977.

———. *Magic Names of Fashion.* Englewood Cliffs, N.J.: Prentice-Hall, 1980.

Castelbajac, Kate de. *The Face of the Century: One Hundred Years of Makeup and Style.* New York: Rizzoli, 1995.

Chariau, Joelle. *Gruau.* New York: Te Neues, 1999.

Charles-Roux, Edmonde. *Chanel and Her World.* London: Vendome, 1979.

Clark, Fiona. *Hats.* New York: Drama, 1982.

Coleman, Elizabeth. *The Genius of Charles James.* New York: Holt, Rinehart, and Winston, 1983.

Cooper, Wendy. *Hair: Sex, Society, Symbolism.* New York: Stein and Day, 1971.

Craik, Jennifer. *The Face of Fashion: Cultural Studies in Fashion.* London: Routledge, 1994.

Cunningham, Patricia, and Susan Voso Lab, eds. *Dress in American Culture.* Bowling Green, Ohio: Bowling Green State University Popular Press, 1993.

Daves, Jessica. *Ready-Made Miracle.* New York: G. P. Putnam's Sons, 1967.

DeLong, Marilyn. *The Way We Look: A Framework for Visual Analysis of Dress.* Ames: Iowa State University Press, 1987.

De Marly, Diana. *Christian Dior.* New York: Holmes and Meier, 1990.

———. *The History of Haute Couture 1850–1950.* London: B. T. Batsford, 1980.

———. *Worth: Father of Haute Couture.* New York: Holmes and Meier, 1991.

Devlin, Polly. *Vogue Book of Fashion Photography, 1919–1979.* New York: Simon and Schuster, 1979.

Eichler, Lillian. *The Customs of Mankind.* New York: Doubleday, 1924.

Evans, Mike, ed. *Key Moments in Fashion: The Evolution of Style.* New York: Octopus, 1999.

Ewing, Elizabeth. *Dress and Undress.* New York: Drama, 1978.

———. *History of Twentieth Century Fashion.* New York: Charles Scribner's Sons, 1974.

Farrell-Beck, Jane, and Colleen Gau. *Uplift: The Bra in America.* Philadelphia: University of Pennsylvania Press, 2002.

Finlayson, Iain. *Denim: The American Legend.* New York: Fireside, 1990.

Fischer-Mirkin, Toby. *Dress Code: Understanding the Hidden Meanings of Women's Clothes.* New York: Clarkson Potter, 1995.

Frankel, Susannah. *Visionaries: Interviews with Fashion Designers.* New York: Harry N. Abrams, 2001.

Fraser, Kennedy. *The Fashionable Mind.* New York: Knopf, 1981.

Gaines, Jane, and Charlotte Herzog, eds. *Fabrications: Costume and the Female Body.* New York: Routledge, 1990.

Gernsheim, Alison. *Fashion and Reality.* London: Faber and Faber, 1963.

Glynn, Prudence, and Madeleine Ginsburg. *In Fashion: Dress in the Twentieth Century.* London: George Allen and Unwin, 1978.

Golbin, Pamela. *Fashion Designer.* New York: Watson-Guptill, 1999.

Gold, Annalee. *One World of Fashion.* New York: Fairchild, 1987.

Graveline, Noel. *Jeans: Levi's Story.* Paris: Minerva, 1990.

Gross, Elaine, and Fred Rottman. *Halston: An American Original.* New York: Harper Collins, 1999.

Hall, Lee. *Common Threads: A Parade of American Clothing.* Boston: Bulfinch, 1992.

Hansen, Joseph, et al. *Cosmetics, Fashions, and the Exploitation of Women.* New York: Pathfinder, 1986.

Harrison, Martin. *Beauty Photography in Vogue.* New York: Stewart, Tabori, and Chang, 1987.

Haye, Amy de la. *Fashion Source Book: A Visual Reference to Twentieth Century Fashion.* Secaucus, N.J.: Wellfleet, 1988.

Haye, Amy de la, ed. *The Cutting Edge: Fifty Years of British Fashion, 1947–1997.* Woodstock, N.Y.: Overlook, 1997.

Haye, Amy de la, and Cathie Dingwall. *Surfers, Soulies, Skinheads, and Skaters.* New York: Overlook, 1996.

Haye, Amy de la, and Shelley Tobin. *Chanel: The Couturier at Work.* New York: Overlook, 1995.

Haye, Amy de la, and Elizabeth Wilson, eds. *Defining Dress: Dress as Object, Meaning, and Identity.* Manchester, U.K.: Manchester University Press, 1999.

Hoobler, Dorothy, and Thomas Hoobler. *Vanity Rules: A History of American Fashion and Beauty.* Brookfield, Conn.: 21st Century, 2000.

Howell. Georgina. *In Vogue: Seventy-Five Years of Style.* Rev. ed. London: Condé Nast, 1991.

Joselit, Jenna Weissman. *A Perfect Fit: Clothes, Character, and the Promise of America.* New York: Metropolitan, 2001.

Jouve, Marie-Andree. *Balenciaga.* New York: Universe, 1997.

Kaiser, Susan. *The Social Psychology of Clothing.* New York: Macmillan, 1990.

Keenan, Brigid. *Dior in Vogue.* New York: Harmony, 1981.

Kennedy, Shirley. *Pucci: A Renaissance in Fashion.* New York: Abbeville, 1991.

Kunzle, David. *Fashion and Fetishism.* Totowa, N.J.: Rowman and Littlefield, 1992.

Kurella, Elizabeth. *The Complete Guide to Vintage Textiles.* Iola, Wis.: Krause, 1999.

Lancek, Lena, and Gideon Bosker. *Making Waves: Swimsuits and the Undressing of America.* San Francisco: Chronicle, 1989.

Lee, Sarah Tomerlin, ed. *American Fashion.* New York: Fashion Institute of Technology, 1975.

Lee-Potter, Charlie. *Sportswear in Vogue since 1910.* New York: Abbeville, 1984.

Lehnert, Gertrud. *A History of Fashion in the Twentieth Century.* Cologne: Konemann Verlagsgesellschaft, 2000.

Levin, Phyllis. *The Wheels of Fashion.* Garden City, N.Y.: Doubleday, 1965.

Ley, Sandra. *Fashion for Everyone: The Story of Ready-to-Wear, 1870s–1970s.* New York: Charles Scribner's Sons, 1975.

Leymarie, Jean. *Chanel.* New York: Rizzoli, 1987.

Liberman, Alexander, ed. *On the Edge: Images from One Hundred*

Years of Vogue. New York: Random House, 1992.

Lipovetsky, Gilles. *The Empire of Fashion.* Trans. Catherine Porter. Princeton, N.J.: Princeton University Press, 1994.

Lloyd, Valerie. *The Art of Vogue Photographic Covers.* New York: Harmony, 1986.

Lynam, Ruth, ed. *Couture.* Garden City, N.Y.: Doubleday, 1972.

Martin, Richard. *American Ingenuity: Sportswear 1930s–1970s.* New York: Metropolitan Museum of Art, 1998.

———. *Fashion and Surrealism.* New York: Rizzoli, 1996.

———. *The St. James Fashion Encyclopedia: A Survey of Style from 1945 to Present.* Rev. ed. Detroit: Visible Ink, 1997.

———. *Versace.* New York: Universe, 1997.

McDowell, Colin. *Hats: Status, Style, and Glamour.* New York: Rizzoli, 1992.

———. *A Hundred Years of Royal Style.* London: Muller, Blond, and White, 1985.

———. *McDowell's Directory of Twentieth Century Fashion.* Englewood Cliffs, N.J.: Prentice-Hall, 1985.

———. *Shoes: Fashion and Fantasy.* London: Thames and Hudson, 1992.

Meller, Susan, and Joost Elffers. *Textile Designs: Two Hundred Years of European and American Patterns.* New York: Harry N. Abrams, 1991.

Mendes, Valerie, and Amy de la Haye. *Twentieth-Century Fashion.* London: Thames and Hudson, 1999.

Milbank, Caroline. *New York Fashion.* New York: Harry N. Abrams, 1996.

Mo, Charles. *Evening Elegance: One Hundred Fifty Years of Formal Fashions.* Charlotte, N.C.: Mint Museum of Art, 1998.

Morris, Bernadine. *The Fashion Makers.* New York: Random House, 1978.

———. *Valentino.* New York: Universe, 1996.

Mulvagh, Jane. *Costume Jewelry in Vogue.* London: Thames and Hudson, 1988.

———. *Vogue: History of Twentieth Century Fashion.* London: Viking, 1988.

Mulvey, Kate, and Melissa Richards. *Decades of Beauty: The Changing Image of Women, 1890s–1990s.* New York: Reed Consumer, 1998.

Newman, Cathy. *Fashion.* Washington, D.C.: National Geographic Society, 2001.

Nystrom, Paul. *Economics of Fashion.* New York: Ronald, 1928.

O'Hara, Georgina. *The Encyclopaedia of Fashion.* New York: Harry N. Abrams, 1986.

O'Keefe, Linda. *Shoes: A Celebration of Pumps, Sandals, Slippers, and More.* New York: Workman, 1996.

Osma, Guillermo de. *Fortuny: His Life and Work.* New York: Rizzoli, 1980.

Packer, William. *The Art of Vogue Covers, 1909–1940.* New York: Bonanza, 1980.

———. *Fashion Drawing in Vogue.* New York: Thames and Hudson, 1983.

Peacock, John. *Fashion Accessories: The Complete Twentieth-Century Sourcebook.* New York: Thames and Hudson, 2000.

Pietri, Stephen de, and Melissa Leventon. *New Look to Now.* New York: Rizzoli, 1989.

Probert, Christina. *Hats in Vogue since 1910.* New York: Abbeville, 1981.

———. *Lingerie in Vogue since 1910.* New York: Abbeville, 1981.

———. *Shoes in Vogue since 1910.* New York: Abbeville, 1981.

———. *Swimwear in Vogue since 1910.* New York: Abbeville, 1981.

Rhodes, Zandra, and Anne Knight. *The Art of Zandra Rhodes.* Boston: Houghton Mifflin, 1988.

Ross, Josephine. *Beaton in Vogue.* New York: Clarkson N. Potter, 1986.

Saint Laurent, Yves. *Images of Design, 1958–1988.* New York: Alfred A. Knopf, 1988.

Sato, Pater. *Fashion Illustration in New York.* New York: Graphic-sha, 1985.

Scaasi, Arnold, and Bernadine Morris. *Scaasi: A Cut Above.* New York: Rizzoli, 1996.

Seebohm, Caroline. *The Man Who Was Vogue.* New York: Viking, 1982.

Seeling, Charlotte. *Fashion: The Century of the Designer, 1900–1999.* Cologne: Konemann Verlagsgesellschaft, 1999.

Simonds, Cherri. *Costume Jewelry.* Paducah, Ky.: Collector, 1997.

Smith, Desire. *Fashion Footwear 1800–1970.* Atglen, Pa: Schiffer, 2000.

Steele, Valerie. *The Corset: A Cultural History.* New Haven, Conn.: Yale University Press, 2001.

———. *Fashion and Eroticism: Ideals of Feminine Beauty from the Victorian Era to the Jazz Age.* New York: Oxford University Press, 1985.

———. *Fifty Years of Fashion: New Look to Now.* New Haven, Conn.: Yale University Press, 1997.

———. *Handbags: A Lexicon of Style.* New York: Rizzoli, 2000.

———. *Paris Fashion: A Cultural History.* New York: Oxford University Press, 1988.

———. *Shoes: A Lexicon of Style.* New York: Rizzoli, 1999.

———. *Women of Fashion: Twentieth-Century Designers.* New York: Rizzoli, 1991.

Taylor. Lou. *The Study of Dress History.* Manchester, U.K.: Manchester University Press, 2002.

Tolkien, Tracy. *Dressing Up Vintage.* New York: Rizzoli, 2000.

Torrens, Deborah. *Fashion Illustrated: A Review of Women's Dress, 1920–1950.* New York: Hawthorne, 1975.

Trahey, Jane, ed. *One Hundred Years of the American Female.* New York: Random House, 1967.

Tucker, Andrew, and Tamsin Kingswell. *Fashion: A Crash Course.* New York: Watson-Guptill, 2000.

Watson, Linda. *Vogue: Twentieth Century Fashion.* London: Carelton, 1999.

White, Palmer. *Haute Couture Embroidery: The Art of Lesage.* New York: Vendome, 1988.

Wilcox, Claire, and Valerie Mendes. *Modern Fashion in Detail.* Woodstock, N.Y.: Overlook, 1991.

Wilson, Carrie. *Fashions since Their Debut.* Scranton, Pa.: International Textbooks, 1945.

Zahm, Volker. *The Art of Creating Fashion.* Pocking, Germany: Mondi, 1991.

ADVERTISING AND MARKETING

Atwan, Robert, et al. *Edsels, Luckies, and Frigidaires: Advertising the American Way.* New York: Dell, 1979.

Barthel, Diane. *Putting on Appearances: Gender and Advertising.*

Philadelphia: Temple University Press, 1988.

Bartos, Rena. *The Moving Target: What Every Marketer Should Know about Women.* New York: Free, 1982.

Berman, Ronald. *Advertising and Social Change.* Beverly Hills, Calif.: Sage, 1981.

Clark, Eric. *The Want Makers.* New York: Viking, 1989.

Danna, Sammy, ed. *Advertising and Popular Culture: Studies in Variety and Versatility.* Bowling Green, Ohio: Bowling Green State University Popular Press, 1992.

Ewen, Stuart. *All Consuming Images: The Politics of Style in Contemporary Culture.* Rev. ed. New York: Basic, 1999.

Ewen, Stuart, and Elizabeth Ewen. *Channels of Desire: Mass Images and the Shaping of American Consciousness.* Minneapolis: University of Minnesota Press, 1992.

Fox, Stephen. *The Mirror Makers.* Urbana, Ill.: University of Illinois Press, 1997.

Frederick, Christine. *Selling Mrs. Consumer.* New York: Business Bourse, 1929.

Goffman, Erving. *Gender Advertisements.* New York: Harper Colophon, 1979.

Goodrum, Charles, and Helen Dalrymple. *Advertising in America: The First Two Hundred Years.* New York: Harry N. Abrams, 1990.

Hambleton, Ronald. *Branding of America.* Dublin, N.H.: Yankee, 1987.

Hill, Daniel Delis. *Advertising to the American Woman 1900–1999.* Columbus: Ohio State University Press, 2002.

Holme, Bryan. *Art of Advertising.* London: Peerage, 1985.

Janello, Amy, and Brennon Jones. *The American Magazine.* New York: Harry N. Abrams, 1991.

Jones, Duane. *Ads, Women, and Boxtops.* Pleasantville, N.Y.: Printers' Ink, 1955.

Kery, Patricia. *Great Magazine Covers of the World.* New York: Abbeville, 1982.

Marchand, Roland. *Advertising the American Dream.* Berkeley: University of California Press, 1985.

Margolin, Victor, et al. *The Promise and the Product.* New York: Macmillan, 1979.

Meyer, Susan. *America's Great Illustrators.* New York: Galahad, 1987.

Nava, Mica, et al., eds. *Buy This Book: Studies in Advertising and Consumption.* London: Routledge, 1997.

O'Barr, William. *Culture and the Ad.* Boulder: Westview Press, 1994.

Ohmann, Richard. *Selling Culture.* London: Verso, 1996.

Packard, Vance. *The Hidden Persuaders.* New York: David McKay, 1957.

Paganetti, Jo Ann, and M. Seklemian. *The Best in Retail Ads.* New York: Retail Reporting, 1983.

Preston, Ivan. *The Tangled Web They Weave.* Madison: University of Wisconsin Press, 1994.

Rowsome, Frank. *They Laughed When I Sat Down.* New York: Bonanza, 1959.

Sivulka, Juliann. *Soap, Sex, and Cigarettes: A Cultural History of American Advertising.* Belmont, Calif.: Wadsworth, 1998.

Strasser, Susan. *Satisfaction Guaranteed.* Washington, D.C.: Smithsonian Institution, 1989.

Twitchell, James. *Adcult USA.* New York: Columbia University Press, 1996.

Winters, Peggy, et al. *What Works in Fashion Advertising.* New York: Retail Reporting, 1996.

Woodward, Helen. *The Lady Persuaders.* New York: Ivan Obolenky, 1960.

WOMEN'S STUDIES

Brown, Dorothy. *Setting a Course: American Women in the 1920s.* Boston: Twayne, 1987.

Brownmiller, Susan. *Femininity.* New York: Linden, 1984.

Chafe, William. *The Paradox of Change: American Women in the Twentieth Century.* New York: Oxford University Press, 1991.

Faludi, Susan. *Backlash.* New York: Crown, 1991.

Fogarty, Anne. *Wife Dressing.* New York: Julian Messner, 1959.

Freeman, Jo, ed. *Women: A Feminist Perspective.* Palo Alto, Calif.: Mayfield, 1984.

Friday, Nancy. *The Power of Beauty.* New York: Harper Collins, 1996.

Friedan, Betty. *The Feminine Mystique.* Rev. ed. New York: Laurel, 1984.

Greer, Germaine. *The Female Eunuch.* New York: McGraw-Hill, 1971.

Henry, Sherrye. *The Deep Divide.* New York: Macmillan, 1994.

Hymowitz, Carol, and Michaele Weissman. *A History of Women in America.* New York: Bantam, 1978.

Jensen, Oliver. *The Revolt of American Women.* New York: Harcourt, Brace, 1952.

Lehrman, Karen. *The Lipstick Proviso.* New York: Anchor, 1997.

Moog, Carol. *Are They Selling Her Lips?* New York: William Morrow, 1990.

Napheys, George. *Physical Life of Woman.* Philadelphia: George MacClean, 1870.

Newman, Louise Michele, ed. *Men's Ideas/Women's Realities.* New York: Pergamon, 1985.

Pipher, Mary. *Reviving Ophelia.* New York: Grosset-Putnam, 1994.

Rowbotham, Sheila. *A Century of Women.* New York: Viking, 1997.

Ryan, Mary. *Womanhood in America.* New York: Franklin Watts, 1983.

Steinem, Gloria. *Moving beyond Words.* New York: Simon and Schuster, 1994.

Tavris, Carol. *The Mismeasure of Woman.* New York: Simon and Schuster, 1992.

Turow, Joseph. *Breaking Up America.* Chicago: University of Chicago Press, 1997.

Wolf, Naomi. *The Beauty Myth.* New York: Anchor, 1991.

HISTORY AND POPULAR CULTURE

Allen, Frederick Lewis. *Only Yesterday: An Informal History of the Nineteen Twenties.* New York: Harper and Brothers, 1931.

Andrist, Ralph, ed. *The American Heritage History of the 1920s and 1930s.* New York: Bonanza, 1987.

Bailey, Thomas. *The American Pageant.* 4th ed. Lexington, Mass.: D. C. Heath, 1971.

Bowen, Ezra, ed. *This Fabulous Century: Sixty Years of American Life.* 8 vols. New York: Time-Life, 1969–1970.

Cameron, Judy. *The Art of Gone with the Wind: The Making of a Legend.* New York: Prentice Hall, 1989.

Daniel, Clifton, ed. *Chronicle of the Twentieth Century.* Mount Kisco, N.Y.: Chronicle, 1987.

Duncan, Alastair. *Art Deco.* London: Thames and Hudson, 1988.

Eichler, Lillian. *The Customs of Mankind.* New York: Doubleday,

1924.

Ellis, Havelock. *Man and Woman.* Boston: Houghton Mifflin, 1929.

Evans, Harold. *The American Century.* New York: Alfred A. Knopf, 1998.

Gardner, Gerald, and Harriet Gardner. *Pictorial History of Gone with the Wind.* New York: Bonanza, 1983.

Gitter, Michael, and Sylvie Anapol. *Do You Remember? The Book That Takes You Back.* San Francisco: Chronicle, 1996.

Hendrickson, Robert. *The Grand Emporiums: The Illustrated History of America's Great Department Stores.* New York: Scarborough, 1979.

Jennings, Peter, and Todd Brewster. *The Century.* New York: Doubleday, 1998.

Klein, Dan. *All Colour Book of Art Deco.* London: Octopus, 1974.

Lynd, Robert, and Helen Lynd. *Middletown: A Study in Contemporary American Culture.* New York: Harcourt Brace, 1929.

———. *Middletown in Transition.* New York: Harcourt Brace, 1937.

Maeder, Edward. *Hollywood and History: Costume Design in Film.* London: Thames and Hudson, 1987.

Marcus, Stanley. *Minding the Store.* New York: Little, Brown, 1974.

Panati, Charles. *Panati's Extraordinary Origins of Everyday Things.* New York: Perennial Library, 1989.

Schlesinger, Arthur, ed. *The Almanac of American History.* Greenwich, Conn.: Bison, 1983.

Sullivan, Mark. *Our Times: The United States 1900–1925.* New York: Charles Scribner's Sons, 1927.

Susman, Warren. *Culture as History: The Transformation of American Society in the Twentieth Century.* New York: Scarborough, 1980.

ADVERTISING PERIODICALS

Advertising Age (1930–present)
Adweek (1960–present)
Journal of Advertising (1972–present)
Printers' Ink (1888–1967)

FASHION, COSTUME, AND POPULAR CULTURE PERIODICALS

Allure (1991–present)
American Magazine (1876–56)
Bride's (1934–present)
CIBA Review (1937–75)
Delineator (1873–1937)
Dress (1975–present)
Ebony (1945–present)
Elle (1985–present)
Essence (1970–present)
Flair (1950–51)
Glamour (1939–present)
Godey's Lady's Book (1830–98)
Good Housekeeping (1885–present)
Harper's Bazaar (1867–present)
Ladies' Home Journal (1883–present)
Ladies' World (1880–1918)
Life (1936–72)
Look (1937–71)
Mademoiselle (1935–2001)
McCall's (1876–present)
Mirabella (1989–2000)
Modern Bride (1949–present)
Peterson's Magazine (1837–98)
Redbook (1903–present)
Saturday Evening Post (1821–1969)
Seventeen (1944–present)
Vanity Fair (1913–36, 1983–present)
Vogue (1892–present)
Vogue Pattern Book (1925–present)
W (1971–present)
Woman's Day (1937–present)
Woman's Magazine (1896–1920)
Women's Wear Daily (1910–present)

INDEX